Feeling A Draft:
Baseball Scouting and the
First 50 Years of the
Amateur Player Draft

Frederick J. Day & Raymond J. McKenna

In memory of Daniel J. Crowe, Rev. Bob DeLeon, C.S.C., and Arthur W. Phinney III, classmates and treasured friends, each of whom tossed his final pitches in 2021.

– Fred Day

With love to my home team – my lovely wife, Shawn, and seven adorable children, Chris, Mary, Joe, Nick, Meg, Sarah, and Amelia.

– Ray McKenna

A special thank you and note of appreciation to Francie and Doug

FEELING A DRAFT
BASEBALL SCOUTING AND THE FIRST 50 YEARS
OF THE AMATEUR PLAYER DRAFT

iUniverse books may be ordered through booksellers or by contacting:

iUniverse
1663 Liberty Drive
Bloomington, IN 47403
www.iuniverse.com
844-349-9409

Front and back cover design by Hung Pham, Washington, D.C.
Graphic layout by Catherine Hébert, Vail, CO

Quaerite et invenietis

ISBN: 978-1-6632-3170-3 (sc)
ISBN: 978-1-6632-3171-0 (hc)
ISBN: 978-1-6632-3169-7 (e)

Library of Congress Control Number: 2021923286

Print information available on the last page.

iUniverse rev. date: 11/17/2021

You spend a good piece of your life gripping a baseball and in the end it turns out that it was the other way around all the time.

– Jim Bouton, former Major League pitcher, in *Ball Four: My Life and Hard Times Throwing the Knuckleball in the Big Leagues*

Table of Contents

Acknowledgment

During the process of researching and writing *Feeling A Draft*, we encountered many individuals who would become treasured friends. The narration of these individuals transported us through time and space to a special place of baseball lore. We were enthralled by the bittersweet story of Harry Minor's clutch home run that catapulted the Savannah Indians deep into the South Atlantic League playoffs and, in the process, denied Harry his one and only opportunity to reach the Major Leagues. We felt the dejection and pain of young flame-throwing Ron Rizzi as he was pulled from a college game with a no-hitter in the works and then, still seething, attempted to throw his fastball through the proverbial brick wall in a subsequent batting practice session – only to suffer an irreparable arm injury.

We were amused by the enthusiastic recollections of an eighty-eight year-old Al LaMacchia from his draft-room battles in the early days of the Toronto Blue Jays. We were humbled by Augie Schmidt's anguish-filled journey from second overall pick in 1982 to bedeviled minor leaguer to wildly successful head coach at Carthage College. We experienced, along with Bill Livesey, the dramatic tension and subsequent elation of the 1992 New York Yankee draft room as the Yankees sweated out the selection of Derek Jeter. We marveled along with Stan Meek as he recalled his sheer good fortune in discovering future all-star catcher J.T. Realmuto during a high school football game in which Realmuto quarterbacked Carl Albert High School to victory in the 2009 Oklahoma Class 5A championship game. We shared Greg Smith's amazement as he spied five-foot, four-inch eighth-grader, Tim Lincecum, looking "like he was in the fourth grade" yet dominating his junior high school opponents.

We are all the richer for the stories of triumph and disappointment so graciously shared by those with whom we spoke. We are deeply indebted to all who allowed us a glimpse into the noble pursuit of seeking out the talented individuals who possess the unique ability to survive and flourish in professional baseball.

Listed in alphabetical sequence, we are grateful to: Bill Almon, Russ Ardolina, Richie Bancells, Sal Bando, John Barr, Jeff Bittiger, Billy Blitzer, Gib Bodet, John Boggs, John Boles, Bob Boone, Bill Bordley, Chris Buckley, Matthew Burns, Joe Caro, Ben Cherington, Fred Claire, Ned Colletti, Pat Corrales, Mark Cresse, Bobby Darwin, Dan Duquette, Jim Fleming, Orrin Freeman, Pat Gillick, Brian Golden, Dick Groch, Bill Harrison, Bob Harrison, RJ Harrison, Roland Hemond, Chuck Hernandez, Amanda Hopkins, Ron Hopkins, Gary Hughes, Sam Hughes, Stan Jefferson, Dan Jennings, Dave Jennings, Terry Kennedy, Bobby Keppel, Kevin Kerrane, Wayne Krivsky, Al La-Macchia, Gary LaRoque, Jim Leyritz, Bill Livesey, Adam Loewen, Carl Loewenstine, Doug Mapson, Mark Marquess, Joe McIlvaine, Jack McKeon, Ben McLure, Stan Meek, Doug Melvin, Frank Menechino, Darrell Miller, Bob Minor, Harry Minor, Bill Moore, Pat Murtaugh, Gary Nickels, CJ Nitkowski, Ed Randall, J.P. Ricciardi, Jim Riggleman, Ron Rizzi, Jax Robertson, George Rose, Augie Schmidt, Buck Showalter, Bill Singer, Matt Slater, Greg Smith, Reggie Smith, Chris Speier, Craig Stammen, Art Stewart, Jeff Suppan, Mike Sweeney, Mike Toomey, John Tumminia, Mike Wallace, Logan White, Mickey White, Tim Wilken, Earl Winn, Phil Wood, Stan Zielinski and George Zuraw.

We thank them all.

Photo Credits

Page 190: Photograph of George Brett and Mike Toomey. Courtesy of Mike Toomey. Used with permission.

Page 190: Photograph of Yogi Berra and Ron Rizzi. Courtesy of Ron Rizzi. Used with permission.

Page 190: Photograph of Charlie Sheen and Ron Rizzi. Courtesy of Ron Rizzi. Used with permission.

Page 190: Photograph of Gib Bodet and Jean Bodet. Courtesy of Gib Bodet. Used with permission.

Page191: Photograph of Ben McLure. Courtesy of Ben McLure. Used with permission.

Page 191: Photograph of Billy Blitzer. Courtesy of Billy Blitzer. Used with permission.

Page 191: Photograph of Tony La Russa and Matt Slater. Courtesy of Matt Slater. Used with permission.

Page 192: Photograph of John Tumminia. Courtesy of John Tumminia. Used with permission.

Page 192: Photograph of Darrell Miller. Courtesy of Darrell Miller. Used with permission.

Page 192: Photograph of Joe Caro and Gene Michael. Courtesy of Joe Caro. Used with permission.

Source for Player Statistics

The player statistics and related data used in this volume are drawn from www.baseball-reference.com. The authors gratefully acknowledge the contributions of Baseball-Reference.com in providing an authoritative reference for the baseball community and for fans of the game.

Preface

Baseball scouts are storytellers. Perhaps this trait comes from sitting in ballparks for extended periods – something to do in between taking radar gun readings. Greg Smith, special assistant to the general manager of the Texas Rangers, is a ready example. Smith tells of the time that a veteran scout sent him to check out a prospect who was pitching for Sandra Day O'Connor High School in Phoenix. The veteran instructed Smith to see if the kid "could live up to his name."

The kid's name was Maverick Lasker. Smith thought to himself, "Top Gun? Really?" Smith went to see Lasker pitch. And the kid threw 94 mph, with a decent curveball. Smith reported back, "Yes, the kid can live up to his name." Lasker played professionally for four years in the Brewers organization, but suffered a serious back injury and never advanced beyond the lower levels of the pro ranks. He was out of baseball at the age of 22. Today, he is on track to become an orthopedic surgeon, with hopes of enabling injured athletes to get back to the playing field. Meanwhile, Maverick's own baseball experiences live on in the stories that Greg Smith tells.

Our purpose in writing this book is threefold. *First*, we wanted to analyze the results of baseball's amateur draft during the first 50 years of the draft's existence, 1965 to 2014. *Second*, we wanted to report on and assess, in the era of the amateur draft, the role of the scouts who go to investigate high school and collegiate prospects such as Maverick Lasker. *Third*, we wanted to relate the vibrant experiences and anecdotes of the scouting community.

We have felt both a need and an obligation to record on paper the very compelling stories spun by the scouts with whom we talked. In satisfaction of this mission, we have inserted, throughout the book, brief accounts in the form of sidebars. These sidebars relate the stories of the unique individuals who search the back roads, school yards and college campuses in the hope of finding that one ballplayer who can fill out a Major League uniform. Throughout the book, we have used quotes and anecdotes from scouts and others in baseball whom we interviewed. Unless otherwise noted, all quotes and anecdotes attributed to individuals are derived directly from our interviews.

San Francisco Giants senior advisor John Barr says that baseball scouting is all about keeping an eye on the future. The hope is that good decisions at the scouting level will translate, someday, into victories at the Major League level. In Barr's view, "that is what gets a scout in his car every day or getting on an airplane every day to see a game in a distant city." The scout's mentality, Barr says, must be, "Today I have got to make a difference."

We hope that this book, in at least a small way, will make a difference as well.

Introduction

I loved Jim McLaughlin [former scouting director for the Baltimore Orioles] telling me that when he watched Bubby Brister playing baseball, he said, 'I really see a Mike Schmidt body there.' I was reading the Mike Schmidt report when he was at Ohio University. Some scouts said, 'reminds me of Jim Fregosi.' If you could uncover a report on Jim Fregosi when he was an amateur, somebody might have said, 'He looks like Al Rosen.' And if you could get an Al Rosen report, it might have said, 'Looks like Whitey Kurowski.' Each player you see as a scout calls to mind another player from an earlier generation.

— Kevin Kerrane, author, in *Dollar Sign on the Muscle: The World of Baseball Scouting*

In the days leading up to the 2020 World Series, much of the media discussion focused on the analytic acumen of the two participants, the Los Angeles Dodgers and the Tampa Bay Rays. However, Los Angeles' ultimate victory was predominantly the result of the team's scouting excellence. Almost all of the key contributors to the Dodgers' world championship were products of the amateur drafting savvy of former scouting director Logan White and his top-notch scouts. Although White had departed Los Angeles in 2014 for a front office position with the San Diego Padres, his fingerprints were all over the script for the Dodgers' success.

Los Angeles ace Clayton Kershaw, who led the way on the mound with two World Series wins, was drafted by White way back in the first round of 2006. Shortstop Corey Seager, who was named the Most Valuable Player of both the National League Championship Series and the World Series, had been drafted by White in the first round of 2012. Center fielder Cody Bellinger, who provided key middle-of-the-order power and superior outfield defense, was a fourth-round Logan White special in 2013. While star right fielder Mookie Betts was acquired by the Dodgers' current president of baseball operations, Andrew Friedman, in a trade with the Boston Red Sox, Boston only agreed to part with the 2018 American League Most Valuable Player when the Dodgers included prized prospect Alex Verdugo in the deal. Verdugo was a second-round pick in 2014 by – you guessed it – Logan White.

When a baseball scout such as Logan White sees a prospect, he often actually sees two players; he sees the player before him and another player from his memory bank whom the player at hand calls to mind. In 2014, when scouting legend Stan Zielinski saw Kyle Schwarber hit at Indiana University, in his mind's eye, he also saw Babe Ruth. Zielinski's scouting report, filled with references to Ruth, captured the full attention of the Chicago Cubs organization.[1] The fact that Schwarber was a high draft pick who ascended quickly through the Cubs' system to play a pivotal role in their 2016 World Series Championship season has the makings of legend and lore that would make the Babe himself proud.

Zielinski's evaluation of Schwarber provides a prime example of the intuitive or subjective nature of baseball scouting. Most amateur scouts believe they can "feel" whether a player has "the right stuff" to succeed in the big leagues. In contrast to the gut feel of traditional scouts, many observers today believe all aspects of baseball – including amateur scouting – may be understood through the prism of objective criteria, or statistical analysis. Kevin Kerrane probed this divide over 30 years ago in his seminal work on baseball scouting, *Dollar Sign on the Muscle*, as he examined whether scouting is an art or a science.[2]

Feeling A Draft focuses on the continuing importance of scouts in baseball and most especially examines the vital role these scouts play in evaluating the talent under consideration in Major League Baseball's annual amateur player draft. Even in the age of advanced statistical analysis, scouts remain the lifeblood of professional baseball, yet they receive preciously little professional recognition. When they have received recognition, it has often been unduly negative and harsh. As the title, *Feeling A Draft*, implies, scouting is much more of an art than a science.

Baseball was once America's unrivalled national pastime. It was the game that captivated youngsters like none other. Kids played baseball always and everywhere, from the congested streets of Manhattan to the cornfields of the Midwest and west to the shores of sunny California. Today, the National Football League has loudly zoomed by Major League Baseball in almost every measurable way. Interest among youngsters has declined precipitously to the point where baseball has been compelled to create a program, "Reviving Baseball in Inner Cities" (RBI), and establish facilities in inner cities devoted to generating greater interest among youths.

Nonetheless, baseball remains extremely popular in the United States, as over 68 million fans paid to attend Major League games in 2019. Across the nation, on any given day when there is a full schedule of Major League games, an average of 2.4 million fans watch games on television. Beyond overall viewing numbers, baseball still retains the capacity to captivate its most devout fans. The passion and interest of baseball devotees, once manifested by the purchase of trading cards and an obsessive devotion to their favorite teams and players, has matured into a more generic fandom that has led them to become true students of the game. Their curriculum is baseball statistics – mundane stats like batting average, home runs and earned run average, and the newer, more esoteric measures such as On-base Plus Slugging (OPS), Batting Average on Balls In Play (BABIP), Wins Above Replacement (WAR) and Home Run to Fly Ball ratio (HR/FB).[3] More than ever before, these statistically minded baseball fans are committed to learning about player performance.

Of course, these savvy, statistically-oriented fans have not developed in a vacuum. Since the early twenty-first century, team management, and baseball culture as a whole, have come to recognize and employ sabermetrics in new and exciting ways.[4] Today most teams employ high level executives trained in statistical analysis who oversee a cadre of analysts exploring the depths of new sabermetric analysis. The embrace of sabermetrics by both executives and fans can be largely attributed to two factors: (1) the research and writing of author Bill James, who was at the forefront of the use of advanced metrics in baseball; and (2) the discussion generated by the 2003 publication of Michael Lewis' book *Moneyball*, which chronicles the creative and innovative methods of Oakland A's general manager Billy Beane.[5] As knowledge spread of Beane's use of sabermetrics to gain competitive advantages over his more well-funded competitors, statistical analysis began to seep into the consciousness of the average fan.

By the time that *Moneyball* was made into a successful Hollywood motion picture starring Brad Pitt as Beane in 2011, a false and misleading narrative had grown that sabermetrics could and would replace old-time scouting in the selection of amateur players through the annual draft or via international free agency. However, as former Toronto Blue Jays executive Keith Law asserts in his book on the smart statistical analysis of baseball, "the problem with the [narrative] is that it is not true."[6]

The best organizations employ both scouts and statistical analysts working together to complement each other. Kevin Kerrane underscores the extreme exaggeration of the perceived conflict between quantitative analysis and qualitative scouting.[7] He once debated the supposed conflict with baseball writer Alan Schwarz, author of *The Numbers Game*. "Neither of us won," Kerrane says, "because we weren't talking about the same thing."[8]

Former Cubs' general manager, Theo Epstein, much like Billy Beane, is an avant-garde leader in incorporating statistical analysis into his scouting appraisals. Yet under Epstein, the Cubs relied heavily on the input of old-time scouts, as the story of Stan Zielinski's discovery of Kyle Schwarber demonstrates. During the team's 2014 draft deliberations, Epstein asked Zielinski to explain his conviction on Schwarber. Zielinski had long since proven his scouting mettle by discovering many future Major League players, including notable stars Cliff Floyd and Jeff Samardzija.

Zielinski argued forcefully and persuasively for the Cubs to take Schwarber with the fourth overall pick in 2014. In scouting parlance, Zielinski *pounded the table* for Schwarber. Zielinski was willing to put his stellar reputation and storied career on the line because he was so convinced that he had found the next Babe Ruth. As recounted in an article in *Sports Illustrated*, Zielinski pulled clips of Schwarber's swings and those of Babe Ruth, and called his wife and children over to his laptop. "Don't you see it?" he asked his family, his fist zealously clenched. "Don't you see it?" Zielinski then filed his scouting report for the Cubs that read, in part, "Squint your eyes and imagine a grainy film of Babe Ruth hitting a ball in the stands, I swear I saw that reenacted today as the ball flew out over the 2nd fence in right field … I believed today … squint again and you can see him Call His Shot and point to the center field bleachers in Wrigley Field."[9]

Epstein may not have seen Babe Ruth when he watched Zielinski's videos of Schwarber, but he repeatedly heard Zielinski's whispering voice saying he loved Schwarber. Epstein also was enamored by Schwarber's swing and just as impressed by an in-person interview he conducted with Schwarber in February 2014. Schwarber's personality and confidence, combined with Zielinski's zealous and unqualified recommendation, convinced Epstein to select Schwarber with the fourth overall pick. While Epstein undoubtedly conferred with his sabermetric experts prior to the selection, it is clear that the selection was driven by the intuition of an old scout and Epstein's own subjective feelings about Schwarber.

Feeling A Draft aims to present a more complete picture as it examines the performance of scouts in the era of the amateur draft. Scouts are an unusual breed and the "old-time" scouts are, sadly, a dying breed. Stories abound of the hijinks and shenanigans that baseball scouts engaged in prior to the advent of the draft, in the days of "pure free agency." In those days, scouting was comparable to a Wild West environment where no holds were barred. While most of the old-timers were truly characters – brimming with competitiveness, savvy and enough scouting stories to fill a library – they also were mostly men of great character. Although scouts were relatively poorly compensated for the many hours and miles they logged each year, their work was as much a labor of love as it was their livelihood.

Although the hyperbolic embrace of sabermetrics by baseball insiders and commentators has presented the unfair perception that scouts are going the way of the dinosaur, they remain as important to the success of Major League franchises as ever. Further, scouts will *always* be the lifeblood of the game precisely because it is so very hard to predict the future success of high-school and college players in baseball. Ted Williams, widely acknowledged as the greatest pure hitter in baseball history, famously and accurately said, "I think without question the hardest single thing to do in sport is to hit a baseball." From our vantage point, predicting the future success of teenage players is even harder than hitting a baseball. As the old adage goes, a hitter who fails seven out of ten times goes to the Hall of Fame; identifying those players who will succeed in the Major Leagues is even more of a risky proposition, as less than two out of ten players drafted even *make* the Major Leagues. This apparently unspectacular record may ostensibly seem like the basis for justifiable criticism of the baseball brain trust (general managers, player personnel executives, and scouts) that makes the draft decisions. Upon closer examination, it serves to underline their unmatched evaluative brilliance and unique gimlet "eye" for the game.

A scout's intuition or "gut feel" is an essential component of player evaluation and, especially, player projection. For example, veteran scout Doug Mapson had a gut feel that Greg Maddux would develop into an elite pitcher when he first viewed Maddux at Valley High School in Las Vegas. On the issue of a scout's gut feel, we part company with many baseball experts who trust more in empirical evidence and measurable statistics such as the newer yardsticks of spin rate and Win Probability Added (WPA).[10] While hardly any reasonable baseball person disputes the need for both the scouts and sabermetric analysts, the debate over whether the draft is an art or science is likely to continue to rage. *Feeling A Draft* aims to present the successes and failures of the draft, both of which abound, and allow the reader to make his or her own determination on the subject.

Baseball instituted the first-ever amateur player draft in 1965. The primary impetus for implementing the draft was the desire of baseball's owners to eliminate the frenzied bidding wars to sign the top talents. The competition between the New York Yankees and Los Angeles Angels in 1964 to sign Big 10 batting champion Rick Reichardt was costly; the Angels ultimately won the Reichardt sweepstakes, signing the University of Wisconsin grad for a $205,000 bonus. As intended by Major League Baseball's hierarchy, the institution of the draft dramatically changed the nature of the game. The draft changed, especially, the work of the individuals who select the players. Veteran scout Howie Haak once commented,

> *The draft has more or less made every club equal, and maybe it's made baseball better, but I think it's changed scouting for the worse. … Say that you are a scout in California, and there's eight top prospects there, and your team drafts twenty-third. They're all gone, and your whole year is gone. And the draft has taken a lot of the fun away.*[11]

While scouting may be less fun in the draft era, the draft hasn't made the scouting process any easier. Only 42 percent of all players selected in the first five rounds of the draft – players who represent the cream of the crop – actually reach the Major Leagues. Further, very few of the players selected after the first five rounds of the draft actually spend even a day in the Major Leagues. While making the Major Leagues is a significant accomplishment, that milestone alone provides little insight into whether a player made a meaningful contribution to the team and the organization.

There is a widespread belief among baseball people that it takes at least five years to evaluate the effectiveness of a player draft. By the time five years have passed from draft day, the reasoning goes, the players selected in a given draft class will have begun to show whether they are capable of fulfilling the promise foreseen on draft day. Therefore, this book will evaluate the first 50 Major League Drafts, from 1965 to 2014. The results of the more recent drafts, 2015 through 2021, are still unfolding; too little time has passed to allow for a fair assessment. Six years after Stan Zielinski pounded the table for Kyle Schwarber, we have limited proof that Schwarber's power numbers are strong (one home run every 14.9 at-bats, compared with 11.6 for the Babe), yet Schwarber's paltry career batting average of .230 lags the Babe by 112 points. While Schwarber's swing does conjure up an image of the Babe, it is doubtful that even Zielinski thought his statistics would compare with those of the Sultan of Swat.

Beyond the statistics, baseball is a game of people and their stories – stories about a 62nd round draft pick who hit his way into baseball's Hall of Fame, stories about an overall number one pick who never appeared in a Major League game, stories about baseball people who beat the bushes to find prospects, and stories about baseball people bearing Ivy League diplomas.

Historian and philosopher Jacques Barzun famously declared, "Whoever wants to know the heart and mind of America had better learn baseball, the rules and realities of the game."[12] There is no better way to learn the reality of the game than through the stories accumulated by baseball's scouts. Many of those stories appear in the pages that follow.

"Something Most People Could Never Do"

In the first 50 years of the Major League Baseball Amateur Draft, baseball teams drafted a total of 59,864 players. Of all the players drafted, a total of 8,716 reached the Major Leagues. The number of players who reached the Major Leagues equates to 14.6% of all players drafted.

The 14.6% figure is misleading, of course, because it fails to distinguish between those players who carved out significant careers in the majors and those who spent only brief periods at the Major League level. Thus, a player such as pitcher Larry Yount, the brother of Hall of Famer Robin Yount, is included in the number of players who spent time in the Major Leagues.

The Houston Astros drafted Larry Yount in the fifth round of 1968. Officially, Larry Yount spent one day – September 15, 1971 – in the majors. The Astros had brought him up from their top minor league club, the Oklahoma City 89ers, to fill out their 40-man roster. Yount was called upon to pitch the ninth inning of a losing game against the Atlanta Braves. He was announced as the Astros pitcher and took the mound. However, Yount explains, "I knew before going to the mound that my elbow was in pain, but figured that the excitement of the moment would make the pain go away."

The pain persisted. Yount threw his warmup pitches and, fearing further injury, pulled himself out of the game. He retired from baseball at the age of 25, never having thrown anything more than warmup pitches in the Major Leagues. "I now have a great family," he says, "and could not be much happier, except that void of not accomplishing my boyhood dreams."*

Of course, even stepping on the rubber in a single big-league game represents an accomplishment. As broadcaster Phil Wood says, "This is such a difficult sport to play on an elite level. By 'elite', I mean professional. If you get to professional baseball for five minutes, you have done something that most people could never do."

While every player who reaches the Major Leagues has done something that most people could never do, it is safe to say that the number of players who actually forged significant Major League careers is a lot less than 14.6% of the players drafted.

* Swirsky, Seth. *Every Pitcher Tells A Story: Letters Gathered By a Devoted Baseball Fan* (New York: Random House, Inc., 1999), 183.

The Early Years of the Amateur Player Draft
(1965 – 1979)

Scouting is very competitive. Each team competes against the others with scouting. That competition goes as far back as the high school games.
  –John Barr, assistant general manaager, San Francisco Giants

M ajor League Baseball instituted its amateur player draft in 1965. Baseball was late to the dance, so to speak, as it was the last of the major U.S. professional sports leagues to implement an amateur draft. While there had been proposals over the years for a draft, opposition from the most successful teams – the teams with the largest scouting infrastructures – had held them at bay. What changed was the large and increasing bonus payments teams were forced to pay in the absence of a draft. The true tipping point was the battle over signing top prospect Rick Reichardt in 1964.

The six-foot-three, 210-pound Reichardt, a spectacular two-sport athlete from the University of Wisconsin, set off a fierce bidding war when he decided to pursue a professional career in baseball. Eventually, the bidding came down to a two-team battle between the New York Yankees, who were looking to replace their aging superstar, Mickey Mantle, and the upstart Los Angeles Angels and their well-heeled owner, former cowboy actor and singer Gene Autry. The Angels won out by offering Reichardt a record $205,000 bonus, which exceeded the salaries of the top Major League stars, Mickey Mantle, Al Kaline, Willie Mays and Ernie Banks.

In terms of economics, the effect of instituting the amateur draft was immediately obvious. The first overall player drafted in 1965, Arizona State University outfielder Rick Monday, signed with the Kansas City Athletics for $104,000, or roughly 50 percent of the Reichardt bounty. The advent of the draft also significantly altered the time-honored competition among scouts to sign the best ballplayers. Prior to the draft, scouts would engage in cutthroat competition to sign a prospect. Perhaps the best example of the "Wild West" nature of the competition in the days before the draft involved long-time Boston Red Sox scout Chuck Koney.

Koney had once been a very promising ballplayer in the Red Sox organization but he suffered a disabling injury and doctors were forced to amputate one of his legs at the knee. The Red Sox hired him as a baseball scout; his disability rarely held him back. Aided by an artificial leg, he was capable of doing everything required of a scout and was instrumental in signing, among many others, Boston legend Carl Yastrzemski. Only once did Koney's disability prove to be a liability.

Koney was staying at a hotel in the hometown of a promising ballplayer, intent on meeting with the player and his family at their home the next morning. Following the meeting with Koney, the family was scheduled to meet with scouts from rival organizations during the remainder of the day. As was his practice, Koney detached his artificial leg before going to sleep and placed it under his bed. During the night, however, a rival scout quietly removed the artificial leg and placed it in the trunk of his car. With his leg missing, Koney had no option but to skip his meeting with the prospect.

Once the draft was established, there was no longer an advantage in being the first scout to show up at a prospect's house. Similarly, there was no longer a competitive advantage to be gained by pilfering the prosthetic leg of a rival scout. While a scout might be the first to "discover" a player, the scout could only wait to see if the player was still available when it came time for the scout's team to make its pick. The draft has eliminated the need for scouts to develop a bond with prospects. Scouts no longer face the pressure of having to "ink" a prized prospect. The implementation of the draft has eliminated the personality and charm of a scout as factors in persuading a player to sign with a given team.

The scout's task has been reduced to one of identifying prospects, evaluating their skills, and formulating recommendations for the front office. The essential question is no longer whether a scout can convince a prospect to sign for a certain sum. Rather, the paramount concerns for a scout are, *first,* whether he can persuade his superiors to expend a highly valued draft choice on his preferred prospect and, *second,* whether a rival club will snap up the player before the time comes for the scout's team to make a selection.

While the scout's role became greatly reduced with the advent of the draft, the importance of the team's scouting director grew exponentially. Someone needed to take the disparate scouting reports and synthesize them to prioritize the team's prospect list and create a national draft board. In the early years of the draft, the Kansas City Athletics experienced considerable success. After snagging Rick Monday, third baseman Sal Bando and catcher Gene Tenace in the inaugural draft of 1965, Kansas City selected future Hall of Fame outfielder Reggie Jackson with the second overall pick in 1966. In the second round of 1967, the A's selected another future All-Star in fire-balling left-hander Vida Blue.

The success of the Athletics in the early years of the draft was no accident. Joe Bowman served as the Athletics' director of scouting from November 1961 until the team moved to Oakland in 1968. Like most of his peers, Bowman was a baseball "lifer." The Kansas City native had pitched for eleven seasons in the Major Leagues before joining the scouting profession. While most teams and scouting directors in the 1960s struggled mightily in adjusting to the draft, Bowman thrived. He used the insights developed over his 35 years in baseball to identify particularly promising prospects. In some quarters, Bowman is considered to be the best scouting director in the draft era.[13]

The primary reason for instituting the amateur draft was to address the concerns about runaway bonuses. However, establishing parity among the teams was another motivating factor. In the years preceding 1965, there were three teams that were disproportionally successful, the Yankees, Dodgers and Cardinals. Ideally, the amateur draft is a vehicle for the "have nots" to gain parity or surpass the "haves" by benefitting from being awarded higher draft picks. The rise of the Athletics' dynasty followed the blueprint to perfection.

The Athletics' haul of talent over the three years from 1965 to 1967 would become the nucleus for their three subsequent world championship teams in 1972-1974. The role that Bowman played in Oakland's success in the 1970s is often overlooked, however, because he moved on from the team before his draft choices developed into Major League stars.

The Kansas City Athletics fit perfectly into the category of a well-deserving "have-not." The team's fans had suffered through some very poor teams in the early years of the franchise. Chicago real estate magnate Arnold Johnson had purchased the Philadelphia Athletics franchise in 1954 from the family of the legendary Connie Mack and moved the team to the Midwest. The move to Kansas City appeared inspired, as it was a rabid baseball city. Kansas City had enthusiastically supported the New York Yankees' Triple-A affiliate, the Kansas City Blues, for the previous 18 years. In addition, the city was home to the most successful Negro League franchise, the Kansas City Monarchs, and its legendary player, Buck O'Neil.

From the time the Athletics arrived in Kansas City in 1955, the team finished at or near the bottom of the standings every year. When Arnold Johnson passed away in 1960, the Kansas City franchise was sold to an insurance mogul, Charles O. Finley. Under Finley's ownership, the Kansas City fans endured an entirely new level of suffering. Finley intruded himself in all aspects of team management, including decisions that historically had been left to the team's on-field manager. Finley tried one gimmick after another, such as dressing the grounds crew in space suits, promoting the use of an orange baseball, and installing a zoo beyond the outfield fence that housed a pet mule named "Charlie-O." With Finley in charge, the Athletics performed poorly, both on the field and at the box office. After much initial opposition to relocating the franchise, Major League Baseball permitted Finley to move the team to Oakland in 1968. In Oakland, bolstered by Joe Bowman's draft picks from 1965 to 1967, the Athletics would win their historic three consecutive World Series championships.

So, in one sense, the draft worked exactly as designed. The worst team in baseball was rewarded for its years of futility with high draft picks, which they used wisely to lay the foundation for future championships. Unfortunately, the beneficiaries of the Athletics' new-found success were the Bay Area inhabitants, not the long-suffering Kansas City fans.

The Athletics' success led to another delicious irony. Even though Charlie Finley had little or no baseball training, he reportedly served as his own chief scout. After Joe Bowman accepted a position with the Atlanta Braves in 1968, Finley began to play a larger role in the draft process for the Athletics. To lower his operating costs, he cut back on the team's scouting staff. Finley did not rely solely on his own player evaluations, but instead would make his draft decisions by picking the brains of scouts from opposing teams. While such blatant pirating of proprietary information seems incredible today, Sal Bando explained, "Finley was masterful at calling multiple scouts prior to the draft to supposedly interview them for the A's general manager position but, in the conversation, he would elicit their views on key draft eligible players." Of course, Finley never hired the scouts after the "interviews."

Finley's penurious instincts contained the seeds of the eventual dismantlement of the Athletics' dynasty. In short order, Finley became as unwelcomed in Oakland as he had been in Kansas City. He created internal tension and discontent among the players due to his failure to pay a wage comparable to their talents. In one of the greatest ironies, baseball arbitrator Peter Seitz declared Oakland pitching ace and future Hall of Famer Jim "Catfish" Hunter a free agent because the *insurance* mogul, Finley, failed to make a timely payment on an insurance policy mandated by Hunter's contract. As a result, Hunter left Oakland for New York City and the Yankees in 1974. Hunter's exit from Oakland began a stream of departures by other Oakland stars, reducing the team to a shell of its former self. To the delight of almost everyone, Finley sold the franchise in 1981. Finley left the sport as baseball's bête noire, having inadvertently opened the door for free agency – one of the most radical changes in baseball history.

The 1965 draft and its early successors were chaotic and disorganized. While the Athletics' selection of Rick Monday would stand the test of time, most of the early drafts were filled with poor choices at the very top. From 1965 to 1975, the majority of the players selected with the first overall pick in the draft produced little or no improvement for the struggling franchises that drafted them. Over time, however, teams began to improve both their selections and their organizational structures to better navigate the draft. Eventually, insightful scouting directors in the mold of Joe Bowman would become adept at using the draft to help their franchises build championship-caliber teams.

Wooing A Prospect

In the days before Major League Baseball instituted the amateur draft, it was not uncommon for a scout to watch a prospect whom he was following play in ten to twelve games. Scouts would invest a considerable amount of time in wooing a player and his family. When the draft came into existence in 1965, it became rare for a scout to see a player more than two or three times. For any team other than the team holding the overall No. 1 pick, there was no guarantee that a player would be available when it came time for a team to make its selection. The uncertainty removed the incentive for scouts to invest a significant amount of time on any one player.

Long-time Los Angeles Dodgers scout Carl Loewenstine speaks fondly of the role of scouts in the days before the draft. In Loewenstine's view, no scout was better at the business of wooing a prospect than Tony Lucadello. Loewenstine recalls, "Tony would get to know the player's family in the off-season through Christmas cards and birthday cards and gain the trust of the family."

Broadcaster Phil Wood cites another example. "Look at the Allen brothers," he says. Scout John Ogden signed all three of the brothers – Dick, Hank and Ron – for the Phillies. According to Wood, Ogden got to know the boys' mother, Era Allen, really well. John was able to charm the mother in a way that left Dick and his brothers no choice but to sign with the Phillies.

In the years before the draft, charm abounded. When the Pittsburgh Pirates were courting pitcher Vernon Law, Pirates scouts showed up at the Law household in Meridian, Idaho, with chocolates and roses for Law's mother. At the time, famed singer and movie star Bing Crosby was a minority owner of the Pirates and a vice president with the franchise. Crosby made a telephone call to Law's home. At least in Meridian, Idaho, Crosby's name was magical. "My mom about fainted," Law would say when recounting the phone call.

With the institution of the draft, a phone call from Bing Crosby or roses for a player's mother lost significance. The sole determining factor in whether a team would be in a position to sign a prospect was whether the player remained unclaimed when it came time for the team to make its draft selection.

1965

I don't think anyone knew what to expect. It was brand new to people who had been signing players in a different way. People were feeling their way along. At that time, it was very difficult to construct a board and get the players in the proper perspective because we didn't have what we now call cross-checkers... As far as comparing a player on the West Coast with a player on the East Coast and formulating some kind of a board, that didn't happen, certainly not in our organization during the 1965 draft.

−Pat Gillick, then assistant farm director for the Houston Astros

The 1965 draft was held at the Commodore Hotel, near Grand Central Station, in New York City. It was a raucous and disorderly affair that bore no resemblance to the staid and well-orchestrated draft events of recent years.

Although the inaugural draft was held on a Tuesday, it will forever be known as "the Monday draft." Outfielder Rick Monday, who had starred at both Santa Monica High School in California and Arizona State University, has the distinction of being the first player ever drafted. The Kansas City Athletics got the draft off to an auspicious start when they selected Monday. By September of the following year, he would be in the Major Leagues. Monday would remain an impact player for 19 seasons, compiling a .264 batting average and hitting 241 home runs. His career included two All-Star Game appearances and a World Series Championship. However, he is best remembered for his role in preventing two protesters from burning an American flag on the field at Dodgers Stadium during a live broadcast on April 25, 1976 while playing center field for the Chicago Cubs.

The late Orioles and Red Sox executive Lou Gorman remembered that many clubs "prepared" for the draft the night before by sharing drinks and swapping stories late into the morning at the nearby Toots Shor's Restaurant.[14] Indicative of the chaos, the Boston Red Sox only drafted 20 players while the Houston Astros drafted an astounding 72 players. The results were just as uneven. Five of the 20 players drafted by the Red Sox would later play in the Major Leagues; only eleven of Houston's 72 picks reached the majors. Three of the Cincinnati Reds' first six picks, Bernie Carbo, Johnny Bench and Hal McRae, would become legitimate stars, while none of the first 17 players selected by the Pittsburgh Pirates would ever play in the big leagues.

Viewed through the prism of what could have been, the Athletics missed on two players, Johnny Bench and Nolan Ryan, who had even more productive careers than Rick Monday. These two future Hall of Famers were both passed over by every team in the first round of the draft. Bench would rise out of the second round to become one of the greatest catchers of all time. The Reds deserve much credit for discovering him, but retrospective eyebrows will always be raised by the fact that the Reds took Bernie Carbo over Bench in the first round of the draft. Ryan lasted until the 12th round, when he was selected by the New York Mets.

Long-time Cincinnati scout Tony Robello first encountered Bench at a high school game in Binger, Oklahoma. With Robello and a host of other scouts in the stands, Bench was the starting pitcher for Binger High School. In a story that would be played out time and time again with other prospects, circumstances conspired to give Robello a leg up on the competition. When the Binger coach replaced Bench with a relief pitcher, all of the scouts other than Robello exited the park. Robello stayed to watch the rest of the game. His dedication was rewarded. Bench shifted from the pitching mound to catcher and displayed the tools that would propel him to the Hall of Fame.

Bench reached the Major Leagues with Cincinnati in 1967 and remained with the Reds for the next 17 years. Over the course of his career, Bench belted 389 homers and drove in 1,376 runs, but his most memorable contributions were on defense. Most everyone in baseball would come to agree with Bench's renowned teammate Pete Rose, who said, "if you want to be a catcher, watch Johnny Bench." With Bench, Rose and Hall of Famers Joe Morgan and Tony Perez leading "the Big Red Machine," Cincinnati finished first in the National League seven times between 1970 and 1981. The Reds were World Series champions in two of those years, 1975 and 1976.

The Athletics selected two players in the later rounds of the 1965 draft, Sal Bando and Gene Tenace, who, arguably, had even better careers than Rick Monday. Bando was drafted in the sixth round, Tenace in the 20th. Each would become mainstays on the A's three consecutive World Series championship teams from 1972 to 1974.

Sal Bando was a teammate of Rick Monday on the same power-house Arizona State team that had won the 1965 College World Series. While Monday was voted as the collegiate player of the year, many scouts thought Bando was at least on a par with Monday. "I was surprised I was drafted so far after Rick," Bando commented, "I think we were very comparable players at ASU."[15] Bando would go on to serve as the Athletics' captain during the team's championship years of 1972-1974.

The New York Mets used the second overall pick in 1965 to select pitcher Les Rohr, who would appear in only 41 Major League games during his career. However, the draft brought a bright silver lining for the Mets in the person of Lynn Nolan Ryan, whom New York selected in the 12th round. In hindsight, it is mind-boggling that the "Ryan Express" was still available to the Mets in the 12th round. In fact, it represents one of the first of what would be many examples of future Hall of Fame players waiting to be drafted long after hundreds of other less notable players had already been selected.

By 1965, Mets' scout John "Red" Murff had become a legend in Texas scouting circles. A pitcher by trade, Murff had spent two seasons, 1956 and 1957, as a pitcher for the Milwaukee Braves. He did not begin playing professional baseball until he was 29 years old and was 35 years old when he finally made his Major League debut. During his scouting career, Murff traveled over a million miles in his Oldsmobile Delta 88 in search of undiscovered prospects. He spoke with thousands of ordinary folks in Texas in his quest to find talent. On one unforgettable day, Murff heard that there was a youngster named Ryan with a "live arm" at Alvin High School in Alvin, Texas.

When Murff first observed the youngster unleash his blazing fastball, he was certain he had found a special talent. Though scouts did not yet use radar guns, Murff's well-honed observation skills told him that the tall, skinny youngster's fastball was traveling at least 95 miles an hour. In the days before the advent of the draft, a scout's excitement of discovery was always tempered by a well-placed fear that his "find" would be discovered by scouts from other organizations. This fear was the genesis of the many imaginative and often hilarious efforts by old-time scouts to hide prized prospects from the prying eyes of their competitors.

Having discovered Ryan, Murff was faced with the new challenges posed by the upcoming first-ever Major League amateur draft. Before implementation of the draft, Murff's challenge would have been limited to convincing his bosses in the Mets' front office to give him the money to sign Ryan. With the advent of the draft, however, Murff had to convince his superiors to draft Ryan ahead of all the other prospects that other Mets scouts were recommending. He also had to persuade the front office to select Ryan sufficiently early in the draft to prevent any other organization from snatching away his prospect. Thus, in a very real sense, the draft made the life of a scout much more difficult.

With the draft looming, Murff knew that he and the Mets had to keep news of Ryan and his blistering fastball away from his competitors. He accomplished this feat by means of stealth and disinformation. Murff's trademark dress shirt and tie were so recognizable in Texas baseball circles that he intentionally stayed away from Ryan's games and sent a subordinate to report back to him on Ryan. In the case of the very few scouts from other organizations who did observe Ryan, Murff intentionally mislead them about his interest. As Ryan had questionable mechanics at the time and a below-average curveball, Murff pointed to both as plausible reasons he was not interested in the kid.

The stealth and disinformation were successful, but Murff still had to surmount his biggest hurdle in acquiring Ryan – convincing Bing Devine and the Mets to select him in the draft. Murff's faith in Ryan never wavered, and he argued for the Mets to draft him with their first selection. Unfortunately, Murff's conviction was not enough to overcome a significant impediment that had developed. Devine came to Alvin, Texas to see Ryan pitch on a day when the prospect had a horrendous performance.

Ryan had warmed up for 45 minutes the day before Devine arrived. Nonetheless, Ryan's coach agreed to pitch him again the next day to accommodate Devine. Ryan's pitches lacked their usually movement and hung over the heart of the plate. The coach pulled Ryan after three innings, seven runs and numerous hard-hit missiles. Both Ryan and Murff feared they had blown their chance with Devine and the Mets, but Murff never stopped pushing for Ryan. His scouting report stated, "this skinny right-handed high school kid has the best arm I've ever seen in my life." When the name of another pitching prospect came up in the

Mets' pre-draft discussions, Murff would interject, "he does not have the velocity of Ryan." Murff repeated this mantra so often and unceasingly that the Mets' hierarchy came to roll their eyes every time Murff mentioned Ryan. In the end, the Mets chose eleven players ahead of Ryan, including their number one pick, pitcher Les Rohr, four other pitchers and six position players.

When the 1969 "Miracle Mets" shocked the baseball world by winning the World Series, Murff's contribution were quite apparent. In addition to Ryan, Murff had also signed second baseman Ken Boswell, catcher Jerry Grote, and free agent pitcher Jerry Koosman. Ironically, the Mets' selection of Ryan will always be a bittersweet event because, in 1971, the team traded him to the California Angels in exchange for infielder Jim Fregosi. The trade would come to be viewed as one of the worst deals in baseball history.

Ryan went on to become the all time Major League strikeout king and was inducted into the Hall of Fame in 1999. In an ironic footnote, Ryan would have his number retired by three separate teams, California, Houston and Texas, but not by the Mets.

The Father of On-Base Percentage

During the 1953 baseball season, Ferris Fain held down first base for the Chicago White Sox for much of the season. Fain was a reliable hitter who had put together two excellent seasons for the Philadelphia Athletics in 1951 and 1952. He hit .344 in 1951 and .327 in 1952, winning the American League batting title both times. Fain's weakness lay in his lack of power. He had hit only two home runs in 1952 and never hit more than 10 in a single season.

Prior to spring training of 1953, the Athletics traded Fain to the Chicago White Sox. Despite Fain's limited power, White Sox manager Paul Richards occasionally installed Fain in spots usually reserved for power hitters. The stretch from August 30 to September 12, 1953, is illustrative. Fain batted third in the order in four games and fifth in five others. By 1953, Fain seemed to be losing some of his touch at the plate; he would bat only .256 for the season in 128 games. Even so, Fain frequently found himself perched on first base, in large part due to his uncanny ability to draw walks. He would walk 108 times in 1953. By comparison, New York Yankees slugger Mickey Mantle drew only 79 walks for the year. With his penchant for walking, Fain successfully reached base in 40% of his total plate appearances, second only to Minnie Minoso among White Sox regulars.

Long-time broadcaster Phil Wood, who ranks among the most knowledgeable of baseball historians, credits Paul Richards with pioneering the use of on-base percentage as a managerial tool. Wood maintains that many of the statistics that are popular in today's game have long been in use but were not maintained as official records. On-base percentage itself did not become an official statistic until 1984. Nonetheless, according to Wood, Richards regularly kept track of the on-base percentages for his players as far back as the early 1950s. The terminology that Richards used was different but the concept was the same. Richards took on-base percentages into account when setting the batting order for games. The approach produced some truly unorthodox lineups. Critics were quick to find fault; the lineups were said to be bizarre, perhaps no more so than when Richards had Fain hitting third in the order.

Richards responded to the criticism by telling observers to wait and see what happened. During Richards' tenure as manager of the White Sox, experience showed that his teams would often end up with more runners on base than their opponents. Richards led the White Sox to 89 wins in 1953 and 91 wins in 1954.

1966

Predicting who will be able to hit in the Major Leagues is the hardest single thing to do in any sport. Round ball, round bat, you've got to square it up.

—Joe Caro, long-time scout for the New York Yankees

In 1966, catcher Steve Chilcott became the second overall number one pick of the draft when he was selected by the New York Mets. The Chilcott selection would come to be considered one of the worst overall number one draft picks of all time. Chilcott never played a day in the Major Leagues. The Mets' error in selecting Chilcott as number one is magnified greatly because they chose him over Reginald Martinez Jackson, better known as Reggie. While rarely would the number one overall pick be without controversy in future years, the Mets' failure to select Jackson may be considered the greatest draft blunder ever.

Chilcott was a powerful left-handed hitting star at Antelope Valley High School in California. However, after being drafted number one by the Mets in 1966, he severely injured his shoulder in a game in the Florida State League in 1967 and was never the same player again. The Mets released him in 1971. The selection of Chilcott not only looks bad in retrospect, but was subject to criticism the day it was made. Many observers believe the Mets avoided the often flamboyant and controversial Jackson because of so-called "character issues." In Jackson's case, "character" appears to have been euphemistic for race; he was a Black man dating a White girl in a time when interracial dating was not widely accepted.

George Weiss, the Mets' general manager in 1966, was not believed to hold enlightened views on race. During his very successful tenure with the cross-town New York Yankees in the 1950s, Weiss was one of the last baseball executives to sign Black players. As noted by author David Halberstam in his excellent work, *October 1964*, Weiss' failure to integrate the Yankees after Jackie Robinson broke baseball's color line in 1947 ultimately led to the decline of the storied Yankee franchise in the mid-sixties.[16]

Officials in the Mets organization such as Bing Devine, Weiss's assistant general manager, defended the selection of Chilcott as a pick that was based on need. Mets manager Casey Stengel defended the pick as well, noting that, "if you don't have a catcher, you're gonna' have a lot of passed balls."

After the Mets' selection of Chilcott, the Oakland Athletics, with the enthusiastic backing of legendary scout Bob Zuk, made Reggie Jackson the second overall pick. Jackson would become a foundational building block for the soon-to-be world champion Athletics. The muscular Jackson would go on to have a 21-year Hall of Fame career, blasting 563 homers and driving in 1,702 runs. He led the Athletics to three World Series championships and then led the New York Yankees to world championships in 1977 and 1978.

In addition to winning an American League Most Valuable Player Award and appearing in fourteen American League All-Star Games, Jackson won two World Series Most Valuable Player Awards, earning him the nickname "Mr. October." During his lengthy career, Jackson publicly feuded with firebrand Yankees manager Billy Martin and several other teammates and opponents. He infamously referred to himself as "the straw who stirred the drink" in a 1978 *Sport Magazine* interview. Oakland A's teammate Darold Knowles famously quipped that "there isn't enough mustard in all the world to cover that hot dog."

1966

The Legend of Harry Billie

Pittsburgh Pirates scout George Zuraw had seen the arm. He knew what was coming. As 21-year-old Harry Billie prepared to unleash a throw from right field at the Pirates' spring training site in Fort Myers, Florida, Zuraw tried to warn the catcher, Sam Narron. "Be careful," Zuraw yelled to Narron. Narron took the warning as an insult. He had been a catcher with the 1935 St. Louis Cardinals, when Dizzy Dean was in his prime. He had caught some of the best arms in baseball. Then the throw came whizzing in from right field. Narron handled it cleanly, but it left an impact. Zuraw heard Narron exclaim, "Wow!"

There was a time when Harry Billie prompted a similar reaction from coaches, scouts and fellow players alike. He was a full-blooded Seminole who had grown up on the Big Cypress Seminole Reservation near Everglades City, Florida. He stood five feet, eleven inches and weighed 180 pounds but played much bigger, a man among boys. He was listed as a shortstop, third baseman, and catcher but he could play every position on the diamond. He also excelled in football and basketball.

Zuraw once saw Billie play in a game for the Naples High School football team. A flanker, Billie leaped for a pass that had been overthrown. As he jumped, Billie tipped the ball over the defender with his right hand. Still in the air, he caught the ball with his left hand and went in for the touchdown. For Zuraw, it was the greatest play he had ever seen at any level of football.

In 1964, Billie signed with the Pirates. In spring training that year, he hit against Virgil Trucks, who had retired a few years earlier after a 17-year Major League career. Trucks threw 15 balls. Billie hit 10 of them out of the park. Billie spent four years in the Pirates' organization, mostly in the low minors. He never hit well, compiling a .230 batting average over the four seasons. Some say that Billie never had a chance, that he was unable to adjust to living off the reservation and in a "White man's world."

There were reports that he had bounced some checks. Whatever problems Billie may have had with the law, Zuraw termed his conduct "harmless." More than 50 years after first seeing Billie play baseball, Zuraw insisted that he had "as good a set of tools as anybody I have ever worked out."

1967

I figured I would be taken in the top three, but when I heard I was going to the Yankees, I was elated. That changed my mind about attending college. I was a Yankees fan, and the opportunity to play for my favorite team was too good to pass up.

– Ron Blomberg, as recounted in *Designated Hebrew: The Ron Blomberg Story*

The Mets' cross-town rival, the New York Yankees, held the first pick of the 1967 draft. The Yankees had enjoyed unparalleled success from the 1920s to the early 1960s. However, the Yankees' fortunes had turned south dramatically just two years into the draft. The fabled Bronx Bombers finished dead last in the American League in 1966.

Ironically, the historical success of the Yankees was a significant factor leading to the adoption of the draft. The draft was seen as a way to limit the ability of the Yankees to attract and sign the best prospects throughout the country. Now, the Yankees franchise was an immediate beneficiary, as they held the number one overall selection in 1967. The Yankees used the pick to choose Atlanta high school star Ron Blomberg. Atley Donald, who had pitched for the Yankees in the 1941 and 1942 World Series before turning to scouting, was the scout most responsible for recommending Blomberg.[17]

A native of Louisiana, Donald followed Blomberg's high school career closely and was present at a high school All-Star Game in Atlanta-Fulton County Stadium when Blomberg hit a 420-foot home run to dead center field. Blomberg was an accomplished athlete who lettered in four sports in high school. In addition to his power, Blomberg hit for average and possessed great running speed for a muscular six foot, two inch athlete.

The Yankee management drooled over the prospect of the left-handed, power-hitting Blomberg routinely depositing baseballs into Yankee Stadium's short right-field porch. The team envisioned that he would succeed the aging Mickey Mantle as the Yankees' next great superstar. As a further bonus, Blomberg's Jewish ethnicity would be welcomed in New York, a market with a very large Jewish population. As the Yankees had been late to integrate their team, they also had very few Jewish players over the years. Blomberg seemed to be a "home run" on every count.

Unfortunately, persistent and recurring shoulder and leg injuries prevented Blomberg from fulfilling his great promise. He began his Yankees career by hitting an impressive .322 in 1971. However, the team's hopes for Blomberg had faded by 1975, as injuries sapped him of his power and his ability to contribute defensively. He played in parts of eight Major League seasons and hit well over .300 in three of them but only hit 52 lifetime homers and stole a paltry six bases. He signed a lucrative four-year deal with the Chicago White Sox in 1977 but only managed 169 plate appearances for the "pale hose" before he was cut, never to return to the game.

Blomberg's greatest and most lasting contributions to baseball are mostly as a footnote – in addition to being the first player chosen in the 1967 draft, he also became, in 1973, the first designated hitter in the history of the Major Leagues. As Blomberg recounts in his autobiography, *Designated Hebrew*, while his popularity continues to remain high in New York and especially with the Jewish community, he never came close to fulfilling the expectations of being a number one overall selection in the draft.[18] Blomberg's career Wins Above Replacement value pales in comparison with the career WAR numbers of several of the players whom the Yankees passed over in the 1967 draft, including Dusty Baker, Bobby Grich, Don Baylor, Vida Blue, Jon Matlack, Jerry Reuss, and Ted Simmons.

Good Prospect, Bad X-ray

Veteran scouts describe the scouting profession as both collegial and competitive. It's an exclusive club. Scouts often run into each other at ballparks across the country. Friendships develop. There are times when scouts from competing teams will help out a friend on a rival team. White Sox scout John Tumminia gives an example based on his experiences as a pro scout. Tumminia says that if a scout is lacking information on a certain player, opposing scouts who have become friends will provide data to fill in the gaps.

For Tumminia, it was always a small group that he would trust, perhaps no more than six or seven. While the friendships formed among rival scouts are lasting, the job is distinctly competitive. Tumminia shared a close bond with Billy Blitzer of the Chicago Cubs, but he never wanted to see Blitzer get a player for the Cubs whom Tumminia liked. "I want to get that player at a higher pick than the Cubs," Tumminia says.

Tumminia spent 32 years as a scout. For roughly half of his career, he scouted amateur players at the high school and college levels. He spent the latter 16 years scouting professional players at all levels, from rookie ball to the majors. From his years scouting amateur players, Tumminia fondly recalls the excitement that developed as the teams prepared for the amateur draft each June. "When it comes to the draft," Tumminia says, "that's a special couple of days where your name is attached to a player – and there's a lot of pride and ego involved in this too – there's a lot of pride in getting a player." Over the years, the "pride and ego" that Tumminia experienced in getting a player – and, indeed, the very competitive nature of the business – has led scouts to employ an assortment of tricks to ward off rival scouts.

Veteran Dodgers scout Carl Loewenstine started in scouting in 1973. He was assigned to cover the Midwestern states. For Loewenstine, when he came across a legitimate prospect in the Midwest, it was something special. "You can go a couple of weeks in the Midwest before you see a hotshot prospect," Loewenstine says, whereas in areas like California, Florida or Texas, "they see hotshots twice a week."

In the late 1970s, at a time when Loewenstine was still very much in the learning stages of his career, he became enthralled with a pitcher from the University of Kentucky. Loewenstine found it difficult to contain his excitement. One day while the prospect was pitching, Cincinnati Reds scout Gene Bennett, a wily veteran, approached Loewenstine, pointed to the mound and said, "He's a pretty good pitcher, isn't he, Carl?" Loewenstine responded, "Man, I tell you what, Gene, he looks pretty good to me. I really like him."

Bennett replied, "The only thing wrong is, it's a shame about his back." Loewenstine asked, "What are you talking about, Gene?" Bennett then pulled out a radiology film from his briefcase. Loewenstine recalls, "the film showed a man's spine and it's got two or three screws in it." Bennett held the film up to the sun and you could see the screws and all the patch jobs on the spine. "That's his x-ray there," Bennett said. "His back isn't very good."

Only years later did Loewenstine learn that Bennett had often pulled out the same x-ray for any number of pitchers, trying to run other scouts off a prized prospect.

1968

Any time a player does not live up to our expectations, we try to evaluate and go back and see how we reported on him. We look at the reports and see if they matched the tools. That's fairly easy to do and you can do that within the first year. With most players, other than injuries, it is player make-up and work ethic and his determination. Those things are usually the contributing factors more than any other factors.

    –Jim Fleming, long-time baseball scout for the Montreal Expos and Miami Marlins

The New York Mets won only 61 games during the 1967 season, ending with the worst record in the Major Leagues. As a result, for purposes of the 1968 draft, the Mets were back in the catbird seat, possessing the first overall pick. It would be the third consecutive year that a New York team held the number one overall selection.

The Mets chose 17-year-old shortstop Tim Foli out of Notre Dame High School in Sherman Oaks, California. The fiery Foli made it to the majors with the Mets in just two years but was never able to hit at the level one would expect from the number one overall pick. The Mets' director of player development, Nelson Burbrink, projected that Foli would be able to hit with power. Burbrink noted that "each time Mets' general manager Bob Scheffing saw [Foli], he hit a home run." The irony was that Foli did not hit a single home run in the 102 Major Leagues games in which he played for the Mets.

Foli's combustible personality led to numerous arguments and altercations, including one with Mets coach Joe Pignatano. The Mets traded Foli to the Montreal Expos in 1972. In 16 Major Leagues seasons, Foli earned the reputation of a solid fielding but mediocre hitting journeyman shortstop.

With the second overall pick, the Oakland Athletics selected Palm Beach high school pitching star Pete Broberg. However, Broberg chose to attend college and so enrolled at Dartmouth University. Broberg became eligible again for the draft in 1971, when he would be selected by the Washington Senators. Broberg would play for eight seasons in the Major Leagues but, in every season, lost more games than he won. He closed out his baseball career in 1978 with a record of 41 wins and 71 losses.

With the fifth pick in the draft, the Los Angeles Dodgers chose Stamford, Connecticut high school star Bobby Valentine. His selection provides some interesting parallels to the Mets' selection of Foli. Both Valentine and Foli had irascible personalities, both were drafted by teams across the country and both were considered to be shortstop candidates.

Valentine starred in both baseball and football in high school. Unlike Foli, Valentine was the epitome of the rare five-tool player, excelling in hitting, hitting for power, throwing, running, and fielding. He could also do most things off the field as well or better than anyone else. In his first few years in professional baseball, Valentine was as good as he was in high school. He impressed his managers and twice won his league's Most Valuable Player Award.

Valentine's first manager was Tommy Lasorda. Though Lasorda was given to overstatement in evaluating young Dodger talent, he truly believed that Valentine was destined for greatness. During the 1971 and 1972 seasons, Valentine played 220 games for the Dodgers. His overall performance was mediocre but he did show flashes of greatness. In retrospect, it seems the Dodgers were overly impatient with his development, perhaps because the strongly-opinionated Valentine often clashed with management. In 1972, the Dodgers shipped Valentine 30 miles down the freeway to the California Angels. Valentine went on to play for ten years in the Major Leagues.

Valentine's name and story would be but another casualty on the long list of "can't miss prospects who missed" but for the fact that he went on to have a long and colorful managerial career in baseball. He managed for 23 seasons, including for the Mets and in Japan, where he became a revered celebrity.

Though the first round of the June 1968 draft was largely an exercise in drafting futility, the New York Yankees found a gem with the fourth overall pick in Kent State University catcher Thurman Munson. In 1970, Munson's first full season in the Major Leagues, he hit .302 and won the American League Rookie of the Year Award. He made seven All-Star Game appearances during his career. Most importantly, he became the captain and foundation of the Yankees' world championships in 1977 and 1978.

Despite the relative failure of the Los Angeles Dodgers' first pick in Valentine, the Dodgers' 1968 draft is considered one of the greatest of all time. Most of the credit belongs to their director of scouting, Al Campanis, who was both a baseball and Dodgers "lifer." Campanis was one of the many unsung and underappreciated Dodgers scouts who helped the legendary Branch Rickey build the Brooklyn team into a perennial National League contender.

Campanis literally wrote the book on the "Dodger Way of Playing Baseball." In almost 300 pages, his book explained things such as the organization's preference for speed and agility and provides advice to young players on how to comport themselves as Dodgers. Working under Branch Rickey, Campanis is credited with finding baseball legends Sandy Koufax and Roberto Clemente. He also was involved in the signing of stellar outfielders Tommy Davis and Willie Davis.

Campanis and the Dodgers organization had a rocky start in the 1965 draft, selecting only five players who would ever play in the majors. In 1966, they improved greatly, snaring pitcher Charlie Hough, infielder/outfielder Bill Russell, and infielders Billy Grabarkewitz and Ted Sizemore. Hough pitched for the Dodgers for more than ten years. Russell arrived in the majors in 1969 and remained for 18 years. Sizemore, a fifteenth-round draft choice from the University of Michigan, also joined the Dodgers in 1969 and won the Rookie of the Year Award. Grabarkewitz's star burned out quickly in Los Angeles but he is remembered for his quips and quick-witted retorts. Aptly nicknamed "Gabby," Grabarkewitz uttered some of the most memorable lines in baseball this side of Yogi Berra.

In 1972, Grabarkewitz quipped that he knew the Dodgers were not going to trade him after they went to the trouble and expense of stitching all the letters of his name on his jersey. The Dodgers then traded him to the California Angels after the season. Injuries dampened Grabarkewitz's career but not his comedic wit. "I've been x-rayed so much I glow in the dark," he would say.

By 1968, Campanis and the Dodgers finally hit their draft stride in a big way. Los Angeles added 15 major leaguers through the draft in 1968, including pitchers Doyle Alexander and Geoff Zahn, outfielder Tom Paciorek, catcher Joe Ferguson, third baseman Ron Cey, first baseman Steve Garvey, second baseman Davey Lopes and outfielder/first baseman Bill Buckner. The 1968 draft became the nucleus for the Dodgers' success in the 1970s and into the 1980s, which included a World Series championship in 1981. The Dodgers were one of the first teams to "figure it out" in the draft era and use the draft as a foundation for future success.

Five years after the 1968 draft, Garvey, Lopes and Cey joined Bill Russell in Los Angeles to form one of the greatest infields in baseball history. From 1973 to 1981, day in and day out, Garvey, Lopes, Cey and Russell were the most famous foursome to perform at Dodger Stadium since the Beatles packed the house in August of 1966. While Garvey was the last member to join the "fab four" he was also the most famous and productive. His movie-star good looks and potent bat quickly made him the face of the franchise. Garvey was the National League's Most Valuable Player in 1974. He was a very productive clutch hitter for most of his 19-year big league career and became a ten-time All-Star selection. For his career, Garvey drove in 1,308 runs and had a batting average of .294.

Bill Russell, Davey Lopes, Ron Cey, and Steve Garvey played together for a record eight and a half years, becoming the longest running infield in baseball history. Collectively, they garnered 23 All-Star Game appearances. Anchored by these four All-Stars, the Dodgers battled with the Cincinnati Reds for supremacy in the National League West almost every year from 1973 to the end of the decade. The historic 1968 draft provided the Dodgers with the core players responsible for the team's sustained success.

The First Rule of Scouting

For Buck Showalter, former manager of the Yankees, Diamondbacks, Rangers and Orioles, the first rule of scouting is to find out where the mother and father of a prospect are sitting at a game and sit right behind them. Showalter firmly believes that a scout will get more useful information for evaluating a player from the mother and father than he will get from on-field scouting.

"Hell, everybody's got the statistics, that's easy," Showalter says. He has greater interest in the information that a scout can bring in on a player that other scouts couldn't get.

Showalter advises scouts to watch the player interact with his mother and father, sister and brother. "Watch in between innings," he says, "watch the player with his teammates, watch them in the parking lot after the games, what car they get into, that's scouting."

Pirates associate scout Matthew Burns takes a similar approach. Burns says that it is easy to find the family of the star high school or college player "because everyone is talking to them." Burns wants to hear what the family says about a prospect and what other people are saying.

Burns is not reluctant to ask other students, "How is this guy as a human being?" He is confident that the students are not going to lie. "If they don't like another person," he says, "they are going to tell you and they are going to give you information that no one else can give you."

Burns also questions umpires. ""How is this guy as a player?" he will ask an umpire. "Is he respectful to you?"

For Showalter, "There is a picture to be painted about every player." Unless a scout has spoken with the player's high school counselor or with the parking lot attendant who interacts with the player, Showalter says, the picture will not be complete.

1969

You never really know. As much as anything, it is the ability to make adjustments. It's a game of constant adjustments. For the average player, it takes five or six seasons in the minors to learn to make the adjustments. Then, once a guy reaches the majors, it probably takes three years or 1,500 at-bats to know what kind of a big-league hitter you have. There's going to be peaks and valleys. Hopefully, it's not all valleys. Some people stay in those valleys a little longer, they don't have the make-up to stick with it. Who knows?

    – Bill Livesey, scout and former director of player development, New York Yankees

Enthusiasm was running high in June of 1969 when the Washington Senators selected power-hitting prep star Jeff Burroughs, a product of Long Beach, California, with the first pick in the draft. No less a hitting authority then Ted Williams had labeled Burroughs "as the best 18-year-old hitter I've ever seen."[19] The Senators' chief scout, Jack Sheehan, was similarly impressed. When taking batting practice at Anaheim Stadium before the draft, Burroughs had put on such a power display for scouts that Sheehan described him as having the best power of any 18-year-old he had ever seen. Other scouts concurred in the assessment. With the Senators' selection of Burroughs, baseball fans in the Nation's capital expected better times ahead for their Senators.

Burroughs spent the 1969 season in rookie ball. After he had played four months with the Denver Bears in 1970, the Senators promoted him to the majors. He made his debut for Washington on July 20, 1970 at the age of 19. Facing Al Downing of the Milwaukee Brewers, Burroughs went hitless in three at-bats. In subsequent games, Burroughs continued to struggle with Major League pitching. He also incurred the wrath of Senators' manager Ted Williams. Burroughs managed to stay in Washington only 10 days. On July 30, Williams banished the hot-tempered Burroughs and his .167 batting average to the minors to "heat his bat and cool his head." Burroughs had little appreciation for Williams at the time but, over the years, came to be thankful for his tutelage.

By the time the 1972 season opened, the Senators had been recast as the Texas Rangers and were playing their home games in Arlington,

Texas. Burroughs opened the season in Denver, where he hit .303 in 84 games and earned a promotion to the parent club.

By 1973, Burroughs was in the big leagues to stay. He slugged a home run in the second game of the season, the first of 30 homers he would hit that year. For the season, he hit .279 in 151 games for the Rangers. In 1974, Burroughs' star shone even brighter, as he slugged 25 home runs, had a league-leading 118 runs batted in, and was named the American League's Most Valuable Player. Burroughs appeared to be on a path to stardom and perhaps even to Cooperstown. However, throughout the final 11 years of his career, Burroughs was never able to replicate the success of his banner 1974 season. He did go on to have a fine 16-year Major League career, amassing 240 lifetime homers and 882 runs batted in.

While it has been very rare for the number one overall draft pick to transform a team's fortunes in short order, almost all picks look good in the light of the draft day shine. Burroughs' experience is not uncommon and counsels caution in projecting greatness based on early success. Burroughs' career counsels against extrapolating future success on the basis of a relatively short sample.

If one had evaluated the 1969 draft class following the 1980 season, Burroughs' selection would clearly have been ranked as the best choice in the draft. By comparison, pitcher Bert Blyleven, whom the Minnesota Twins selected in the third round, had only 12 more career wins than losses at that point and had been named to only one All-Star Game. From 1981 on, however, Burroughs endured a precipitous decline. In contrast, Blyleven would go on to pitch effectively for 11 more years and would become the only player from the 1969 draft to be enshrined in the Hall of Fame.

The Dutch-born Blyleven came to the attention of Twins scout Jesse Flores while playing at Santiago High School in Garden Grove, California. Flores was one of the first Mexican-born players to reach the big leagues but made his real contribution to the game as a scout in Southern California. In addition to Blyleven, Flores signed a breath-taking 70 future Major League players, including Lyman Bostock, Rick Dempsey and Jesse Orosco.

Flores not only signed Blyleven but played a key role in the pitcher's development. The scout served as Blyleven's first pitching coach in the instructional league. More importantly, Flores helped Blyleven in making the transition to professional baseball and life away from home. When the naive young pitcher cooked and ate a spoiled steak, it was Flores whom Blyleven called to nurse him back to health. Nicknamed the "Frying Dutchman" for his penchant for setting the shoelaces of his teammates on fire, Blyleven possessed one of the best curveballs in Major League history. He amassed 287 wins during his 22-year playing career.

See Ball, Hit Ball

Dr. Bill Harrison pitched for two years at the University of California in the mid-1960s. He eventually became the number one starter for the Cal Bears. The Baltimore Orioles were sufficiently impressed with Harrison to offer him a pro contract. However, Harrison blew out his shoulder the day before he was to sign with Baltimore. With his dream of playing professional baseball derailed, Harrison went on to become a doctor of optometry.

For the better part of 40 years, Harrison trained baseball players and other athletes to improve their vision, concentration, and focus. Harrison worked with more than a hundred major leaguers, including stars George Brett of the Kansas City Royals and Mark McGwire of the Oakland Athletics and St. Louis Cardinals.

Over the course of his career, Harrison observed many batters whose eyes failed to work in tandem to identify pitches. The difficulty, Harrison would say, is that when a batter's two eyes do not work together, every pitch looks to be the same speed. Even when a batter knows that a curveball is coming, the pitch would look to be the same speed as a fastball.

Harrison used an analogy to explain the adverse effect on a ballplayer. "One way to think about it," he said, "is that each eye is capable of 100 watts but the brain says, 'let's just use the left eye, we don't need the right one.' That's okay in just about everything a person does, but it's not okay when you are trying to hit a baseball. When a player wants to see a high-velocity pitch, it's an asset to have both eyes at 100 watts."

On the other hand, Harrison would say, "the players who have an exceptional level of depth perception – not merely average and not merely very good – and have the ability to use their two eyes together, they see slight changes in speed without even knowing that they see it."

With reference to the ability of individual players to use their two eyes together, Harrison said, "Rod Carew had it. Tony Gwynn had it. John Kruk had it. Barry Bonds had it. Bobby Bonilla had it. Don Mattingly had it. Sammy Sosa had it. Adam Dunn had it."

Harrison did not include either George Brett or Mark McGwire on his list of players who "had it." The reason? "George Brett didn't have it, but we trained him so that his two eyes would work together." In Harrison's view, McGwire didn't have it either. However, like Brett, McGwire "trained it."

1970

The two biggest risks in the draft are high school catchers and high school right-handed pitchers. History will show you that. The failure rate is astronomical. Yes, you can also get some good ones going that route. When you look at how many high school catchers have been picked, there are not a whole lot that were taken up high and became what you thought they would become.

– Ron Hopkins, special assistant to the general manager, Pittsburgh Pirates

No draft occurs in a vacuum; each one is the product of the unique circumstances of the times. The June 1970 draft took place with the backdrop of Johnny Bench leading the Cincinnati Reds to 102 regular season wins and the World Series. Bench hit 45 home runs in 1970 and drove in an astounding 148 runs, won the National League Most Valuable Player Award and provided the best defense available outside of the Pentagon. On-field success always has a subtle influence on the draft. It was no coincidence, therefore, that the 1970 draft would become the so-called "Year of the Catcher." Teams selected a record six backstops in the first round, including three of the first four draft choices.

The San Diego Padres held the first pick. Running the Padres' baseball operations was a transplanted New Yorker, Emil Joseph Bavasi, known to all by his childhood moniker of "Buzzie." Baseball was literally the Bavasi family business. Buzzie Bavasi had started with the Dodgers in 1938 under Larry MacPhail and quickly became one of MacPhail's most trusted lieutenants.

With the first pick in 1970, Bavasi and his team selected a strapping six-foot-four power-hitting catcher from Walker High School in Atlanta, Mike Ivie. In one 21-game period at Walker High, Ivie had hit 21 home runs. Understandably, the Padres saw him as the next Johnny Bench – a catcher who would provide dominant power in the middle of the lineup for years to come.

Ivie spent all of the 1972 and 1973 seasons in the minor leagues, playing first base exclusively. The Padres had determined, to their great chagrin, that Ivie did not have the ability to catch at the Major League level. Ivie's failure as a backstop remains something of a mystery. No less an authority than Cincinnati's Hall of Fame catcher Johnny Bench had once declared, "Ivie has the softest hands, the best catcher's hands I've ever seen."[20] According to San Diego scout Leon Hamilton, Ivie "got some kind of mental block about throwin' the ball back to the pitcher. Couldn't even lob it back."[21] Hamilton suspected that some of Ivie's friends had convinced him that he would last longer in baseball if he played first base.

Although Ivie spent time with the Padres in 1974, he did not play a meaningful role with the team until 1975. His power potential was so prodigious that players on the opposing teams would gather to watch him take batting practice. Although he hit for a decent average in his three full seasons with San Diego, Ivie never reached double-digit home runs in any of those years. By 1977, the Padres had concluded that his batting practice power would never translate into the game-time power they had been expecting and made him available for trade.

In 1978, the Padres traded Ivie to a divisional rival, the San Francisco Giants. From 1978 to 1980, while alternating between first base and the outfield for the Giants, he had his best years in baseball. He hit a career high .308 for the Giants in 1978 and followed that up with 27 home runs and a .286 batting average in 1979.

While the first round in 1970 was focused on catchers, a re-evaluation of the draft may more accurately depict it as the year of the relief pitcher. The Chicago White Sox were led by general manager Edwin Short. Short and the Sox struck it rich in the second round with pitcher Terry Forster and followed up with a bona fide "steal" in the ninth round in pitcher Rich "Goose" Gossage. Roland Hemond, then the farm director for the White Sox, would describe Forster and Gossage as the best young relief pitching tandem he had ever seen.

The early careers of Forster and Gossage would be very much tied together. Though Gossage's Hall of Fame career would qualify him as the most successful player drafted in 1970, Forster made a more immediate impact. By 1972, Forster had become Chicago's stopper out of the bullpen. He saved 29 games that year, the second highest total in the American League. Forster led the White Sox in saves again in 1974 but succumbed to an arm injury, which opened the door for Gossage to become Chicago's primary stopper. Gossage excelled in the role of closer, leading the American League in saves in 1975.

Even though *The Sporting News* had named Forster and Gossage as the American League "Firemen of the Year" in 1974 and 1975, respectively, the White Sox moved both pitchers to the starting rotation in 1976. After the season, Chicago then traded the pair to the Pittsburgh Pirates in exchange for slugger Richie Zisk. Both Forster and Gossage were granted free agency after the 1977 season and, on November 22, 1977, each signed lucrative free agent deals, Gossage with the New York Yankees and Forster with the Los Angeles Dodgers.

Gossage went on to become a dominant closer for the Yankees for the next six years. Over the course of his 22-year career, the "Goose" appeared in nine All-Star Games. Forster put together a stellar 16-year Major League career in which he had a 3.23 earned run average and posted 127 saves, primarily as a middle innings reliever.

Joe McIlvaine, General Manager

For a long time, Joe McIlvaine's preferred career choice appeared to be out of reach. A pitcher by trade, McIlvaine had dreamed of playing pro ball ever since childhood. He grew up on Hampden Avenue in Narbeth, Pennsylvania. Less than two miles away was the imposing presence of St. Charles Borromeo Catholic Seminary. For as long as McIlvaine could remember, there were two constants in his life, baseball and the Catholic Church.

Playing for the St. Charles Borromeo Seminary High School baseball team, McIlvaine compiled a credible record. His résumé included games against Cheltenham High School and its star, future Hall of Famer Reggie Jackson. However, McIlvaine stood five feet, eleven inches and weighed only 130 pounds. It was not the kind of physique that would attract baseball scouts.

If a career in baseball was McIlvaine's first choice, becoming a Catholic priest was a close second. When he graduated from high school without any prospects for playing pro ball, McIlvaine turned to "Plan B." St. Charles Borromeo Seminary became his home for the next four years.

While in the seminary, McIlvaine studied Latin, philosophy and theology and, during the summer months, played on a semi-pro baseball team in Philadelphia. McIlvaine's time in the seminary coincided with an unexpected growth spurt. By the end of his second year at the seminary, he had gained six inches and 30 pounds. Two years later, McIlvaine stood six-feet-six, and the baseball scouts were in pursuit. In June 1969, McIlvaine left the seminary to embark on a career in baseball. "The seminary really takes a commitment," he would say later. "I don't think I was committed to making the sacrifices."

McIlvaine played minor league ball in the Detroit Tigers organization for five years, from 1969 to1973. In 1972, with the Class A Lakeland Tigers, he pitched in 43 games, all in relief, and had a record of 9 wins and 6 losses, with a 1.57 earned run average. The majors seemed a realistic reach. A year later, however, the dream unraveled. Playing for the Clinton Pilots in the Midwest League, McIlvaine saw his earned run average balloon to 5.22. He consulted with Clinton manager Jim Leyland to discuss his future. When Leyland encouraged him to pursue options other than pro ball, McIlvaine decided to quit. The Tigers released him after the 1973 season.

Unsure of his next step, the 24-year-old McIlvaine wrote letters to Major League organizations across the country asking for a job. Only the Baltimore Orioles indicated any interest. McIlvaine interviewed with the Birds' general manager Frank Cashen, who dangled a position as a scout. McIlvaine took the job, the first step in a lengthy career that included serving as general manager for both the New York Mets and the San Diego Padres.

1971

The players' dreams of glory are no more compelling than the scouts' dreams of discovery, of seeing the crystal through the carbon, the future shining through the present.

– Kevin Kerrane, author of *Dollar Sign on the Muscle: The World of Baseball Scouting*

The 1971 draft represented another year of growing pains for teams participating in the draft. Just as a baseball bat has a "sweet spot," the first ten picks of the amateur draft are considered to be "the sweet spot" of the draft – the ideal place to secure high-impact, foundational building blocks. In hindsight, the teams holding the first 10 picks in the 1971 draft failed miserably. The draft produced one of the most inept performances by team executives in the early first round in the entire history of the draft.

In 1971, Danny Kay Goodwin was the first overall selection by the Chicago White Sox. By all accounts, Goodwin was a consensus choice among scouts due to his prodigious power and canon-like arm. Rampant comparisons to the reigning National League MVP, catcher Johnny Bench (1970 MVP), made the choice seem all but a foregone conclusion. In fact, some scouts even took to referring to Goodwin as the "Black Johnny Bench," and others even amplified the compliment by adding that Goodwin possessed the one tool Bench lacked – speed.

In contrast to many other talented prospects who toiled in relative obscurity, Goodwin's exploits at Peoria Central High School were widely viewed by a growing number of admiring scouts as his legend continued to grow by word of mouth. In addition to hitting .477 in his senior high school campaign, Goodwin would periodically clout tape measure home runs. On one occasion he slugged a gargantuan home run that traveled out of the ballpark and landed on the second deck of a swimming pool well over 400 feet away. The majestic blast was fondly remembered more for its height and hang time than its distance, recalling to mind the legendary shots of Negro League star Josh Gibson or even the Bambino himself.

Chicago General Manager Roland Hemond, who would become a legend in the world of scouting over his 65-year baseball career, assumed the White Sox would be able to sign the intelligent and likeable Goodwin with their $65,000 bonus offer but Goodwin counteroffered with a $100,000 demand. Hemond and Sox did not accommodate the demand and miscalculated Danny's genuine desire to attend college unless his bonus demands were met. Consequently, Goodwin enrolled in the premed program at Southern University and thus became the first overall one number one draftee not to sign a professional baseball contract.

The nine draft picks after Danny Goodwin went on to have very undistinguished careers in baseball. Four of the picks never even made it to the majors and only one top 10 pick – the Phillies' Roy Thomas – played longer than two years in the big leagues. If the early picks of the first round were indicative, 1971 would be remembered as the worst draft in baseball history. However, in the second half of the first round, the selections improved dramatically. With the 13th pick, the California Angels selected Frank Tanana. Two picks later, the Red Sox struck it rich with future Hall of Fame slugger Jim Rice. Despite these two selections, however, the first-round picks of 1971 were historically unimpressive.

In the second round, the Phillies and Royals selected future Hall of Famers Mike Schmidt and George Brett with successive picks. While both were selected as shortstops, each converted to third base. Both went on to have stellar careers. The Phillies had the opportunity to take Schmidt in the first round but made a calculated gamble and deferred selecting him until the second round. The Royals took the same gamble with Brett. In each case, the gambles paid off. Such stories serve to emphasize the difficultly of predicting the future success of young baseball players.

Instead of selecting Schmidt in the first round, the Phillies chose to take Roy Thomas, a promising 6'5" right-handed pitcher from Lompoc, California. Thomas would spend 20 years in pro ball, but the majority of those years were in the minor leagues. He would win 116 games in the minor leagues, more than any other pitcher selected in the first round. Clearly, if Philadelphia had the opportunity to re-visit the 1971 draft, it would elevate Schmidt over Thomas on their draft board.

Similarly, with the clarity of hindsight, the Kansas City Royals would take George Brett in the first round of 1971 instead of the team's actual pick, right-handed pitcher Roy Branch. At the time, however, the Royals were convinced that Branch was poised to become "the next Bob Gibson." In high school, Branch brandished a blazing fastball. In his senior year, he had a 7-0 won-lost record and a microscopic 0.59 earned run average. Branch injured his right arm the day before the draft in a workout for Bob Gibson's team, the St. Louis Cardinals. The Royals believed the injury to be minor. Unfortunately, however, the Royals underestimated the severity of the damage to the pitcher's arm. Branch would only play in two games at the big-league level in his entire career.

The draft stories of Brett and Schmidt share many interesting similarities: (1) they were drafted with successive picks in the second round; (2) they were each passed over in the first round by their respective teams for right-handed high school pitchers; (3) they were shortstops in high school but would be shifted to third base in the minors; (4) each played under the radar in high school but became second-round picks due to the foresight and perception of scouts; and (5) they each possessed a rare determination to become outstanding Major League players.

Tony Lucadello was the scout who signed Schmidt. Lucadello ranks among the greatest scouts of all time. After playing for a few years in the minor leagues, Lucadello began scouting in 1942 for the Chicago Cubs. His scouting career extended until 1989. Lucadello was one of the authentic characters in the game. He would arrive at ballparks, always driving his trademark Chevrolet Caprice. He not only scouted for baseball talent but would also scour the area under the grandstands for loose change. Unlike many scouts, he was always nattily attired in suit and tie and wore an ever-present houndstooth fedora. His biographer, Mark Winegardner, described Lucadello as a gentleman, dignified, polite, well-mannered, patient and caring.[22]

Most scouts sit together behind home plate during games. Lucadello rarely joined the pack. Instead, he roamed the field to observe the play from a variety of different angles. He reportedly climbed trees and descended into coal mines to observe talent. Lucadello had his own unique scouting theories. He believed that every player's body had eight sides and that a scout had to continually shift his viewing angle until he had formed a three-dimensional image of the player. While the theory struck many as peculiar, Lucadello's methods proved successful. He signed more than 50 Major League Baseball players during his time as a scout.

Lucadello's most notable signees were Schmidt and Ferguson Jenkins, each of whom would be elected to the Hall of Fame in Cooperstown. In a profession where scouts often exaggerate their role in signing Major League players, Lucadello would not take credit for recommending the signing of Chicago Cubs great Ernie Banks because Banks was already a professional player in the Negro Leagues at the time. Long-time scout Carl Loewenstine learned his trade as an apprentice to Lucadello. Loewenstine considered Lucadello to be "the best scout ever at projecting the future baseball development of players from young teenagers to mature major leaguers."

Mike Schmidt was not even drafted upon graduating from Fairview High School in Dayton, Ohio. By his own admission, he was only the fifth or sixth best player on his high school team. In a day and age when strikeouts were unacceptable, Schmidt made infrequent contact with the baseball. A promising high school prospect might hit for a .500 batting average in high school. Schmidt, however, could not even muster a .300 average in high school. Further, while he was equipped with a cannon for an arm, he was unsuited to playing shortstop. Lucadello was able to look past these limitations to see Schmidt's uncommon power and smooth fielding. Lucadello labeled Schmidt a classic "late bloomer" and projected him as an above average prospect.

Years after he had become a success in baseball, Schmidt recalled that, after the draft, Lucadello arrived at Schmidt's home in his Caprice carrying a typewriter. Lucadello was there to negotiate Schmidt's contract. Schmidt signed for $37,500. His pro career started slowly. In 1971, Schmidt's first minor league season, he hit only .211 in 74 games with the Reading Phillies in the Eastern League. But, one season later, he reached the big leagues. In 1973, Schmidt's first full season with the Phillies, he hit only .196 and struck out in one of every three at-bats.

Schmidt's detractors complained of his inability to make contact. At one point, Phillies owner Ruly Carpenter took seriously the barrage of criticism that his baseball people were directing toward Schmidt. Carpenter called Lucadello to inform him that the Phillies were considering releasing Schmidt. Lucadello quickly rattled off Schmidt's attributes, listing his above average power, speed on the bases, stellar glove and rocket arm. Lucadello appealed to Carpenter to give the "late bloomer" more time.

Schmidt responded, reducing his strikeouts to less than one in every four at-bats. He would star for the Phillies for 18 seasons, hitting 548 home runs and driving in 1,595 runs to go with a .267 lifetime batting average. Along the way he won 10 Gold Gloves for his deft fielding, six Silver Slugger Awards, three National League Most Valuable Player Awards, and a World Series Most Valuable Player Award in 1980. When he was enshrined in the Hall of Fame in 1995, few people remembered the rocky start to his career. Schmidt remembered, however. He thanked Lucadello in his induction speech for never losing faith in his ability.

As with Schmidt, no one predicted stardom for George Brett during his early high school career. Despite all the similarities in the draft stories of Schmidt and Brett, there was one large difference. While Schmidt played at a small college in Ohio, Brett played high school ball under the watchful eye of numerous scouts in talent-rich Southern California. Unlike most future Hall of Famers, George Brett was not the best player in his high school and wasn't even the best player in his family. Brett had three brothers, all of whom would play professional baseball. Brett's older brother, Ken, was considered the most talented of the crew. Red Sox scout Joe Stephenson was effusive in his description of Ken Brett, calling him "the best prospect I ever saw."

The Red Sox drafted Ken Brett with the fourth pick of the 1966 draft. He reached the Major Leagues the next season and, that same year, became the youngest pitcher ever to appear in a World Series game. As with Babe Ruth years earlier, many Red Sox observers thought Ken Brett was a better hitter than pitcher. Brett drew comparisons to pitchers Sandy Koufax and Lefty Grove and power-hitting Yankee star Roger Maris. George Brett, five years younger than Ken, claims that Ken was always the better hitter in the family. Ken Brett missed the 1968 season after spending six months on active duty with the Army Reserves. Upon his return, he suffered an arm injury. Like so many phenoms before and after, Ken Brett was never again an elite pitcher after the injury.

As a short and skinny high school freshman, George Brett nearly failed to make the freshman baseball team at El Segundo High School. Dodgers scout Gib Bodet remembers Brett as "a skinny five-foot, one-inch high school freshman weighing only 90 pounds." If not for the intervention of the El Segundo High head coach, Brett would have been cut from the freshman team. At that stage of Brett's high school career, it was a stretch to envision that he would develop into a Major League superstar.

Kansas City Royals owner Ewing Kauffman possessed the foresight to hire excellent baseball people to staff his front office. He brought in Cedric Tallis to serve as general manager and oversee the team's development. Kauffman then proceeded to hire scouts Art Stewart from the Yankees and Ross "Rosey" Gilhousen from the Angels. Both were masters of their trade. Gilhousen's résumé included the signing of many quality big-league players. However, it was as the Royals' West Coast scouting director that Gilhousen established himself as one of the best talent evaluators in baseball. In 1969, Gilhousen signed Doug Bird, Jim York and Al Cowens for the Royals. In 1970, he added Jim Wohlford and Greg Minton.

In the 1971 draft, Gilhousen put his name into the pantheon of scouting greats with the selections of Steve Busby, John Wathan and George Brett. In future years, he drafted and signed Dan Quisenberry, Jamie Quirk, Darryl Motley and Ken Phelps. Kansas City celebrated its first World Series championship in 1985; Gilhousen was credited with signing five of the key players on the team. The most significant, of course, was George Brett.

Art Stewart was not involved in scouting George Brett but keenly remembers the early stages of Brett's development as a pro. In Stewart's view, Brett possessed good but not great talent. The key to Brett's development, says Stewart, was his dedication to improving as a player. Stewart says that Brett had the best work ethic of any player he had ever observed in seven decades of scouting.[23] Gilhousen's scouting report reflected a similar evaluation of Brett's tools. Yet Gilhousen also saw the intangible qualities that suggested possible greatness ahead.

Like Schmidt, Brett was not an immediate success in the minors. However, he was able to change his hitting approach under the tutelage of the Royals' hitting guru, Charlie Lau. Brett's work ethic allowed him to exceed the most optimistic hopes and projections of Gilhousen and his other advocates in the organization. Twenty-eight years later, Brett was inducted into Cooperstown as a first-ballot Hall of Famer.

Brett ended his career with a batting average of .305 to go with 317 home runs and 1,596 runs batted in. He remains the only player in baseball history to win batting titles in three different decades. Brett and Schmidt ended their careers as two of the best third basemen of all time. Not even their most ardent supporters could have anticipated their extraordinary success.

In addition to Hall of Famers Rice, Schmidt, and Brett, the 1971 draft also produced pitching stars Frank Tanana and Ron Guidry. The Yankees drafted Guidry in the third round. He went on to have a stellar fourteen-year career. In 1978, Guidry put together one of the most dominant years of any pitcher in history. He won 25 games and lost only three, with an earned run average of 1.74. In doing so, he led the Yankees to a World Series title and won the American League Cy Young Award.

The Eleventh Guy

In 1976, pitcher Bill Bordley concluded his highly successful baseball career at Bishop Montgomery High School in Torrance, California by being named California Player of the Year. It was the second year that he had received the honor. Bordley was left-handed and stood six-foot-three, features that Major League teams coveted.

The Milwaukee Brewers took Bordley with the fourth pick in the June 1976 draft. At the conclusion of the draft, a Milwaukee scout opened negotiations with Bordley and his family. The Brewers' initial offer was in the $60,000 - $65,000 range. Bordley and his father pushed for more, but the Brewers remained firm.

Hoping to close the deal, the Brewers' scout decided to give the Bordley family a brief explanation of how the bonus system worked. According to the scout, it was all very simple. "Well, you know," the scout said, "the number one guy always gets $90,000 to $100,000; the second guy gets $80,000 to $90,000; the third guy always gets $70,000 to $80,000; and the fourth guy always gets $60,000 to $70,000."

After the scout had completed his explanation, Bordley's father remarked, "Boy, I'd hate to be that eleventh guy."

The negotiations broke down, and Bordley accepted a scholarship to pitch for the University of Southern California. The Cincinnati Reds later selected him in the first round of the January 1979 draft. However, Commissioner Bowie Kuhn found that the California Angels had engaged in pre-draft discussions with Bordley that were tantamount to tampering. The Commissioner's office negated the Reds' selection of Bordley and assigned his rights to the San Francisco Giants. Shortly thereafter, the Giants and Bordley agreed on a bonus of $250,000, the largest sum of money ever paid to an amateur to that date.

Bordley spent the 1979 season and the first part of 1980 with the Triple-A Phoenix Giants. San Francisco called him up to the majors on June 30, 1980. He started six games for the Giants in 1980 before encountering arm troubles that would end his career.

Bordley's final game for the Giants came on September 9, 1980, when he pitched two-thirds of an inning in relief. He ended his Major League career with a record of two wins and three losses.

1972

I try not to say that somebody is a great player because great players are in the Hall of Fame.
– Jim Fleming, former vice president of player development and scouting for the Florida Marlins

The San Diego Padres again held the first overall pick in the 1972 draft. The Padres used the pick to select shortstop-third baseman Dave Roberts, of the University of Oregon. Thus, the infielder became the first collegiate player to be drafted with the top pick since Rick Monday in 1965.

Roberts was drafted on June 6, and signed a Major League contract on June 7. The Padres thought so highly of him that they immediately placed him on the Major League roster and activated him in time to play in the second game of the team's June 7 doubleheader. Roberts became only the sixth player ever drafted who began his career at the Major League level without playing a day in the minors. He would post creditable numbers in his first season, hitting .244 with five home runs and driving in 33 runs in 100 games.

In 1973 Roberts started the season slowly. He had only one hit in his first 16 at-bats. By the sixth game of the season, manager Don Zimmer had removed him from the starting lineup. The Padres demoted him to Hawaii of the Pacific Coast League, where he hit .375 in 22 games and earned a promotion back to San Diego. Upon his return, Roberts continued to hit with authority, batting .286 with 21 home runs and 64 runs batted in. At that point, his star appeared to be rising. There was every indication that the Padres had chosen wisely with the first pick of the 1972 draft.

Unfortunately, the success that Roberts experienced was short-lived. He was never able to duplicate his 1973 season. Over his 10-year Major League career, Roberts averaged a mere five home runs and 20 runs batted in each year, with a paltry .239 career batting average. In 1976, the Padres converted Roberts to catcher, but he never was able to hit well enough to justify a full-time Major League job. For the Padres and their fans, Roberts' selection as the first overall pick in 1972 qualifies as a severe disappointment.

While 1972 was a relatively poor draft class, the third round of the draft was clearly "the money round." In another interesting coincidence reminiscent of the back-to-back selections of Brett and Schmidt in 1971, the two best players and only Hall of Famers from the 1972 draft were selected three picks apart in the third round. The Cleveland Indians drafted right-handed pitcher Dennis Eckersley with the second pick in the third round. Three picks later, the Montreal Expos chose Gary Carter. In another irony of the draft, it was Carter who would follow in Bench's footsteps – from behind the plate to Cooperstown – and not any of the six catchers drafted in the first round of 1970.

Eckersley became an excellent starting pitcher for Cleveland but was shipped to the Boston Red Sox in a 1978 trade. Eckersley was a dominating starter for the first half of his career, amassing almost 200 wins and 2,400 strikeouts. However, he only reached an elite Hall of Fame level when Oakland Athletics manager Tony La Russa moved him to the bullpen in 1987. As Oakland's stopper, Eckersley's performance was, at times, otherworldly. In his career year of 1992, he won both the American League Most Valuable Player Award and the Cy Young Award with 51 saves and a 1.91 earned run average. In his 11 years as a closer, Eckersley earned 390 saves. He was elected to the Hall of Fame in his first year of eligibility in 2004.

Carter played primarily as an outfielder at the appropriately named Sunny Hills High School in Fullerton, California; his outlook and demeanor were perpetually cheery. Though Carter had played only a handful of games at catcher in high school, scout Bob Zuk was adamant that his skills and intangibles were exceptionally suited to the catcher position.

Once Carter signed, the Expos tutored him on the finer points of catching. After he had settled in behind the plate for the Expos, he began to draw comparisons to Bench. Carter brought an infectious enthusiasm to the game. He constantly hustled, bringing to mind Cincinnati Reds legend, Pete Rose. Along the way to the Hall of Fame, Carter appeared in 11 All-Star Games, won three Gold Gloves, five Silver Slugger Awards, hit 324 home runs and drove in 1,225 runs.

Measuring A Scout's Impact

Is there any way to measure the contributions of a baseball scout? Is it possible to compare, statistically, the relative impact of competing scouts?

In a 2012 profile of scout Bob Zuk for the New York Times* and a related biographical piece prepared for the Society of American Baseball Research**, author John Klima offered a provocative comparison of Zuk and his contemporary, George Genovese. Klima, a graduate of Major League Baseball's Scout Development Program, describes Genovese as "a social animal." By comparison, Klima says, Zuk was a self-described loner. In Klima's telling, Genovese "had more friends and fewer enemies."

According to Klima, Zuk took great pride in his ability to identify and sign power hitters. As a measure of his own success, Zuk would point to the number of career home runs accumulated by the players he had signed. His oft-stated goal was for his signees to reach the 3,000-homer mark.

Ultimately, Zuk fell short of that goal. Led by Reggie Jackson (563 career home runs), Willie Stargell (475 home runs), Darrell Evans (414 homers) and Gary Carter (324 homers), Zuk's signees had clubbed a total of 2,444 career home runs by the time that Zuk retired.

Using homers as the measure of a scout's success, it can be argued that Genovese, the more congenial individual, was also the better scout. By the count of ProBaseballScouting.com, players whom Genovese signed – a group that includes Bobby Bonds, Will Clark, George Foster, Dave Kingman, Matt Williams and Gary Matthews – accounted for 3,335 career homers.

So was Genovese the better scout? It depends, of course, on the measure used. Three of the players whom Zuk signed – Jackson, Stargell and Carter – are in the Hall of Fame. While Genovese is regarded by some as the greatest scout in baseball history, none of the players whom he signed have ever been elected to Cooperstown.

*John Klima, *Wily Scout Schemed to Acquire Carter*, THE N.Y. TIMES, February 18, 2012, https://nytimes.com/2012/02/19/sports/baseball/wily-baseball-scout-schemed-to-sign-gary-carter.html.

** John Klima, "Bob Zuk," SABR Project, https://sabr.org/bioproj/person/bob-zuk/

1973

A rule of thumb for me, everything else being equal, I would be more inclined to take a high school hitter and a college pitcher. On the college end, you are probably closer to looking at a finished product. With a college pitcher, what I like is that he has probably gotten a lot of coaching, he's shown that he can compete at the next level beyond high school, he's played against college hitters, he's probably shown that he can withstand the amount of innings that has been placed on him in college, he's held up to that. You are not going to pass on a Kerry Wood and other great pitchers, but over the next few years you will be putting them through some things they haven't gone through yet and you don't know how their body will react to that.

–Jim Riggleman, former Major League manager

The top four picks of the 1973 draft reached the big leagues faster than did the first four selections in any draft before or after. In some cases, starting at the top was a mistake. Other draft choices fit in immediately. The 1973 draft also produced some of the most prodigious power hitters to come along in any draft year, but many of the pitching prospects selected burned out early.

David Clyde, a left-handed fireballer from Westchester High School in Houston, Texas, was the consensus choice as the best player available in the draft. At the time, Clyde was compared to some of the immortal pitchers of all time and, most frequently, to Los Angeles Dodgers legend Sandy Koufax. Clyde was a "man among boys" at Westchester High in 1973 as he compiled an 18-0 record with a microscopic 0.18 earned run average. Veteran scout Howie Haak's take on Clyde was filled with superlatives. Haak concluded that Clyde's fastball and curve were better than the repertoire of most pitchers then in the big leagues.

Phillies scout Lou Fitzgerald considered Clyde to be the best player available by far. Most other scouts agreed. While every team would have likely drafted Clyde with the first pick, the choice was a "no-brainer" for the home state Texas Rangers. Having just relocated to the Dallas area from Washington D.C., the Rangers were struggling to draw fans. The Texas high school star was a surefire remedy for the attendance issues.

Consequently, the Rangers brought Clyde immediately to the Major Leagues. It was the same approach that the Padres had taken a year earlier with Dave Roberts. But unlike Roberts, Clyde was a mere 18 years old. He would be the youngest player to play in the majors in 1973.

Football was dominant in Dallas. The decision of Rangers owner Bob Short to relocate the franchise to Texas appeared especially foolhardy, as the Rangers were not doing well at the gate or on the field. In his first few years in Texas, Short undoubtedly heard and, perhaps came to lament, the old axiom that "the two biggest sports in Texas are football and spring football."

The initial plan was to start Clyde in two home starts and then send him to the minors for seasoning. That plan was soon scrapped, however, because Clyde fared well in each of the two starts. In his first start, he struck out eight hitters in five innings, allowed two runs and led the Rangers to victory. More significantly for Short, Clyde debuted to a sold-out stadium. He also pitched well in his second start before he was forced to leave the game with a blister in the sixth inning. The plan to send him to the minors for the rest of the season was soon forgotten. Rangers teammate Tom Grieve called the decision to keep Clyde on the team "the dumbest thing you could ever do to a high school pitcher. In my opinion, it ruined his career." Dallas sportswriter Randy Galloway describes it as one of the worst cases of "mishandling" a young player in baseball history.

Despite his early success, Clyde was now just a boy among men. Even with his two impressive starts, he finished the 1973 season with a 4-8 won-lost record and a 5.01 earned run average in 18 starts. His trademark curveball, which was his "out pitch" and had prompted the numerous comparisons with Koufax, mysteriously deserted him. Without his devastating curve, Clyde was very mortal and very hittable.

In 1974, the fairy tale seemed to be back on track. Clyde began the season with a 3-0 record, but new Texas manager Billy Martin was less than enamored with the pitching phenom. According to most observers, Martin badly misused Clyde for the rest of season. After his initial three wins, he lost his next nine starts. In 1975, Clyde injured his shoulder after only one start. His Major League career was over by 1979, with a career record of 18 wins and 33 losses. As Hall of Fame baseball writer Tracy Ringolsby noted, this fairy tale had an unhappy ending.

As Major League teams were preparing for the 1973 draft, the University of Minnesota's Dave Winfield was in the process of dominating the College World Series. Winfield's performance overshadowed the series as he almost single-handedly defeated the powerhouse University of Southern California Trojans. He turned in a masterful pitching performance and was named the Most Valuable Player of the series. USC would go on to win the NCAA title and continue their impressive championship run, but it was Winfield's heroics on the mound and at bat that had the scouts talking.

The San Diego Padres eagerly chose Winfield with the fourth pick. The only real question was whether to use Winfield as a pitcher or play him every day in the field. The Padres' director of scouting and player development, Bob Fontaine, concluded, "With his ability to run and hit and throw, we think he would be more an asset in the lineup every day."[24] The Padres also decided that Winfield was capable of making an impact in the big leagues immediately. As the Rangers had done with Clyde, the Padres assigned Winfield to the Major League roster as soon as he signed his contract.

In an era filled with multi-sport phenoms, Winfield stood out. He was a hulking 6'6" and 220 pounds and was the perfect combination of power and grace. The hometown Minnesota Vikings drafted him as a tight end, even though he had not played football in school. In addition to the Padres in baseball and the Vikings in football, he was also drafted by teams in two other professional leagues, the Atlanta Hawks in the National Basketball Association and the Utah Stars of the American Basketball Association.

Winfield proved to be ready for prime time. He made his debut with the Padres on June 19, 1973. In 1974, his first full season, he hit 20 home runs and drove in 75 runs. The Padres helped Winfield acclimate to the Major Leagues by keeping him out of the lineup when San Diego was facing elite hurlers such as Bob Gibson or Tom Seaver. Padres manager Don Zimmer also helped by keeping Winfield away from coaches who wanted to change his swing.[25]

In 1977 Winfield was elected to his first All-Star Game – the first of 12 straight appearances in the All-Star Game. Over his 22-year big-league career, Winfield won seven Gold Gloves and six Silver Slugger Awards. Winfield exceeded the magical 3,000 hit mark, with 3,110 career hits, and also had 465 career homers and 1,833 runs batted in. He was enshrined in Cooperstown in 2001.

No team, the Padres included, found a more impactful player than the Milwaukee Brewers when they selected shortstop Robin Yount of Taft High School in Woodland Hills, California. The Brewers claimed Yount with the third pick of the draft, immediately before the Padres took Winfield. Yount was another in the long and continuing line of California high school standouts. No less an authority than Red Sox scout Joe Stephenson labeled him as the best prospect in the draft. Scouts flocked to Taft to observe Yount. At times, there were more scouts in the stands at Yount's high school games than fans.

The Brewers' scouting director, Jim Baumer, signed Yount after protracted negotiations. Though Yount did not go immediately to the majors, he spent only 64 games in the minors. Yount joined the Brewers at the start of the 1974 season. He was only 18 years old when he started at shortstop for the Brewers on opening day of 1974. He would be a fixture in the Major Leagues for the next 20 years. Over the course of his career with the Brewers, Yount accumulated 3,142 hits and twice won the American League's Most Valuable Player Award. He was inducted into the Hall of Fame in 1999.

The Red Sox found an impact player in the second round in Fred Lynn, a smooth center fielder with a sweet left-handed stroke from the University of Southern California. Lynn most assuredly would have been drafted in the first round, if not for a woeful showing in a game against Arizona State University. Facing Eddie Bane, Lynn struck out four times. His performance in that game is believed to have caused him to slip to the second round. Red Sox scout Joe Stephenson signed Lynn to a contract for $40,000, which was equivalent to first-round money. In Lynn's case, it was money well spent. Even with all the emphasis on drafting immediate impact players and bringing them quickly to the Major Leagues, it would be Lynn who would make the most significant early impact out of all the 1973 draftees.

After spending most of 1974 in the minors, Lynn came up to Boston for a cameo appearance at the end of the season. By 1975, he had fully arrived in Boston and had one of the greatest seasons ever by a rookie. Lynn and another young outfielder, Jim Rice, led the Sox to the World Series in 1975. Lynn won the American League Rookie of the Year

Award *and* the League's Most Valuable Player Award. For the season, he hit 47 doubles, 21 homers, and 105 runs batted in, with a .331 batting average. He also won a Gold Glove for his excellent play in center field.

Over the remainder of his years in the big leagues, Lynn would never be able to replicate his magical season of 1975. However, he went on to have an excellent career, winning four Gold Gloves, a batting title and earning nine All-Star Game appearances. He played for five teams over his 17-year Major League career and was a model of consistency. Toward the end of his career, injuries would take a major toll, causing his batting average to dip below .250 in four of his last five seasons.

In the third round, the Baltimore Orioles struck gold in California, when they drafted Eddie Murray out of Locke High School in Los Angeles.[26] Murray came from a family of 12 children in East Los Angeles. Four of his brothers would go on to play professional baseball.

Orioles scout Ray Poitevint signed Murray for $20,000. Murray was named the American League Rookie of the Year in 1977, when he smashed 27 home runs and drove in 88 runs. He would eventually become a switch-hitter for the Orioles and drew comparisons to Mickey Mantle for his power from both sides of the plate. He would typically hit 30 home runs and drive in over a hundred runs each year during his time in Baltimore. Over a 21-year career, he played more games at first base than any other player in the history of the game. For his career, he hit 504 home runs, drove in 1,917 runs and garnered over 3,000 hits. He was inducted into the Hall of Fame in 2003.

The tenor of the Oriole's protracted – but mostly positive – negotiations with Murray and his family in 1973 were later negatively portrayed in a 1979 article by the *New York Daily News*. The controversial tone of the article, which included references to details of the original negotiations provided by Poitevint, would drive Murray to adopt a reticent attitude toward the media for most of his career. For the remainder of his life, Poitevint was left to regret sharing details of the negotiations, as the incident severed the customary bond between player and scout.[27]

The San Francisco Giants drafted first baseman/outfielder Jack Clark in the 13th round. He became the power source that ran manager Whitey Herzog's "go-go" Cardinals of the 1980s. Clark was a dependable middle-of-the-order run producer with prodigious power. He made a lot of money and spent even more. St. Louis Cardinals teammate Vince

Coleman remembers that the profligate Clark rarely packed a suitcase for road trips. Rather, he bought new clothes in every city. At the end of the trip, he would give the newly purchased clothes away to a person in need.

Clark was scouted and signed by Giants scout George Genovese. Genovese was responsible for signing many other stalwarts for the Giants from the 1960s, 1970s, and 1980s, including Bobby Bonds, Matt Williams, Gary Maddox, Gary Matthews, and Dave Kingman.

Genovese is revered as one of the greatest scouts of all time. He was born in 1922 on Staten Island, New York to an Italian-American family of eight children. His experience was representative of many baseball men of the mid-twentieth century. He grew up playing baseball on the streets with his eight brothers and sisters. All of his brothers would continue playing baseball in some professional capacity, as did Genovese's sister, Josephine, who played briefly for the All-American Girls Professional Baseball League.

Genovese's baseball career, like so many others of the time, would take a giant detour due to the onset of World War II. Genovese spent three years in the Pacific Theater. After the war, he continued his baseball career in the St. Louis Cardinals organization but his prospects declined due to a wartime injury. He played for the Hollywood Stars of the Pacific Coast League in 1949 and 1951 and helped the Stars to a league-leading 109-78 record in 1949.

After the 1951 season, Branch Rickey persuaded Genovese to leave the Stars and join the Pirates organization as a scout. Rickey assigned Genovese to run tryout camps with some of the great names in baseball. In Pittsburgh, he teamed with Pirates' Hall of Famer Pie Traynor. In Mexico, he partnered with Rickey's trusted confidants, Howie Haak and Clyde Sukeforth. The camps would be the platform for Genovese to launch one of the greatest scouting careers of all time.

When Rickey retired, the Pirates released Genovese, but he caught on with the San Francisco Giants. With the Giants, Genovese hit his stride in scouting. Initially, he served as the manager of minor league teams in the Giants organization. In that capacity, he proved his ability as a superior teacher of young players. In 1963, the Giants moved him to the position of scouting supervisor for Southern California. Genovese began holding tryout camps for prospects. In one of his tryout camps, he discovered a raw yet talented youngster named Bobby Bonds from Riverside, California. Genovese tutored and signed Bonds for the Giants.

Like many scouts of the day, Genovese would take raw talents and work with the players every day on the field to develop their baseball skills. "Nobody in the history of the game was better at recognizing raw talent," according to fellow scout Artie Harris. Genovese worked with Garry Maddox in 1968 and then signed him for the Giants. He also discovered Gary Matthews in 1968 while Matthews was playing American Legion baseball. Genovese convinced the Giants to draft and sign Matthews. With Genovese's help, Matthews developed into the National League Rookie of the Year in 1973.

The Giants had at least one player signed by Genovese on their roster from 1965 to 1996. His scouting fame quickly spread and a younger generation of scouts would simply follow him around to try to identify the players whom he was scouting.[28]

A Scout's Insight

Daniel Palka, an outfielder with the Chicago White Sox, made his Major League debut on April 25, 2018 against the Seattle Mariners. Inserted into the lineup as Chicago's designated hitter, Palka went 0 for 4 with one strikeout. Palka was back in the lineup the next day against the Kansas City Royals but again went 0 for 4. He sat out the next game but started in right field on April 28th and had four hits in five at-bats, including a double and a home run. The following day, Palka collected a triple and a double in two at-bats, along with two runs batted in.

With four Major League games under his belt, Palka was batting .400, with two doubles, a triple, one home run and five runs batted in.

White Sox scout John Tumminia had seen it all before. Tumminia had scouted Palka in 2017 when he was playing for Triple-A Rochester, a Minnesota Twins affiliate. The book on Palka portrayed him as a swing-and-miss guy who rarely made contact. Tumminia saw something more. He recalled one game in Rochester when Palka, a left-handed hitter, hit a bomb to left-center field. Tumminia returned the next day and watched as Palka struck out in his first three times at bat. That same day, however, in his fourth at-bat, Palka hit a homer to right field, a ball that Tumminia says went "as far and as high as it could go." Tumminia had heard what the numbers said about Palka but didn't care. For Tumminia, Palka's power was "off the charts."

On November 3, 2017, based on Tumminia's recommendation, the White Sox claimed Palka off waivers from the Twins. Palka played in 124 games for the White Sox in 2018, batting .240, with 27 home runs and 67 runs batted in.

During his seasons in the minor leagues, Palka never put up good numbers against left-handed pitching. White Sox manager Rick Renteria was well aware of Palka's inability to handle left-handers and, as a result, Palka rarely faces southpaws. "Does Palka strike out?" Tumminia asks rhetorically. Yes, he does, with roughly one strikeout in every three official plate appearances. The key for Tumminia, however, was that Palka provided good power from the left side of the plate. In his rookie season at least, Palka proved to be more than a swing-and-miss guy. For his part, Tumminia correctly sensed that, when Palka was used as a corner outfielder or at designated hitter as part of a platoon, he could help the White Sox win.

1974

The first September when I got called up, 1974, I got to play. I got to be around the league a bit. I felt that I would be comfortable at the Major League level and that I would be capable of playing in the big leagues. I just had to learn how to play Major League Baseball but I knew I would be comfortable when I got there.

– Bill Almon, former Major League infielder and overall number one pick in the 1974 amateur draft

In 1973, the San Diego Padres finished with 102 losses, vesting the team with the first overall pick in 1974. Well before the draft, Bob Fontaine, the Padres' director of scouting and player development, and general manager Peter Bavasi, had a good idea that shortstop Bill Almon of Brown University would be their choice.

The Padres had drafted Almon in the 11th round of the 1971 draft. He had starred at Warwick High School in Warwick, Rhode Island. The Padres took Almon on the recommendation of area scout Ken Bracey, a key scout and advisor with the Padres from their inception until 2009. Fontaine and Bavasi quickly realized after the 1971 draft that Almon was unalterably set upon attending Brown University. In the process of courting Almon, the Padres became so enamored with his maturity and humility and his range of interests beyond baseball that they eagerly awaited their next opportunity to draft him.

Almon excelled at Brown, winning honors as the 1974 College Baseball Player of the Year while posting a .350 batting average with 31 runs batted in and 20 stolen bases. Throughout Almon's collegiate career, the Padres made it a point to stay in touch with him. When it came time for the 1974 draft, San Diego was focused on selecting Almon with the number one pick. However, under the rules in effect at the time, the Padres needed Almon's consent if they were going to draft him again. Almon recollects, "I was in the right place at the right time. The Padres needed a shortstop and they already knew who I was."

Almon was quite content with the San Diego organization and readily gave his consent. Thus, the Padres picked Almon with the first overall pick. They also signed him to a Major League contract, which was uncommon at the time. Almon was a September call-up to the Padres in 1974 and played in 16 games. He hit .316 in that limited stint. Almon spent most of 1975 and 1976 with the Padres' Triple-A club in Hawaii, playing only 20 games at the Major League level. By 1977, however, Almon had established himself as San Diego's regular shortstop.

Almon was a pronounced improvement over Mike Ivie and Dave Roberts, the Padres' number one picks in 1970 and 1972, respectively. Almon would play for 15 Major League seasons with seven different teams. Throughout his career, he fielded a solid shortstop and learned to play several other positions in the infield and outfield. He hit a career high of .301 with the Chicago White Sox in 1981 but, five years later, could manage only .219 with the Pittsburgh Pirates. He finished his career with a lifetime batting average of .254.

After his playing days, Almon returned to Rhode Island to coach at Brown University and work with the Special Olympics program. He remains the only Ivy League player in history to be selected as number one overall in the Major League Baseball Draft. Considering both his own experiences and the ways in which the draft has developed over time, Almon finds the efficiency of the scouting system to be remarkable. "If you can play," he says, "the scouts will find you." He is quick to point out, however, that "scouting and the draft are inexact sciences." Almon's own career provides supporting evidence. Though he was a versatile and productive major leaguer, he never emerged as the impact player the Padres were expecting when they drafted him as the overall number one pick.

Notwithstanding the Padres' commitment to Almon, many scouts considered Lonnie Smith, a speedster from Los Angeles, to be the best talent available in the 1974 draft. The Philadelphia Phillies took Smith with the third pick in the draft. Smith never showed much power. In only one of his 17 Major League seasons did he ever hit more than nine home runs. What he did possess, however, was the ability to get to first base and then use his speed to advance on the base paths. In his first four big league seasons after he began playing on a somewhat regular basis, Smith had a batting average of .320 and stole 165 bases. He finished his career with a batting average of .288 and 370 stolen bases.

The Atlanta Braves had the fifth overall pick in the 1974 draft. Mike Miley, a shortstop from Louisiana State University, was the consensus candidate in the Braves' front office. Miley was a versatile athlete who had played quarterback for the LSU football team. Braves scout Al La-Macchia sounded the only discordant note in Atlanta's scouting department. LaMacchia advocated for drafting catcher Dale Murphy from Portland, Oregon. Murphy stood six-foot, four-inches and reminded scouts of two other catchers of similar height, the Yankees' Bill Dickey and Cleveland's Jim Hegan. LaMacchia likened Murphy to Johnny Bench, especially with regard to arm strength.

LaMacchia went to bat, in his inimitable way, for Murphy in pre-draft meetings with Braves general manager Eddie Robinson. When it looked as if the Braves were poised to use their first-round pick on Miley, LaMacchia told Robinson, "I don't think you need me to work for you." Eventually, LaMacchia prevailed and the Braves selected Murphy. Before Murphy's career took off in 1978, he had to switch from catcher to center field. Like Mike Ivie, Murphy had developed a mental block that prevented him from throwing the ball back to the pitcher with accuracy. Braves' manager Bobby Cox told LaMacchia, "He's spooked." Cox moved Murphy to center field, where his arm became an asset rather than a liability.

Once Murphy was positioned in center field, his bat came alive. In 1980, his second season as a regular, he hit .281 with 33 home runs and 89 runs batted in. Murphy went on to become the mainstay of the Braves for the next seven seasons. In the decade from 1980 to 1989, he made the National League All-Star team seven times. During his career, he hit 398 home runs and was named the National League's Most Valuable Player in back-to-back years, 1982 and 1983.

A Stand-up Guy

Doug Mapson's first full-time job in scouting came with the Chicago Cubs in 1982. Gene Handley was one of Mapson's mentors with the Cubs. Handley was a veteran of the game, having spent over fifty years as a player, minor league manager, and scout.

Handley taught Mapson to look for three attributes in a player – attitude, aptitude and ability. "It's the three A's that matter," Handley would say, adding that if a player doesn't have a lot of ability, he'd better have a whole lot of attitude and aptitude. For Mapson, aptitude comes down primarily to one trait, the ability to adjust.

Mapson identifies former Boston Red Sox infielder Kevin Youkilis as a player who possessed a unique ability to adjust. Mapson first saw Youkilis play at the University of Cincinnati. At the time, Youkilis possessed an unorthodox stance at the plate. Mapson describes the stance as ridiculously spread out and crouched. The effect was to make Youkilis' six-foot, one-inch frame seem much smaller.

During one of Youkilis' college games, Mapson sat next to Youkilis' mother. Mapson asked the mother, "How did he come up with that stance?" Her response startled Mapson. She said, "I'm tired of people asking me about his stance. When the pitcher delivers the ball, you can look and see that he's in a good position to hit. Give him a break." Mapson said to himself, "Wow, this is a mom!"

Youkilis' mother had more to say. She told Mapson that her son had originally been a shortstop and that when people complained that he did not steal enough bases for shortstop, he stole 27 bases in the season. According to Mrs. Youkilis, the next year scouts wanted to see more power, so her son started hitting home runs in bunches. Mapson came away from the game with a very favorable impression of Youkilis and deep respect for his mother.

Boston drafted Youkilis in the eighth round of 2001. According to Mapson, one of the first things the Red Sox coaches did was to tell him to "stand up and hit like a big guy."

As always was the case, Youkilis adjusted. He stood up and kept on hitting. During the course of his baseball career, Youkilis always made the adjustments necessary to accomplish what was asked of him. In 10 years in the Major Leagues, he hit 150 home runs, batted .281 and made three All-Star teams.

1975

My whole career I have been linked with one person. For 19 years, Lou Whitaker and I formed the longest running double-play combination in the history of baseball. I doubt that record will ever be broken. Lou and I were called up to the big leagues from Double-A on the same day. We both played in our first big-league ballgame at Fenway Park on the same day. We both got hits in our first Major League at-bats off the same pitcher, Reggie Cleveland, and we both got our last hits of our careers off the same pitcher, Mike Fetters. Can you believe that?

– Alan Trammell, former shortstop, Detroit Tigers, speaking at his Hall of Fame induction ceremony on July 29, 2018

Just when it seemed as if teams were starting to get the draft right, the 1975 draft represented a huge step backwards. Only two of the 24 selections in the first round, catcher Rick Cerone and infielder Dale Berra, would merit first-round consideration based on their career production. Almost half of the first-round picks, including four of the first five selections, did not make it to the big leagues. And the lone draft pick among the first five who "made" the big leagues had one of the most disappointing careers in the history of baseball.

The California Angels were desperate for catching help and salivating at the prospect of drafting Southern University's star catcher Danny Goodwin, the first overall selection of the 1971 draft. Since he spurned the White Sox, Goodwin continued to excel at and behind the plate in college. The Angels selected him with the first pick and paid him a record $150,000 bonus. He became the first, and to date only, player to ever be drafted twice with the overall number one selection. Angels management, including owner Gene Autry – the "Singing Cowboy" of motion picture fame – expected to have Goodwin in the majors after a brief stint in the minors.

Unfortunately, Goodwin suffered a serious shoulder injury that sapped him of his stellar throwing ability for the rest of his career. While he continued to hit well in the minors, the injury required the Angels to move him from his natural catching position to more hitter oriented positions such as first base and designated hitter. Disappointingly, Goodwin was only able to hit 13 lifetime home runs over parts of seven years – a far cry from the power expectations he had created in high school, college and even the minors.

As is the case with even the worst drafts, there are always very good players who slip beyond the first round. Outfielder Andre Dawson, who was perhaps the best player of the entire 1975 draft, dropped all the way to the 11th round. The Montreal Expos selected Dawson with the 250th pick of the draft, based largely on the efforts of the team's scouting director, Mel Didier.

Didier was truly "old school."[29] However, even though he was still scouting at the age of 90, he never really grew old. Didier always seemed to retain the youthful enthusiasm that he possessed when he had started scouting. He loved the work. A former collegiate football player at Louisiana State University, Didier left the Bayou to play in the Detroit Tigers' system in 1948. An injury ended his playing career, but Tigers executive John McHale signed him as a scout.

From all accounts, Didier truly enjoyed all of his more than 60 years in baseball. Every day he set out hoping, and even expecting, to find the next great player. Even though his own experience and the evidence around him suggested that scouts only find a great player "once in a blue moon," Didier seemed to earnestly believe that each day was the day he would find that exceptional prospect. Other than his family, he had very few interests away from the field. He would encourage other scouts to take time off to play golf and engage in other leisurely pursuits, in part so that he might find the next great player while they were teeing it up at the country club.

Even more so than his love and enthusiasm for baseball, Didier's simple and straightforward integrity is what people who knew him most admired – and after all his years in the game, everyone seemed to know him. Angels manager Mike Scioscia knew Didier most of his baseball life and testifies that his most attractive quality was his adherence to a strong moral code of right and wrong. Didier would always offer his unapologetic and unvarnished opinions on players and on baseball, without any guile or self-protective instincts. Dodgers general manager Fred Claire knew Didier would always give him his truthful opinion, whether he thought it would be well-received or not.

Not surprisingly, Didier loved to tell stories about his days in the game. He wrote a book about his years in scouting and in working with players.[30] The book includes, as an example, Didier's recollection of the time that he had to ride a donkey to a mud hut in rural Puerto Rico to sign outfielder Pepe Mangual. Mangual proved to be worth the trip; he made his Major League debut with the Expos at the age of 20 and played for six years with Montreal and the New York Mets. In his days with Atlanta, Didier discovered many excellent players, including relief pitcher Cecil Upshaw and outfielder Ralph Garr. Garr, known as "the Roadrunner," was blessed with amazing footspeed. In classic Cajun speech, Didier described Garr's footspeed with a homespun metaphor. Garr, he said, was able "to run faster than a scalded dog."

Didier discovered future Hall of Famer Andre Dawson while scouting another player at a Florida A&M game in 1975. Didier immediately realized that Dawson, playing center field for A&M, was the best player on the field. Didier saw that Dawson was a five-tool player. He could hit, hit with power, run, throw, and field. Didier saw an image of the great Henry Aaron in Dawson's quick wrists – "just like Hammering Hank." Didier also recorded one crucial intangible that Dawson possessed. "He loves the game of baseball," Didier wrote, "He just loves to play."

Often times, scouts play a role akin to that of an intelligence agent. In talking with Dawson after he had first seen him play, Didier learned that few other scouts had come to see him. In a follow-up conversation with Dawson the day before the draft, Didier confirmed that no other teams had contacted Dawson. Armed with this knowledge, Didier made a calculated gamble to wait longer to draft Dawson than his talent would have suggested.

Didier tells the story of the heated argument that he and another noted scout, Bobby Mattick, had in Montreal's draft room concerning Dawson. With each passing round, Mattick argued ever more strenuously for the Expos to take Dawson. At one point, prior to the 11th round, Mattick jumped up and yelled to Didier, "You hard-headed Cajun, you better take him now or you will lose him." Mattick then stormed out of the draft room. Reflecting on the incident later, Didier admitted that he would have been heartbroken if he lost Dawson that day.

Dawson far exceeded even the most optimistic projections of Didier, Mattick and everyone else. The "Hawk" would star for the Expos, and later the Cubs, in a brilliant 21-year big league career. Didier was beaming when Dawson won the National League Rookie of the Year Award in 1977, just two years after he was drafted. Dawson would go on to appear in eight All-Star Games, win eight Gold Gloves and be named the National League's Most Valuable Player in his career year of 1987. In his 2010 acceptance speech at Cooperstown, Dawson succinctly and poignantly summed up his view of baseball, which was likely inspired by his mentor, Mel Didier: "If you love the game of baseball, it will love you back."

For all his success in amateur scouting, Didier is perhaps best remembered for the advice he gave as a professional advance scout in 1988. Didier was then with the Los Angeles Dodgers, who were squaring off against the Oakland Athletics in the 1988 World Series. Prior to the start of the Series, Didier had written a scouting report that has been spoken about with reverence in baseball circles ever since.

When the Dodgers' injured left fielder, Kirk Gibson, limped to the plate as a pinch hitter in the ninth inning of the first game of the Series, Didier's scouting report loomed large. Gibson was facing Oakland's closer, Dennis Eckersley. During an epic battle brilliantly described in real time by Hall of Fame announcer Vin Scully, Gibson had worked the count to three balls and two strikes. In his head, Gibson heard Didier's unmistakable Cajun drawl saying, "Podnuh, as sure as I am standing before you breathing, you can take it to the bank, if the count gets to 3 and 2, Eckersley will throw a backdoor slider!" With the count full, Eckersley unleashed the backdoor slider, just as Didier had predicted. An expectant Gibson hit the ball out of the park to win the game.

As Gibson rounded third base, he yelled to the Dodgers' third base coach, Joe Amalfitano, "backdoor slider, Joe." Didier was beaming as proudly after Gibson's home run as he did on the day he discovered Dawson. Didier's written scouting report on Eckersley sits among the World Series memorabilia in Cooperstown.[31]

In addition to Dawson, the 1975 draft produced another future Hall of Famer in pitcher Lee Smith. The Chicago Cubs selected Smith in the second round. He spent the next six seasons working his way through the Cubs' minor league system. For the first four of those seasons, Smith pitched almost exclusively as a starter and recorded 25 wins against 27 losses.

In 1979, Smith's fifth minor league season, the Cubs decided to make him a relief pitcher. As a member of the Double-A Midland Cubs, he appeared in 35 games, 26 as a reliever. However, the conversion to relief pitching did not sit well with Smith, and he considered retiring from baseball. "I thought it was a slap in the face," Smith said, "like I wasn't good enough to be a starter."[32] Former Cubs outfielder Billy Williams, then recently retired, helped persuade Smith to continue playing.

In his sixth minor league season, Smith pitched in 48 games in relief, with a 3.70 earned run average. The performance earned him a promotion to Chicago in September 1980. Smith pitched as a reliever in 18 games for the Cubs during the months of September and October, with an earned run average of 2.91. From that point on, Smith's role as a reliever was firmly established. Over 18 Major League seasons, Smith appeared in 1,022 games, earned 478 saves and had an earned run average of 3.03. He was inducted into the Hall of Fame in 2019. Smith's 478 saves rank as the third highest total of all time, trailing only Trevor Hoffman and Mariano Rivera.

By almost any measure, the career of second baseman Lou Whitaker, who was drafted by the Detroit Tigers in the fifth round of 1975, is also worthy of admission to the Hall of Fame. Whitaker was the Rookie of the Year in 1978. During his career, he won three Gold Gloves, four Silver Slugger Awards and was named as an American League All-Star five times. Baseball historian Bill James has declared Whitaker to be the 13th greatest second baseman of all time.

Whitaker's career accomplishments compare favorably to the records of several second basemen already inducted in Cooperstown. Along with Joe Morgan and Rogers Hornsby, Whitaker is one of only three second basemen to post more than 1,000 runs, 1,000 runs batted in, and 200 home runs.

While the 1975 draft also yielded third baseman Carney Lansford, pitcher Dave Stewart, and first baseman Jason Thompson, it will largely be remembered as a year of unfulfilled expectations. As Mel Didier would often tell scouts, however, "Podnuh, tomorrow you might find the next great major leaguer."

Baseball Stories

The New York Mets drafted first baseman Marshall Brant in the fourth round of the 1975 amateur draft. Standing six feet, five inches and weighing 185 pounds, Brant was an excellent athlete capable of crushing monstrous home runs. He enjoyed considerable success in the minor leagues, collecting 185 homers and batting .270 in nine seasons. However, he was never able to find a home on a Major League roster. His Major League experience was limited to eight games, three with the New York Yankees in 1980 and five with the Oakland Athletics in 1983. In those eight games, Brant went to bat 20 times and produced two hits, both singles.

Midway through Brant's baseball career, he spent three seasons with the Triple-A Columbus Clippers, during which he hit 79 home runs and drove in 283 runs. Brant was so productive and so popular in Columbus that, when his tenure with the Clippers ended, the team retired his uniform number 33 – the only number ever to be retired in the history of the Columbus team. Not even future Hall of Famer Derek Jeter, who played shortstop for Columbus for two seasons in the 1990s, earned that honor.

"People ask me about my baseball career," Brant once said. "I don't have great stories to share. The next step never happened for me. But when I do talk, it's always about Columbus."

For Danny Graham, also a journeyman ballplayer, the experience of playing baseball brought both greater success at the Major League level and more stories. Like Brant, Graham was drafted in 1975, going to the Minnesota Twins in the fifth round. As a minor leaguer, Graham did his best work in 1978, when he clouted 23 home runs and drove in 85 runs. The next season, however, Graham went into a tailspin, and the Twins traded him to the Baltimore Orioles. For Graham, the trade worked wonders. The Orioles summoned him to the Major Leagues in May 1980 and, over the course of two seasons, Graham appeared in 141 games with the Orioles.

Shortly after joining the Orioles, Graham told *Washington Post* baseball writer Thomas Boswell, "A few months ago, I figured I was going to end up 60 years old, driving a taxi and telling Triple-A stories. Now, I may still be 60 and driving a taxi, but I'll be telling big league stories."

Only a small percentage of the more than 1,200 players drafted each year ever get to tell "big league stories." Dan Graham is one of the fortunate few.

1976

Dick Wiencek, the scout who signed me, deserves a lot of credit. Dick was able to convince Bill Lajoie, who was the Tigers' scouting director, to draft a skinny, 165-pound shortstop with no power. Looking back, Bill respected Dick's judgment. Dick Wiencek would sign 72 Major League players, the most in baseball history. I remember Dick telling me if I hit .250 and played good defense, I would play in the big leagues a long time.

– Alan Trammell, Detroit Tigers, at his July 29, 2018 Hall of Fame induction ceremony

The Houston Astros led off the 1976 player draft by selecting pitcher Floyd Bannister with the number one pick. Bannister was a six-foot-one left-handed pitcher from Seattle, Washington. He was a logical choice. As a high school senior, he led his John F. Kennedy High School team to the state championship, posting a sterling 15-0 won-loss record. Bannister was practically unhittable in high school. As a senior, he did not yield an earned run the entire season.

In the 1973 draft, Charlie Finley's Oakland Athletics had selected Bannister out of high school. However, the penny-pinching Finley did not make a competitive offer and Bannister enrolled at Arizona State. He went on to dominate collegiate competition, winning 38 games and losing only six over three years. In Bannister's final season at Arizona State, the *Sporting News* named him the College Player of the Year.

After protracted negotiations, Bannister signed with the Astros for $100,000. Bannister readily agreed to start in the minors, where he again dominated his opponents. His first-year manager, Julio Linares, was extremely impressed. "I think he's got to be the best young pitcher I've ever seen," Linares said.

After a year of seasoning in the minors, Bannister made the Houston roster out of spring training in 1977. On April 19, 1977, he made his Major League debut, pitching in relief against the San Francisco Giants. He made 23 starts in his rookie year, going 8-9 with a 4.04 earned run average. Bannister spent two seasons with the Astros before being traded to the Seattle Mariners. He would spend 15 seasons in the Major Leagues, pitching for six different clubs. He closed out his Major League career with 134 wins, 143 losses and an earned run average of 4.06.

Bannister had his best years in Seattle with his hometown Mariners, where he made the All-Star Game in 1982 while leading the American League in strikeouts. He became the most successful overall number one pick since the selection of Rick Monday in 1965.

The 1976 draft produced two other pitchers, Bruce Hurst and Jack Morris, who enjoyed even more success than Bannister. The Red Sox selected Hurst with the 22nd overall pick. Morris went to the Tigers in the fifth round, the 98th overall pick.

Hurst won 145 games over the course of his 15-year career while losing 113. The Utah native played the first nine years of his career with the Red Sox. He excelled for Boston during the 1986 World Series, winning two games and allowing the New York Mets only five runs in 23 innings.

The Detroit Tigers had an outstanding draft in 1976. The lion's share of the credit belongs to Michigan native Bill Lajoie, a long-time scout and an excellent judge of talent. Lajoie served as Detroit's scouting director from 1974 to 1978. A direct line can be traced from his time as scouting director to the Tigers' 1984 World Series championship. Detroit started out the 1984 season with 35 wins and only 5 losses. The team went on to win 104 regular season games before dominating the post-season. Lajoie oversaw the acquisition of the key players on that team and drafted at least eight impact players during his tenure as Detroit's scouting director. While he had selected star talents such as Lance Parrish and Lou Whitaker in earlier drafts, 1976 was Lajoie's most impressive draft year.

A talented draft class usually contains at least two and possibly three Hall of Famers. By comparison, in 1976, the Tigers alone drafted three future Hall of Famers, Jack Morris, Alan Trammell and Ozzie Smith. While Smith never signed with Detroit, the Tigers' 1976 draft nonetheless stands as one of the astonishing feats in baseball history. No other team had ever before selected two Hall of Famers in the same draft. In this regard, the 1976 Tigers' draft was off the charts.

In the second round, Detroit drafted Trammell, a shortstop from Kearny High School in San Diego. Tigers scout Dick Wiencek had highly recommended Trammell. As a member of the Tigers' 1984 world championship team, he was named the most valuable player of the World Series. Lajoie trusted and relied on Wiencek's player evaluations. Lajoie praised

Wiencek as "good at getting to know players before he signed them."[33] Trammell credited Wiencek at his Hall of Fame induction, calling him a "great man" who deserved much of the credit for the success experienced by the Detroit team and by Trammell in particular.[34]

It was far from a foregone conclusion that Trammell would succeed at the Major League level. Tigers' scout Rick Ferrell turned in a pre-draft report on Trammell that offered faint praise. Ferrell predicted that Trammell would develop into a fine *defensive* shortstop along the lines of Ray Oyler. The comparison was particularly noteworthy because Oyler had a batting average of .180 during his four seasons as Detroit's shortstop in the 1960s.

Trammell had signed a letter of intent to play college baseball for the UCLA Bruins but, after Detroit drafted him in the second round, he thought "Wow, [the Tigers] really must like me." Trammell signed for $35,000. He would become a mainstay for the Tigers within two years, teaming with second baseman Lou Whitaker to form one of the best double play combinations in history.

Trammell played over a hundred games at shortstop in 1978 and would remain at that position for the Tigers until 1996. He played for 20 Major League seasons, all with Detroit. The only other players with longer careers for the Tigers are legends Ty Cobb and Al Kaline. In Trammell's 20 seasons in Detroit, he would win four Gold Gloves and make six All-Star appearances. He had six seasons where he batted over .300 and hit at least twelve home runs. As a member of the Tigers' 1984 world championship team, he was named the most valuable player of the World Series.

Due in large part to Wiencek, Lajoie went on to draft right-handed pitchers Dan Petry and Jack Morris in the fourth and fifth rounds, respectively. Both would become mainstays in the Detroit rotation. Petry was from El Dorado High School in Placentia, California. He joined the Tigers in 1979 and was a steady and reliable workhorse as a starting pitcher for Detroit for 10 seasons. He contributed 18 wins to the championship team of 1984.

Morris, a native of St. Paul, Minnesota, joined the Tigers for a cup of coffee in 1977 and became a fixture on the Tigers' roster in 1978. In 1979, he established himself as the team's ace and proved to be a reliable big-game starter for the next 11 years. Morris was a fierce competitor on the mound, who used his devastating split-finger fastball to great effect. In 14 seasons with the Tigers, he won 198 games.

In 1991, Morris went home to play for the Minnesota Twins and was the Most Valuable Player of the 1991 World Series. He pitched a 10-inning shutout in the seventh game of the Series, one of the most impressive clutch performances in baseball history. He won another world title with the Toronto Blue Jays in 1992. Over 18 seasons, he won a total of 254 games and was inducted into the Hall of Fame with Trammell in 2018.

In the January 1976 supplemental draft, the Tigers used the first overall pick to select Steve Kemp, a hitting star for the powerhouse University of Southern California team. Kemp started in Detroit the very next year and provided a key middle-of-the-order bat for the emerging Tigers. In his career year of 1979, Kemp hit .318, clubbed 26 home runs and drove in 105 runs. Kemp played in Detroit for five seasons and subsequently played for four other teams before closing out his career.

In the fourth round of 1976, the Oakland A's hit it out of the park when they selected local Oakland product Rickey Henderson. Henderson would become one of the greatest players in the history of the game. Football was Henderson's first love; as a child, he dreamed of playing for the Oakland Raiders. Henderson starred at running back in high school and drew comparisons to O.J. Simpson. Baseball scouts widely assumed that he would choose to play football in college rather than sign a baseball contract. However, Henderson's mother was fearful that he would be injured in football and pushed him to baseball. Oakland scout Jim Guinn's report on him stated, "Henderson is the best-looking prospect in the Alameda County League and the Oakland Athletic League." At that time, Guinn couldn't have anticipated that Henderson would also be the best and most celebrated player in the entire 1976 draft.

Henderson hit well in the minors. He credited much of his success in baseball to veteran baseball man Tom Trebelhorn, who tutored Henderson in base stealing. Henderson arrived in the majors as a full-time player in 1980. His timing was perfect. The fiery Billy Martin had just taken over the managerial reins in Oakland. In 1979, the Athletics had finished with a record of 54 wins and 108 losses. The team was moribund, demoralized and in last place in the Western Division of the American League. In just one year, Martin pushed and prodded the Athletics to a second-place finish in the division, with a record of 83 wins and 79 losses.

Martin's aggressive style of play was known as "Billy Ball." For Henderson, the style was ideal. He hit .303 for the season and stole 100 bases, earning selection to the first of his 10 All-Star teams. "Rickey is a once in a lifetime player," Martin proclaimed. Henderson would become as synonymous with the stolen base as Babe Ruth was with the home run. When Henderson first mentioned that he was targeting Lou Brock's iconic single-season stolen base record of 118 thefts, the claim appeared to be the words of a braggart. When he smashed the record by stealing 130 in 1982, it seemed very matter of fact.

Henderson could steal bases almost at will. In his 25 Major League seasons, he shattered baseball's career stolen base record by stealing an astounding 1,406 bags. He is also the all time Major League leader in runs scored with 2,295. Henderson was also a good power hitter for such a base-stealing threat. During his career, he hit 297 home runs, with 1,115 runs batted in. He won the American League Most Valuable Player Award in 1990 during his second tour with the Athletics and was elected to the Hall of Fame in 2009.[35]

In several ways, Henderson's career and persona mirrored that of fellow Hall of Famer Reggie Jackson: (1) both started with the Oakland Athletics but played prominently for the New York Yankees in the prime of their careers; (2) both felt they were underappreciated and misunderstood; (3) both spoke about themselves in the third person; and (4) both were blessed with generational talent and were inducted into the Hall of Fame.

The Boston Red Sox grabbed future Hall of Famer Wade Boggs in the seventh round. No less an authority than Red Sox great Ted Williams once stated that Boggs had "a hell of a stance… he ought to become a great hitter." Unsurprisingly, Williams' prediction did not hold much weight at the time, because he was basing it on a picture of Boggs at only 18 months old.

The scouts were on the lookout for five-tool stars. Unfortunately, Boggs did not run well, did not hit for power, and did not field or throw particularly well either. However, the one tool he did have – hitting for average – was exceptional.

Red Sox scout George Digby was impressed enough with Boggs' bat to argue strongly for Boston to grab him in the 7th round. Known as a "hitting scout," Digby was particularly adept at projecting hitters. He saw great potential in Boggs' smooth swing. Digby had been looking for talent for 64 years and had discovered Bob Montgomery, Jerry Moses and Reid Nichols for the Red Sox. Digby's greatest regret was Boston's refusal to sign a young outfielder from Birmingham in 1949 named Willie Mays.

If they had heeded Digby's advice, the Sox could have signed Mays for only $4,500.

Long-time scout and baseball executive Dan Jennings remembers Digby as a mentor. Jennings once approached Digby, a genteel Southern gentleman, and asked him if he could pick Digby's brain on hitting. Digby nodded agreeably and said "you got a pen?" Jennings produced a pen and paper and prepared to write down Digby's pearls of wisdom. "You've got to see bat speed, aggressiveness and contact," Digby said. Jennings looked up and asked, "Okay, what else?" Digby simply said, "That's it, son. Don't complicate it." Jennings pondered Digby's words, concluding that when a great scout speaks, it all sounds easy.

With the help of Digby, Ted Williams and hitting guru Walt Hriniak, Boggs would work hard to develop his hitting talents. Boggs would accumulate five batting titles and eight Silver Slugger Awards and made 12 All-Star appearances. His work ethic helped him to develop into a good fielder. Working under the tutelage of former Yankees third basemen Clete Boyer, Boggs won two Gold Gloves. He joined the New York Yankees later in his career and was part of their 1996 World Series championship. In his 18-year Major League career, Boggs reached the magical 3,000 hit mark and was elected to the Hall of Fame in 2005 – his first year of eligibility – with 92 percent of the votes.[36]

"Bigfoot"

Long-time scout Gilbert "Gib" Bodet grew up in northern New Jersey. As a high school player, Bodet once attended a workout organized by the Boston Red Sox. At the workout, Bodet met Neil Mahoney, Boston's scouting supervisor for the East Coast. Several years later, after service with the U.S. Army in Korea, Bodet wrote a letter to Mahoney seeking a job in baseball. Mahoney referred Bodet to veteran Boston scout Joe Stephenson. Stephenson took a liking to Bodet and, soon thereafter, Bodet began working for Stephenson as a bird dog.

By 1976, Bodet had graduated to full-time scout and was working the southern California area for the Montreal Expos. Shortstop Glenn Hoffman, a product of Savanna High School in Anaheim, California, was then drawing considerable attention. During the Easter recess, Bodet drove to LaPalma Park, which straddled the cities of Anaheim and Fullerton, to see Hoffman in action. On his way into the park, Bodet encountered Stephenson, still in the employ of the Red Sox.

Stephenson asked Bodet what he was doing. Bodet replied that he wanted to take a look at Hoffman. Stephenson said, "Don't worry about Hoffman." Bodet's curiosity was piqued. "Why's that?" he asked. Stephenson countered with a question, "Have you ever seen a guy play shortstop with feet like that?" Taken aback, Bodet responded, "To be honest with you, I didn't notice that." Stephenson explained, "This guy wears size 13 shoes, Gib. His feet won't work, not at shortstop. It just won't work." Stephenson then talked Bodet into joining him for a beer at a local bowling alley.

When it came time for the 1976 draft, the Red Sox took none other than Glenn Hoffman with their second-round pick. The next time that Bodet ran into Stephenson, he said to him, "What happened to that shortstop with the big feet? I see you drafted him." The wily Stephenson replied, "Hey, kid, if I didn't think you could scout, I wouldn't have tried to steer you in the other direction."

Hoffman and his big feet advanced quickly through the Red Sox farm system. He made his Major League debut in April 1980 and would spend nine seasons in the majors, playing 615 games at shortstop and 151 more at other infield positions.

1977

I went into Columbia, South Carolina a day early and I was reading the newspaper. I read that the University of South Carolina was playing a night game, so I decided to go watch the night game. I had Mookie Wilson down but not as a top prospect. Playing for South Carolina, Mookie had a great game, and I was the only scout there. The next day, there were 25 scouts there for the doubleheader to see the pitcher who was pitching for South Carolina. Mookie had a terrible day in the doubleheader, threw the ball all over the place, struck out a couple of times, didn't look good. But I had seen him the night before and he looked great, so I turned in a pretty good report on him. Mookie became the Mets' second round pick in 1977. I saw a couple of scouts at the College World Series and they asked me, 'How come you took that guy Wilson in the second round? We had the guy way down.' I told them, Oh, we kind of liked him.

– Harry Minor, former scout, New York Mets

For three consecutive years, 1974 through 1976, the team holding the first overall draft pick selected a college player. In 1977, the Chicago White Sox held the first overall draft choice and went back to the high school ranks to select left-handed hitting outfielder Harold Baines of Easton, Maryland. Baines had been on the White Sox's radar for a long time. Chicago's owner, Bill Veeck, had first spotted Baines when he was playing Little League baseball as a 12-year-old.

Veeck, who would purchase ownership of the White Sox in 1975, long maintained that he had seen Baines playing in Little League in 1971. Baines does not confirm Veeck's account but does say, "I must have had a pretty decent day in Little League that day."

Veeck was a life-long and insightful baseball man. As famed sportswriter Red Smith commented, "[Veeck] was a promoter at heart but a baseball man at bottom." Veeck was not the only individual affiliated with the White Sox who was favorably impressed with Baines. Veeck directed his two best talent evaluators, general manager Roland Hemond and player personnel advisor Paul Richards, to watch Baines prior to the draft. Both concurred with Veeck's positive assessment. Richards was impressed by Baines' prodigious power and, as is the wont of all scouts, he compared him to another talented left-handed hitter, Billy Williams of the Chicago Cubs.

Nonetheless, the selection of Baines raised questions. Most draft observers were focused on Joliet Catholic High School pitcher Bill Gullickson or Florida State catcher Terry Kennedy as the potential overall number one pick. While Baines was considered the best hitter in the draft, his lack of footspeed and spotty defensive play were considered liabilities. When Veeck signed Baines for an historically low $32,000 bonus contract, the doubts about Baines were further amplified. With the signing of Baines, the concept of drafting based on financial concerns rather than talent was introduced to the Major League Baseball Draft.

In 1978, the 19-year-old Baines was assigned to play for Chicago's Double-A farm team, the Knoxville Sox. Tony La Russa was slated to be Knoxville's manager. Paul Richards told La Russa that Baines was "the best hitting prospect in all of baseball."

Baines would not have quite the career of Billy Williams. However, Baines's numbers demonstrate that his selection was one of the better choices historically. Over 22 seasons, he was a six-time All-Star, batted .289 for his career, and had 384 home runs and 1,628 runs batted in. Baines did more than enough to validate his selection as the first overall draft pick. He was inducted into the Hall of Fame in 2019.

After the White Sox selected Baines, the Montreal Expos took pitcher Bill Gullickson with the second overall pick. Early in his career, Gullickson appeared to be well on his way to fulfilling the high expectations placed on him. He reached the Major Leagues at age 20 and, the next year, struck out 18 batters in one game while pitching to a 10-5 record. However, he was diagnosed with diabetes the following year and never again was a dominant big league pitcher. Nonetheless, he remained in the Major Leagues for 14 years and finished with 162 career wins.

The Milwaukee Brewers hit it big with the third overall pick, Paul Molitor from the University of Minnesota. Molitor made a name for himself in college with his bat and his speed. Teaming with Robin Yount in Milwaukee, Molitor continued to do the same with the Brewers, earning the moniker "the Ignitor." By the end of his 21-year career, Molitor had joined the storied 3,000-hit club while driving in over a thousand runs and swiping 504 bases. He was a first-ballot Hall of Famer in 2004.

The San Diego Padres struck it rich in the fourth round when they drafted shortstop Ozzie Smith from California Polytechnic State University at San Luis Obispo. Padres scout Bob Fontaine, Jr. scouted and signed

Smith for the Padres. Smith had starred with Eddie Murray at Locke High School in Los Angeles and then would follow Murray into All-Star status and, ultimately, Cooperstown. Unfortunately for the Padres, Smith's career only took off after San Diego had traded him to the St. Louis Cardinals.

Smith is considered by many astute observers to be perhaps the best defensive shortstop of all time. He would win an astounding 13 consecutive Gold Glove Awards and make 15 National League All-Star teams. Smith possessed extraordinary athleticism; his pre-game somersaults were his signature move. New York Mets shortstop Bud Harrelson offered perhaps the best insight into Smith's defensive genius: "The thing about Ozzie is if he misses a ball, you assume it is uncatchable. If any other shortstop misses a ball, your first thought is 'would Ozzie have had it?'"[37] Early in his career, Smith was not considered a good hitter. However, he worked hard to improve during his time with the Cardinals and would end up with 2,460 career hits and a memorable walk-off home run for St. Louis in the 1985 National League Championship Series. He was inducted into Cooperstown in 2002.

The Expos found another gem in Tim "Rock" Raines in the fifth round. Raines would follow Ozzie Smith into the Hall of Fame but it would take until 2017 for him to be inducted. One of the greatest leadoff hitters of all time, Raines scored 1,571 runs and stole an astounding 808 bases over his 23-year career.

A Long Swing

Bob Boone was a catcher in the Major Leagues for 19 seasons, from 1972 to 1990. He caught 2,225 big league games in his career – more than 18,000 innings. He has seen plenty of swings that scouts would describe as "too long."

Boone uses the example of Hall of Fame pitcher Nolan Ryan to explain the cause and effect of a long swing. In 1974, Ryan's fastball was timed at 108.5 miles per hour.

"When guys would face Nolan Ryan," Boone says, "their first thought was 'Holy crap! What am I going to do?'" Boone explains that the anxiety makes a batter move a lot and causes him to swing real hard. When the anxiety takes over, the hitter's arms flare out and the batter loses control of his swing.

Ideally, according to Boone, when a hitter makes his turn, his hands should form a straight line to get the bat to the ball, making the swing shorter. "If you don't have that shortness to the ball," Boone says, "you can't catch up with a 95-mile-per-hour fastball thrown from sixty-feet-six-inches." Boone would often observe the swings of Paul Molitor and Tony Gwynn, both Hall of Famers. In his view, from the time that Molitor and Gwynn started to swing to the point where they made contact with the ball, their swings were among the quickest, i.e., shortest, in all of baseball.

1978

When I started in baseball, players spent the winter getting themselves out of shape and spent spring training getting back in shape. Cal [Ripken] had this notion, 'How about if I just never get out of shape?' He was ahead of his time.

    – Richie Bancells, former trainer, Baltimore Orioles

On the field in 1978, the defending champion New York Yankees and their archrival Boston Red Sox engaged in an epic year-long battle that concluded in a classic one-game playoff in Fenway Park. The Yankees would defeat the Sox in the playoff and then beat the Kansas City Royals in the American League Championship Series to advance to the World Series. The Yankees then disposed of the Los Angeles Dodgers in six games to repeat as World Champions. Many of the key players selected in the early drafts, including Reggie Jackson, Thurman Munson, "Goose" Gossage, Carlton Fisk, Jim Rice, George Brett, Mike Schmidt, Steve Garvey and Rick Monday, starred for the teams participating in the 1978 playoff series.

In 1978, the first overall pick was again a product of the powerhouse Arizona State University team. The Atlanta Braves held the first pick and chose ASU's power-hitting third baseman, Bob Horner.

The Braves' scouting director, Paul Snyder, preferred outfielder Kirk Gibson of Michigan State University to Horner. After observing Gibson's combination of power and speed, Snyder compared him to Mickey Mantle. However, Gibson, a star wide receiver at Michigan State, was believed to be headed to the National Football League. The Braves concluded that they would not be able to sign him if they were to draft him.

Horner was Atlanta's second choice. The Braves were thrilled to "settle" for him. Horner came highly recommended. The Major League Baseball Scouting Bureau rated him as the top player in the draft. He had won the Golden Spikes Award as the best collegiate player in the nation. Most scouts drooled over his compact power stroke and his ability to play all four infield positions.

After drafting Horner, the Braves immediately placed him on the Major League roster. He made his debut on June 16, 1978, joining David Clyde and Dave Roberts as one of the few number one picks to start their professional careers at the Major League level. Horner started his pro career even more impressively than had Clyde, homering in his first-ever Major League game against future Hall of Fame pitcher Bert Blyleven.

In the first eighty-nine games of his Major League career, Horner hit 23 home runs, drove in 63 runs, and compiled a slugging percentage of .539. His twenty-three dingers led all National League third sackers, and he was selected as the National League Rookie of the Year. Clearly, to that point, he had put together the best rookie season of any player taken with the number one pick over the first fourteen years of the draft. The future looked very bright for Horner and the Braves.

Things only got better in the early part of Horner's career. He batted .314 with 33 home runs and 98 RBI's in his second season. The next year, 1980, Horner hit 35 homers and drove in 89 runs. In the strike-shortened 1981 season, he still managed to hit 15 home runs and drive in 42 runs in only 79 games. In 1982, Horner continued the success of his early career with 32 home runs and 97 runs batted in.

As the 1983 season approached, it appeared that the Braves may have made the best number one selection in the history of the draft to that date. However, in 1983, things started to unravel for Horner as he struggled with weight issues and injuries. Though he still slugged 20 home runs in 1983 and hit .303, he fractured his wrist while sliding and missed the last quarter of the season. The next year he broke the same wrist and missed almost the entire season. He bounced back in 1985 to play 130 games and hit 27 home runs, with 89 runs batted in. In 1986, he again demonstrated his remarkable power, hitting 27 home runs, including four in one game.

While Horner was one of the bright young stars of baseball as he approached free agency in 1987, he did not receive any legitimate offers due to salary collusion among the owners. Horner said "sayonara" to Major League Baseball and signed to play for the Yakult Swallows in Japan. He would return to the United States to play for the St. Louis Cardinals in 1988, but he injured his shoulder after only 60 games and was never the same player. Horner played his last Major League game on

June 18, 1988, retiring at the age of 30. Much like the earlier case of Jeff Burroughs, Horner remains another cautionary tale advising against predicting Hall of Fame status too early in a player's career.

Bill Lajoie, general manager of the Detroit Tigers, brought Michigan State football and baseball star Kirk Gibson in for a pre-draft workout at Tiger Stadium the night before the draft. Lajoie coaxed Gibson into promising that the Tigers were the only baseball team he would play for if he opted against a career in professional football. Armed with this inside information, the Tigers drafted Gibson with the 12th pick in the first round.

The Tigers agreed to Gibson's demand that he be allowed to play football during his senior season at Michigan State. Detroit also paid Gibson a whopping $150,000 bonus, almost twice as much as the highest bonus awarded in 1977. Gibson was the final addition to the exceptional 1975 and 1976 Tigers' draft classes that would propel Detroit to the team's runaway World Championship in 1984.

In the second round, the Baltimore Orioles selected a high school third baseman from nearby Aberdeen, Maryland, Cal Ripken Jr. Ripken would go on to become not only the most celebrated draftee of 1978 but one of the greatest players in the game. Ironically, Orioles scouts were divided on Ripken's abilities. He had starred on the mound at Aberdeen High School, and many scouts questioned his hitting ability and thought he projected better as a pitcher than a position player. Longtime scout Joe Consoli favorably compared Ripken to the Orioles' pitching ace, Jim Palmer. Even more ironic, there were some in the organization who viewed the choice of Ripken as a favor to his father, Cal Ripken Sr., a veteran Orioles minor league player and manager.

It was determined that Ripken would begin in the minor leagues playing the shortstop position. He struggled in his first exposure to pro ball, committing 33 errors in only 62 games in rookie ball, without a single home run. Later, however, in two seasons at Double-A and Triple-A, respectively, Ripken would blast 25 and 23 homers. His minor league production earned him a full Major League season in 1982, when he would slug 28 home runs.

Ripken remained a fixture in Baltimore for a legendary 21-year career, during which his name became synonymous with the shortstop position. In fact, he redefined the position, which had been considered primarily a defensive position prior to his arrival. Ripken shattered the stereotype for shortstops, introducing middle-of-the-order hitting and power and would set the record for most lifetime home runs by a short-stop. His career numbers include 431 home runs, 3,184 hits, 19 All-Star selections and two American League Most Valuable Player Awards.

Ripken became the "Iron Man" by breaking Lou Gehrig's longstand-ing record for most consecutive games played. Prior to Ripken, Gehrig's record of 2,130 straight games was widely considered to be unbreak-able. However, in 1995, Ripken had the eyes of everyone in the game, if not the nation, focused on him as he surpassed Gehrig's record and then went on to play another 501 consecutive games.

To provide context for Ripken's achievement, no current Major League player has ever played in even 500 straight games. In fact, very few players even play 2,632 games in their entire career. Ripken's streak was a testament to his dedication, durability and stubbornness. When inducted into Cooperstown as a first-ballot Hall of Famer in 2007, Rip-ken credited long-time Orioles trainer Richie Bancells. In turn, Bancells summed up the Ripken mystique well: "Sometimes when he gets hit by a pitch, I am almost embarrassed to ask him about it. By the time he gets back to the dugout, the bruise is gone."

A second future Hall of Famer, Ryne Sandberg, was drafted by the Philadelphia Phillies in the 20th round. Sandberg was a well-regarded high school shortstop at North Central in Spokane, Washington and was on the radar of most Major League teams. However, like Kirk Gibson, Sandberg was a star football player and had signed to play quarterback at Washington State University. Most everyone assumed he would honor that commitment – everyone but the Phillies' Northwest area scout Bill Harper. Harper had followed Sandberg for a long time and had devel-oped a close relationship. Harper was confident that Sandberg would choose baseball over football.

Harper and the Phillies were able to sign Sandberg for a report-ed bonus of $35,000, a sum unheard of for a 20th round draft choice. Sandberg made it to the majors with the Phillies in 1981 but five-time All-Star Larry Bowa was firmly entrenched at shortstop for Philadelphia. The Phillies traded Sandberg to the Chicago Cubs before the start of the 1982 season, and it was in Chicago, playing second base, that Sand-berg put together his 16-year Hall of Fame career. His career numbers represent some of the most prolific of any second sacker in history: 282

1978

home runs, 1,061 runs batted in, 344 stolen bases, 10 All-Star Games, nine Gold Gloves, seven Silver Slugger Awards and a National League Most Valuable Player Award in 1984.

Saving Henry Mack for the Phillies

Dick Teed was a baseball "lifer." He spent 17 seasons in the minor leagues as a catcher, mostly in the Brooklyn Dodgers system. During those 17 minor league seasons, Teed appeared in exactly 1,400 games. He also had one Major League game on his résumé. In 1953, the 27-year-old was playing for the Mobile Bears in the Southern Association when the Dodgers' backup catcher, Rube Walker, suffered a bruised thumb. In need of a reliable substitute, the Dodgers called Teed to the majors. Teed's one Major League game came on July 24, 1953 at Ebbets Field when he pinch hit – and struck out – against the Milwaukee Braves.

After his playing career, Teed managed for two seasons in the minor leagues. He then turned to scouting and became a highly regarded cross-checker for the Philadelphia Phillies. Teed would sometimes work in tandem with legendary Phillies scout, Tony Lucadello.

In the spring of 1976, Lucadello got wind of a hard-throwing high school pitcher in Winchester, Kentucky. The details were sparse. The pitcher was African-American and was reputed to throw smoke. Lucadello sent Carl Loewenstine, then a young part-time scout, to hunt for the pitcher. In time, Loewenstine found his way to George Rogers Clark High School in Winchester. He learned that the young fireballer was named Henry Mack. "I think I found your guy," Loewenstine reported back to Lucadello.

The next week, Lucadello and Teed traveled to Kentucky to see Mack pitch. Mack had a game befitting a phenom, pitching a no-hitter and striking out some 20 batters. Lucadello and Teed knew that word of the no-hitter would travel quickly. They did not welcome the competition.

For Mack's next game, there were eight or more scouts in the stands. However, the Henry Mack on display bore little resemblance to the pitcher who had authored a no-hitter. Curiously, he had morphed into a knuckleball pitcher. For the remainder of his high school season, Mack threw exclusively knuckleballs. Scouts would ask him to throw hard. Mack would reply, "I throw the heat when I need it. I can strike these guys out with my knuckleball."

When it came time for the 1976 draft, the Phillies took Mack in the 13th round. No other team dared to use a draft pick on a pitcher who threw only knuckleballs. Mack's sudden transformation from fastballer to knuckleballer had "saved" him for the Phillies. Lucadello, as crafty a scout as ever existed, and Teed, the cross-checker with one Major League at-bat to his name, were surely left smiling.

Mack would go on to have two stellar seasons in the minors, 1978 and 1979, but then hurt his arm. By the age of 22, he was out of baseball.

1979

NFL Hall of Famers Dan Marino [a pitcher] and John Elway [an outfielder] were drafted ahead of Don Mattingly in the 1979 MLB Draft. To go from being a pick in the 19th round to be the Most Valuable Player of the American League and have your number retired in Monument Park, that told me that this man was a worker who dissected his swing and dissected the game and so I always had the utmost respect for Donnie, because he came from where he came from and he did what he did. He was not afraid and he knew the value of hard work.

    – Ned Colletti, former general manager, Los Angeles Dodgers

In 1979, the Seattle Mariners owned the first overall selection. The Mariners used the pick to draft Harrisburg, Pennsylvania high school star Al Chambers. There was widespread support for the choice in the scouting community. However, the selection of Chambers turned out to be one of the worst choices of all time.

Chambers was a physically imposing six-feet-four, 215-pound specimen who could punish a baseball. He had starred at John Harris High School in Harrisburg, attracting the attention of the Seattle Mariners scouting staff. Bill Kearns, a Mariners scout, said, "Chambers had the most power of any free agent I've seen." He predicted that in a few years from draft day, "people will pay just to watch this guy take batting practice."

Mariners scout Bob Harrison, who scouted and signed Chambers, was just as fulsome in his praise. Harrison described Chambers as a combination of Dave Parker and Dave Winfield, both five-tool superstars. In other words, Chambers was huge, athletic and could hit a baseball a very long way. In fact, Harrison thought Chambers might even have more power than Parker and Winfield. Others in the organization compared Chambers to Jim Rice, the reigning American League Most Valuable Player. Rice had slugged 46 home runs in 1978 with a .315 batting average.

Even though the Mariners held the first pick, they had to compete with Arizona State University, with whom Chambers had signed a letter of intent to play football. In one of the great lines uttered by any two-sport star in history, Chambers noted, "I enjoy hitting a baseball more than getting hit in football." The Mariners won out over Arizona State by offering Chambers a signing bonus of $85,000. The Mariners expected that Chambers would be in the middle of their lineup in a few years. The team first called Chambers to the Major Leagues in July 1983. Chambers made the decision to elevate him easy by batting .331 and driving in 75 runs in 99 games at Triple-A Salt Lake City that season. His play at Salt Lake City seemed to herald the success that the Mariners had anticipated.

In his first 31 games with the Mariners, Chambers struggled, batting only .209 with one home run and seven runs batted in. He spent the bulk of the next two seasons back in Triple-A. Chambers showed the ability to hit in the minor leagues but never managed to make an impression at the Major League level, due in large part to a shoulder injury. The Mariners released him on March 25, 1986, one day after his 25th birthday. Chambers finished his Major League career with a .208 batting average and two home runs.

Former Toronto Blue Jays area scout Ben McLure fondly remembers the displays of prodigious power that Chambers showed in high school games. McLure believes Chambers would have had a productive Major League career if not for his shoulder problems. Chambers attributes his dismal showing to the fact that he did not receive sufficient opportunity with the Mariners. "I didn't get an opportunity," he says, arguing that "any high picks that don't get an opportunity will be in the same position I'm in." For Chambers, the experience was extremely disappointing. He says, "There was a time after I left the game, I didn't want to watch a baseball game or pick up a paper."[38]

In the 19th round of the draft, the New York Yankees found a hidden gem in Don Mattingly. A left-handed batter, Mattingly stroked balls to left field with maddening consistency. Bill Livesey, former director of player development for the Yankees, was impressed with Mattingly's bat control from the first time that he saw him play. Livesey says, "If you sat in the stands when Mattingly was up and you didn't know who was hitting, you would think it was a right-handed batter because he hit all of them that way."

In the minor leagues, Mattingly made his mark as a doubles hitter. In one at-bat after another, he would drive the ball to left-center field.

In 1984, his first full season with the Yankees, Mattingly led the American League with 44 doubles. He followed that season with 48 doubles in 1985 and 53 doubles in 1986, leading the league both years. Livesey recalls that opposing teams never really developed a good approach for pitching to Mattingly. "They said we've got to pitch this guy in because you can't get him out away," Livesey says. "When they pitched him in, he would turn on it and hit it into the stands. And he was so cerebral." Mattingly ended his Major League career in 1995 with a lifetime batting average of .307.

What Don Mattingly Taught the Scouts

When the New York Yankees kicked off spring training in 1984, the common perception was that veteran Roy Smalley and 22-year-old Don Mattingly were in competition for the first base job. Smalley had played in 22 games at first base for the Yankees in 1983. He had also played 91 games at shortstop, but with limited range. Overall, playing in 130 games in 1983, Smalley had collected 24 doubles and 18 home runs to go with a .275 average.

The Yankees had called Mattingly up from Columbus in June 1983 and he remained with the parent club for the rest of the season. Before being called up, Mattingly had hit for a .332 average over five minor league seasons. In those five seasons, however, he had managed only 37 home runs. So, entering spring training of 1984, the first base position was thought to be a choice between Smalley's power and Mattingly's history of hitting for average.

On May 6, 1984, Mattingly started at first and went four for six. That game started a streak in which Mattingly had 15 hits in 43 at-bats, a .348 clip. From then on, aside from occasional days off, first base belonged to Mattingly. For the season, he had 44 doubles, 23 home runs and a .343 average in 153 games, 133 of them at first base. His performance severely cut into Smalley's playing time, leading the Yankees to trade Smalley to the Chicago White Sox midway through the season.

Mattingly's 23 home runs in 1984 came as a pleasant surprise to Bill Livesey and other Yankee scouts. Livesey used to watch Mattingly in 1981 when he was playing for the Double-A Nashville Sounds as a 20-year-old. The majority of Mattingly's hits went to left-center. He made a practice of driving the ball the opposite way and ending up at second base with a double. Later, as opposing pitchers adjusted and began pitching him more inside – especially at the major league level – Mattingly would turn on the pitches and hit them with power to right field.

As Livesey watched Mattingly develop, he was particularly impressed with his cerebral approach to hitting. "We learn so much from these guys, from all of them, as they progress through the minor leagues. We would study them and we realized that if you have a 70 or 75 on a guy's tool, especially with hitting, you've probably got the power well undergraded."

With Mattingly as his prime example, Livesey concluded that even though a young hitter may not be showing the ability to hit for the fences early in his pro career, once he gets bigger and stronger, he's going to hit with power. Livesey says, "That is what Don Mattingly taught us."

The Golden Age of the Amateur Draft
(1980 – 2001)

Eighty percent of big league players are what the backs of their baseball cards say they are. The key is to identify which 10% of the remaining players are declining and which 10% are ascending.

—Longtime scout Ken Bracey

While the first pick alone does not make or break a successful draft, it does carry a special symbolic significance. A successful first overall pick can validate and trademark a draft. Success with the first overall pick demonstrates that a team has surveyed the entire nation and found the best player available.

In 1980, the Mets had the first overall draft pick for the third time in their short history. When they selected outfielder Darryl Strawberry with that pick, the third time was indeed a charm. The selection of Strawberry, a student at Crenshaw High School in Los Angeles, as the number one overall pick was a "bull's-eye." The pick has stood the test of time; Strawberry turned out to have the best career of any player drafted in 1980. In future years, there would be players selected with the overall number one pick who would experience even greater success than Strawberry. However, the selection of Strawberry was especially significant because it ushered in a new era of success and celebrity for the draft.

In the period from 1980 to 2001 – the period we have labeled "The Golden Age of the Amateur Draft" – there were five years in which the teams holding the overall number one pick scored a "bull's-eye." In addition to the Mets' selection of Strawberry in 1980, the Seattle Mariners drafted Ken Griffey Jr. in 1987; the Atlanta Braves took Chipper Jones in 1990; the Mariners selected Álex Rodríguez in 1993; and the Minnesota Twins drafted Joe Mauer in 2001. All five players were taken with the overall number one pick. All five were "bull's-eyes" – indisputably, the best players to come out of the draft in their respective draft years.

Griffey Jr., Jones, Rodríguez and Mauer would all be far more transcendent players than Strawberry. Both Griffey Jr. and Jones have already been inducted into the Baseball Hall of Fame. Mauer is expected to join them when eligible.[39] Álex Rodríguez would no doubt also be on his way to Cooperstown, but his prospects for admission remain clouded due to his admitted use of performance-enhancing drugs.

Beyond the symbolic number one choice, the amateur draft also hit its stride and began to produce deeper and more talented early round choices, such as the heralded 1985 draft class. The players drafted in the first round of 1985 have a collective career Wins Above Replacement (WAR) value of 496. This total exceeds the collective WAR values of every other draft – by a wide margin. The 1985 class has already produced three Hall of Famers in Barry Larkin, Randy Johnson, and John Smoltz. The careers of two other candidates, Rafael Palmeiro and career home run leader Barry Bonds, seem worthy of admission to the Hall of Fame, but their election is in doubt because of suspected or confirmed use of performance enhancing drugs. Almost each and every class in the golden years possessed superstar quality and seemingly a Hall of Famer or two for good measure. Luminous stars such as Greg Maddux, Tom Glavine, John Smoltz, Derek Jeter, and Craig Biggio were among the draft hauls. The 1989 class alone produced three Hall of Fame first basemen in Frank Thomas, Jeff Bagwell, and Jim Thome.

The golden years of the draft, 1980-2001, mostly coincided with the narrow yet special window of time when baseball was included in the Olympic Games. Consequently, the era had the special cache of name recognition and buzz otherwise absent from the amateur draft. Due to his participation in the 1984 Olympics, University of Southern California slugger Mark McGwire was a well-known commodity when he was drafted. His moonshot home runs for the Oakland Athletics and St. Louis Cardinals helped rejuvenate baseball after a player strike had led to widespread fan disinterest. While McGwire's records have also been sullied by his admission of steroid use, his home run spree that broke Roger Maris's single season home run record will always be remembered as a legendary part of the game.

The period of the golden years also produced extraordinary dual-sport players like Bo Jackson. While Jackson's career was cut short by injury, he captivated the sports world and performed unprecedented feats of greatness on the diamond that have not been seen before or since. The period also produced one of the greatest hitters in the game in slugger Manny Ramírez. Like many others of this period, Ramírez is also tainted by suspensions for using performance enhancing drugs. However, his clutch batting remains a singular testament to his ability to hit a baseball as well as almost anyone who has ever played the game.

Two Questions

The San Francisco Giants drafted catcher Kirt Manwaring in the second round of the 1986 draft. Manwaring quickly signed his professional contract and reported to the Class A Clinton (Iowa) Giants to begin his pro career. By the end of the next season, Manwaring was in the Major Leagues.

Mike Toomey, then a scout for San Francisco, followed Manwaring closely during his college career at Coastal Carolina University. Toomey liked everything about Manwaring. Toomey offers a concise but apt appraisal of Manwaring's abilities. "He could catch and throw and had survival skills with the bat," Toomey says, adding, "I knew in my heart that he was going to make it. He had tremendous desire."

According to Toomey, Manwaring asked the Giants two questions after he was drafted: (1) where am I going to play? and (2) when do I leave?

Two days after the draft, Toomey and fellow scout Jim Fairey signed Manwaring at a Howard Johnson's Motor Inn in Elmira, New York. In his second season of pro ball, Manwaring hit .267 in 98 games for the Shreveport Captains, earning a September call-up to the Major Leagues.

During his 13 seasons in the Major Leagues, Manwaring played for three clubs, San Francisco, Houston and Colorado. His best year came in 1993 with the Giants when he hit .275 in 130 games and won the Gold Glove Award. Manwaring was particularly adept at blocking pitches in the dirt. Toomey says, "Manwaring was an excellent catch-and-throw guy. Pitchers loved throwing to him."

These days, Toomey notes, players who are drafted are less inclined to ask the same questions that Manwaring asked in 1986. In the current era, Toomey says, the most common questions are: (1) what round? and (2) how much?

1980

I don't have a ton of Major League highlights but I got Wade Boggs out three times on cut fastballs that he hit on the ground to second base. They told me in the pre-game scouting report not to throw the ball away to him because he will hit it over the left fielder's head and don't throw it inside because he will pull it over the right field fence. I said, 'What do I do?' They said, 'Throw it down the middle; he won't know what to do with it.' I threw cutters down the middle. They started right down the middle and cut a little bit and he rolled over to second base three times.

– Jeff Bittiger, former pitcher for the Phillies, Twins and White Sox and current scout for the Oakland Athletics

The New York Yankees won 103 regular season games in 1980, more than any other team in baseball that year. However, New York finally succumbed in the playoffs to their perennial rival, the Kansas City Royals. The Royals were led by George Brett, Dennis Leonard, and Willie Wilson, players whom they had stockpiled in recent years due to shrewd choices in the draft. Led by Mike Schmidt, the Philadelphia Phillies defeated the Royals in the 1980 World Series. The Phillies captured their first-ever World Series championship, winning four games to two.

Eddie Bockman, a former player who scouted for the Phillies for 30 years after his playing career, was responsible for signing seven members of the 1980 Phillies. Bockman's signings included catcher Bob Boone, pitcher Dick Ruthven and shortstop Larry Bowa. Unlike Boone and Ruthven, Bowa was not drafted. Bockman signed him out of Sacramento City College as an undrafted free agent.

Bowa was both the sparkplug and the antagonist of the 1980 Phillies. He was considered to be stubborn, cocky and obnoxious. He ignored baseball scouts who told him he was not good enough to play in the majors. Only one team, Philadelphia, was interested in Bowa prior to the draft. The Phillies sent Bockman to scout him on a day when Bowa's team played a doubleheader. Bowa managed to be ejected by the umpires in *both* ends of the doubleheader. The Phillies decided not to draft Bowa but continued to follow him. Bockman's scouting report told the Phillies everything they needed to know about Bowa: "Have always liked his potential, but his attitude will make you throw up. A definite Major League prospect if he keeps the bugs out of his head."[40]

The Phillies were chocked full of excellent scouts in the 1980s. One of the most famous was Hugh Alexander. Alexander was known as "Uncle Hughie," for his warm and avuncular personality. In his youth, Alexander was considered to be an excellent prospect. However, his playing career was tragically cut short by an off-season machinery accident that severed his left hand. Cy Slapnicka, another legendary scout, had signed Alexander to play for the Cleveland Indians.[41] After the accident, Slapnicka signed the 20-year-old Alexander as a scout for the Indians. Alexander proved Slapnicka to be as good a judge of scouting talent as he was of baseball talent. Uncle Hughie would sign over 60 big leaguers, including three extraordinary players: Allie Reynolds, who would win 182 games and became a mainstay of the great New York Yankee teams of the early 1950s; Frank "Hondo" Howard, who would hit almost 400 Major League home runs; and Dodger pitcher Don Sutton, who would win 324 career games and be enshrined in the Hall of Fame in 1998.

Like every great scout, Alexander always had a story about "the one who got away." His best story was about a fellow Oklahoman. One day a friend gave Alexander a tip on a young player in Commerce, Oklahoma. The friend wrote the player's name on a piece of paper that he then handed to Alexander. When Uncle Hughie went to see the player at his high school, the principal told him the lad suffered from arthritis in his legs and that the school did not have a baseball team. Alexander left the school without speaking to the player. As he exited the school parking lot, the scrap of paper blew away in the wind. Alexander often thought, with remorse, of that piece of paper and the name that his friend had written – "Mickey Mantle."[42]

The Philadelphia Phillies did not have a monopoly on great scouts in 1980. Two of the best scouts of all time worked for the New York Mets, national cross-checker Harry Minor and chief scout Roger Jongewaard. Both Minor and Jongewaard were very involved in the scouting and drafting of Darryl Strawberry in 1980.

Like many of the great baseball scouts from "back in the day," Jongewaard was a colorful personality, with a varied career off the field to boot. For many years, he and his wife, Carol, operated a famous coffee shop, Jongewaard's Bake-n-Broil, in Long Beach, California. The restaurant was renowned for its cakes and pies. On the baseball diamond, Jongewaard was renowned for his ability to evaluate and project talent. Jongewaard described Strawberry as "a power hitter who runs like a deer." Although a little slender by the standard of most power hitters, the six-foot-six Strawberry possessed a sweet left-handed swing and power that brought to mind Reggie Jackson and Willie McCovey.

Minor, an excellent talent evaluator in his own right, concurred with Jongewaard and most every other scout. "Strawberry was the best available talent in the draft," Minor said. However, Minor and many other Mets scouts were also intrigued by the possibility of drafting two other California-bred outfielders in Darnell Coles of Los Angeles and San Diego phenom Billy Beane. Long after the draft, Minor remembered the draft room "like it was yesterday." Even with a generational talent such as Darryl Strawberry, not all of the Mets scouts agreed with taking Strawberry as the first pick.

Minor recalled, "We had three first-round picks and a split of opinion on our draft board. Some argued for Strawberry and others pushed for Beane. Roger and I were very much on the side of drafting Strawberry. I had scouted Beane extensively and liked him a great deal also. He had the whole package, just like "Straw," but I offered that Beane could fall to us with our second pick as a lot of teams feared he was going to Stanford. Mets general manager, Frank Cashen, ultimately chose Strawberry and then we got very lucky when Beane was still available for us at pick number 23. We got both our guys and some of our very good scouts sincerely thought Beane would have the better Major League career."

Both Strawberry and Beane advanced quickly through the Mets' farm system. By 1982, they were both with the Double-A Jackson Mets in the Texas League. On the Jackson Mets, Strawberry and Beane played with other players drafted by the Mets in 1980, most notably pitcher Jeff Bittiger. The Mets had selected Bittiger in the seventh round. Strawberry, Beane, and Bittiger were all 20 years old and full of promise.

A year later, Strawberry arrived in New York and won the Rookie of the Year Award. Bittiger progressed to the Mets' Triple-A club in Tidewater. Beane hit only .211 for Jackson in 1982, causing his progress to stall. He would spend the better part of the next two seasons with Jackson, where his average improved only marginally. Bittiger pitched creditably for the Tidewater Tides in 1983, winning 12 games and losing 10. However, his progress was hindered by the depth of the Mets' pitching at the Major League level. The Mets ultimately traded Bittiger to Philadelphia, where, on September 22, 1986, he won his first Major League game and hit his first and only big-league home run on the same day.

Strawberry would go on to play a pivotal role in helping lead the Mets to the 1986 World Series championship. Over his seventeen-year Major League career, Strawberry was selected to eight All-Star teams and played on four World Series champions. Strawberry hit 335 career home runs, stole 221 bases and accumulated an even 1,000 runs batted in. He was an impact player; many of his 335 home runs were the type of "moon beams" that had fans sitting on the edge of their seats.

At Strawberry's introductory press conference with the Mets after the 1980 draft, the Beatles' iconic tune, "Strawberry Fields Forever," blared in the background. Understandably, the Mets were anticipating a long and sustained run of success with Strawberry as their linchpin. While Strawberry was a key contributor for the Mets during the period 1983-1990, his baseball biography will be forever qualified by "what-ifs." His career was derailed at its zenith by alcohol and cocaine addiction problems that greatly diminished his rising star. Individuals such as Harry Minor, who watched and admired Strawberry's powerful left-handed swing, believed that "Straw" would have been on a par with the all time greats if not for his addiction problems and, later, a series of injuries. Nonetheless, Strawberry's performance certainly was sufficient to banish the ghosts of the Mets' earlier number one miscues in drafting Steve Chilcott in 1966 and Tim Foli in 1968.

The Mets paid Billy Beane a whopping $125,000 bonus to sign, more than any other first rounder other than Strawberry. Beane, unlike Strawberry, was a major disappointment for Harry Minor and the Mets. Beane hit only .219 with three homers in his six-year big league career. Minor believed that if Beane had stuck with playing baseball, he would have eventually had a productive career. As Michael Lewis's *MoneyBall* so magnificently points out, Billy Beane has repeatedly lamented his first-round selection by the Mets and his decision to turn pro instead of accepting a scholarship to Stanford University.[43]

The 1980s are considered to be a major step forward for the Major League draft. In a sense, the Strawberry pick turned the page on the largely unsuccessful efforts of the early years. While the number one overall pick is largely symbolic, it is a tribute to the Mets that their selection of Darryl Strawberry would be the first to stand the test of time. The 1980 draft appeared to usher in a new era, where teams would "get it right" with greater frequency than in the early years.

While a greater sense of optimism may have taken root in 1980, success was anything but widespread. Although almost seventy-five percent of the first-round choices in 1980 would go on to play in the Major Leagues, the figure is misleading. Other than Strawberry, no other first-round choice became a true impact player. Kelly Gruber, whom the Cleveland Indians selected with the tenth overall pick, was the only other first-rounder to have a good career. Other than Strawberry, the most celebrated first-round picks in 1980 made their names in the dugout or, in Beane's case, in the front office. In a strange coincidence, three current or former managers – Rick Renteria, Terry Francona, and John Gibbons – were all drafted in the first round of 1980.

One Strikeout Away from the Majors

Harry Minor's name does not appear in the *Baseball Encyclopedia* but, on paper at least, he made it to the Major Leagues. In 1953, the Philadelphia Athletics recalled Minor toward the end of the season. He was to join the Athletics as soon as his minor league team, the Savannah Indians, completed its games.

In the last game of Savannah's regular season, Minor and his teammates took on the Jacksonville Braves, a team that featured future major leaguers Henry Aaron, Felix Mantilla, and Ray Crone. A loss to the Braves would wrap up Savannah's schedule and put Minor on a bus to the big leagues. Late in the game, Savannah trailed Jacksonville by one run. Savannah had a runner on second base but was down to its last out. Crone, winner of 19 games that season, was on the mound for Jacksonville. In 253 innings, he had yielded only seven home runs.

With the game on the line, Harry Minor strode to the plate. Minor worked the count to two balls and two strikes. Crone let loose with a pitch but Minor did not bite. Confident the pitch had found the plate, Crone began to walk off the field. The umpire, however, yelled "ball," prolonging Savannah's season for one more pitch. With the count at 3-2, Crone went back to work. On the next pitch, Minor took a hearty cut and connected. As the broadcasters are inclined to say, "the ball wasn't coming back." Minor circled the bases and crossed the plate with the winning run.

Minor's blast allowed Savannah to finish one game ahead of the Macon Peaches, earning the Indians a spot in the South Atlantic League playoffs. Savannah then embarked on an extended march through the playoffs. Weeks later, Savannah's season ended. Minor promptly called the Athletics to tell them he was on his way. By then, however, the Athletics were on their final road trip of the season, with two games against the Yankees in New York and a season-ending series against the Senators in Washington. Philadelphia told Minor not to bother making the trip. "We'll do it next year," the front office said.

For Minor, "next year" never came. He again had a productive season in 1954 but, at the age of 26, time was not on his side. Minor played pro ball for seven more years but never again came within striking distance of the Major Leagues. His career took him south to Birmingham and west to Little Rock and Salinas but never north to the majors. In the ultimate irony, Minor's home run deprived him of his ticket to the big leagues. "If I had struck out," he would say wistfully, "we wouldn't have been in the playoffs, but you don't think about those things."

1981

Tony Gwynn as a kid, he didn't just wake up and be a great hitter, he worked. Even after Tony was in the big leagues, he would be in the batting cage hitting for hours, talking about hitting, learning the game. Some guys make it their goal to be drafted high, some guys have a goal of just getting to the big leagues, others like Tony really strive to be the best player they can be and they put in the work to achieve that goal. The guys like Tony Gwynn are going to succeed because they work at it and work at it properly.

— Orrin Freeman, former special assistant to the general manager, Miami Marlins

The 1981 season was a very strange year in the annals of baseball. For almost two months of summer, there was no Major League Baseball at all because of a players' strike. The strike lasted from June 12 until August 9 and resulted in the cancellation of 713 games. When play resumed, the Major Leagues adopted a split season format. Eventually, the Los Angeles Dodgers met the New York Yankees in the World Series, with the Dodgers prevailing, 4 games to 2. While it was a great time for Dodger Blue, the whole season seemed quite amiss.

The draft was also a strange affair. Unlike most every other year, a majority of the successful first-round draft picks made their mark with a different team than the team which drafted them. Most of the stars of the 1981 draft were shipped out of town, sometimes in short order, before they reached the zenith of their careers. Such was the case with the first two players selected in 1981, Mike Moore and Joe Carter. Both Moore and Carter hailed from Oklahoma. The Sooner state had given baseball some of its greatest players, such as Mickey Mantle, Warren Spahn, Johnny Bench and Willie Stargell, but never before or since were the first two players in the draft both from Oklahoma.

The 1981 season was also the year the draft went to college or, more precisely, college players became much more prevalent in the first round than in prior years. The 1981 draft presented a clear example of the evolution of the college game and its ever-increasing prominence in the draft. In addition to being from Oklahoma, the first two selections were both collegian players, as were fifteen other first-round choices.

In all, two-thirds of the first round picks were from college, a significant reversal from the inaugural draft, when high school players accounted for 75% of the players drafted.

A college game played just a few short weeks before the draft became the most remembered event of the 1981 amateur season. On May 21, in New Haven, Connecticut, pitcher Ron Darling of Yale University and Frank Viola of St. John's University matched up in the first round of the NCAA baseball tournament. The matchup produced a classic game that is still discussed with awe, especially in scouting circles. Many observers have labeled it the best college game in history. Although the supply of players in the draft was continuing to migrate to the Sunbelt region, there were still some very good baseball players in the Northeast.

Yale University was hardly a baseball powerhouse. Yet Darling had captured the scouts' full attention in 1981. With the stands packed with as many scouts as fans, Darling pitched a dominating game. He handled a potent St. John's lineup with a mix of fastballs and an unhittable slider. In an eleven-inning masterpiece, Darling struck out sixteen batters while allowing no hits. As overpowering as Darling was, Viola matched him, scoreless frame for scoreless frame. Both pitchers were so dominating that, at the end of nine innings, no runner from either team had reached third base.

In the twelfth inning, St. John's managed to score on a bloop single and an error to end Darling's no-hit bid and win the game. Amazingly, each pitcher threw close to 170 pitches, a mind-numbing total. As the game ended, even the players from St. John's rose to the top step of their dugout to cheer Darling.

If Darling wasn't already at the top of the draft list, his dominating performance against St. John's ensured that he would be at the top. The Mariners again held the number one pick in the draft. Costs were still a concern for the Seattle franchise. When Darling took the then unprecedented step of hiring an agent, the Mariners, as well as other teams, became leery. Seattle resolved not to break the budget on its first-round selection. Instead of selecting Darling, the Mariners chose Mike Moore, who had starred at Oral Roberts University in Tulsa.

The six-foot-four Moore was the first right-handed pitcher ever to be selected as the number one pick in the draft. Mariners scout Bob Harrison played a key role in the scouting of Moore, who featured a 97-mph fastball. The Mariners envisioned him anchoring their staff for years to come. While he was far from the disappointment that Al Chambers turned out to be, Moore never became a top-of-the-rotation starter for the Mariners. Although he did win 17 games for the Mariners in 1985, his most successful season came in 1989 when he won 19 games for the Oakland Athletics. Moore pitched to a career mark of 161 wins and 176 losses over his 14 Major League seasons. After the Mets had scored big with Darryl Strawberry in 1980, the selection of Mike Moore was clearly a regression.

With the second pick, the Chicago Cubs made another solid but unspectacular pick in selecting outfielder Joe Carter from Oklahoma City. Carter had starred collegiately at Wichita State and was signed by Negro League legend Buck O'Neil. Carter seemed to be ready to star in the Cubs' outfield for years to come but it was not to be. After Carter had played only 23 games with Chicago, the Cubs traded him to the Cleveland Indians in 1984. Carter became a reliable middle-of-the-order power hitter in Cleveland, but he truly blossomed with the Toronto Blues Jays from 1991 to 1997. As a Blue Jay, Carter was selected for five All-Star Games. He would have his most memorable baseball moment with Toronto—a walk-off home run for the Blue Jays to win the 1993 World Series. Over his career, Carter belted 396 homers, drove in 1,445 runs and stole 231 bases. While his career statistics would suggest that Carter was an impact player, his relatively low on-base percentage (.306) and subpar defense depress his historical valuation.

Beyond Moore and Carter, the 1981 draft also provided many excellent players. Ron Darling fell all the way to the ninth pick of the draft and was selected by the Texas Rangers. Like Carter, Darling made his impact in the majors with a different team than the team that drafted him. The Rangers traded Darling to the New York Mets less than a year after he was drafted. He pitched for 13 big-league seasons and made one All-Star Game appearance but never fulfilled the expectations he had created at Yale.

Frank Viola, who was drafted by the Minnesota Twins in the second round, went on to have a much better Major League career than Darling. "Sweet Music," as Viola was known, led the 1987 Minnesota Twins to the World Series championship, won the American League Cy Young Award in 1988, and was selected to three All-Star Games. Over the course of his career, Viola won 176 games.

Feeling A Draft

The San Diego Padres and the team's general manager, Jack McKeon, would become the success story of the 1981 draft by selecting Tony Gwynn from San Diego State University in the third round. "Trader Jack" McKeon had seen just about every San Diego State baseball game he could get to because his son, Casey, played for the team. McKeon was well aware that San Diego State boasted one of the top 1981 draft prospects in shortstop Bobby Meacham.

In March of 1981, Tony Gwynn caught McKeon's eye. As Gwynn hit line drive after line drive, McKeon asked his scouts who Gwynn was and how he had escaped their attention previously. The scouts answered that Gwynn was primarily a basketball player at San Diego State and had only recently joined the baseball team. McKeon told his scouts that he wanted to draft Gwynn. On draft day, McKeon remained adamant about selecting Gwynn. However, the San Diego scouts assured McKeon that Gwynn had flown under the radar and that very few teams had him on their draft boards. Meacham, the more celebrated San Diego State player, was drafted eighth overall by the St. Louis Cardinals but no other team targeted Gwynn.

When the second round began, McKeon was eager to select Gwynn but his scouts convinced him instead to take Miami of Ohio pitcher Bill Long with the pick. The scouts remained convinced that no other team was interested in taking Gwynn as high as second. Reluctantly, McKeon agreed. When the third round began and Gwynn was still on the board, McKeon was adamant that the Padres had to draft him. Some of his scouts still believed they could wait until a later round, but McKeon's tone and demeanor told them they could not both counsel him to wait and still keep their jobs. Therefore, with the 58th pick, the Padres selected Tony Gwynn. Gwynn immediately proved that he belonged. He played in 23 games for the Double-A Amarillo Gold Sox in 1981 and hit .462. By July 1982, he had joined the Padres and was there to stay for the next 20 years.

In a testament to Gwynn's athleticism, he was drafted by both the Padres and the San Diego Clippers of the National Basketball Association in 1981. Although Gwynn was only five-foot-eleven, many believe he was a better basketball player than baseball player. In time, however, he made himself into an outstanding baseball player. McKeon marveled at Gwynn's work ethic and points out that he worked hard at improving his defense as well as his hitting. "When we signed him," McKeon says, "he could not throw from home plate to second base. Two years later, he was a Gold Glove outfielder."

Gwynn would go on to appear in fifteen All-Star Games over his twenty-year Major League career. He amassed 3,141 hits and compiled a .338 career batting average. He earned the title, "Mr. Padre," and is regarded as one of the greatest hitters of all time.

In Gwynn's 2007 acceptance speech at his Hall of Fame induction, he thanked Jack McKeon for drafting him. McKeon jokes that the drafting of Gwynn reminds him of the old saying, "success has many fathers but failure is an orphan." By the time Gwynn became a perennial All-Star, six different San Diego Padre scouts claimed credit for his signing. McKeon once reviewed the team's draft day scouting reports for 1981 and found that one of the six scouts projected Gwynn as a 20th round pick and the other five did not even have his name on their list.

With the selection of Darryl Strawberry in 1980, the New York Mets began a sustained run of excellence in drafting, led by general manager Frank Cashen and scouting director Joe McIlvaine. Starting in 1980, the Mets' drafts yielded a bonanza of talent that culminated in a World Championship in 1986 and fueled strongly competitive teams throughout the remainder of the 1980s. Yet, after hitting on their selection of Strawberry in 1980, the Mets missed badly with their first-round pick in 1981, speedy Tennessee State outfielder Terry Blocker. The Mets were thrilled to see Blocker still on the board at number four and paid him the highest bonus in the 1981 draft. However, he was never able to adjust to Major League pitching and wound up with only 244 lifetime atbats over three seasons in the Major Leagues.

Jim Riggleman, Hard Hat

In 1973, Bill Livesey was the coach of the Falmouth Commodores in the Cape Cod League. Among other responsibilities, he had to recruit players for his summer team. He had locked up his shortstop, Bill Almon from Brown University. He needed to find other infielders.

Livesey called Jim Riggleman, a standout at Frostburg State University in the western reaches of Maryland. The Cape Cod League was the premier summer collegiate baseball league. Riggleman was flattered to receive a call. When Riggleman indicated that he was interested in playing for the Commodores, Livesey filled in the details. As with other players in the Cape Cod League, Riggleman would have to work a daytime job. Livesey promised to get Riggleman a job at the Holiday Inn in Falmouth.

Livesey's talk of the Holiday Inn piqued Riggleman's interest. "So, I'm thinking that I was going to be serving tea to the ladies out by the swimming pool," Riggleman recalled. He had visions of being at the swimming pool by day and at the ballpark by night.

When Riggleman arrived in Falmouth for the summer, Livesey drove him to his summer job. To Riggleman's dismay, the Holiday Inn was under construction. Riggleman would spend the summer as a "hard hat." His job was to help build the Holiday Inn. Riggleman played well for the Commodores that summer, impressing, among others, the Los Angeles Dodgers. Based largely on Riggleman's performance for Falmouth in the summer of 1973, the Dodgers drafted him in the fourth round of 1974.

Riggleman played in the minor leagues for eight years, spending time in the farm systems of both the Dodgers and the St. Louis Cardinals. His best season came in 1980, when he hit .295 with 21 home runs for the Double-A Arkansas Travelers. In 1981, Riggleman retired as an active player at the age of 28.

Riggleman never made it to the Major Leagues as a player. However, he has spent 13 years as a Major League manager, working for the San Diego Padres, Chicago Cubs, Seattle Mariners, Washington Nationals and Cincinnati Reds.

1982

Baseball is totally about dealing with failure. The number one thing a player has to learn is that, some days, baseball just wins. Some days are not yours, 'not my day.' So you wake up the next day and try to make it your day. That's the hardest thing about baseball is all the damn failure. If you don't know how to deal with failure or maybe you don't expect it, it can crush you. You can get in a downward spiral where you put so much pressure on yourself. I walked into spring training and I watched Alfredo Griffin and Tony Fernandez playing shortstop – my position – and I said 'Holy shit, I can't do what these guys do.'

– Augie Schmidt, shortstop selected by the Toronto Blue Jays with the second overall pick in the 1982 draft

Brats and beer were at center stage in the 1982 baseball season as the St. Louis Cardinals defeated the Milwaukee Brewers in an exciting and highly competitive World Series that went to seven games. Although both teams represented Middle America, they could not have been any more different in composition and style. The Brewers were dubbed "Harvey's Wallbangers." Manager Harvey Kuenn and the Brewers clearly relied on the long ball, having slugged 216 home runs during the regular season. In contrast, Whitey Herzog's Cardinals hit only 67 home runs during the season and won their games with speed on the bases, solid pitching and excellent defense.

The manner in which the Brewers and the Cardinals constructed their rosters was also a study in contrasts. The Brewers built their roster through the draft. Core pieces Robin Yount and Paul Molitor were recent first-round picks who would both be elected to the Hall of Fame. The Cardinals were led largely by late-round picks and undrafted free agents. Keith Hernandez, who played first base for the Cardinals, was selected in the 42nd round of 1971. Starting pitcher Joaquin Andujar, winner of 15 games during the regular season and two more in the World Series, was signed as a free agent, as was second baseman Tommy Herr.

Ironically, the Cardinals' catcher, Darrell Porter, who was the only player on the team who had been a high first-round pick, was drafted by the Brewers in 1970. The Cardinals signed Porter as a free agent in 1980. Porter played a pivotal role in the Cardinals' march to the 1982

Championship, earning Most Valuable Player honors in both the National League Championship Series and the World Series.

The 1982 draft also had a distinctly Midwestern flavor. The Chicago Cubs held the number one overall pick. The Cubs had a new management team, led by general manager Dallas Green. As the manager of the Philadelphia Phillies from 1979 to 1981, Green had seen Philadelphia build a respectable team through judicious drafting. He was committed to helping the Cubs follow the same approach. Green's first order of business in Chicago was to assemble a first-rate scouting staff.

In the 1982 draft, the Cubs' scouts were especially focused on the state of Florida, as were most other organizations. Draft experts considered Florida to have a bumper crop of prospects in 1982, well beyond the typical haul. Former Cleveland Indians general manager John Hart noted at the time that "Florida is usually good for a couple of number one picks every year but [1982] was an exceptional year. ... Every cross-checker and general manager was there because there was so much talent."[44]

Unlike the 1981 draft, when there was no clear number one choice, a consensus developed around high school shortstop Shawon Dunston from Brooklyn, New York. Dunston was considered by many scouts as a rare talent, having a potential similar to that of Darryl Strawberry. Pittsburgh Pirates area scout Dutch Deutsch, who had signed New York City natives John Candelaria and Willie Randolph, called Dunston "the best player to come out of the New York area since Carl Yastrzemski."[45]

Dunston's production in high school was prodigious. As a senior, he had a batting average of .790 and swiped 37 bases without being caught once. He had good power, especially for a middle infielder, and possessed a cannon for a right arm. The Cubs' scouting director, Gordon Goldsberry, believed Dunston had more potential than anyone else in the draft and signed him for $135,000. Dunston enjoyed a successful career in the big leagues that spanned 18 seasons. While he came up short of the Cubs' lofty expectations, he made two appearances as a member of the National League All-Star team and hit 150 lifetime home runs.

Ned Colletti, former general manager of the Los Angeles Dodgers, started scouting for the Cubs shortly before the 1982 draft. He had seen Dunston play in high school. Colletti recalls Dunston as having "athleticism, the arm, electricity." The Cubs were trying to build from the ground up, Colletti says, and Dunston was a good pick. Colletti commented, "When I was with the Giants, we acquired [Dunston] twice and then hired him as a coach after that. So I have had to make a decision on Shawon three or four times – always glad I did, by the way."

The Toronto Blue Jays held the second pick in the draft. The Blue Jays also opted for a shortstop, Augie Schmidt of the University of New Orleans. Schmidt was acclaimed as the best collegiate player in the nation in 1982. He struggled immediately upon joining the Blue Jays' organization. Toronto was deep at the shortstop position, with incumbent Alfredo Griffin and top prospect Tony Fernandez ahead of Schmidt on the depth chart. Schmidt admits to being overwhelmed by the adjustment to pro ball.

The Blue Jays attempted to work with Schmidt on both his fielding and his approach to hitting, but he was never able to advance to the big leagues. He played three seasons with Toronto's minor league teams before the Blue Jays traded him to the San Francisco Giants. Schmidt spent 1985 and 1986 in the minor leagues and retired from baseball after the 1986 season.

Toronto scout Al LaMacchia came to regret the selection of Schmidt. LaMacchia regarded the choice of Schmidt as "the worst mistake" he ever made in the draft. LaMacchia believed that Schmidt did not work hard enough to become a successful player. Long after his playing career had ended, Schmidt reflected on his time in pro ball. "Baseball is a grueling thing," he said. "You really have to love the game. You have to love the process and doing all the work that goes into refining your game."

After his professional career, Schmidt remained in baseball and eventually succeeded his father as the head coach at Carthage College in Kenosha, Wisconsin. As the Carthage coach, he has enjoyed a long and storied career, finding the success that had eluded him with the Blue Jays. Schmidt is honest about the difficult time he faced with Toronto, noting that he lacked the self-confidence that is an essential ingredient for success in the Major Leagues.

Schmidt's nephew, Gavin Lux, was a first-round draft pick by the Los Angeles Dodgers in the 2016 draft. In September 2019, the Dodgers brought Lux to the Major Leagues and he played a significant role for the Dodgers in the latter part of the season. Augie Schmidt worked with his nephew and helped mold him into a promising infielder.

With the fifth overall pick in 1982, the New York Mets selected right-hander Dwight Gooden from Hillsborough High School in Tampa, Florida. Gooden made it to the big leagues as a 19-year-old. By his 21st birthday, he had won 41 games for the Mets. Nonetheless, in June of 1982, the Mets' selection of Gooden with the fifth overall pick was quite controversial. The Major League Scouting Bureau had ranked Gooden as only the 25th best player in the draft. Gooden's high school coach preferred to play him at third base and in the outfield. The coach had numerous other pitchers who possessed arms of Major League caliber, so he could easily afford to put Gooden at other positions. On those occasions when Gooden did pitch, his fastball readings were diminished by playing in the field every game. Moreover, Gooden did not develop his signature curveball until late in his senior year of high school.

The Mets' scouting director, Joe McIlvaine, had personally scouted Gooden when he pitched at Hillsborough High. McIlvaine believed he could be a 20-game winner. While the pick raised eyebrows at the time, Gooden arrived in the majors like a meteor in 1984. He made his debut as a starting pitcher for the Mets on April 7, 1984. He would go on to dominate Major League hitters in an almost unprecedented way. Gooden's first year with the Mets was an eye-popping success. He won 17 games, struck out 276 batters, and was named the National League Rookie of the Year. In 1985, he was even better, winning 24 games against only four losses while posting a microscopic 1.53 earned run average. Gooden won the Cy Young Award in 1985. In 1986, his 17 wins and 200 strikeouts helped lead the Mets to the World Series championship.

Early on in his tenure with the Mets, Gooden gained the nickname "Doc," for the surgical way he struck out National League batters. His fastball was nearly unhittable. Batters testified that Gooden's fastball defied gravity by rising as it approached home plate. His curveball, which he had fully developed in his first years as a pro, was a devastating out pitch that had its own nickname, "Lord Charles." According to one baseball scribe, the curve "headed for the batter's head, waited for the poor guy's knees to buckle, then veered over the plate like a heat-seeking missile."[46]

The Blue Jays more than made up for their mistake in selecting Augie Schmidt by taking left-handed hurler David Wells in the second round. Al LaMacchia "pounded the table" for Wells, as he had done for Schmidt. This time, LaMacchia was vindicated. Wells pitched for 21 years in the Major Leagues and had 239 lifetime wins. "Character issues" were believed to have scared some teams away from drafting Wells. The "Boomer," as he was known, lived a large and colorful life, complete with motorcycle riding and Ruthian-like carousing habits.

Toronto struck gold again in the third round of the 1982 draft when it drafted pitcher Jimmy Key. Tim Wilken, a young Toronto scout who would go on to become a highly respected talent evaluator, found Key while scouting a game at Clemson University. Key developed into the epitome of a crafty left-hander. He played for 15 years in the big leagues, winning 186 games.

In the 15th round of 1982, the Oakland Athletics drafted outfielder José Canseco. Canseco had flown under the radar. Oakland scout Camilo Pascual discovered Canseco playing in Miami, Florida. Pascual, a Cuban-born pitcher for the Washington Senators in the 1960s, was aware of Canseco because Pascual's son played on Canseco's high school team. Pascual knew that very few, if any, scouts were aware of Canseco. On the day of the draft, Pascual argued forcefully and demonstratively for the A's to select Canseco; instead of pounding the table, he opened his wallet, dropped all his cash on the table, and said he would give it to Canseco if the A's drafted him.

The Athletics proceeded to draft Canseco and signed him for $10,000. It turned out to be a wise investment. Canseco dominated the minor leagues and, in 1985, was named Minor League Player of the Year by *Baseball America*. When Canseco arrived in the big leagues in 1986, he won the American League Rookie of the Year Award. His 1988 season was historic; he became the first Major League player ever to hit 40 home runs and steal 40 bases in the same season. His feats earned him the American League's Most Valuable Player Award.

Over his seventeen-year career, Canseco slugged 462 home runs, drove in 1,407 runs, and stole 200 bases. Even Pascual was amazed by Canseco's achievements. After retiring from baseball, Canseco confessed that he had used performance-enhancing steroids to assist with his power development. For that reason, his accomplishments will remain forever tarnished.

Batting Woes

The gentleman on the telephone was J.P. Ricciardi, former minor league infielder, former general manager of the Toronto Blue Jays. He had played college ball at St. Leo College in Florida and then spent two years as a player in the New York Mets organization.

A gritty player and smooth fielder during his playing days, Ricciardi found it difficult to convert effort into production at the plate. The talk turned to Augie Schmidt, a contemporary of Ricciardi, who had endured similar struggles as a minor leaguer with the Blue Jays. There was a comment that Schmidt would sometimes wake up in his hotel room at 2 a.m. to work on his swing. Ricciardi said, "If Augie was up one night a week swinging his bat, I was probably up seven nights a week swinging my bat."

Ricciardi related that he once was traveling from Florida to his home in Massachusetts with two of his college teammates. Traveling on Interstate 95, the three students encountered engine troubles in Connecticut. They stopped at a truck rest area for repairs. With nothing better to do, Ricciardi took out his baseball bat and started swinging. A Mayflower van passed by. The driver tooted his horn. Ricciardi continued swinging.

Fifteen minutes later, the same Mayflower truck pulled into the rest area. The driver had known Ricciardi from his time at Worcester State College. Ricciardi and the driver exchanged greetings. The driver told Ricciardi, "I knew there would only be one nut swinging a bat on I-95 at this truck stop. I knew it had to be you."

Ricciardi concluded the story with a ballplayer's observation: "You never stop trying to get better. And when you don't have success, you never stop trying to figure out why and how."

1983

In July 1981, I went with the ball club down to Houston and I made it a point to see [Roger Clemens] pitch. Unfortunately, the game was rained out. I never saw him do anything. I came back the next trip to Texas with the ball club and went out to see Roger again and it was rained out again. I never saw him the next time. When Vin Scully was announcing the 1986 World Series, he told the story of how we had tried to see him pitch. I guess I told the story to a reporter who put it in the newspaper. I told the reporter, 'Sometimes things just aren't meant to be.'

      –Joe McIlvaine, former general manager, New York Mets

The 1983 amateur draft was considered one of the weakest crops in history. The first-round selections were certainly some of the poorest choices. The Minnesota Twins held the number one overall pick and selected right-handed pitcher Tim Belcher. The process of selecting and signing Belcher played out in a strange, almost bizarre, way.

Belcher epitomized the "player who came out of nowhere." He pitched at Mount Vernon Nazarene College, an obscure Bible college in Ohio. He was unspectacular in his first two seasons at Mount Vernon Nazarene, barely exceeding a .500 record against a poor level of college competition. He began the 1983 college season by losing four out of five starts. But then Belcher's fast ball started to reach the mid-nineties on the radar guns and Midwestern scouts flocked to see him. Belcher wound up striking out 95 batters in only 66 innings. His performance led the Major League Scouting Bureau to assign him its number one overall ranking.

Minnesota Twins scouting director George Brophy described the 1983 draft as the weakest, both in terms of first-round candidates and overall depth."[47] Belcher's meteoric rise led Brophy and the penurious Twins to select him number one overall. While being drafted number one in the draft seemed to be almost a dream for Belcher, the contentious negotiations quickly turned it into a nightmare. The Twins refused to even match the signing bonus that the Cincinnati Reds paid to the second overall pick, Kurt Stillwell, a shortstop from Thousand Oaks, California.

Eventually, Belcher was amenable to accepting $25,000 less than Stillwell received but, by that time, the Twins had substantially reduced their offer. Belcher rejected the reduced offer and, following in the footsteps of Danny Goodwin, became the second overall number one pick to decline to sign. Instead, Belcher entered the 1984 January draft and was again drafted number one overall, this time by the New York Yankees.

The Belcher saga would quickly become even more bizarre. Shortly after the 1984 January draft, the Oakland Athletics lost a veteran pitcher, Tom Underwood, to the Baltimore Orioles in free agency. The loss entitled the Athletics to compensation, giving them the right to pick an unprotected player from another franchise. The Athletics claimed Belcher from the Yankees before New York was able to add Belcher to its protected list. The Yankees protested the decision to the Commissioner's office. Commissioner Bowie Kuhn acknowledged the unfairness of the rules as applied in Belcher's case but nonetheless ruled against the Yankees.

Aside from the Belcher drama, the 1983 draft is most notable for two other individuals who would have a profound and significant impact on the game for the next generation and beyond. One, right-handed Texan pitcher Roger Clemens, was "underdrafted" and would become the shining star of the 1983 draft class. The other, an undistinguished former infielder named Scott Boras, had been drafted almost a decade before by the Kansas City Royals. The names Roger Clemens and Scott Boras were little known to the average baseball fan in June of 1983 but, in a relatively short period of time, their names would be well-known and, in time, lightning rods for controversy.

Clemens hardly labored in obscurity. He had starred for the 1983 College World Series champion, the University of Texas Longhorns. Yet, most scouts and even his own college coach, Cliff Gustafson, rated Clemens as only the third best starter on the Texas team. All of the buzz was focused on fellow starter Calvin Schiraldi, who had won the 1983 College World Series Most Valuable Player Award. However, Red Sox scout Danny Doyle was impressed with Clemens' intense focus on the mound and had a feeling that Clemens was the crown jewel of the class.

Doyle put his reputation on the line in arguing for the Red Sox to select Clemens with their first-round pick, which would be the 19th overall. Doyle had significant credibility with the Red Sox as he had signed pitcher Jim Lonborg out of high school in 1963. Lonborg went on to become the Red Sox's ace and won the Cy Young Award in Boston's magical year of 1967. Doyle believed Clemens had the best arm of any college player but, even more, loved the intangible toughness that Clemens brought to the mound in every start. Red Sox scouting director Eddie Kasko pushed Doyle to explain his high ranking of Clemens. Doyle responded, "Eddie, I like what the boy has behind his belt buckle."[48]

While Kasko and the other members of the Red Sox brass were sufficiently convinced by Doyle's conviction on Clemens, they were most likely unaware of the drama unfolding in the Blue Jays' war room that could have made Clemens unavailable to the Sox. Toronto was slated to pick at number nine. Al LaMacchia and Bobby Mattick were again at odds over the Blue Jays' first selection. LaMacchia, a Texan, was as high on Clemens as was Doyle. LaMacchia had numerous opportunities to observe Clemens pitch for the University of Texas and was certain he was the best player in the whole draft. Unfortunately for the Blue Jays, Mattick and most of the rest of the scouting community had observed Clemens pitch at Texas on a day when he was sick and should not have been pitching. Predictably, Clemens had an awful outing. Mattick and the other scouts in attendance came away with a negative impression of Clemens.

When the talk in Toronto turned to Clemens, voices became loud and the tension escalated. Ultimately, Blue Jays general manager Pat Gillick sided with Mattick and ruled against drafting Clemens. Instead, Toronto opted for a hulking high school catching prospect named Matt Stark. The six-foot-four, 220-pound Stark was a football star and appeared set to play tight end at the University of Southern California. However, when the Blue Jays offered $130,000, Stark accepted the offer and soon signed.

Stark's bonus was $9,000 more than Clemens would receive from the Red Sox. Mattick, who had scouted Stark in high school, believed that with his big arm and powerful bat, Stark would become a mainstay for the Jays behind the plate for many years. However, Stark was slowed by injuries and never realized the potential that Mattick had envisioned. Stark would appear in only five games for Toronto and managed only one hit in twelve plate appearances. He returned to the big leagues in 1990 with the White Sox and played in eight more games.

Clemens would go on to have one of the best pitching careers in history. He dominated the minor league competition in 1983 and pitched for Boston in 1984. By 1985 Clemens was already a mainstay of the Red Sox staff. Ben McLure, a Toronto scout, observed Clemens pitching in the minor leagues. McLure reported to the Blue Jays brass that Clemens "was one of the best pitchers I have seen at any level." McLure was taken aback when Mattick screamed at him, "Who in the hell put you up to this?" McLure remembers that general manager Pat Gillick heard the outburst and "was hiding behind a newspaper ... and Al [LaMacchia] had the biggest grin on his face I had ever seen." Mattick would say to McLure, "You just write this down. Clemens will never see the big leagues." Years later, after Clemens had established himself as the ace of the Red Sox staff, McLure would taunt Mattick, saying, "Bobby, whatever happened to that Clemens guy?"

Over the years, of course, "that Clemens guy" did just fine. From almost every standpoint, his achievements compare favorably with the numbers compiled by the best pitchers in the game. Nicknamed the "Rocket," Clemens earned 354 wins during his 24-year career, had 4,672 strikeouts, and a 3.12 earned run average. He also won a record seven Cy Young Awards. Clemens was selected for the All-Star Game eleven times and pitched for two World Series champions.

On paper, Clemens clearly deserves to be enshrined in the Hall of Fame. However, Clemens was accused in baseball's "Mitchell Report" of having used anabolic steroids.[49] Clemens vehemently denied the charge. Yet the members of the Baseball Writers of America, who are charged with determining which players are worthy of admission to the Hall of Fame, appear to have discounted Clemens' denials. To date, the members have not voted Clemens into the Hall. Regardless of whether he is ever inducted into the Hall of Fame, Clemens remains undoubtedly one of the best draft choices of all time.

In his college days, Scott Boras made the University of Pacific baseball team as a walk-on and led the team in hitting. He spent four years in the minor leagues, advancing as high as Double-A. In 1977, his last year of minor league ball, he hit .275 in the Texas League. After his playing days, Boras enrolled in law school and then decided to try his hand at the relatively new business of sports representation.

Though Boras never made it to the big leagues, it may be credibly argued he has had more of an impact on the draft than anyone else in history. While in law school, he realized that draftees had little negotiating power and believed they were undervalued and grossly underpaid for their services. Over time, Boras designed clever negotiating ploys for his clients that have reworked the salary structure for players in the draft. Much like Clemens, mere mention of Boras's name evokes strong reactions and emotions. Some team executives refer to him, off the record, with four-letter words. One executive, speaking on the record, has called him "the devil."[50] The pejorative references notwithstanding, it is undeniable that Boras has changed the salary structure of the draft more profoundly than anyone in baseball history since Rick Reichardt.

Boras represented Tim Belcher in his negotiations with the Minnesota Twins after the 1983 draft. It was the first draft in which Boras represented any amateur players. By the prevailing standards, Boras's demands on behalf of Belcher were eminently reasonable. Boras was seeking an amount identical to what the first overall selection in 1982, Shawon Dunston, had received. Boras also represented the second pick in 1983, Kurt Stillwell, who received his full $135,000 asking price from the Cincinnati Reds. Stillwell was considering a scholarship offer from Stanford University. Boras had sensed that the Reds were eager to pry Stillwell away from Stanford and so were willing to entice him with a generous offer.

In 1983, the New York Mets were armed with four draft picks among the top 32 picks. The Mets seemed primed to continue their successful run of drafts picks that had yielded Darryl Strawberry, Lenny Dykstra, Roger McDowell and Dwight Gooden in the prior three drafts. However, New York's first two picks, third baseman Eddie Williams and outfielder Stanley Jefferson, turned out to be significant disappointments. Williams played ten years in the big leagues but never consistently demonstrated the skills that he had displayed at San Diego's Hoover High School. Jefferson played six seasons in the majors but never showed the ability to hit consistently.

The Signing of Bobby Bonilla

The first time that scout Billy Blitzer laid eyes on Bobby Bonilla, Bonilla was playing shortstop for his Bronx High School baseball team in New York. The year was 1981. Blitzer was then a scout for the Major League Scouting Bureau. To Blitzer, shortstop seemed a strange fit for Bonilla. At six-foot-three and 200 pounds, Bonilla had the look of a corner infielder perhaps but not a shortstop. What Blitzer would learn later was that Bonilla was not one to question his coach; he played where he was told to play.

Blitzer sent in a favorable report on Bonilla. In time, the report was distributed to all the clubs that were members of the Scouting Bureau. Within weeks, Blitzer started receiving feedback from various teams. The New York Yankee area scout called Blitzer and said, "Billy, this guy can't pitch." The next day, another scout called Blitzer and reported, "Billy, this guy can't catch." Blitzer quickly called Bonilla and told him, "Bobby, I have a good report in on you but scouts are going to see you and one day you pitch and one day you catch. What's going on?" Bonilla responded, "Mr. Blitzer, I play wherever the coach puts me." Blitzer was emphatic, telling Bonilla, "You are hurting yourself because they are not getting to see the true player."

The 1981 June draft came and went. Through the entire 50 rounds, no team selected Bonilla. Blitzer was not surprised. He knew that scouts had spread the word that Bonilla couldn't play. After the draft, Bonilla's high school coach called Blitzer and asked why Bonilla wasn't drafted. Much as he had told Bonilla, Blitzer explained to the coach that scouts were not able to appreciate Bonilla's talent because he was constantly shifting between different positions.

Upon realizing his mistake, the coach worked to place Bonilla on an All-Star team that would be traveling to play in the Netherlands. The coach also raised money to pay for Bonilla's travel expenses. In the Netherlands, Syd Thrift, who had spent ten years with the Pittsburgh Pirates as a scouting supervisor and instructor, saw Bonilla play and recommended that the Pirates give Bonilla a shot. In short order, Peter Gebrian, an area scout stationed in New Jersey, worked Bonilla out for the Pirates.

Days later, Blitzer received a phone call from Bonilla. "Mr. Blitzer," Bonilla said, "there's a Mr. Gebrian here and he wants to sign me. What should I do?" Not one to pull his punches, Blitzer replied, "If I were you, I would lock the door and don't let him out of your house until he signs you."

Bonilla laughed, hung up the phone, and told Gebrian, "Give me a pen. I'm signing the contract."

1984

The first time I ever talked with Greg Maddux was when I went to sign him. He had gone on a college trip to Hawaii. He had shorts and a T-shirt on. I told him, jokingly, that I would never have the guts to sign someone who looked like him. He's probably five-ten or five-eleven. He came back after his first year of pro ball and he weighed 145 pounds. In that era, scouts frowned on signing small right-handed pitchers. Guys with freckles and red hair were a 'No' also. They had all these cliches. Getting the Cubs to look past a smaller right-handed pitcher was the thing.

    –Doug Mapson, former Chicago Cubs scout

The Detroit Tigers "Bless You Boys" began the 1984 season by winning 35 of their first 40 games. From the beginning of the regular season to its end, the Tigers were never out of first place in the American League East Division. The Tigers steamed to a wire-to-wire World Series championship, becoming only the third team in history to accomplish the feat and the first since the vaunted 1927 New York Yankees.

The Tigers' 1984 championship was the product of the drafting acumen of Bill LaJoie, who had joined the Tigers as a scout in 1968. Lajoie was Detroit's scouting director and, later, assistant general manager before becoming the Tigers' general manager in 1984. Lajoie drafted and signed the mainstays of the 1984 team, Alan Trammell, Lou Whitaker, Jack Morris, Dan Petry, Steve Kemp and Kirk Gibson.[51] A Detroit sportscaster was so enamored of the 1984 team that he consistently referred to Trammell and his teammates as the "Bless You Boys." The phrase stuck and, when the season was finished, it served as the title of a book published by Detroit manager, Sparky Anderson.[52] Anderson's book sold out in Detroit and elsewhere and was generally lauded.[53]

While the Tigers were running away with the championship in 1984, baseball fans were captivated by an unprecedented collection of collegiate stars assembled to represent the United States for the first time ever in the Summer Olympics. The International Olympic Committee had added baseball as a demonstration sport. The excitement surrounding the Team USA "dream team" was palpable. The Olympics ran from July 28 to August 12. Team USA captured the nation's attention and steamrolled their competition all the way to the Gold Medal game, which the USA lost to Japan. Major League Baseball agreed to a special arrangement in which Olympic players who were drafted in June were allowed to continue playing all summer for Team USA before joining their respective professional teams. Baseball correctly realized that the exposure and experience would benefit their draftees much more than playing a few extra games in the minor leagues.

Fifteen of the 20 members of Team USA entered the 1984 June draft and became the talk of baseball.[54] In all, 18 out of the 20 "dream teamers" would be first-round selections. All but three would play in the Major Leagues. Unlike prior years of the draft, when the draftees were relatively anonymous, most of the players selected in the first round of 1984 were well known due to the publicity leading up to the Olympics. The timing allowed members of the fan base for Major League teams to cheer for both Team USA and the specific college stars who had already been drafted.

In the first round of the 1984 draft, Major League teams drafted 20 college players. The total represented the most college players ever selected in the first round of the draft. The Mets were back in the familiar position of holding the number one overall pick. For months prior to the draft, the Mets were set to use the first pick to take University of Southern California slugger Mark McGwire.

The Mets' West Coast scouting team, led by Harry Minor and Roger Jongewaard, were in full agreement that "Big Mac" was the best player available in the draft. In college, McGwire had starred both as a hitter and a pitcher. The Mets' only question was whether he projected as a pitcher or a hitter. The Mets attempted to reach a contractual agreement with McGwire in the days leading up to the draft. However, at almost the very last minute, the negotiations broke down. Each side traded recriminations. It became clear that McGwire did not want to sign with the Mets. McGwire's father dropped a bombshell on the Mets the night before the draft, telling them that his son would only sign with a West Coast team. The McGwire family maintained that the Mets tried to exert undue influence to have McGwire commit to signing before the draft.

When it became clear that McGwire was unsignable, the Mets pivoted to the player whom they had rated second to McGwire, high school prospect Shawn Abner of Mechanicsburg, Pennsylvania. Abner, a quint-essential "tools player," became the number one overall pick in the draft. McIlvaine enumerated Abner's attributes: "quickness, power, good runner, above average outfielder with a strong arm."[55] Although McIlvaine didn't explicitly mention "hitting for average," Abner had batted .580 in his senior season at Mechanicsburg High School. In addition, McIlvaine considered Abner to be "a great kid with a wonderful attitude."

McIlvaine did notice one negative with Abner. McIlvaine thought he had a long swing, causing Abner to take a long time to get his bat through the hitting zone and make contact. While a dominant player's superior talent can compensate for a long swing at lower levels of competition, scouts know that a long swing is usually exposed at higher levels of competition. However, McIlvaine was confident the Mets' developmental instructors would be able to fix the problem.

During his minor league career, Abner displayed many of the qualities that had attracted the Mets. He hit with some power, was a good run producer and hit .300 at two of his minor league stops. Yet the organization concluded that he was not able to overcome the flaw in his swing. The Mets felt that as Abner progressed up the minor league chain, he was swinging and missing too frequently. Further, the Mets had long been fascinated by San Diego outfielder Kevin McReynolds. As a result, in December 1986, the Mets traded Abner, Stan Jefferson, Kevin Mitchell, Kevin Brown and Kevin Armstrong to the Padres for McReynolds and two minor leaguers. The deal almost certainly set a record for the most "Kevins" ever traded in the same deal.

In parts of six big league seasons, Abner was never able to overcome the problems with his long swing to make sufficient hard contact. He finished his Major League career with a .227 batting average and only 11 home runs. Most observers rank Abner as one of the worst overall number one picks in history.

The Mariners continued to perform poorly on the field and consequently found themselves with the number two overall pick in 1984. The Mariners opted for pitcher Billy Swift, who was slated to be one of the starting pitchers for Team USA. Swift was the 14th child born in a family of 15 children. His professional baseball career was slowed by injuries. However, he possessed great patience and dedication. In 1991, Seattle converted Swift from starter to full-time relief pitcher and he recorded an earned run average of 1.99 in 71 appearances. Swift had a dominant sinker that opposing batters routinely pounded into the ground. Just as he began to hit his stride in Seattle, the Mariners traded Swift to the San Francisco Giants in 1991 as part of a deal for slugger Kevin Mitchell. Thus, in one of the many oddities of the draft, the number one and number two overall players selected in 1984 were traded by their respective teams in separate deals involving Kevin Mitchell.

Mark McGwire still remained available as the Oakland Athletics prepared to draft at number ten. The Athletics moved quickly to take McGwire. In short order, McGwire confirmed the Mets' scouting analysis. In 1987, he took the American League by storm, winning the American League Rookie of the Year Award. He slugged a league-leading 49 home runs and drove in 118 runs. McGwire joined with Jose Canseco to form the "Bash Brothers"– one of the most potent middle-of-the-order power tandems in the history of baseball. From 1986 to 1992, McGwire and Canseco combined to hit 446 home runs for the Athletics.

The Athletics traded McGwire to the St. Louis Cardinals in the middle of the 1997 season. In 1998, McGwire and Sammy Sosa of the Chicago Cubs captivated the baseball world when they engaged in an historic home run battle. Both McGwire and Sosa eclipsed the single season record of 61 home runs that Roger Maris had set in 1961. McGwire slammed 70 home runs; Sosa finished with 66.

When he retired after the 2001 season, "Big Mac" had hit 583 lifetime home runs and had collected 1,414 runs batted in. In the process, he made twelve All-Star Game appearances. McGwire's home run record was short-lived, as Barry Bonds surpassed it with 73 home runs in 2001. Years after the end of his baseball career, McGwire confessed to having used steroids, a fact that has dimmed his chances of being admitted to the Hall of Fame.

Two high school picks in the second round would prove to be the most important draft selections of 1984. With their second-round pick, the Chicago Cubs took Greg Maddux of Valley High School in Las Vegas, Nevada.

Doug Mapson, a young scout whom Cubs' general manager Dallas Green had brought over from Philadelphia, was the person most responsible for selecting Maddux. Mapson believed that Maddux might be the best player in the entire draft. In his report, Mapson noted, "If he was six-foot-one, he would be the first pick in the draft." Though Maddux barely reached 90 miles an hour on the radar gun, Mapson identified great late movement on his fastball and an otherworldly quality to his curveball. More importantly, Maddux's ability to locate was second to none; he possessed an uncanny ability to throw any pitch in the precise location he wanted. Maddux would go on to use these skills to win four Cy Young Awards over a sterling 23-year career in which he won 355 games with 3,371 strikeouts. He was elected to the Hall of Fame in 2014.

Later in the second round, the Atlanta Braves would select another future Hall of Famer, left-handed pitcher Tom Glavine of Billerica Memorial High School in Massachusetts. Glavine was a first-round talent but had been drafted by the Los Angeles Kings in the fourth round of the National Hockey League draft. Glavine fell in the baseball draft due to the possibility that he might choose a career in hockey instead of baseball. The Braves were able to lure him away from hockey. He reached the majors with Atlanta in 1987 and would star there for 14 seasons, winning two Cy Young Awards.

Maddux joined Glavine in Atlanta in 1993. Together, they formed one of the best one-two pitching duos in baseball history. The two led the Braves to an impressive run of eight straight National League East championships. Glavine would win 305 games over 22 years in the Major Leagues, while appearing in ten All-Star Games. The two long-time teammates were elected to the Hall of Fame in 2014.

The 1984 draft was unique. For the first time in draft history, all of the first twelve players drafted would make it to the majors. While the best talent actually would come from the second round, the success of the members of Team USA focused attention like never before on the collegiate ranks.

Darrell Miller's "Major Crush"

There was a time when Darrell Miller had his sights set on going to medical school. Toward that end, in addition to the standard core of high school science classes, Miller took three years of Latin during his time at Ramona High School in Riverside, California. In Miller's junior year, he developed a "major crush" on Cindy Cohenour, the social chairwoman for the Class of 1975.

As luck would have it, Cindy occupied the seat immediately in front of Miller in Latin class. One day during the class, perhaps in a bid to make an impression on Cindy, Miller began quietly singing Elton John's hit song, *Bennie and the Jets*. Miller admits to having butchered the lyrics. "What are you singing?" Cindy asked over her shoulder. *"Bennie and the Jets,"* Miller replied. "Those aren't the words," Cindy chided him. She quickly scribbled the correct lyrics on a piece of paper and passed the words to Miller. Properly humbled, Miller sang no more. "Wow!" he could only think, "who knows the lyrics?"

More adept at baseball than he was at singing, Miller proved to be a solid hitter and an agile catcher throughout his high school career and began drawing the attention of Major League teams. He continued his education at California Poly-technic State University in Pomona, where he gained a reputation as an excellent defensive catcher and a clutch hitter.

The local California Angels, among other teams, were paying close attention. One day while Miller was playing for Cal Poly, an Angels scout introduced himself. "Lou Cohenour," the scout said. Miller immediately recognized the name. The scout was, of course, Cindy's father. The Angels ended up drafting Miller in the 9th round of the 1979 amateur draft. It was Lou Cohenour who signed Miller to his first professional contract.

In 1984, Miller's sixth year in pro ball, he hit .326 for Triple-A Edmonton, earning a promotion to the Angels. Miller would spend the next five seasons in the majors as a reserve outfielder and catcher, hitting .241 in 224 games.

1985

A guy like [Barry] Bonds is just so gifted and his confidence level is so high. We played Bonds in Toronto in a three-game series. He walked three times the first night and three times the second day, maybe four, and on Sunday, he got his one pitch and hit it off the windows of the restaurant that overlooks the ballpark. I remember telling some of our players, that's the perfect example of what a complete player Bonds is offensively. He kept taking his walks and that one pitch, he didn't miss it. He was ready for that pitch. It was an amazing feat to watch all weekend because he never expanded the strike zone, he never chased pitches, he just took his walks but when he got his pitch to hit, he hit it. That, to me, is the epitome of greatness as a hitter.

– J.P. Ricciardi, former general manager, Toronto Blue Jays

In 1985, the World Series was again a Midwestern affair as the Kansas City Royals defeated the St. Louis Cardinals in seven games. The series included controversy over a very questionable umpire's call at first base in the 9th inning of the 6th game, which Cardinals' fans believe cost their team the title.

The Royals' success was directly attributable to the wisdom and dedication of their general manager, John Schuerholz, and the excellent scouting staff he had assembled, including Art Stewart and Rosey Gilhousen. They were led by future Hall of Famer George Brett, World Series Most Valuable Player Bret Saberhagen and recent draft picks such as Willie Wilson, Mark Gubicza, and Dennis Leonard. The Cardinals, in contrast, were a combination of players acquired in clever trades with other teams (Jack Clark, Ozzie Smith, Willie McGee, Lonnie Smith and Darrell Porter), supplemented by some of their key recent draft picks such as Terry Pendleton, Vince Coleman and Andy Van Slyke.

1985 was a magical year for the June draft. Many long-time draft observers consider it the most talented and deepest class in draft history. The draft was in its twenty-first year; it had truly grown up.

Hitters, especially left-handed power hitters, were plentiful in 1985. For the most part, the best hitters were considered somewhat surly, selfish and arrogant. Nonetheless, clubs were salivating over the possibility of drafting them because, as the saying among scouts goes, "you can't teach power." Three collegiate players – Will Clark, Barry Bonds, and Pete Incaviglia – stood out for their pure hitting ability and power potential even in the hitting-rich 1985 draft class.

The warm afterglow of Team USA permeated the 1985 draft as the remaining undrafted Olympians dominated the early first round selections. All four of the first picks were from Team USA. The Milwaukee Brewers owned the first pick for the first time in team history and used it on Olympic star B.J. Surhoff, a left-handed hitting catcher from the University of North Carolina. Surhoff was versatile enough to have played shortstop in high school. In the view of Brewers director of player procurement, Ray Poitevint, even if Surhoff had remained at shortstop in college, the Brewers would still have taken him as the overall number one pick.[56]

The Tar Heels moved Surhoff behind the plate because another member of the North Carolina team, Walt Weiss of Suffern, New York, was also a stellar shortstop. The Oakland Athletics would select Weiss ten picks after Surhoff. Over his collegiate career, Surhoff hit .392 with 32 homers and stole 84 bases. Brewers general manager Harry Dalton believed Surhoff was the most complete player available in the draft.[57] Their confidence was rewarded in less than two years as Surhoff made Milwaukee's roster in 1987 and shared catching duties with Bill Schroeder. Surhoff went on to have a 19-year Major League career, playing for three teams.

Using the second pick, the San Francisco Giants selected Will Clark, who had starred for both Team USA and a powerhouse Mississippi State team. While Clark was labeled at times as cocky, brash and arrogant, his demeanor did not concern the Giants. San Francisco viewed those qualities as a reflection of Clark's ultracompetitive nature. More importantly, the Giants and many other teams were infatuated with his prodigious hitting ability.

The sweet swinging Clark, who won the 1985 Golden Spikes Award, was described by Giants' hitting instructor Jim Lefebrve as the "best pure hitter I have seen come along in a long time."[58] E.M Swift of *Sports Illustrated* described his swing as "the sweetest swing anyone has seen in history."[59] Giants' hitting coach Dusty Baker called the swing "tension free, using leverage to drive the ball instead of muscle it." Clark's swing drew comparisons to those of hitting legends Stan Musial and Ted Williams.[60]

In a game where nicknames abound, Clark acquired a slew, all of them a testament to his prodigious hitting ability. At Mississippi State, Clark had teamed with another 1985 draftee in Rafael Palmeiro to form one of the most formidable middle-of-the-order hitting duos in college history. Clark and Palmeiro were dubbed "Thunder and Lightning."

Clark had almost no difficulty adjusting to professional baseball. His quick start for the Giants earned him the nickname "The Natural," a reference to fictional baseball star Roy Hobbs. Indeed, Clark's immediate success seemed to have a storybook quality about it. He homered in his very first minor league at-bat. On opening day of 1986, Clark homered on his first Major League swing, less than a year from the 1985 draft. To make the story even more improbable, he hit the home run off strikeout king Nolan Ryan and then he homered in his first Candlestick Park at-bat a few days later. His early hitting heroics prompted Giants' catcher Bob Brenley to dub him "The Thrill."

Will Clark continued to enjoy success for the Giants. In his second season in the majors, he smashed 35 homers with 91 runs batted in. The very next year, he had 29 home runs and a league-leading 109 runs batted in. He was selected to the National League All-Star Game in 1988. For the next four years he established himself as one of the premier first basemen in the game. In 1989, Clark teamed with Kevin Mitchell to form another fearsome hitting duo that became known as "The Pacific Sock Exchange." The well-traveled Mitchell won the 1989 Most Valuable Player trophy but Clark finished second in the voting and was named the Most Valuable Player of the National League Championship Series. Clark's bat carried the Giants to the 1989 World Series.

Clark's early success led to a big payday. The Giants rewarded him with a massive four-year, $15 million contract that made him the highest paid player in the game. Giants general manager Al Rosen stated, "he plays like a Hall of Famer, and he should be paid like one."[61] After signing the large contract, Clark's numbers, especially his power numbers, declined the very next year. After the season, he revealed that he had suffered from a foot ailment all year that forced him to hit to the opposite field. While he bounced back after off-season surgery to have another big year in 1991, another injury hampered his production late in the season.

Most observers, and even Clark himself, expected 1992 to be his career year, but it didn't materialize. Opposing teams often pitched around him, mostly because the Giants had traded Kevin Mitchell after the 1991 season. With Mitchell no longer hitting behind Clark, pitchers could afford to be more careful when pitching to Clark. In 1993, Clark's numbers continued to decline, even though the Giants had added the potent bat of Barry Bonds through free agency.

Clark was granted free agency following the 1993 season and signed with the Texas Rangers. Although he appeared in the All-Star Game in 1994 for the Rangers and posted good numbers, he never again approached the greatness for which he once seemed destined. Clark played in the majors for 15 years and finished with 284 home runs, 1,205 runs batted in and an impressive .303 batting average.

With the third pick, the Texas Rangers selected another Olympian in right-handed starting pitcher Bobby Witt of the University of Oklahoma. Witt came with high expectations. Many scouts believed he had more potential than his Olympic counterpart Billy Swift, the number two overall pick in 1984. Witt's fastball was electric and it captured the imagination of scouts, who projected him as a future staff ace. Witt also had a nasty slider to confuse batters who were loading up on his fastball. Many scouts thought Witt was the best prospect in the entire draft class and he actually received the largest bonus of all players in the draft.

Like many hard throwers, Witt struggled with his control. Scouts often compared him to a young Nolan Ryan, who had similar control issues early in his career but had become a Texas icon by 1985. Witt was never able to harness his pitches. Nonetheless, he pitched in the majors for 16 years, finishing with a record of 142 wins and 157 losses. He is viewed as a disappointment because of the huge, mostly unfulfilled expectations.

The Cincinnati Reds, who had previously selected only one college player in the first round in the draft's history, jumped at the opportunity to draft Olympic shortstop Barry Larkin from the University of Michigan. Reds super scout Gene Bennett had first seen Larkin at an All-Star Game when he was 15 years old and immediately compared him to Davey Concepcion of the Big Red Machine.

Bennett and the Reds followed Larkin all through his high school career at Cincinnati's Moeller High School. The Reds first drafted him in the second round of the 1982 draft, but he opted to attend the University of Michigan. Prior to the 1985 draft, Bennett remained high on Larkin, but many others in the organization had cooled on his prospects. Bennett went to bat in a big way for Larkin as he pleaded his case directly to Reds general manager Bob Howsam. Howsam queried Bennett as to how long it would take for Larkin to make the big leagues. Bennett's response has entered the pantheon of scouting legend. Bennett looked at his watch and told Howsam "ten minutes after nine on June third." Inasmuch as the draft began on June third, Bennett was telegraphing that, in his view, Larkin was ready to go straight to the majors.[62]

Bennett's estimate was off the mark. It took Larkin 175 minor league games to reach Cincinnati, but once he did he stayed for nineteen years. Once Larkin acclimated to Major League pitching, he made the All-Star Game in 1988 and in eleven other seasons during his stellar nineteen-year career. For his career, Larkin batted .295 with 198 home runs and 960 runs batted in. He won the National League Most Valuable Player Award in 1995 and was inducted into the Hall of Fame in 2012.

The Pittsburgh Pirates would select Barry Bonds with the sixth pick of the draft. If some thought Will Clark was churlish, he was a regular Mr. Congeniality when compared with Bonds. The abrasive Bonds offended almost everyone he played with or against in high school. One scout wrote him off and cursed him out in his scouting report due to the arrogance he displayed when among his teammates. The scout wrote, "Ass _ _ _ _" under the attitude section of the report.[63] Bonds's behavior did not improve appreciably at Arizona State. His coach Jim Brock considered him rude, inconsiderate and self-centered and bemoaned his pronounced lack of people skills. "I don't think he ever figured out what to do to get people to like him," Brock said.[64] A majority of his teammates voted to remove Bonds from the team, but Brock kept him nonetheless.

The Pirates' selection of Bonds proved to be the best pick in the best draft of all time. In retrospect, it is hard to understand how Bonds lasted until the sixth pick. He had literally been born into the game; he was the son of former Giants star Bobby Bonds and the godson of all time great Giants center fielder, Willie Mays. Even at the age of three, Bonds roamed the Giants' clubhouse while playing catch with his dad. He starred at Junipero Serra High School in the Bay Area and the Giants drafted him in the second round of the 1982 draft.

Given Bonds's lineage, the Giants may have thought getting his signature would be easy. However, they were mistaken. The Giants and Bonds were a mere $5,000 apart in bonus money but could not reach agreement, so Bonds headed to Arizona State. While the character issues obviously played a big role in devaluing his draft stock, some scouts also had concerns about his power projections. Bonds's real calling card was his amazing combination of hitting and speed. In college and in his early years in Pittsburgh, Bonds was very thin, almost skinny. He led off for the Bucs; his speed was clearly his first tool to manifest itself in the big leagues.

Bonds played only 115 games in the minors before he was promoted to Pittsburgh. Unlike Clark, Bonds was not an immediate success. He batted only .223 in 113 games but he did hit 16 dingers and, most impressively, stole 36 bases. In his next three seasons in Pittsburgh he averaged 23 homers and 27 stolen bases with mediocre batting average figures. No one was predicting Ruthian numbers for him at this point but in 1990 he broke out in a big way, winning the National League Most Valuable Player Award. Bonds finished the 1990 season with 33 homers, 114 RBI's, 52 stolen bases and a .301 batting average. He continued to post similarly sterling numbers in his next two years and again won the Most Valuable Player Award in 1992.

Despite all of Bonds's accomplishments, the fans in Pittsburgh never fully warmed up to his prickly personality. He left the Pirates in free agency after the 1992 season. Owner Peter McGowan and the San Francisco Giants finally were able to lure him back to the Bay Area. While the Giants refused to sign him over a difference of $5,000 in 1982, it cost them a whopping $43 million in 1992 to bring him back home. The Giants hoped that Bonds and Clark would form a new "Sock Exchange." However, the two stars were more like ships passing in the night. In his first year in San Francisco, Bonds won his third Most Valuable Player Award. Hitting in front of either Bonds or third baseman Matt Williams, Clark hit .283 with 14 home runs in 132 games. Bonds was now providing the thrills for Giant fans. Clark would depart for Texas as a free agent after the 1993 season.

While Clark's performance in San Francisco declined precipitously after his record contract, Bonds was just warming up. He would go on to play for fourteen more seasons in San Francisco and establish his credentials as one of the greatest players of all time. He won four more Most Valuable Player Awards and, in 2001, shattered the record for most home runs in a season. For his career, Bonds established the record for career home runs with 762 and was named to 14 All-Star Games. Based on talent alone, Bonds was the most talented player in the draft.

Perhaps the most overlooked statistic of Bonds's illustrious career is his record number of intentional walks, 688. Diamondbacks manager Buck Showalter had such respect for Bonds that he once intentionally walked him even though the bases were loaded. As Bonds's legend grew, so did his physique and so did the whispers that his growth and his power were chemically enhanced. Bonds initially denied any use of steroids but later altered his story to admit he had inadvertently taken a steroid cream without knowing it was a steroid. His numbers alone are certainly deserving of first ballot Hall of Fame induction. To date, Bonds has not been elected to the Hall because of the cloud of allegations regarding his use of steroids.

With the eighth pick, the Montreal Expos chose Oklahoma State University slugger Pete Incaviglia. Of all the talented hitters in the 1985 draft, it was Incaviglia who re-wrote the NCAA records book in 1985. He hit .464 with 48 home runs and 143 runs batted in. He also had 100 career home runs, which remains an NCAA record. Like Clark and Bonds, Incaviglia's reputation for brash talk preceded him. "Inky," as he was known, had a special swagger in his gait and would never back down from anyone. According to baseball writer Tracy Ringolsby, Incaviglia once challenged the entire University of Texas team to a fight.[65]

The Expos were happy to see Incaviglia still available at number eight. They were not bothered by his combativeness or, at least, not until they entered into signing negotiations. The California native did not want to play in the cold of Montreal. As negotiations dragged on, the Expos eventually signed him with the intention of trading him before they lost his rights. Montreal then shipped him to the Texas Rangers.

With the Rangers, Incaviglia went straight to the majors and started out impressively, hitting 30 home runs, driving in 88 runs and hitting a respectable .250. When he hit the ball, he usually hit it hard. However, Incaviglia also missed a lot, striking out a league-leading 185 times. Incaviglia hit over twenty homers in each of his five seasons with the Rangers but he continued to be susceptible to strikeouts. He was released by the Rangers and bounced around with a few other teams before landing with the Phillies in 1993, where he hit 24 homers and posted a respectable .274 batting average. When he retired in 1998, he had played twelve seasons in the Major Leagues. While he hit 206 home runs, he also struck out 1,277 times.

Despite the enormous promise that Incaviglia brought to the 1985 draft, his greatest contribution to the draft was the rule that Major

League Baseball enacted to prohibit teams from trading a draftee immediately after signing him. In what became known as the "Pete Incaviglia rule," teams could not trade a drafted player until he was under contract for at least a year. The rule was changed in 2015 to allow teams to trade drafted players after the World Series.

With the 20th pick, the New York Mets selected shortstop Gregg Jefferies of Junipero Serra High School in San Mateo, California. Jefferies was a consistent hitting machine and one of the most prolific minor league hitters of all time. He was voted the minor league Player of the Year in both 1986 and 1987. Jefferies's minor league career drew rave reviews for his hitting prowess and work ethic. Joe McIlvaine credited Jefferies's father for teaching his son to switch hit in the family swimming pool and thus learn to complete the full swing through the resistance of the water. Mets minor league manager Bobby Floyd said, "I've never seen a switch-hitter handle the bat and hit with power from both sides like Gregg. You hate to make such heavy-handed comparisons, but Mickey Mantle is the only player who has come along with that type of power from both sides."[66]

Hitting was clearly Jefferies's strongest suit. Like the great sluggers who preceded him in the 1985 draft, he was hampered by a brash and abrasive personality. Ironically, Jefferies graduated from the same San Mateo high school as Barry Bonds and apparently the same charm school as well. His self-confidence often veered towards arrogance. "God put me on this earth to play baseball," he was heard to say. After joining the Mets in 1987, he boldly and foolishly told reporters, "I'm here to break Ty Cobb's records."[67]

The Mets were just coming off a celebrated victory in the 1986 World Series. Grizzled veterans in the Mets' clubhouse took offense at Jefferies's words. Teammates resented the implication that Jefferies was going to save the Mets. In light of the emphasis Jefferies placed on hitting, he was preoccupied with his bats. He insisted that the Mets' equipment managers keep his bats separate from his teammates' bats. Jefferies would explain in detail to anyone who would listen exactly where on the bats he had made contact for his hits.

Annoyed with the attention that Jefferies was receiving from the media, Mets relief ace Randy Myers and a few other veterans surreptitiously "borrowed" a few of Jefferies's bats and returned them in the form of sawdust. In a 1989 game against the Phillies, Jefferies charged the mound with the intent of attacking Phillies reliever Roger McDowell, a popular former member of the Mets. A bench-clearing brawl ensued. Phillies manager Nick Leyva quipped, "There were 30 of our guys rooting for Roger and 20 of theirs rooting for him too."[68]

Jefferies played in New York for the Mets for three full seasons and parts of two others. Although he had plenty of pop for a second baseman, he never fulfilled the lofty expectations he had set in the minors. He was traded to Kansas City after the 1991 season and then moved to the Cardinals in February 1993. His best years came for the Cardinals, where he hit well over .300 and made two All-Star squads at first base. He played for fourteen years in the Major Leagues and hit 126 home runs in his career.

With the 22nd pick, the Chicago Cubs drafted Will Clark's Mississippi State running mate, Rafael Palmeiro. Professional baseball proved to have a stiff learning curve for Palmeiro. He struggled with transitioning from the aluminum bats used in college to wooden bats. In his first few years with the Cubs he displayed very little power. Even though he was selected to the All-Star Game in 1988, he only hit eight home runs and drove in 53 runs. Chicago traded Palmeiro to the Texas Rangers after the 1988 season. In Texas, his collegiate power stroke began to emerge. He averaged 20 home runs per year. After five years in Texas, Palmeiro signed as a free agent with the Baltimore Orioles. In Baltimore his power continued to surge. When all was said and done, Palmeiro played 20 years in the big leagues and hit 569 homers and collected 3,020 hits.

In March 2005, Palmeiro vehemently denied using steroids in a riveting, nationally televised Congressional hearing. Five months later, he tested positive for anabolic steroids. He is now remembered more for simultaneously wagging his finger in the face of the Congressional committee and denying he ever used steroids than for his picture perfect swing.

While the first round was exceptional, it could have been better if it had included pitcher Randy Johnson. Montreal struck gold with the huge six-foot-ten Johnson in the second round. While it would have been impossible for the scouts to overlook the largest player in the nation, there was far from universal agreement about his pitching ability. One scout pegged Johnson as the tenth best pitching prospect in the draft. Another scout didn't even rank him as a prospect at all, commenting, "I just can't project his delivery and arm action to the big leagues."[69]

The choice was clearly a projection; the gangly Johnson was truly a project. There were flaws in Johnson's delivery and, consequently, in his results. The biggest problem was his erratic control. It would take years for Johnson to develop control. Yet, his blazing fastball and his dominating stature made him a worthy project. Montreal's minor league instructors did an excellent job to help Johnson harness his natural ability. However, Montreal did not fully reap the fruits of its efforts. In 1989, the Expos traded Johnson to the Seattle Mariners for fellow pitcher Mark Langston.

With the Mariners, Johnson continued to struggle with his control at first. While he continued to rack up strikeouts, he also led the American League in walks for three straight years from 1990 to 1992. No less of a pitching authority than Nolan Ryan advised Johnson to develop a secondary pitch to go with his fastball and to continue to work on his control.[70] Johnson worked hard to develop a biting slider. Once he was able to control the pitch, he elevated his game to an elite level.

Johnson would go on to become one of the most dominating pitchers of all time. His Major League career spanned 22 seasons. He won five Cy Young Awards, struck out an astounding 4,875 hitters, won 303 games and had a 3.29 lifetime earned run average. The "Big Unit," as Johnson was nicknamed by teammate Tim Raines, was inducted into the Hall of Fame in 2015, his first year of eligibility. As a testament to the golden age of the draft, three of the ten greatest pitchers in the history of baseball would come out of the three successive drafts of 1983 (Roger Clemens), 1984 (Greg Maddux), and 1985 (Randy Johnson).

In the 22nd round, the Tigers snagged a future Hall of Famer in high school pitcher John Smoltz of Lansing, Michigan. Smoltz's talent was no secret to scouts, many of whom projected him as an early round pick. However, Michigan State University had offered Smoltz a scholarship. It was pretty much a foregone conclusion that Smoltz would pass up the pros in favor of playing college ball. In a story reminiscent of Detroit's signing of Kirk Gibson in 1978, Smoltz decided at the twelfth hour to sign with the Tigers. However, Smoltz never wore a Tigers' uniform. In 1987, Detroit traded him to Atlanta.

By 1989, Smoltz was an All-Star for the Braves. He would pitch for the Braves until 2008. Over that time, he was both a dominant starter, and when the team needed bullpen help, a dominant reliever. Only Hall of Famer Dennis Eckersley has been able to perform so well in both roles. Smoltz was selected to eight All-Star Games and won the Cy Young Award in 1996. When Greg Maddux joined Smoltz and Tom Glavine in the Braves' rotation in 1993, they would form perhaps the best starting pitching trio in baseball history. In 2015, Smoltz was elected to the Hall of Fame, joining Maddux and Glavine in Cooperstown.

The Chicago Cubs found a late-round gem in the 24th round in Mark Grace, who played at San Diego State University. Over Grace's 16-year career, most of which was spent with the Cubs, the three-time All-Star hit .303 with 173 home runs and 1,146 runs batted in.

Amazing Grace

In two full minor league seasons and part of a third, Mark Grace hit .332. Over thirteen full seasons with the Chicago Cubs and three more with the Arizona Diamondbacks, he hit .303. He possessed, as scout Gary Nickels says, "the magic wand."

Fortunately for the Cubs, Nickels was one of the few scouts to get a good glimpse of the magic wand during Grace's days as an amateur. Other teams surely knew of Grace when he was playing in college but didn't hold him in high regard. When the Cubs drafted Grace in the 24th round of the 1985 draft, there were 621 players taken ahead of him. Only 133 of the players drafted before Grace ever reached the majors. Of those 133 players, only three – B.J. Surhoff, Rafael Palmeiro and Barry Bonds – played in more Major League games than Grace.

Grace played his college ball at San Diego State University, where his magic wand was a well-kept secret. Nickels suggests that, at the time, most of the San Diego State hitters were taught to be inside-out hitters. For that reason, even hitters capable of producing power tended to hit the ball the opposite way. Grace, a left-handed batter, would typically hit the ball to left-center.

After San Diego State finished its 1985 season, Grace headed to Alaska to play summer ball. Grace was assigned to the North Pole Nicks, a team managed by University of Southern California coach Mike Gillespie. While playing for Gillespie, Grace began to pull balls more consistently. The results were dramatic. Grace hit .367 with 52 runs batted in during Alaska's regular season, earning the nickname "Amazing Grace."

Grace signed with the Cubs in August 1985. He spent the 1986 season with the Class A Peoria Chiefs, where he hit .342 with 15 home runs and 95 runs batted in. For the next 17 seasons, Grace and his magic wand continued to produce. When Grace retired from baseball at the age of 39, he left with 173 home runs, 1,146 runs batted in, four Gold Glove Awards and three All-Star appearances. It was an amazing career, especially so for a player who didn't get drafted until the 24th round.

1986

I was in my third year with the Tigers. John Young [scouting director for the Detroit Tigers] said to me, 'I want you to go to go to McAdory High School, right outside of Birmingham, and go see this kid Bo Jackson. I don't know what he can do, but I know he's a great athlete.' I went into his little high school early in the season. Only one other scout was there. Bo had not been a popular prospect in baseball circles. We got there real early, just the two of us. The coach was hitting ground balls to all these kids. I ask the coach, 'Is there a kid named Bo Jackson around here?' I just keep peeking at the gym door and then this stud comes walking out the door and strolling down the hill. I'm thinking, 'Man, this is him.' Bo looks around, picks up his glove, goes out to shortstop, where he played in high school, and the coach is hitting ground balls. They had a skin infield, hard as a rock. Bo couldn't catch a cold. He was awful catching ground balls. Coach says, 'Anybody out here hasn't hit yet?' Bo raises his hand. About six more ground balls bounce off Bo's shin. He still hasn't caught a ground ball. Coach says to Bo, 'All right come on in, get a bat.' He doesn't swing, doesn't loosen up or anything. Bo hits this one iron shot into the trees in center field. I start thinking, 'Holy cow, this guy's really something.' Then they played the game. Bo's team won by a lot. He played shortstop and caught almost every ball hit to him. He lined shots to right field, left field. He hit everything. It was by far the best athletic display on a baseball field I have ever seen.

   –Jax Robertson, long-time scout, Detroit Tigers and special assistant to the
   general manager, Pittsburgh Pirates

In 1986, the Pittsburgh Pirates owned the overall first pick in the draft for the first time ever. Coming off the drafting of Barry Bonds in 1985, the Pittsburgh Pirates appeared positioned to make another splash. Yet it was the defending World Series champion Kansas City Royals who would make the biggest headlines in the 1986 draft. In the fourth round, the Royals drafted the uber-talented Bo Jackson of Auburn University. The drafting of Jackson represents one of the greatest scouting stories and biggest draft coups in history.

   Scouts are forever looking for and speaking about the mythic "five-tool player." Rarely, if ever, do they get to sign one. Vincent Edward "Bo" Jackson was the epitome of a five-tool player. Often scouts engage in at least a small degree of hyperbole when they label a prospect as a five-tool player. In the case of Bo Jackson, the label was an understatement. In fact, he was a modern-day Jim Thorpe. He excelled at any athletic endeavor that he attempted. He could hit a baseball and hit it very, very far; he could run like a deer and catch almost any ball that remained in the park. In addition, he could throw a baseball with accuracy and with the thrust of a howitzer. The Royals' scouting report gave Jackson an extremely rare grade of "80" for both speed and power and called him "the best athlete in America."[71] Legendary scout Hugh Alexander said of Jackson, "He can run like hell and he can hit the ball out of Yellowstone Park." Uncle Hughie went on to say, "You've got to go back to Mays and Mantle to find anyone with that kind of combination."[72]

Bo hit 20 homers in only 25 high school games in Bessemer, Alabama and some of them were hit over 500 feet. Tigers scout Jax Robertson watched Bo in high school take the first pitch he saw in batting practice, a pitch almost on the ground, and hit it out of the park and over the trees behind the center field fence. Bo ran the sixty-yard dash in 6.15 seconds. By comparison, Royals center fielder Willie Wilson, whose speed was a major part of the Royals' drive to the 1985 World Championship, ran the sixty-yard dash in 6.3 seconds.

At Auburn, playing against outstanding Southeastern Conference football teams, Jackson won the Heisman Trophy as the best college football player in America. At the National Football League Combine, he ran the 40-yard dash in a breath-taking 4.12 seconds.[73] In spite of all his talents, Jackson was not the overwhelming favorite to be drafted with the overall first pick in 1986. The almost universal belief among Major League franchises was that he was "unsignable" because he intended to play pro football. He had previously rebuffed both the New York Yankees, who had drafted him out of high school, and the California Angels, who had selected him after his junior year at Auburn. After Jackson's 1995 Heisman season, the Tampa Bay Buccaneers drafted him with the first pick of the NFL draft. The Buccaneers offered Jackson a huge pay day, $7.6 million. Almost everyone in baseball was now resigned to losing his extraordinary talents to football – everyone except Royals area scout Kenny Gonzales.

After Bo's legend was firmly established, Nike ran a memorable "Bo Knows" ad campaign, which accentuated Bo's incredible aptitude to seemingly master any sport. The real story of the signing of Bo Jackson may aptly be called "Kenny knows Bo." Gonzales had developed a special bond with Jackson and his mother. The relationship was reminiscent of the ties that scouts built with players and their parents in the era of scouting before the institution of the draft. Royals scouting director

Art Stewart, who had been involved with the New York Yankee dynasties of the 1950s and 1960s, called Gonzales's signing of Bo Jackson "the greatest scouting story of [my] life."[74]

Gonzales believed that Jackson wanted to play baseball. Jackson's mother, Florence Bond, worked at the Ramada Inn in Bessemer, Alabama, where Gonzales would often stay. Gonzales made a point of finding out Florence's morning break time and often met with her during her breaks. Eventually he spent so much time over coffee and meals with Florence and Bo, they came to consider him a member of the family. Gonzales knew through his discussions with Florence that Bo would not sign with any team out of high school for any amount of money. Although Florence was a single mom with eight children and undoubtedly could have used the bonus money, she was determined to have Bo accept his scholarship to Auburn and graduate from college.

When the New York Yankees drafted Jackson in 1982, the team was prepared to offer him $250,000 to sign. Jackson and his mother were not even willing to discuss the offer, so strong was his commitment to enrolling in college. Gonzales had wisely advised the Royals not to waste a draft pick on Jackson in 1982. Three years later, when the Angels drafted him in the 20th round and offered him $1 million to sign, Gonzales accurately predicted to his Royals' superiors that Bo would spurn the Angels too. After turning down two Major League teams and a boatload of money, Bo was drafted by the Buccaneers.

Kenny Gonzales had learned that Bo was offended by the Buccaneers' lack of transparency in dealing with him and knew that Jackson was reluctant to sign with Tampa Bay. However, even Gonzales had doubts regarding his true intentions. He advised the Royals not to use an early draft pick on Jackson. On the day of the Major League Draft, Jackson called the Royals general manager, John Schuerholz, to tell him that he was genuinely interested in playing for the Royals. When three rounds of the draft passed without Jackson's name being called, Stewart said to Schuerholz, "We have to believe in Kenny."[75] The Royals trusted Kenny and rolled the dice. Bo signed with the Royals for the same $1 million the Angels had offered, plus a $100,000 bonus. The Tampa Bay Buccaneers became just another spurned suitor.

Schuerholz trumpeted the fact that baseball had been able to prevail over the National Football League in signing Jackson. Other Major League teams appeared to be thrilled by Jackson's signing too. New York Mets scouting director Joe McIlvaine thought it was "a good thing for baseball, particularly getting a high-class athlete." San Diego Padres manager Jack McKeon described Jackson's signing as "the best damn free-agent signing in the history of the game."[76]

The Royals called Jackson up to the majors after only 53 games in the minors. From 1986 to 1988, Jackson played all three outfield positions for the Royals and amazed the baseball world with his tape measure blasts, but never hit above .250. In 1989, it all came together for him. He was selected to the All-Star Game, in which he hit a monster 450-foot home run and was named the Most Valuable Player. Jackson finished the 1989 season with 32 homers, 105 runs batted in, and 26 stolen bases. He also led the league in strikeouts, with 172, but clearly his talent was coming to the fore.

As many in baseball feared, however, the prospect of playing in the National Football League still attracted Jackson. When the Oakland Raiders drafted him in the seventh round of the 1987 draft, he signed an unprecedented contract that would allow him to play with the Royals but join the Raiders at the end of the baseball season. When Jackson joined the Raiders in mid-season of 1987, he was just as dominant as he had been at Auburn. He became the only player to become an All-Star in both the National Football League and in Major League Baseball. However, his decision to play year-long eventually took a toll on his body and his performance. The Royals released him in March 1991. While he bounced around the majors for a few more years, he never came close to fulfilling his enormous potential. Yet, if a metric can be designed to measure pure athletic plays and thrills, Vincent Edward Jackson would be at or near the very top.

The Southwest Conference was the focus of the top two picks in the 1986 draft. University of Texas pitcher Greg Swindell and University of Arkansas third baseman Jeff King were the top two consensus picks. The Pirates held the first pick. They considered both Swindell and King, but ultimately chose King. For his college career, King had slugged 42 homers and driven in 204 runs.

Pittsburgh scouting director Elmer Gray was hoping King would follow in the footsteps of Barry Bonds. Gray's expectation proved to be unrealistic. Bonds had reached the majors less than a year after he was drafted, but it took King three years in the minors before he arrived in Pittsburgh. It took King six seasons to hit with consistency in the majors. Not until his eighth Major League season, 1996, did he hit more than 18 home runs. Following the 1996 season, the Pirates traded him to the Kansas City Royals. King enjoyed two respectable seasons with the Royals before retiring in the middle of the 1999 season at the age of 34. King never fulfilled the potential the Pirates had envisioned. He did, however, hit two home runs in the same inning twice in his career, a feat accomplished only by baseball greats Willie McCovey and Andre Dawson.

Swindell fell to the Cleveland Indians with the second overall pick. He would play for 17 seasons in the Major Leagues and finished his career with a lifetime record of 123 wins and 122 losses. Swindell was a starter for the first ten years of his career but had only one season in which he recorded more than 13 wins. For the last seven years of his career, he pitched almost exclusively in relief and served as a valuable part-time closer for the Twins, Red Sox and Diamondbacks.

Fresh off selecting Will Clark with the second pick in 1985, the San Francisco Giants used the third overall pick to take a gamble on short-stop Matt Williams of the University of Nevada at Las Vegas. President Al Rosen and the Giants surprised many teams with the early selection of Williams because he was not as highly regarded as many other prospects in the draft. However, Williams was in San Francisco by the next year and was starting at shortstop for the Giants. In 1990 he moved to third base and joined with Will Clark to form another potent middle-of-the-order duo for the Giants. The move to third base led to a breakout season for Williams, as he slugged 33 homers, hit .277 and had a league-leading 122 runs batted in. The next year he won the Gold Glove Award while hitting 34 home runs. For the next five years, he would continue to post big power number for the Giants while flashing his leather at third base. In 1994, he smashed a league-leading 43 home runs and drove in 96 runs while winning another Gold Glove at third base.

The Giants traded Williams to the Cleveland Indians before the 1997 season. He continued to hit well in the junior circuit, clubbing 32 homers and driving in 105 runs in 1997. The Indians traded him to the fledgling Arizona Diamondbacks after the 1997 season. Williams closed out his Major League career with six seasons in Arizona. He wound up playing 17 big league seasons while hitting 378 homers and driving in 1,218 runs.

With the fourth pick of the draft, the Texas Rangers selected right-handed Georgia Tech pitcher Kevin Brown. Brown had a stellar junior season at Tech that propelled him to the top of many draft boards. In one respect, Brown was the biggest surprise of the draft because he was not even drafted when he finished high school in 1992. At Georgia Tech, Brown was able to add velocity to his fastball and become an unexpected sensation. By 1989 he became the Rangers' second starter behind Nolan Ryan and won 12 games against 9 defeats. In 1992, he established himself as a dominant pitching force, winning a league-leading 21 games and making the All-Star team. He joined the Florida Marlins after the 1995 season as a free agent, posted a league-leading earned run average of 1.89 in 1996, and helped the Marlins to the World Series championship in 1997. He joined the Los Angeles Dodgers in 1999, when he signed baseball's first $100 million contract. Over his nineteen-year career, Brown recorded 211 wins.

The Milwaukee Brewers drafted Gary Sheffield with the sixth overall pick. Sheffield was a natural hitter and possessed a quick swing. The Brewers traded him to the San Diego Padres in 1992. Sheffield enjoyed an outstanding season with San Diego in 1992, hitting 33 homers and leading the National League with a batting average of .330. The Padres traded him to the Florida Marlins the very next year in a deal that brought future Hall of Famer Trevor Hoffman to the Padres. Sheffield was a productive hitter for the Marlins for the next five years and put together a brilliant season in 1996, when he hit .314 with 42 home runs and 120 runs batted in. The Marlins traded him to the Dodgers in 1998 in exchange for a future Hall of Famer, Mike Piazza. When Sheffield retired in 2009 at age 40, he had slugged 509 home runs, driven in 1,676 runs and had a career average of .292. He was selected to nine All-Star teams. Like many of his colleagues, Sheffield's chances of being elected to the Hall of Fame have been adversely affected by allegations of steroid use.

The Royals not only snared Bo Jackson in the fourth round but made a very astute choice in the sixth round when they drafted pitcher Tom "Flash" Gordon. Gordon stood five-feet-nine. He possessed a live fastball and one of the best curveballs in the history of the game.

Scouts frequently refer to Tom Gordon as the exception that proves the rule. The "rule" prescribes that a team should not draft a right-handed pitcher who is less than six feet tall. The "exception" allows for right-handed pitchers under six feet if they possess a curveball that is unhittable. As Bill Livesey, the former New York Yankee director of player development, said of Gordon, "Oh my, with his curveball, he's six-foot-three." Gordon pitched for twenty-one seasons in the major leagues.

A Franchise Rebounds

In the seven-year stretch between 1977 and 1983, the New York Mets were a dismal team. They lost six out of every ten games they played in those years and finished last in the National League East five times.

By 1983, however, there was reason for hope. With prudent drafting, the Mets were able to build strong teams up and down their farm system. The Mets fielded five teams from A ball to Triple-A. In 1983, their five teams won a total of 372 games and lost only 259. The 1984 season was nearly as good, with 369 wins and 259 losses. The lights shone especially brightly at Lynchburg City Stadium, home of the Class A Lynchburg (Virginia) Mets.

Two products of the Mets' 1981 draft, outfielders Lenny Dykstra and Mark Carreon, had exceptional years for Lynchburg in 1983. So too did pitcher Dwight Gooden, a 1982 draftee. Dykstra hit .358 and Carreon hit .334. Gooden won 19 games and lost only 4. The three led Lynchburg to 96 wins and the 1983 Carolina League championship.

The 1984 Lynchburg Mets were even more successful, winning 97 games and claiming the league championship. Gooden had moved on to the parent club, but Mitch Cook, Randy Myers and Rick Aguilera led a formidable starting rotation. Cook, newly acquired from the Cubs, started 27 games and compiled a 16-4 record. Myers, selected by the Mets in the secondary phase of the 1982 June draft, started 22 games and finished with 13 wins against 5 losses. Aguilera, the Mets' third-round pick in 1983, went 8-3 in 13 starts.

Twenty-year-old Stanley Jefferson, fresh off his first season in pro ball with the Little Falls (NY) Mets, joined the 1983 Lynchburg team during its playoff run. Jefferson did not see any action in the playoffs but benefited from watching the manner in which Dykstra, Carreon, and first baseman Randy Milligan went about their business. Jefferson, a speedster, would become an integral member of the 1984 Lynchburg team, hitting .288 and stealing 45 bases. Jefferson remembers his time in Lynchburg fondly. "There was great camaraderie," Jefferson says. "That was probably the best time, the most innocent time. We were winning so much."

By 1986, with the promotion of several recent draft picks and the acquisition of Gary Carter and other key veterans, the New York Mets had assembled a roster that was more talented than in past years. When the Mets defeated the Red Sox in the World Series, Dykstra, Carter, third baseman Ray Knight and pitcher Ron Darling led the way. It was a time-honored recipe for success: judicious drafting and inspired trades.

1987

I was with Texas in 1987. I learned a lesson. I was driving home from Plant City, Florida to Arlington, Texas. I stopped off in Pensacola on a Monday. I wanted to see Travis Fryman, who was playing for Gonzalez Tate High School, a very famous high school in Florida. It had produced Jay Bell, Don Sutton, and now Travis Fryman. Their next game was on Tuesday. I got to my hotel room and called the coach to check in on him. The team had just lost two games in a row, which was unheard of at Tate High School. They lost about one game a year. So the coach told me he was going to put his players through a simulated game, they were going to play until it got dark. 'We're going to play situational baseball, everybody's going to hit. You're welcome to come out to the park.' I was the only scout there. I saw Travis hit 20-25 times. I saw every aspect of his game. I went to the game the next day but I pretty much already had my card filled out on Travis Fryman. I loved what he could do on a baseball field. I got such a tremendous look. I learned that you can see more at a practice than you maybe can at a game. It was one of my favorite scouting days ever.

    –Wayne Krivsky, scout and former general manager, Cincinnati Reds

The 1987 amateur draft represented another step forward in the maturation of the draft. The Seattle Mariners held the number one overall pick and selected Ken Griffey Jr. from Moeller High School in Cincinnati. Griffey would supplant Darryl Strawberry as the best overall first pick in the history of the draft and would become the standard for judging all future number one selections going forward. The delicious irony is that the Mariners almost did not select Griffey.

The Mariners franchise was hanging by a thread in 1987. Owner George Argyros was trying to sell the team when the 1987 draft came around. As with George Steinbrenner, owner of the New York Yankees, Argyros was very involved with all of his team's baseball decisions, including the amateur draft. Argyros was somewhat skeptical of the baseball people in his organization, particularly since the Mariners had already missed on the number one overall pick twice in their brief history. Al Chambers, selected by Seattle in 1979, and Mike Moore, Seattle's draft choice in 1981, represented failures as far as Argyros was concerned. Like Griffey, Chambers had been a high school phenom "who could not miss." Argyros was therefore wary of drafting another high school star with the first pick. Rather, he favored taking pitcher Mike Harkey from

California State University at Fullerton. Harkey was a hulking six-foot-five right-handed fireballer coming off a very successful college season.

The Mariners' front office, led by general manager Dick Balderson, scouting director Roger Jongewaard and senior scout Bob Harrison all preferred Griffey over Harkey. Jongewaard had joined the Mariners in 1985 and had earned respect for his judgment in the scouting world. During his tenure with the New York Mets, he had been instrumental in identifying, among others, Darryl Strawberry, Lenny Dykstra, and Kevin Mitchell for the Mets. Propelled by the talent that Jongewaard had helped to accumulate in New York, the Mets had just won the 1986 World Series.

Jongewaard was certain that Griffey had more natural ability than every one of the players he had signed in the past, including Strawberry. Jongewaard had observed Griffey in the spring at Moeller High when he hit a towering home run over a grove of trees that stood 20 yards behind the fence. When the ball landed, Jongewaard asked fellow Mariners scout Tom Mooney to identify the tree that the ball had hit. Mooney told him that the ball had cleared all the trees, impressing the normally unflappable Jongewaard.

Almost every scout and organization that had seen Griffey raved about his talent. One scouting report described him as follows: "live athletic body, rare combination of power and speed, makes game look easy, bat speed with HR power, great arm and center field glove, similar in style but much better than Barry Bonds at the same stage." Atlanta's general manager Bobby Cox, who had scouted Griffey at Moeller High, said, "He was the best prospect I have seen in my life. There was nobody even close to him."[77] Griffey could truly do it all. He hit for average, hit for power, ran very well, threw with great accuracy and authority, and patrolled center field like Willie Mays.

Argyros resisted Jongewaard's urgent pleas for Griffey. He reminded Jongewaard that the scouts had also raved about the Mariners' first round selection in 1986, outfielder Patrick Lennon. The Mariners had taken Lennon, a North Carolina high school star, with the eighth overall pick.[78] Lennon was struggling greatly in the minors at the time. He would not be promoted to Seattle until 1991, and even then only for eight at-bats. Jongewaard persisted in pushing Griffey and, in doing so, clearly put his job on the line with Argyros.

Unfazed by the pressure, Jongewaard conspired with Balderson and Harrison to engage in some "creative accounting" to tip the scales in Griffey's favor. Mariners scouts had rated both Harkey and Griffey with a perfect 80 out of 80 as their final grade. Balderson and Jongewaard convinced Harrison, who had the complete trust of Argyros, to reduce Harkey's grade so that Griffey would be the clear choice.[79] The gambit worked and Argyros signed off on Griffey. The next hurdle would be for the cash-strapped Mariners to find the money to sign Griffey. The night before the draft, the Mariners were able to get Griffey to agree to a $160,000 signing bonus, which was lower than the highest bonuses of the prior two drafts. Griffey's agent, Brian Goldberg, expressed concern that Griffey was leaving tens of thousands of dollars on the table. Griffey, with extreme confidence in his abilities, said, "I'll make up for that later. Let's be Number One."[80]

Griffey spent the rest of 1987 and all of 1988 rising through the Mariners' system. He arrived in Seattle, ahead of schedule, in 1989. He had hit so well in spring training that the Mariners could not hold him down any longer. On opening day of the 1989 season, Griffey started for the Mariners in center field. In his rookie season, Griffey quickly put to rest any lingering doubts that Argyros may have had. In his first Major League at-bat, he slammed a double to left-center against Oakland Athletics ace Dave Stewart. He began to exhibit the uncanny flair for dramatic moments that would characterize his entire big-league career. He homered in his home debut in Seattle on the first pitch he saw. He hit a game-winning two-run home run in his first pinch-hitting appearance. In June, on Ken Griffey Jr. Poster Day, he hit another game-winning home run.

Griffey's rapid early success and emerging legend grew so fast that an enterprising Seattle company produced a candy bar named after him and sold almost one million bars. He seemed to be a lock for the Rookie of the Year Award but a fractured right hand forced him to miss a whole month in the middle of the season. The injury continued to affect him even after he returned to the lineup, robbing him of his power. He had hit 13 home runs prior to the injury but hit only three after his return. He finished a disappointing third in the Rookie of the Year voting.

In 1990, the story got even better when the Mariners signed Griffey's father, Ken Griffey Sr., who had been a member of the Big Red Machine in Cincinnati. Griffey and his father made history when they played together in the same outfield on August 31, 1990. The father-son legend continued to grow as both Senior and Junior hit back-to-back home runs in a game against the California Angels on September 14, 1990.

If any player in the game ever had a Hall of Fame pedigree and predestination, it was Griffey Jr. In addition to being born into a baseball family, he was born in the same city, Donora, Pennsylvania, and on the same date, November 21, as St. Louis Cardinals Hall of Famer Stan Musial. While Barry Bonds grew up playing at the feet of Willie Mays and Willie McCovey, Griffey grew up playing ball near Big Red Machine greats Johnny Bench, Tony Perez and Joe Morgan. At Moeller High School, Griffey Jr. followed in the footsteps of another Cincinnati Hall of Famer, Barry Larkin.

On the field, Junior was a human highlight reel. In Yankee Stadium, he scaled the eight-foot wall in left-center field to rob Jesse Barfield of a home run. While he would repeat the feat many times over during his career, it left observers stunned when it first happened. In 1993, he played in the All-Star Game in Baltimore's Camden Yards, and, during the Home Run Derby competition, he hit the first and only ball ever to the strike the iconic B&O Warehouse beyond right field on the fly.

In a game where comparisons with legends are the highest compliments, Griffey collected the comparisons as routinely as young fans acquire trading cards. He was so fluid and effortless that he supplanted San Francisco's Will Clark as "the Natural."[81] He arrived in the Major Leagues so quickly and achieved stardom at such an early age that he became known as the "Kid," a moniker previously reserved for Ted Williams. Hall of Famer Reggie Jackson fashioned his own compliment. Jackson said, "He is creating excitement and making headlines just by his presence. There hasn't been anyone like that since … Reggie Jackson."[82] Griffey was also compared to Hall of Famer Al Kaline for his early batting success and to Willie Mays for his over-the-head running catches, and to Roberto Clemente for his cannon-like arm. As *Sports Illustrated* writer E.M. Swift commented, "It's almost as if Griffey were born to do this kind of work."[83]

In his 22-year career, Griffey's accomplishments were innumerable: 13 All-Star Game selections, ten Gold Gloves, seven Silver Slugger Awards, and the American League Most Valuable Player Award in 1997, when he hit 56 home runs and drove in 147 runs. For his career, he hit 630 home runs, had 1,836 runs batted in, and stole 184 bases. As his career progressed, Griffey was slowed by injuries, preventing him from making a run at the all time home run record. He was elected to the Hall of Fame in 2016. In doing so, he received the highest percentage of votes of any inductee up to that point in history. From his first at-bat to his last, Griffey Jr. brought a distinct joy to the game.

While Griffey fulfilled the lofty expectations placed on him, the second pick of the draft turned out to be a big miss for the Pittsburgh Pirates. Though it is difficult to understand in retrospect, there was almost an equal split in opinion among Major League teams as to whether Griffey Jr. or first baseman/outfielder Mark Merchant was the best player available. Almost half of the teams considered Merchant, a high school standout from Oviedo, Florida, to be the best player in the draft. Unfortunately for the Pirates, Merchant became one of the most high-profile "can't miss players who missed." As the Florida High School Player of the Year, Merchant hit over .400 and stole over 40 bases. Noted baseball scribe Peter Gammons rated him the second-best prospect in the 1987 draft class. One scout called him the best player to come out of Florida in 30 years. Another compared him to Cincinnati's star outfielder Eric Davis.

Merchant's minor league career had a promising start. He hit .265 and stole 33 bases in his first 50 minor league games. Then he separated his throwing shoulder while diving for a ball, bringing an abrupt end to his first season. In 1990, other injuries caused him to miss much of the season. Merchant tried to overcome the injuries and played for eleven seasons in the minors, but never advanced to the big leagues.[84]

With the fourth pick in 1987, the Chicago Cubs selected the player whom George Argyros had preferred over Griffey, the towering Mike Harkey. The Cubs gave Harkey the same $160,000 bonus that Griffey received. Harkey featured a 95-mph fastball. He started 27 games for Chicago in 1990 and finished the season with a record of 12 wins and six losses and a respectable 3.26 earned run average. He appeared poised to become a fixture as a top-of-the-line starter. However, just as he looked to build on his rookie success, he suffered a series of injuries that largely wiped out his next two seasons. He never recaptured the form that he had displayed in 1990. Although Harkey would pitch for eight Major League seasons, he won only 24 more games after his rookie season.

The Chicago White Sox held the fifth pick and selected another tall, heralded college pitcher in 6'5" Stanford University star Jack McDowell. The right-hander was coming off a season in which he had led Stanford to victory in the College World Series. Nicknamed "Black Jack," McDowell received a larger bonus than either Griffey or Harkey. The White Sox's investment paid immediate dividends. Chicago brought McDowell to the big leagues three months after the draft. By the early 1990s, he was the ace of Chicago's pitching staff and one of the best starters in the American League. In 1993 he won the American League Cy Young Award, winning a league best twenty-two games. McDowell pitched for twelve seasons in the majors, appeared in three All-Star Games, and compiled a record of 127 wins and 87 losses.

The Kansas City Royals continued their recent draft success, selecting pitcher Kevin Appier of Antelope Valley Junior College in Lancaster, California with the ninth pick. Some scouts shied away from Appier because he had an unorthodox delivery. Notwithstanding those concerns, Appier developed into an accomplished and reliable big-league starter. Years after Appier closed out his baseball career, Mickey White, the former director of scouting for the Pittsburgh Pirates, said, "I wouldn't have gone near Kevin Appier because his pitching motion was so awkward, but he ended up pitching for 16 seasons in the big leagues and won 169 games, so you never know."

Other observers thought that using a first-round pick on Appier was a reach. However, for a stretch of five seasons, Appier was the undisputed ace of the Kansas City pitching staff. Appier was not drafted out of high school but he worked hard to improve under the tutelage of Antelope Valley coach Ted Henkel. He was able to increase his fastball from the mid-80s to the low nineties. The Royals' pitching guru, Guy Hansen, helped Appier develop further. In 1993, Appier led the American League in earned run average.

Seton Hall catcher Craig Biggio went to the Houston Astros with the 22nd overall pick. Biggio was not drafted out of high school because he had made it clear that he intended to enroll at Seton Hall. Most observers thought that Biggio needed additional experience before he would be ready for professional ball. Biggio agreed. At Seton Hall, Biggio's baseball skills improved considerably under the guidance of head coach Mike Sheppard. Teaming with future Red Sox slugger Mo Vaughn, Biggio helped to propel Seton Hall to the 1987 NCAA tournament. In his final season of college ball, Biggio hit .407 with 14 homers and 30 stolen bases. His rare blend of power and speed made him an attractive prospect. Scout Phil Rossi noted that Biggio's versatility would allow him to be moved to another position in the infield or outfield as he progressed in his career.

Biggio remained behind the plate in the minors and for his first four years in Houston. In 1992, the Astros shifted him to second base. Although he was already an All-Star catcher, his career really caught fire after the switch. As a second baseman, he made the All-Star team six more times. In his youth, Biggio favored players whose baseball cards depicted a lengthy stretch of consecutive years with the same team. One of his goals as a player was for the reverse side of his baseball cards to show a continuous string of years with a single team. Biggio accomplished that goal and then some, having spent his entire 20-year career with the Astros. During that stretch, he became a fan favorite and a franchise icon. Over the course of his career, he had 3,060 hits, 291 homers, 1,175 runs batted in and a career average of .281. He is the only player in history to have had more than 3,000 hits and over 600 doubles, 250 home runs and 400 stolen bases. He was elected to the Hall of Fame in 2015 and will perhaps be best remembered for his tenacious approach to the game and his relentless hustle.

Louisiana State University outfielder Joey Belle, one of the best college hitting prospects of 1987, fell to the Cleveland Indians in the second round. Belle would have fit better among the surly sluggers of the 1985 class. He was undoubtedly drafted well below where his talent would have suggested, due to his suspect attitude. At LSU, he was once suspended for charging after a fan who had yelled a racial invective at him. It was the most serious of many disturbing encounters that Belle had with fans in college. Philadelphia Phillies scout Eddie Bockman went so far as to predict that Belle's attitude issues would prevent him from ever reaching the Major Leagues.[85]

Bockman underrated Belle's hitting talent but was correct in predicting that anger issues would be a significant impediment to Belle's success. Judged from the purely objective standpoint of talent, Belle was one of the most fearsome run-producing power hitters of all time. Judged from the perspective of his seething anger, Belle was a ticking time bomb.[86] While his powerful bat was hard to ignore or resist, his anger always wound up overshadowing his ability.

Belle's prodigious talent brought him to Cleveland in 1989. In 1991, he clubbed 28 homers and drove in 95 runs. Belle was a model of hitting consistency. In the years from 1991 to 2000, he hit .298 and averaged 37 home runs per season. His special calling card was clutch run production; three times during the mid-1990s, he led the American League in runs batted in. Unlike many power hitters, Belle's batting average did not suffer due to his focus on power.

Belle's temper prevented him from getting the acclaim that his numbers would otherwise have merited. While he changed his preferred name from "Joey" to "Albert" during his time in Cleveland, there was no parallel change in his attitude. In the big leagues, Belle still had occasional outbursts directed toward fans. However, more frequently, his outbursts were aimed at reporters and writers. In one well-chronicled outburst, teammate Sandy Alomar Jr. had to physically separate Belle from a beat reporter. Belle unleashed a verbal assault on ESPN reporter Hannah Storm during batting practice one day, simply because Storm had watched him hit.[87] In one of the greatest understatements in baseball history, Cleveland manager Mike Hargrove lamented, "With Albert, you take the good with the bad."[88]

In the end, Belle produced a lot of good on the baseball side of the ledger. Though his career was cut short by a degenerative hip condition, he hit 381 home runs, drove in 1,239 runs and had a career batting average of .295. His career numbers stack up well with Hall of Famers such as Tony Perez, Harmon Killebrew and Jim Rice, but Belle has never come close to being admitted to Cooperstown. There is no doubt that his chances of being elected to the Hall are hampered by his history of aggressive displays of temper. Belle's enduring reputation will be that of an individual who "never met a fastball he couldn't crush or a writer he wouldn't berate."[89] Late in Belle's career, after it had become clear that his hip condition would cause him to retire, Belle made an effort to show a warmer side to reporters. Once, upon hearing Belle address him in a softer and more welcoming voice, *Washington Post* sportswriter Thomas Boswell was prompted to say, "They learn to say hello when it's time to say goodbye."[90]

Gregg Jefferies's Rocky Start

On September 27, 1989, the Philadelphia Phillies played the New York Mets at Shea Stadium. With the Phillies leading 5-3 and two out in the top half of the ninth inning, Philadelphia manager Nick Leyva called on relief pitcher Roger McDowell to face the Mets' second baseman, Gregg Jefferies. McDowell induced Jefferies to hit into a ground out for the last out of the game. McDowell then directed some unflattering comments at Jefferies. Jefferies erupted, charging McDowell. Players from both teams raced from the dugouts, leading to a full-scale brawl.

The bad blood between McDowell and Jefferies likely dated back to September 1987. McDowell, then 26 years old, was in his third season as the Mets' closer. The 20-year old Jefferies had completed an historic season with the Double-A Jackson (Mississippi) Mets, in which he bashed 20 home runs, drove in 101 runs and hit .367. This followed a campaign in which Jefferies had hit .353 and was named the 1986 Minor League Player of the Year.

In recognition of Jefferies's accomplishments, the Mets summoned him to the Major Leagues in 1987 as a September call-up. Jefferies was on his way, or so he thought. Before his first game as a member of the Mets, a reporter asked him, "What do you hope to accomplish while you are here in the big leagues?" Never lacking for confidence, Jefferies answered, "I'm here to break Ty Cobb's records." As Joe McIlvaine, then the Mets assistant general manager, tells the story, the veterans in the clubhouse almost fell off their stools. With that one remark, Jefferies had turned virtually the entire clubhouse – a clubhouse in which McDowell was a key member – against him.

McIlvaine blames himself for Jefferies's rough start. "Normally when you bring a kid up," McIlvaine says, "you bring him into your office and you say something to him about talking to the press. You want him to know the kinds of questions he will get." Unfortunately, on the day of Jefferies's first game, McIlvaine was preoccupied with something else and didn't have a chance to talk with Jefferies.

Jefferies went on to have a respectable Major League career. In fourteen seasons, he compiled a .289 batting average, with a career best of .342 in 1993 while playing for the St. Louis Cardinals. However, he never came close to breaking the records established by Ty Cobb. In McIlvaine's view, Jefferies's unfortunate comment, uttered on the first day of his Major League career, haunted him for the rest of his career. "Gregg always had trouble on ball clubs because of that remark," McIlvaine says.

1988

Failing to allow your judgment to evolve can be a danger in scouting. Scouts can see a kid in high school and say things like, 'I don't think he's a prospect' or 'He doesn't have a position.' So the kid might go to college and when they see him in college, the scouts might still see the same guy. They disregard the improvement. I think that's what happened in [Mike] Piazza's case. They thought he was still the same guy. But when I saw him, I didn't have any of that background. It was all new to me. Yes, he was the last guy the Dodgers picked in the draft but when he swung that bat in batting practice, he didn't look at all like the last guy you would pick in the draft.

– Gib Bodet, long-time scout, Los Angeles Dodgers

The 1988 season was another big year for baseball. The Los Angeles Dodgers defeated the favored Oakland Athletics in a dramatic seven-game series highlighted by Kirk Gibson's memorable walk-off home run against Oakland's closer, Dennis Eckersley. In the now immortal words of Dodgers announcer Vin Scully, "in the year of the improbable, the impossible has happened." Part of the improbable scenario was the Dodgers, behind ace Orel Hershiser, beating the defending champion New York Mets to win the National League pennant.

The 1988 draft was a mini-reprise of the 1984 draft, as Team USA again set the stage for the draft. As in 1984, Team USA dominated the first round of the 1988 draft. The 1988 version of Team USA actually did something their more celebrated predecessors could not, as they beat Japan to win the Gold Medal in the Olympics. However, as the games were played half-way around the world in Korea and not in Los Angeles, there was less interest in the 1988 version of Team USA. Additionally, the 1988 version was much more focused on pitching than hitting and lacked sluggers such as Mark McGwire, Will Clark or Barry Larkin to captivate the fans.

The Padres were back in the familiar spot of owning the first draft pick. Their history with the number one overall pick was poor at best: Mike Ivie in 1970, Dave Roberts in 1972, and Bill Almon in 1974. The Padres deliberated between Olympic ace Andy Benes and closer Gregg Olson. Benes's stock had risen dramatically in a very short time. He had been a three-sport star in college but, in his junior year, played only baseball in order to narrow his focus. The results were dramatic. He struck out 21 batters in a game and elevated his fastball to touch 100 miles per hour. Almost immediately, scouts flocked to see him. When he shut out highly regarded Arizona State University in the opening round of the NCAA tournament in May, six Padres officials were in attendance. San Diego's scouting director, Tom Romenesko, described his performance as "awesome." The Padres drafted Benes with the number one pick and signed him to a record $235,000 bonus.

With the eighth overall pick, the Angels chose Olympian Jim Abbott, a left-handed pitcher from the University of Michigan. Abbott was the most well-known and most discussed draftee of 1988. He had pitched Team USA to victory in the Gold Medal game against Japan. Due to a congenital defect, Abbott lacked a right hand and therefore had to both throw and catch the baseball with his left arm. Sceptics doubted whether he could overcome the disability to field his position, but Abbott proved them wrong at every level.

Some observers believed the Angels' selection of Abbott was largely about attracting attention for his compelling human interest story. However, the Angels' hierarchy was firmly convinced that Abbott was capable of competing in the Major Leagues. Furthermore, Abbott's make-up, fueled by his tenacious desire to overcome his disability, was his most shining attribute. Angels scouting director Bob Fontaine, Jr. commented at the time, "This is the only kid I've ever signed that I'm 100 percent sure what kind of makeup he has."[91]

Abbott immediately validated the Angels' confidence. He made the team out of spring training in 1989, without ever playing in the minors, and won twelve games that year. His early career with the Angels fluctuated between seasons that were good and not so good. He flourished in 1991 when he won 18 games with a 2.89 earned run average. After the 1992 season, the Angels traded him to the New York Yankees. Though Abbott pitched a no-hitter with New York in September 1993, he never reclaimed the success he enjoyed in 1991. He pitched for ten seasons in the big leagues and won 87 games overall, with 108 losses. However, Abbott's legacy in baseball is less about wins and losses and more about the continuing inspiration he provided to countless individuals with disabilities.

The Chicago White Sox selected third baseman Robin Ventura with the tenth pick in the draft. Ventura turned out to be one of the best players in the draft. He was the 1988 Golden Spikes Award winner as the best player in college baseball and had been a veritable hitting machine at Oklahoma State, where he hit .469 as a freshman. Given Ventura's accomplishments, it was surprising that he lasted until the tenth pick in the draft. He had begun to capture national attention in his sophomore season of college when he put together a 58-game hitting streak. In his junior season, Ventura hit .391 with 26 home runs and 96 runs batted in. His efforts helped lead the Oklahoma State Cowboys to 61 wins. He continued to pound the ball in the Olympics, hitting .409 for Team USA.

Girardi's Promise

Gary Nickels has had a role in drafting several notable big league ballplayers. His signees include pitcher Chad Billingsley and catcher A.J. Ellis, among others. However, it was the signing of catcher Joe Girardi that will always hold a special place among Nickels' baseball memories.

When Girardi was 13 years old, his mother, Angela, was diagnosed with cancer. Her doctors told her that she had three to six months to live. Angela ended up surviving for six years, succumbing in 1984. Girardi tells people that his mother was a woman of faith. "At the end," he says, "she had a vision the Lord had his arms open for her, and it was time for her to come home." In the time before Angela died, Girardi made a promise to his mother that he would continue in school and earn his college degree.

At the time of Angela's death, Girardi was a sophomore at Northwestern University and a fixture at catcher for the university's baseball team. Nickels, then scouting for the Chicago Cubs, had followed Girardi during his college career and believed he possessed Major League potential. In 1985, after three years of college, Girardi was eligible for the Major League Draft. Nickels briefly gave thought to recommending that the Cubs draft him. However, Girardi had made it clear to Nickels that he intended to fulfill his promise to his mother and would remain at Northwestern for his senior year.

The Cubs passed on Girardi in 1985. He received his degree the following year, and the Cubs drafted him with their fifth round pick in June 1986. Three years later, Girardi was catching for the Cubs.

Always high on Girardi, Nickels became even more convinced that Girardi would go far in baseball when he saw his determination to fulfill the promise he had made. Nickels says, "It meant a lot to me that he would make that decision. He was going to honor his commitment to his mother."

Years later, Nickels still cherishes his experience with Girardi. "That was a pleasant one," he says, "because he had a long career as a catcher and a very good career as a manager and has had quite an impact on the game over the last 30 years."

1989

Ben McDonald was one of the more dominant pitchers we had seen. We saw him pitch against Oklahoma State and he struck out sixteen hitters. He was probably recognized as the top arm in the nation that year. The Orioles had gone from the worst team in baseball in 1988 to challenging the Blue Jays for the playoffs in 1989. Part of the pressure when we were trying to sign McDonald was whether he could have helped the Orioles down the pennant stretch that same year. McDonald definitely stood out.

    –John Barr, former scouting director, Baltimore Orioles; former vice
    president and assistant general manager, San Francisco Giants

The 1989 World Series was again an all-California affair. The epicenter of baseball had clearly moved to the West Coast. The Oakland Athletics shook off their devastating loss to the Dodgers in the 1988 series and dominated the San Francisco Giants in the so-called "BART Series." The Athletics took the Series from the Giants in a four-game sweep in which Oakland never trailed.

While the A's made quick work of the Giants on the field, it turned out to be the longest World Series in terms of days spanned from first pitch to final out. The ground at San Francisco's Candlestick Park literally moved underneath the two teams before the start of the third game as the result of an earthquake. The catastrophic Loma Prieta quake measured 6.9 on the Richter scale and claimed 63 lives. The Bay Area suffered over $5 billion in damage, halting the World Series for 10 days.

The increasing significance of the draft was evident in the Series as the Giants were led by recent high first-round picks Will Clark, drafted in 1985, and Matt Williams, drafted in 1986. Similarly, the Athletics received significant contributions from recent early first-rounders Mark McGwire, drafted in 1984, and Walt Weiss, selected in 1985. Further, former overall number one pick, Mike Moore, a 1981 draft pick of the Mariners, truly hit his stride with the Athletics. Moore had 19 wins during the season and then in the World Series won two games against the Giants. In 13 innings of pitching during the Series, Moore allowed only three runs.

While the draft was still evolving in 1989, the seeds of a seismic shift in bonus payment escalation began to take root. Big bonus money had come to the fore with the 1988 class. The prior year's number one selection, Andy Benes, had received a record bonus amount of $235,000. Benes's bonus was more than double the highest bonus of 1977.

In its twenty-fifth year, the draft set a record for the most players ever drafted (1,490) and for the most rounds (87). In addition to being a deep class, it would produce as many Hall of Fame players as any draft class in history. It was also a year of physically big, dominating players.

Big Ben McDonald of Louisiana State University, who stood an imposing six-feet-seven, was the first overall selection. Like Andy Benes the year before, McDonald had starred for Team USA during the team's Gold Medal success of 1988. There was almost unanimous agreement that McDonald was the best talent in the 1989 draft. The Baltimore Orioles, who owned the number one pick as a result of their 107 losses in 1988, scooped McDonald up.

McDonald relied primarily on a blazing fastball and an excellent curve and, perhaps most impressively for a pitcher of his size and velocity, he possessed pinpoint control. While Yankee scouting director Brian Sabean believed McDonald's fastball was good enough for him to be a "pure power-er pitcher" in the big leagues,[92] McDonald also possessed two secondary pitches, a curve and a forkball, to supplement the heater if needed. In his junior year at LSU, Big Ben struck out 202 batters in 152 innings and, at one point, did not allow a run for 45 consecutive innings.[93]

As the draft drew near, Orioles general manager Roland Hemond, scouting director John Barr and their scouts were certain that McDonald would be their choice to help turn around their last-place fortunes. The biggest concern would be signing McDonald – Scott Boras was serving as his agent. Boras's reputation had grown considerably since he first entered the draft day discussions while representing Tim Belcher in 1983. Boras, who could leverage almost any negotiation to his client's advantage, was gifted with a major bargaining chip from New York real estate magnate Donald Trump. Trump was reportedly interested in starting a rival pro-fessional baseball league.[94] Boras bartered a reported offer of $2 million from the unnamed league into a record $350,000 signing bonus from the Orioles, plus other guarantees and incentives that could bring the worth of the contract to a staggering $1.1 million.[95]

After McDonald had pitched in just two games in the minors, Balti-more called him up in September 1989. In July 1990, he made his first start for the Orioles and earned a victory against the Chicago White Sox with a four-hit complete game. He went on to win his next two starts and eight games in all in 1990 while pitching to a stellar 2.43 earned run average. Though McDonald appeared to be on the verge of success, a series of injuries derailed his career. He did not have a winning season again until 1994, when he went 14-7. The Orioles gave up on him after the 1995 season and allowed him to sign with Milwaukee as a free agent. For his career, Big Ben barely won more than he lost. His career won-lost record was 78 wins and 70 losses, and he posted a pedestrian 3.91 earned run average. His performance numbers rank him nearly in the middle of all overall number one picks in the first fifty years of the draft.

The Chicago White Sox and scout Mike Rizzo went big with the seventh pick of the first round when they selected six-foot-five Frank Thomas, a first baseman out of Auburn University. Thomas would quickly prove to be a big hit for the Sox. He became the only first-round selection in the 1989 draft to be elected to the Hall of Fame. Rizzo, the son of a scout, was literally raised on the game. More so than anyone else, Rizzo was convinced that Thomas was the real deal. While Rizzo gave Thomas a maximum "80" rating for his power hitting, many other scouts were mixed in their assessment. The Major League Scouting Bureau didn't even rank him as a first-round talent. Rizzo very clearly and unambiguously stated that Thomas was "the top bat around."[96]

Rizzo also identified that Thomas had a quick bat and a superior batting eye. "He would very rarely get himself out," Rizzo reported.[97] At Chicago's pre-draft meetings, Rizzo doubled down on his bold assessment, calling Thomas "the best amateur in the whole country."[98] He even predicted that Thomas would hit 30 home runs and bat .300 or better every year. Rizzo's firm and unqualified endorsement of Thomas persuaded Sox general manager Larry Himes and scouting director Al Goldis to draft him with the seventh pick. Himes allowed Rizzo to negotiate the contract with Thomas. For a relatively modest $175,000, the White Sox secured a future Hall of Famer.

It didn't take long for Thomas to validate Rizzo's faith in him. He was up with the big club for 60 games the very next year. Then, in 1991, he hit 32 homers, drove in 109 runs, batted .318 and, for good measure, led the American League with 138 walks. His performance in succeeding years was so outstanding that it made Rizzo's predictions seem understated by comparison. Thomas reached the 40 home run mark five times in his brilliant career. In three seasons, he had batting averages of .347 or better. Just four years after he was drafted, he won back-to-back American League Most Valuable Player Awards. Thomas played for 19 years in the Major Leagues. His batting average dipped precipitously in his last decade. He finished his career with a lifetime average of .301, with 521 homers and 1,704 runs batted in. He was elected to the Hall of Fame on the first ballot in 2014.

While the 1989 draft was keenly anticipated for its glut of swift and athletic multi-tooled high school outfielders, it ironically turned out to be chocked full of large and lumbering collegiate first base talents.[99] The Red Sox used the 23rd pick of the first round to select another big slugging first sacker in left-handed power-hitting Mo Vaughn of Seton Hall. Though the six-foot-one Vaughn was not nearly as tall as Thomas, he was much wider and just as fearsome with a bat in his hands. Vaughn's career ended prematurely and abruptly due to injuries, but he still posted excellent career numbers with a .293 batting average, 328 home runs and 1,064 runs batted in.

In the third round, the 1989 narrative again focused on another stellar first baseman. Washington State junior John Olerud was generally considered to be, at worst, the second-best prospect in the class. The biggest question about Olerud was whether he projected as a hitter or a pitcher. He had earned college All-American honors at both first base and pitcher. In 1988, at Washington State, he hit .464 with twenty-three homers and had a 15-0 record as a pitcher. The discussion as to where Olerud would fit in best at the Major League level appeared to be moot when he suffered a life-threatening brain aneurysm in January 1989. In the aftermath of the aneurysm, Olerud publicly announced that he would return to Washington State for his senior season.[100]

Blue Jays general manager Pat Gillick was still determined to sign Olerud. His persistence and a whole lot of bonus money ultimately changed Olerud's mind. The Jays drafted him with the 79th overall pick and then opened up the coffers, which were flush due to the financial success of their new ballpark, the SkyDome. Toronto offered Olerud an unprecedented signing bonus of $575,000. Even as the ink had barely dried on McDonald's record-setting $350,000 bonus, the Blue Jays paid Olerud $225,000 more. For some perspective, Andy Benes's record-setting bonus in 1988 totaled only $235,000.

Amazingly, Olerud went straight to the big leagues that year, making his debut on September 3, 1989. The Jays decided they wanted his left-handed bat in the lineup every day, so Olerud focused on playing first base and abandoned the pitching mound. He established himself as a superior defensive first baseman and as a key middle-of-the-order power source who could hit for a high average. He won the American League batting title in 1993 with a .363 average. The Blue Jays traded Olerud to the New York Mets before the 1997 season and he continued to display his consistency in New York. Near the end of his career, he spent five seasons playing for the Mariners in his home state of Washington. He retired after a 17-year career with 255 homers, 1,230 runs batted in, and a .295 batting average.

The Blue Jays also drafted second baseman Jeff Kent from the University of California at Berkeley in the 20th round. While the Jays traded Kent to the New York Mets after only 65 games, they were able to acquire star pitcher David Cone in exchange. Kent went on to play for six teams over 17 seasons. His best years came with the San Francisco Giants in the period from 1997 to 2002, when he was elected to three All-Star teams. He won the National League Most Valuable Player Award in 2000, when he hit .334 with 33 homers and 125 runs batted in. Over the course of his career, Kent hit 377 homers, drove in 1,518 runs and batted .290. He is the only second baseman in history to have driven in more than 100 runs in eight different seasons.

While any team would have been happy to secure the services of a first baseman like Mo Vaughn in the draft, the Red Sox found an even better first sacker in the fourth round when they drafted hometown native Jeff Bagwell out of the University of Hartford. Although Bagwell was a third baseman at Hartford, his defensive shortcomings required him to shift to first base. Due to his spotty defense and lack of power, Bagwell lasted until the fourth round. Though he was signed by Red Sox scout Erwin Bryant, the credit for Bagwell's development rested mostly with Astros scout Tom Mooney.

Mooney had scouted Bagwell at Hartford. However, his report on Bagwell was less than enthusiastic. He noted Bagwell's obvious defensive shortcomings, his pronounced lack of footspeed and his lack of power. He did, though, project Bagwell to develop power comparable to Kansas City's "all or nothing" slugger, Steve Balboni.[101] As Mooney continued to follow Bagwell in the Red Sox minor league system, he became increasingly impressed with Bagwell's baseball acumen and dedication and highly recommended him to his Houston superiors as a trade target. Scouting director Dan O'Brien recalled, "Tom was very firm in his conviction ... and recommended we acquire [him]. He never wavered on that."[102] The Astros heeded Mooney's repeated pleas for Bagwell and, in one of the most one-sided trades in baseball history, acquired him from the Red Sox in August of 1990 for pitcher Larry Andersen. Not even Mooney could have imagined how well Bagwell would perform in a Houston uniform.

Once Bagwell made the Astros' roster in 1991, he was in Houston to stay. He would team with Craig Biggio as the mainstays of the Astros for the next 15 years. Bagwell was an immediate success, winning the Rookie of the Year Award. His power numbers improved each of the next two years. He learned to drive the ball with backspin and, by 1994, he was the National League's Most Valuable Player, with 39 homers, 116 runs batted in, and a .368 batting average. Bagwell remained in the MVP conversation for most of his career in Houston. He hit 449 lifetime home runs, with 1,529 runs batted in and a .297 batting average. Bagwell was elected to the Hall of Fame in 2017.

The unprecedented procession of first base Hall of Fame talent continued in the thirteenth round as the Cleveland Indians plucked Jim Thome from unheralded Illinois Central College in East Peoria, Illinois. Thome stood six-foot-four. Amazingly, he played shortstop in college, where he was recognized as an All-American. Indians scout Tom Couston discovered Thome when he went to observe another player at Illinois Central. Couston came away from the game far more impressed with Thome. The scout attempted to conceal his interest in the large shortstop by speaking to Thome with his back facing Thome's back.[103] Couston noted, "Thome may have gone 0 for 4, but every ball he hit was a rocket. His swing was so quick and powerful I am surprised he didn't kill somebody."[104] While observing the ball jump off Thome's bat that day, Couston had no doubt that Thome would play in the majors.[105]

Like Bagwell, Thome was moved to first base in the minors. He reached the majors by 1991. It took time for him to acclimate to big league pitching but he began to figure it out by 1994, hitting 20 homers and batting .268. Thome's home run and RBI numbers continued to climb until he truly broke out in 1996, when he hit 38 homers and had 116 runs batted in. In 2002, his final year with Cleveland, Thome slugged a career high 52 homers. He would play at a high level for another ten years, spending time with seven different teams. When he finally hung up his spikes, he had a 22-year Major League career with 612 homers and 1,699 runs batted in. He followed Thomas and Bagwell into the Hall of Fame in 2018. At his induction ceremony, he specifically thanked Tom Couston for believing in him.

In the 11th round, the Cincinnati Reds drafted Trevor Hoffman. Hoffman had played shortstop at the University of Arizona. Jeff Barton, the

Cincinnati scout who signed Hoffman, stated in his report that Hoffman "couldn't hit and couldn't run."[106] However, Barton went on to say, "He has the best arm I'd ever seen."[107] The Reds signed Hoffman for $3,000 and made him a pitcher. Hoffman worked hard in the minors to develop off-speed pitches that would complement his 95-mph fastball. He started to experiment with a change-up. The Florida Marlins selected Hoffman in the 1992 expansion draft and brought him to the majors. As he began to get the hang of pitching, the Marlins traded him to the San Diego Padres in a monster deal that brought Gary Sheffield to the Marlins. Hoffman needed shoulder surgery in 1995 and lost some muscle on his fastball but had refined his change-up to the point that it became his signature pitch.[108]

Hoffman would stay in San Diego for 16 years. It was there that he would accrue the vast majority of his 601 saves and a reputation as one of the best closers of all time. He would enter games as the Padres' closer with his signature AC/DC theme song, "Hells Bells," playing in the background. Hoffman was inducted into the Hall of Fame in 2018.

Chip Ambres

Outfielder Chip Ambres was a first-round pick of the Florida Marlins in 1998, the 27th pick overall. The Marlins were surprised and pleased that Ambres was still available so late in the first round. They had rated him as the sixth or seventh best player in the nation.

In high school, Ambres was a versatile, all-around athlete who possessed great speed. He played quarterback on the West Brook Senior High School football team in Beaumont, Texas and was a second-team All-American in baseball.

Ambres spent six years in the Marlins' system, advancing as high as Double-A. He hit for a .316 average in his first season but saw his average decline in subsequent years. Ambres never developed into the power hitter that the Marlins had expected, though he did hit 20 home runs in 2004 for the Double-A Carolina Mudcats.

Ambres became a free agent after the 2004 season and signed with the Boston Red Sox. Boston then dealt him to Kansas City, and he reached the Major Leagues with the Royals in July 2005. Ambres appeared in 53 games for Kansas City and hit .241 with four home runs. He would make brief appearances with the New York Mets in 2007 and the San Diego Padres in 2008, but did not hit well enough to stick.

Marlins scout Orrin Freeman was a big fan of Ambres and a strong advocate. "He was a great kid," Freeman said, "it was a great disappointment." Freeman suspected that a knee injury deprived Ambres of his exceptional speed. As Ambres advanced in his career, Freeman said, he was never on a team that had a spot open for him to play. "I thought he would have had a much better career," Freeman said.

1990

You watch a guy – I saw it in Mike Mussina when he was in high school – there was no place that he enjoyed more than being right there on that mound, no matter what the situation was. I think that's one thing you look for. When you see it, and it doesn't come around very often, you better get it, because that is the kind of guy who is going to win for you later on. Even in high school, you could tell from his demeanor on the mound how much he wanted to compete. He took that competitiveness with him into the college ranks. He ended up graduating in three-and-a-half years out of Stanford. That gave us an example of his make-up and his determination.

> –John Barr, former scouting director, Baltimore Orioles; former vice president and assistant general manager, San Francisco Giants

The 1990 draft may be thought of as a tale of two teams, two special amateur players and one very talented and significant player agent. The two teams, the Oakland Athletics and the Atlanta Braves, were at opposite ends of the baseball world. The defending World Champion Athletics were on their way to 103 wins and another appearance in the World Series. The Braves languished in last place in the National League West and would lose 97 games in 1990.

In mid-season, Atlanta general manager Bobby Cox would replace Russ Nixon as manager and John Schuerholz would replace Cox as general manager. These moves would be two of the most significant in Major League history, as both Cox and Schuerholz would go on to the Hall of Fame in their new posts. In June of 1990, however, Cox was still the general manager and the Braves, having finished dead last in Major League Baseball in 1989, had the number one pick in the draft.

The nature of the draft itself was changing as bonus payments rose dramatically. In 1990, due to the influx of money coming from baseball's new television contract, the bonuses paid to top prospects escalated significantly.[109] For the first few decades or so after the draft was instituted in 1965, the draft had accomplished baseball's main goal of reversing the rise in bonus payments to unproven amateurs. However, the pendulum was starting to swing back towards the players. This shift was not the result of any new-found altruism by the owners to share more of their increased revenues. Rather, the escalation of bonuses stemmed in large part from the innovative negotiating tactics of player agent Scott Boras.

As was the case in 1989, a consensus had formed that a tall right-handed pitcher was the clear number one player in the class. In fact, Texas school phenom Todd Van Poppel and his 95-mph fastball were drawing comparisons to Nolan Ryan. Montreal Expos scouting director Gary Hughes said, "Van Poppel is head and shoulders above anyone else. Anyone would take him Number One."[110] Al Goldis, the White Sox director of scouting, was even more glowing in his praise. "He has the best arm on any pitcher I've ever seen," Goldis said.[111]

As with Ben McDonald, Scott Boras was the agent representing Van Poppel. Armed with a scholarship offer to play at the University of Texas, Van Poppel had greater negotiating leverage than McDonald. Before the draft, Van Poppel had announced that he was planning to enroll in college. The combustible combination of Boras's relentless representation style and an advantageous negotiating position boded well for Van Poppel.

In most any prior year, the Braves would have been the logical candidate to draft Van Poppel with the number one pick. However, it seemed all but sure that Van Poppel would follow in the footsteps of Clemens, Greg Swindell, Calvin Schiraldi and the many other early draft picks who had played for the University of Texas. Some teams may have dismissed Van Poppel's declaration as "posturing." Bobby Cox and Braves scouting director Paul Snyder offered a reported $1 million to entice Van Poppel to turn pro. However, Van Poppel remained adamant in his decision to attend Texas and would not even meet with the Braves himself. The Braves even tried to have the fabled Red Murff, who had signed Nolan Ryan for the Mets, speak with Van Poppel but it was to no avail.[112] The Braves were extremely disappointed, especially because, in Murff's judgment, Van Poppel "had the best arsenal he had seen since Ryan."[113]

With their hopes of adding Van Poppel to their emerging core of young pitching talent in Glavine, Smoltz and Steve Avery dashed, the Braves moved on to another top prospect, high school star Larry Wayne Jones. Jones himself was planning to play for the University of Miami. The switch-hitting Jones, who went by the nickname "Chipper," played at the Bolles School in Jacksonville, Florida and was considered to be one of the best hitters in the nation. He had hit .488 in his senior season of high school and was named Florida's Player of the Year.

While Jones was considered in some quarters to be a so-called "signability pick" – a euphemistic way to say he was not the Braves' first choice – he would become much more than a consolation prize. Irony, of course, is the draft's constant companion and it was never on more display than in 1990. Chipper Jones would go on to become one of the best overall number one selections of all time. In a further bit of irony, Boras met with Jones and his family in hopes of representing him. As Jones recounts the story in his autobiography, *Chipper Jones, Ballplayer*, he was viscerally turned off by Boras and actually walked out on the meeting with him.[114] Jones chose to be represented by his father, Larry, instead of by an agent. Nonetheless, signability picks would become more and more common in the coming years of the draft, especially when Boras represented one or more of the top talents.

The Braves sent top scout Tony DeMacio, who had signed Tom Glavine, and Dean Jongewaard, brother of Roger, to meet with Jones the night before the draft. The two persuaded Chipper to sign for $275,000, which would be less than the bonuses paid to five other players who were drafted after Jones. At one point, Chipper's father pulled Chipper aside and explained that he was leaving significant money on the table by agreeing to the deal.

In a decision strikingly similar to the one Ken Griffey Jr. had made three years earlier, Jones agreed to accept the below market bonus. He was confident that his ability would yield even bigger returns in the future. The night before the draft, the Braves gladly accepted Jones's signature on the contract.[115] The occasion was the third time that a Jongewaard would be involved in signing an overall number one pick. Dean's brother, Roger, had previously helped to sign Darryl Strawberry for the Mets and Ken Griffey Jr. for the Mariners.

The Braves allowed Jones to proceed through their minor league system at a slow and steady pace. He joined the Braves for good in 1995 and became an integral part of their success in the mid-1990s and early into the next century. Jones would become an eight-time All-Star and the National League's Most Valuable Player in 1999. After David Justice was traded to Cleveland in 1997, Jones provided the most authoritative bat on the Braves' teams. Over his 19-year Major League career, he hit .303, with 468 home runs, 1,623 runs batted in and 150 stolen bases. He was inducted into the Hall of Fame in 2018 with 97.2 percent of the vote. He is considered the third best switch-hitter of all time behind Mickey Mantle and Eddie Murray and perhaps the best "consolation prize" of all time.

While the Braves were disappointed at first when they could not persuade Van Poppel to sign, in retrospect the signing of Chipper Jones was one of the most important and fortuitous events in the history of the franchise. Under the able leadership of Schuerholz and Cox, the Braves were about to have an historic 1991 season, when they went from last place to first place in one season. With Jones providing power and baseball savvy, Atlanta would be a dominant National League powerhouse for the next two decades.

In 1990, the Oakland Athletics appeared to be in a position to execute one of the biggest draft coups in history. Due to additional picks awarded as compensation for players who had departed in free agency, the A's had seven picks in the first two rounds. Oakland had the fourteenth overall pick. The preceding thirteen teams had all passed on Van Poppel, each convinced that he was unalterably committed to Texas.

Sandy Alderson, the A's general manager and architect of their world championship team, gambled that he could sign Van Poppel. In a sense, with seven picks in his pocket, Alderson was playing with house money. When Van Poppel first learned that the A's had drafted him, he said, "If they think they can buy me, they're wrong. Money's not everything."[116] However, Alderson adopted a low-key approach that proved persuasive and enticed Van Poppel to sign for a $500,000 signing bonus and a three-year contract worth $1.2 million. While team executives would become suspicious of any signing that involved Scott Boras, Van Poppel's change of heart appeared genuine. Sincerity aside, the Van Poppel saga served as a primer for future prospects on how to manipulate the signing process, often with the able advice and assistance of Boras.

There was undoubtedly some resentment toward Alderson and the A's for landing Van Poppel. There was also a simmering sense of unfairness that the best team in baseball had landed the player perceived to be the best prospect available. With the benefit of hindsight, however, any such concerns would dissipate because Van Poppel turned out to be one of the biggest busts in draft history. Initially, he moved through Oakland's minor league system with ease and made his Major League debut on September 11, 1991. However, his audition was less than successful, as he yielded five earned runs in 4.2 innings. Oakland immediately returned him to the minors. Everyone agreed that he needed more minor league seasoning. Even with a 95-mph fastball, Van Poppel had to sharpen his breaking pitches to be successful in the majors.

Van Poppel spent the entire 1992 season and much of 1993 with the Triple-A Tacoma Tigers. Under the terms of his contract, Oakland was required to bring him back to the Major Leagues by 1994 or he would become a free agent. He pitched for the Athletics, without success, from July 1993 to July 1996. In August 1996, with Van Poppel's earned run average hovering at well over seven runs per game, Oakland placed him on waivers and he was claimed by the Detroit Tigers. He would go on to play for four other teams over an 11-year career but never realized his potential. He retired at the end of the 2004 season with a 40-52 won-lost record and a 5.58 earned run average. If he had been taken first in the draft, Van Poppel would rank among the most disappointing number one picks of all time.

Oakland had three first-round picks remaining after the selection of Van Poppel. The A's used the picks to draft three college pitchers, Don Peters of the University of St. Francis, David Zancanaro of UCLA and Kirk Dressendorfer of the University of Texas. Shortly after the draft, *Baseball America*, the "bible" for draft analysis, published an edition with Van Poppel and Oakland's other three first-round selections featured under the title, "Four Aces." It looked as if Alderson and the A's had put together a staff to continue their dynasty for years to come. As seen time and time again, however, future developments rarely proceed as anticipated on draft day. The "big haul" that Oakland expected never materialized.

Of the so-called "Four Aces," only Van Poppel and Dressendorfer ever spent time in the Major Leagues. Of the two, Dressendorfer had the far shorter career. He made only seven starts for the A's and finished with a 3-3 won-lost record and a 5.45 earned run average. In total, the "Four Aces" produced 21 wins for Oakland. Oakland had three picks in the second round, all of whom were similarly disappointing. Of the Athletics' second-round selections, only catcher Eric Helfand of Arizona State University reached the majors. Over parts of three seasons with Oakland, Helfand accumulated only 105 at-bats and had a batting average of .171. In the end, all the Athletics had to show for their seven picks in the first two rounds were three marginal players.

After enduring a disappointing 1988 season, in which they were the worst team in baseball, the Baltimore Orioles were on the upswing. Their on-field play improved dramatically in 1989 as they came within two games of wresting the American League East Division from the Toronto Blue Jays. With construction under way for a new ballpark, the iconic Camden Yards, the Orioles' trajectory appeared bright. Scouting director John Barr felt it necessary to add another stud pitcher to team with McDonald and focused on Stanford University pitching ace Mike Mussina. Unlike the prior year when the Orioles had the first overall pick, however, Baltimore was picking at number 20 in 1990. Barr and his scouts Ed Sprague Sr. and Fred Ullman fully expected that Mussina would gone by the time the Orioles picked. When, finally, the San Francisco Giants, picking at number 19, selected catcher Eric Christopherson, elation reigned in Baltimore; Mussina was going to be a Baltimore Oriole.

The Orioles had been eyeing Mussina and his pitching ability for many years, ever since he starred at Montoursville High School in Montoursville, Pennsylvania. Baltimore had drafted him in the eleventh round in 1987 after his senior year of high school. Mussina was hardly a local secret. He had developed a national reputation with the USA Junior Olympic Team, when he defeated the highly touted Cuban team, 1-0. Mussina had pitched a gem against Cuba, striking out 16 batters. "I didn't think it was any big deal," Mussina said, "I struck out 16 in high school games all the time."[117]

The game against Cuba was a big deal, however, because the stands were filled with scouts. Mussina rocketed up the pre-draft rankings. He was considered perhaps the best high school prospect in the 1987 draft and clearly would have been an early first round pick if teams thought he would sign. It was well-known, however, that Mussina intended to attend Stanford. Chicago Cubs area scout Billy Blitzer spoke for most everyone when he noted in his report on Mussina, "He is unsignable. Signed letter of intent to Stanford. Father is wealthy lawyer who will not accept less than $250,000."[118] Another very wealthy and famous lawyer, Orioles owner Edward Bennett Williams, was undeterred and personally led the negotiations for the Orioles. Williams offered Mussina a $175,000 signing bonus. If Mussina had accepted, the deal would have been the largest bonus paid in 1987. Blitzer was right, however. No amount of money was going to keep Mussina from attending Stanford.

On draft day of 1990, many teams devalued their assessment of Mussina. A scout can easily fall into the trap of attaching too much weight to a small or recent sample size. Mussina was both a beneficiary and a victim of this phenomenon. While his gem against Cuba had vaulted him into consideration as the top pick of 1987, Mussina had a poor outing against the University of Georgia on the eve of the 1990 draft. The outing caused many teams to look elsewhere. However, the Orioles were not about to be deterred by one bad game. They were most impressed by Mussina's make-up. In Mussina, both Barr and Sprague had seen a combination of competitiveness and preternatural composure on the mound. In addition, Mussina possessed an excellent repertoire to complement his demeanor: a top-shelf fastball, an excellent curve and a devastating change of pace. Further, he was an extraordinary athlete who gave his team another quality defender in the infield.[119]

This time around, the Orioles were able to get Mussina's signature on a contract. However, it took nearly two months of negotiation and $250,000. For the Orioles, it would prove to be money well-spent. Mussina was an intense competitor for his whole career, and he became a model of consistency, winning at least eleven games for seventeen years in a row. Twice he won nineteen games. Not until his last season, 2008, however, did he manage to win 20 games in a season. In his Major League career, Mussina won 270 games and struck out 2,813 batters. He appeared in five All-Star Games and was inducted into the Hall of Fame in 2019.

70 Power, Soft Hands

Andre Keene was a first baseman/outfielder from Duval High School in Lanham, Maryland. Keene stood six-foot-five and weighed 240 pounds.

Former scout Mike Toomey becomes wistful when he speaks of Keene's talent. According to Toomey, "On a scale of 20-80, with 50 being the Major League average, Keene was 70 power, 60 runner, soft hands." Toomey remembers Major League players coming out to the field during spring training to watch Keene take batting practice. "He had that kind of power," Toomey says.

The knock against Keene was that he lacked a passion for playing baseball. When Toomey would want Keene to take batting practice in front of the Giants' cross-checker, he would have to make a special effort to get Keene to come out of the locker room. "He's the one guy I knew who didn't have the passion to play baseball," Toomey says. He adds, "Some players are just late bloomers."

Toomey was hopeful that Keene would come around. So were the Giants. San Francisco drafted Keene in the 32nd round in 1990. In his first season in the Giants' organization, he batted .348 in 44 games but hit only one home run. Keene played four seasons in the minor leagues but never advanced beyond the Giants' high Class A team in San Jose.

Keene and the Giants parted ways after the 1995 season. In 384 minor league games, he hit .273 with 42 home runs. After his minor league career ended, Keene played baseball for six seasons in the independent leagues.

1991

[Brien Taylor] was a rock star. I don't think I have ever seen anything like it in the minor leagues. In Albany, he had lines of kids asking for his autograph. He needed the challenge of Double-A. He couldn't hold runners on a base. Nobody had ever gotten on base against him before so he never had to learn how to hold runners. It was a nice problem. He'd give up a home run at Albany and it was like it was a new experience for him. Nobody had ever hit the guy in high school. There was never anybody on base against him. The first time I ever saw him pitch was underneath the grandstands in Wilmington, North Carolina. He was throwing 98 mph but it didn't look 98. He was throwing so easy. That's what he was. He was just a rare specimen.

—Bill Livesey, scout and former director of player development, New York Yankees

In the 1991 draft, the first two picks, Brien Taylor and Mike Kelly, were widely considered to be head and shoulders above the competition. Their stories serve as cautionary, yet representative, tales.

The factors accompanying the first overall selection combined for "the perfect storm." Left-handed high school pitcher Brien Taylor was considered to be the best player in the country by far. For the first time since 1967, the financially flush New York Yankees held the first overall pick. Scott Boras, who had negotiated Todd Van Poppel's record shattering $1.2 million bonus in 1990, was retained to serve as Taylor's representative.

Taylor hailed from humble circumstances in Beaufort, North Carolina, on the Carolina coastline. He had dominated hitters at East Carteret High School with a fastball approaching 100 mph. In 88 innings he struck out 213 batters and pitched to an earned run average of 1.25. Scout Ron Rizzi, a former pitcher, considered Brien Taylor to be the best amateur pitcher in high school or college he had ever seen. Almost every scout concurred, including Yankees scouting director Bill Livesey who described Taylor as "the best high school pitching prospect I ever scouted."

Yankees general manager, Gene Michael, was one of the best talent evaluators in baseball. Michael may have faced the most trying circumstances of any general manager in the game because of the consistent and uninformed meddling of the Yankees' principal owner, George M. Steinbrenner III. The Yankees were almost always facing a competitive disadvantage in the draft due to Steinbrenner's penchant for signing "big name" and high-priced free agents. Livesey would bemoan the fact that the Yankees had to forfeit most of their early round picks as compensation for free agent signings. "We lost 18 or 19 picks in the 1980s due to signing free agents. One year, we didn't pick until the fourth round."[120]

The prior two drafts had already exposed cracks in the draft's carefully constructed bonus restraint structure. In 1991, the fissures expanded beyond control. The negotiations between Boras and the Yankees were long and contentious. Ironically, Boras's hand was strengthened by Steinbrenner, who publicly stated that if the Yankees didn't sign Taylor, "someone should be shot."[121] Michael was well aware that he was the "someone." The Yankees opening offer of $350,000 was summarily dismissed by Taylor and his mother Bettie. Bettie Taylor remained adamant that her son would not sign for a penny less than Von Poppel's record amount. She quickly demonstrated that her lack of formal education should not be mistaken for a lack of negotiating savvy. At the end of the day, the Taylors and Boras obtained a record $1.55 million bonus.

Without the slightest recognition of his role in boxing Michael into a negotiating corner, the normally profligate Steinbrenner lambasted the bonus amount. "Never in my wildest dreams would I have paid that kid a million and a half," he railed. "No damn way ... I'm getting damn tired of people spending my money like this."[122] Padres' general manager Joe McIlvaine termed the record signing "not a smart thing. ... If other clubs use these deals as a barometer we'll all go out of business."[123] Despite the many doomsday predictions, the draft would continue to provide larger and larger bonuses for the next decade.

Taylor pitched for two seasons in the minors and exhibited enough of the dominating traits that had been on display in high school for the Yankees to feel confident Taylor was on his way to a long and successful career. Then on one fateful evening in the off-season of 1993 all their hopes and expectations flew out the window as Taylor injured his left shoulder in a bar fight while nobly trying to defend his younger brother.

Taylor had torn his labrum which forced him to miss the entire 1994 season. When he returned in 1995, he had lost significant velocity off his once blazing fastball and he could not even throw his formerly devastating curveball over the plate. Scouts who had seen him prior to the injury could not believe he was the same pitcher. While he continued to play for five more minor league seasons, the injury effectively ended his once promising career. Like Steve Chilcott, he will unfortunately be remembered as another overall number one pick that would never play a single inning in the Major Leagues.

Arizona State University center fielder Mike Kelly was viewed by teams as the best prospect not named Brien Taylor. Kelly had won the Golden Spikes Award as the national collegiate player of the year, hitting .396 with 21 home runs. Long-time scout Carl Loewenstine considered Kelly to be the epitome of the "five-tool player," – "a can't miss prospect." The Braves selected Kelly with the second pick of the draft and expected him to join 1990 first round selectee Chipper Jones to form a dynamic one-two punch in their batting order for many years to come. Instead he would join Taylor as one of the great draft disappointments of all time. Kelly's struggles began in the minors as he only batted .229 at Double-A Greenville. Although he finally made it to the majors in 1995, he hit a paltry .190 with only three homers. Kelly would play in the majors for parts of five years but he never hit more than ten homers in a season.

As was the case with Augie Schmidt in 1982, Mike Kelly undoubtedly wondered how a game that was so easy in college could become so challenging in the pros. Loewenstine explained the apparent contradiction by referencing a time-honored scouting expression: "The game became too fast for him." At the professional level, everything requires a faster response time. Loewenstine believes that Kelly could not adjust to the accelerated pace of the professional game. He lamented: "Kelly could do everything – everything but play Major League Baseball."

While the Yankees appeared to have the biggest and most costly coup of the draft, it would turn out that the best player in the 1991 draft, Manny Ramírez, played at New York City's George Washington High School – only two miles from Yankee Stadium. Ramírez was indeed a transcendent talent, a true hitting prodigy. The first scout to see him, Billy Blitzer of the Chicago Cubs, observed, "The ball just came off his bat differently. I would sit there watching in amazement." Everyone who saw Ramírez in high school believed he was a special player with the potential to be an all time great hitter. Cleveland Indians scout Joe Delucca, who would eventually sign Ramírez, was enthralled with Ramírez's extraordinary bat speed.

Ramírez's family had emigrated from the baseball-crazed Dominican Republic when Ramírez was 13 years old. Baseball was a refuge for Ramírez from the mean streets of the barrio in Washington Heights. It was a place where crack cocaine dealers openly sold their contraband to customers and gun battles often erupted without warning. Blitzer remembered that even scouts were afraid to visit the area unless they traveled together in a pack for safety. Ramírez didn't speak English when his family arrived in New York but, according to Blitzer, his bat did most of the talking. In Blitzer's time watching baseball on Diamond #7 at the Parade Ground in Brooklyn, he had only seen one ball ever hit out of the field. In Ramírez's senior season of high school, he hit five balls over the right-center field fence. In a playoff game against rival Kennedy, Ramírez hit a ball over the dead center field fence so far that it scattered observers from the apartment building well beyond the fence.

Not only was the ballpark an oasis of safety for Ramírez, but the batter's box was a particular comfort zone. Delucca had given Ramírez one rule to follow: "Don't let anyone talk to you about changing your swing." When Ramírez returned to George Washington High School many years later to speak to the players on his former team, he was asked about hitting. He simply explained his hitting philosophy as, "See the ball. Hit the ball." Washington Nationals scout Ron Rizzi marveled at Ramírez's intuitive approach to hitting. "He is a genius with the bat. Few players in the history of the game approached his level of hitting genius," Rizzi said.

According to Rizzi, early in a game, Ramírez would often take a pitch he knew he could hit in order to set up the pitcher for a more crucial at-bat later in the game. By draft day, Ramírez was well-known to all the teams. Blitzer gave the Cubs' front office the names of two players whom he considered worthy of first-round selection. One was Ramírez, and the other was University of Pennsylvania outfielder Doug Glanville. The Cubs, who were picking in the 12th spot, chose the speedy Glanville. The Cleveland Indians held the 13th pick and took Ramírez.

Cleveland's scouting director, Mickey White, had observed Ramírez at George Washington and shared the scouting community's enthusiasm. When queried by the Indians general manager, John Hart, about Ramírez, White was adamant that he would select Ramírez if he fell to them. White told Hart, "His bat reminds me of Roberto Clemente's." White added, "All I needed was to listen to Manny's bat go through the zone."

Ramírez signed for $250,000, which was a bargain compared with the inflated bonus payments of 1991. Ramírez hit from the very beginning with the Indians. He raced through the minors and would become a perennial All-Star and Most Valuable Player candidate. Most everyone who saw Ramírez would agree with his first manager, Mike Hargrove, that he had "probably the prettiest right-handed power swing that I've ever seen."[124]

The Indians lost Ramírez in free agency to the Boston Red Sox after the 2000 season but he continued to rack up big numbers. In 2004, he carried the Red Sox to their first World Series championship since 1918. Over the course of his 19-year career, Ramírez hit 555 home runs, drove in 1,831 runs and batted .312. There were occasions on which Ramírez demonstrated a lack of hustle in the field and made elementary mistakes on the bases. Yet, at the plate, he was always the consummate professional. As Ron Rizzi commented, "Manny may write with crayons off the field, but in the box he is Picasso at work."

Gary Hughes and the Montreal Expos used the 14th pick in 1991 to select left-handed power hitter Cliff Floyd. Hughes referred to the six-foot-four, 230-pound Floyd as a "young Willie McCovey."[125] Floyd suffered a serious wrist injury in 1995 that nearly ended his career. He endured three surgeries to repair the wrist but recovered sufficiently to play 17 productive years in the majors. However, the wrist injury sapped his "McCovey-like" power.

The Toronto Blue Jays selected outfielder Shawn Green with the 16th pick. Green had a scholarship offer to play at Stanford University. To entice him to turn pro, the Blue Jays offered a $725,000 bonus. Prior to the draft, Blue Jays scout Tim Wilken had attempted to convince Blue Jays general manager, Pat Gillick, to use the pick on Washington State pitcher Aaron Sele instead of Green. However, Gillick had personally scouted Green and remained steadfast in the decision to take the outfielder. Green proved to be an inspired choice. He starred for 15 years in the Major Leagues, hitting 328 home runs and batting .283.

The Boston Red Sox used the 23rd pick to take Aaron Sele, the pitcher whom Wilken preferred over Green. Sele, a big right-hander, won 148 Major League games during a career that spanned fifteen years and included two All-Star appearances. Wilken considered the selection of Green over Sele as a beneficial learning experience in his development as a scout. Speaking of that experience, Wilken says, "I learned that if everything is roughly equal and the pitcher doesn't punch you in the face with number one or number two ability, you need to take the everyday player."

In the tenth round of the draft, the Kansas City Royals chose Mike Sweeney, a high school catcher from Ontario, California. Sweeney's father was a former minor league player and served as a part-time scout for the Royals. A tip from Sweeney's father led the Royals to draft the younger Sweeney.[126] Sweeney's first three years in the minor leagues were undistinguished; he failed to hit higher than .240. In his fourth season, however, he hit .301 for the Class A Rockford Royals and his career began to take off. Sweeney appeared as a catcher in 50 Major League games in 1996 and 84 more in 1997, without looking overmatched at the plate. However, his defensive skills were questionable. After the 1998 season, the Royals began to believe that his future would not be at catcher and maybe not with the team at all.

In the spring of 1999, Royals coach Tom Burgmeier told Sweeney that his chances of making the team were slim and none. At first, Sweeney was devastated by the news. He sought solace in a local church, fell to his knees and tried to sort out his future. Sweeney found a calming sense of peace at the church and a renewed commitment to his craft. He not only made the opening day roster for the Royals in 1999 but, two months into the season, became the Royals' starting first baseman. He provided critical power for the Royals, batting .322 and hitting 22 home runs. His 2000 season was even better as he hit 29 homers and had 144 runs batted in, with a stellar .333 average. Sweeney played for 16 seasons in the Major Leagues and made five appearances as an All-Star. He was inducted into the Royals' Hall of Fame and is widely regarded as the best right-handed hitter in Kansas City history.

Joe Caro's Greatest Story

As a high school pitcher, Miami Marlins scout Joe Caro thought he was on track to be the next Tom Seaver. A resident of Tampa, Florida, Caro transferred to Tampa Catholic High School for his senior year. The lure was not the school's religious education program; at the time, Caro wasn't even a practicing Catholic. He transferred because he wanted to play for the best baseball school he could find.

By the time Caro turned 21, his dream of playing professional baseball had ended. Caro turned to coaching. From 1980 to 1993, he was a head baseball coach at three different high schools, including his alma mater. During his time as coach at Tampa Catholic, Caro had the opportunity to work with a young pitcher named Carlos Reyes. Caro calls Reyes his "greatest story in baseball."

Reyes went undrafted out of college but signed with the Atlanta Braves as a free agent in June 1991. In three minor league seasons, he held opponents to an average of 2.29 runs per nine innings. His performance drew the attention of the Oakland Athletics, who acquired Reyes prior to the 1994 season. Reyes made his Major League debut on April 7, 1994. In the hours before the game, when Reyes learned that he was headed to the big leagues, he telephoned Caro to convey the news. Caro immediately broke into tears. Reyes, he explained, is "my surrogate son."

Caro never quite understood the reason for Reyes's success. He doubts that Reyes's fastball ever reached 88 miles an hour. "He never ever should have pitched in the big leagues," Caro says, "but he was the opening day starter for the Oakland Athletics [in 1996]. It's the most unbelievable story I have ever personally heard of."

For Caro, the key to Reyes's success lay in his intangibles. Caro marveled at Reyes's pitching instincts. Reyes, he says, "was blessed with a brilliant pitching mind, knowing how to change speeds and being able to move the ball around and read the swings of hitters." Reyes pitched for eight seasons in the big leagues, appeared in 293 games, and won 20 games against 36 losses, with a 4.66 earned run average.

1992

The Yankees wanted college players. George [Steinbrenner] never rebuilt, he reloaded. You never know what's going to happen with high school players. For Jeter, we were optimistic that he would sign because he wanted to be a Yankee. But he had a girlfriend and she was very close. She was going to the University of Michigan. That always gives us concern, that's a very viable force. So they asked me, 'What do you think? Is he going to go to the University of Michigan?' I said, 'The only place this kid is going is Cooperstown.' That was as strong a statement as I could make. From my perspective, this was the guy and this was what I really felt. He was a very special player. There are not too many guys I can put on that list.

— Dick Groch, scout, New York Yankees

The 1992 draft was unusual to the point of being unique. Florida Marlins scouting director Gary Hughes viewed it as having "the weakest talent in seven or eight years."[127] Most observers shared the assessment. In retrospect, the performances of the players selected in the draft were generally consistent with the distinct lack of pre-draft enthusiasm. While it is not unusual to have a shallow draft pool, it was unusual in the talent-rich era of the late 1980s and early 1990s. The backstory of the first round in 1992 has become the story of a single selection, shortstop Derek Jeter, who was drafted by the New York Yankees with the sixth overall pick.

The Houston Astros used the first pick of the draft to select Phil Nevin, a third baseman for California State University at Fullerton. At the time of the draft, Nevin generated none of the hype that had accompanied the selection of pitcher Brien Taylor in 1991. Nor did Nevin inspire the kind of superlatives that scouts would commonly use when talking about Álex Rodríguez, who would be the top pick in 1993. In a sense, Nevin was "bookended" by celebrities. It would have been a tall order for Nevin or any other player to match either the hysteria or the expectations that were prevalent in 1991 and 1993.

Nevin would go on to have a solid twelve-year big-league career. He spent the 1993 and 1994 seasons in Triple-A and made his Major League debut in June 1995. He did not receive a fair trial with the Astros. After Nevin had played in only 18 Major League games, Houston sent him to the Detroit Tigers in a trade for pitcher Mike Henneman. The trade was prompted, at least in part, by high-profile public disagreements between Nevin and the Astros management. The trade was almost certainly a reflection, also, of the fact that Nevin had hit only .117 in his 18 games with the Astros.

The prevailing narrative surrounding the 1992 draft was not driven so much by Nevin's performance as by Houston's failure to select Jeter. It has become popular sport to question why the Astros passed over Jeter and took Nevin instead. However, there were four other teams that made the same mistake. The Cleveland Indians, Montreal Expos, Baltimore Orioles, and Cincinnati Reds, respectively, held picks two through five; each team passed on drafting Derek Jeter.[128] The teams that passed on Jeter did so for a myriad of reasons, some because they were set at shortstop and others because they had more pressing needs at other positions. The Cincinnati Reds, for example, had perennial All-Star Barry Larkin, then 28 years old, at shortstop and so selected University of Central Florida outfielder Chad Mottola one pick before the Yankees took Jeter.

Houston paid a bonus of $700,000 to sign Nevin. The bonus was well below the $1.55 million that Brien Taylor received in 1991. Even so, the first-round bonus amounts in 1992 remained at historically high levels. The average bonus paid to first-round selections in 1992 was more than 30% higher than the bonuses for first-round draft picks in 1991.[129] Aside from the anomalous bonus that the Yankees gave to Brien Taylor in 1991, the Astros actually paid Nevin more than any other number one selection in history. However, because Astros owner John McMullen placed a cap of $700,000 on the amount that the Astros would spend for their first pick, there was a perception that Houston drafted Nevin – and not Jeter – for cost-saving reasons.

In one of the great draft ironies of all time, the Yankees were able to sign Jeter for the exact same $700,000 that Nevin received. In a further irony, McMullen was a former limited partner of Yankees principal owner George M. Steinbrenner III, and had uttered one of the most insightful observations on Steinbrenner's penchant for control: "Nothing is as limited as being a limited partner of George M. Steinbrenner."

By 1992, the term "signability" had acquired a secondary meaning in draft circles. When a team was said to avoid drafting a player due to signability issues, it typically suggested that Scott Boras was involved as the agent for the player. Boras had represented the number one overall picks in 1988 (Andy Benes), 1989 (Ben McDonald) and 1991 (Brien Taylor), and the perceived best player available in 1990 (Todd Van Poppel). Boras was nowhere to be seen with the first six picks of the 1992 draft. In fact, Boras had become such a lightning rod that the father of high school shortstop Michael Tucker contacted every team prior to the draft to assure them his son was *not* associated with Boras.[130]

The Kansas City Royals selected Florida high school star Johnny Damon with the 35th overall pick. At the beginning of the 1992 school season, the speedy outfielder from Dr. Phillips High School in Orlando was considered a better prospect than Jeter and every other high school player available. However, a poor senior campaign led teams to back off Damon. After the draft, Allard Baird and Art Stewart conducted negotiations at Damon's home on behalf of the Royals. For a period of thirteen hours, Baird and Stewart engaged in contentious discussions with Damon and his family.

During the negotiations, Baird and Stewart became aware that Boras was "advising" Damon and his family by phone. Boras's involvement came to light only because Damon's girlfriend innocently blurted out, "Scott Boras told you you'd get a half-million if you go to Florida and come out after three years."[131] Eventually, Damon agreed on a $250,000 bonus, signing the contract without telling Boras. Damon would star for the Royals and six other Major League teams over a superb 18-year career. He collected 2,769 hits and stole 408 bases while becoming a stellar defensive outfielder. Damon was twice selected to the American League All-Star team and played on two World Series championship teams.

Chad Mottola Reconsidered

Ron Rizzi, former special assistant to Washington Nationals general manager Mike Rizzo, has been involved in scouting, in one capacity or another, for more than 40 years. He grew up in the Bronx, where he attended Columbus High School. A pitcher and third baseman, Rizzi was the Public Schools Athletic League batting champion in 1964 and was named All-City in 1963 and 1964. He captained the baseball team at the City College of New York in the 1960s and once struck out 20 batters in a game against Manhattan College. After a rotator cuff injury in college ended Rizzi's aspirations of playing pro ball, he turned to scouting.

In his youth, Rizzi was an ardent fan of the New York Yankees. He has indelible memories of seeing 24-year-old outfielder Bill Robinson struggle to get acclimated to the Major Leagues. Robinson, whom the Yankees had hoped would succeed Mickey Mantle as the team's next great center fielder, hit a paltry .206 in three seasons in New York. Robinson then spent the next two years in the minors, where he worked to regain both his confidence and his hitting stroke. In 1972, at the age of 29, Robinson made it back to the Major Leagues for good with the Philadelphia Phillies. Over the next eleven seasons, with both Philadelphia and Pittsburgh, Robinson hit .272 with 150 home runs and 546 runs batted in.

Some players, Ron Rizzi says, just take time to develop. Bill Robinson is a prime example. Rizzi maintains that Chad Mottola, the first-round pick of the Cincinnati Reds in 1992, is another example. Mottola failed in his first exposure to the Major Leagues in 1996, batting only .215 for Cincinnati in 35 games. Overall, in 59 games in the Major Leagues, Mottola had a cumulative batting average of .200. However, Mottola's minor league record depicts a vastly different player.

In five minor league seasons from 1997 to 2001, Mottola hit above .300 three times. In those five seasons, Mottola never hit below .292. In 1999, while playing for Triple-A Charlotte, he hit .321 with 20 home runs. In 2000, with Triple-A Syracuse, he hit .309 with 33 home runs. Mottola's career progression seems to have been limited not by a lack of talent so much as by the stigma of his early failure with Cincinnati.

1993

Gary Sheffield and Álex Rodríguez – I never saw bat speed, hand-eye coordination like those two guys had. I saw Álex play when he was seventeen years old and I said to myself, 'What's the difference between this kid and a Major League shortstop?' The answer, 'None.' The most talented player I ever saw as a 17-year-old. And Gary was the most talented hitter I have ever seen as a 17-year-old.

— Joe Caro, former New York Yankees scout

The 1993 draft was considered to be a "two-player" draft at the very top. Scouts were divided over which of the two, collegiate pitcher Darren Dreifort or high school shortstop Álex Rodríguez, was the best player in the nation. The Major League Scouting Bureau rated Dreifort higher than Rodríguez. Other experts were not so sure.

The Seattle Mariners were back in the "catbird seat" with the first pick in 1993, having lost 98 games in 1992 and finishing in last place in the American League West. Mariners scouting director Roger Jongewaard, who was instrumental in the selection of Ken Griffey Jr. in 1987, was adamant that Rodríguez was the best player in the draft. Jongewaard selected Rodríguez despite the preference of Seattle's manager, Lou Piniella, for pitching and for Dreifort.[132] With the selection of Rodríguez, Jongewaard had played a key role in drafting the "trifecta" of Darryl Strawberry for the Mets and Griffey and Rodríguez for the Mariners – three of the top ten number one draft selections of all time.

While most scouts raved about Rodríguez, a tall shortstop from Miami, Jongewaard was especially lavish in his praise. A month before the draft, Jongewaard completed a scouting report on the shortstop. The scouting report described Rodríguez as "better at seventeen than all the superstars in baseball when they were seniors in high school." Jongewaard compared Rodríguez favorably with Derek Jeter but considered him "bigger and better." In view of the thousands of players whom Jongewaard had scouted and reviewed, his highest compliment came when he said that Rodríguez "generates a special feeling when watching him play."

Jongewaard was hardly alone in his assessment. Art Stewart of the Kansas City Royals considered Rodríguez to be "one of the greatest amateur talents in recent baseball history."[133] It was not unusual for a hundred scouts to be in attendance to watch Rodríguez play at Westminster Christian High School in Miami. Milwaukee Brewers scout Russ Bove described Rodríguez as "the prototype shortstop: Tall, lean body, makes all the plays, ... plus runner, instincts on the bases, home run potential, quick bat, ... as good a free agent prospect as you'll ever see." To boot, Bove considered him "intelligent," with a "great feel for the game," and, perhaps most importantly, "he loves to play."

Once Jongewaard was able to overcome the organizational resistance to drafting Rodríguez, he encountered another significant obstacle, Álex Rodríguez. Rodríguez called Jongewaard and told him point blank, "I do not want you to draft me."[134] Jongewaard drafted him anyway, which prompted Rodríguez to fire his existing agent and hire Scott Boras. Notwithstanding the difficulties of negotiating with Boras, the Mariners were able to sign Rodríguez for a bonus of $1 million. The bonus for Rodríguez was a reasonable amount in the context of the recent Brien Taylor signing and the near $1 million that Jeffery Hammonds received in 1992 from the Orioles. Jongewaard never wavered in his pursuit of Rodríguez. He said, "I learned that you don't go the safe way.... You don't worry about agents. You take the best guy available. We knew Álex would be a difficult sign, and he was, but he was the best player out there."[135]

Seattle was able to get Rodríguez to sign a contract at the very last minute before he was scheduled to begin classes at the University of Miami. Rodríguez prophetically predicted, "One day I'll get my market value when I prove myself as an impact player. I just want to get started."[136] Less than a year later, at the age of 18, he arrived in the Major Leagues. After a brief acclimation, he made good on his promise to prove himself as an impact player. In 1996, Rodríguez led the American League in runs scored, doubles, and batting average. He also hit 36 home runs and drove in 123 runs while making his first All-Star team and finishing second in the Most Valuable Player voting. Over the next four seasons in Seattle, Rodríguez continued to post excellent power numbers, especially for a shortstop. Although the Mariners now featured Rodríguez, Randy Johnson, Griffey Jr., and another future Hall of Famer in Edgar Martinez, Seattle only won the division championship once during Rodríguez's years as the regular shortstop for the team.

The Mariners allowed Rodríguez to leave as a free agent after the 2000 season. He quickly made good on his promise to get "market value" when he signed a record contract with the Texas Rangers. Boras and Rangers owner Tom Hicks negotiated a ten-year deal that would pay Rodríguez $252 million. The contract made Rodríguez the highest paid player in baseball. Now widely known by the nickname "A-Rod," Rodríguez continued to excel at bat and in the field and established himself as the perennial All-Star shortstop in the American League.

Rodríguez spent three years with Texas, during which he posted huge power statistics, culminating in his first MVP Award in 2003. Even so, the Rangers never had a winning record with Rodríguez on the team. In 2004, the Rangers traded him to the New York Yankees. Future Hall of Famer Derek Jeter was entrenched at shortstop for the Yankees, causing Rodríguez to play third base. A-Rod continued his success in New York, winning Most Valuable Player Awards in 2005 and 2007. In 2009, Jeter and Rodríguez led the Yankees to the World Series championship.

Rodríguez retired under duress with the Yankees in 2016 when he was only four home runs shy of the magical 700 total. Despite his stellar performance for the Yankees, he was never fully accepted by Yankee fans and became a lightning rod for controversy. In his brilliant 22-year Major League career, he was selected to fourteen All-Star teams, hit 696 home runs, and compiled a lifetime batting average of .295. On the numbers alone, A-Rod would appear to be a certain first-ballot Hall of Fame inductee. Yet, his chances for election to the Hall are greatly clouded by his admission of using performance-enhancing drugs during his career.

Picking second in the 1993 draft, the Los Angeles Dodgers quickly snatched up Darren Dreifort. The Dodgers were enamored with Dreifort's pitching arsenal, which included a blazing sinking fastball and a premier slider. In his junior year at Wichita State University, Dreifort posted a 2.48 earned run average and recorded 120 strikeouts in 102 innings. Dreifort and the Dodgers did not come to terms until three months after the draft. The Dodgers considered Dreifort's skills so advanced that they assigned him to their Major League roster out of spring training in 1994. Unfortunately, Dreifort fell victim to a myriad of injuries that required twenty-two surgeries. He would spend nine years in the Major Leagues and retired in 2004.

The Houston Astros had the12th overall pick in the draft and landed a gem in left-handed pitcher Billy Wagner. Wagner was a small player, standing five-feet-ten, from a small town in Virginia, playing at a very small school, Ferrum College – with a very big arm. Although Ferrum was a Division III school, scouts began to flock to rural Virginia to see Wagner pitch after he set an NCAA record by averaging 19 strikeouts per nine innings.

Though Wagner was a starter at Ferrum, the Astros converted him into a relief pitcher. He became one of the best closers in Major League history. During his 16-year Major League career, he saved 422 games and struck out 1,196 batters in only 903 innings. Wagner's selection as a high first-round draft choice provides a stark reminder that there are unheralded prospects still to be discovered in remote areas of the country.

Jeff Suppan's Best Tool

Former Major League pitcher Jeff Suppan wasn't blessed with a power arm. When Suppan was a senior at Crespi Carmelite High School in Encino, California, his fastball topped out at 88-91 miles per hour. However, Suppan possessed what Boston Red Sox scout Joe Stephenson called "the flash." In the scouting lexicon, "the flash" indicated an inherent ability for a pitcher to pitch best when he needed it the most.

Stephenson was once present for a high school playoff game in which Suppan gave up a home run. When facing the next batter, Suppan produced "the flash," taking his fastball to a higher level and getting a strikeout on three pitches. Then, in his next at-bat, Suppan hit a home run. That playoff game allowed Stephenson to see Suppan's best attribute – the ability to take his game to the next level when he was really motivated.

The Red Sox were sufficiently impressed to draft Suppan with their second-round pick in 1993. Not all teams were as enthusiastic about Suppan's potential. During Suppan's senior year, San Francisco Giants scout George Genovese asked the team's national cross-checker, Bob Hartsfield, to come for one of Suppan's games. Unfortunately for Genovese and the bevy of other scouts in the stands, Suppan "had nothing" that day, turning in a performance that was well below average. The scouts began to leave in droves as Suppan was being battered. Hartsfield joined in the exodus, but not before berating Genovese. "Why did you bring me out to watch this piece of shit?" Hartsfield asked.

Genovese probed Suppan the next day and discovered that the young right-hander had unwisely donated blood the day before his inauspicious start. Suppan's campus ministry advisor had told him, "If you give blood, you can save the lives of four babies." Suppan told the advisor that he was pitching the next day. The advisor responded, "You will be fully recovered in 24 hours." Suppan agreed to donate blood, forgetting that the game was scheduled to start in less than 20 hours.

Suppan told Genovese about the blood donation but the veteran scout knew the explanation would not change his cross-checker's opinion. Genovese then did something that was unusual among old school scouts: he called his friend Joe Stephenson and touted Suppan as "a pitcher, not a thrower." Stephenson began watching Suppan and was similarly impressed. Two years later, Suppan made his debut at Fenway Park. He would go on to play in the big leagues for 17 seasons with seven teams. As a member of the St. Louis Cardinals in 2006, he was named the Most Valuable Player of the National League Championship Series and was a key contributor to the Cardinals' World Series victory.

1994

Like all kids coming out of high school and tasting the pros for the first time, [Josh Booty] struggled. When they go to rookie league, the teams will always have some college pitchers filling out their roster who know how to pitch. There's always an adjustment because hitters have never used a wood bat before. For many, it's the first time in their lives they have struggled. Even when Josh was in pro baseball, LSU kept recruiting him to play football. Even though the Marlins gave him a record signing bonus and even though he did get to the majors for a little bit, his baseball career was a disappointment. There was no reason he should not have been an everyday third baseman in the big leagues.

— Orrin Freeman, former special assistant to the general manager, Miami Marlins

The 1994 season was a tumultuous year for the game of baseball. The team owners entered the season with the intent of implementing a cap on player salaries. The players' union rejected the imposition of a salary cap, finding that the proposal would benefit only the owners, with no advantages for the players. Finding no ground for compromise, the players declared August 12, 1994 as the strike date. When that date arrived without a settlement, the season came to an abrupt end. The strike was a disaster for the game and would dampen fan interest for years to come.

The New York Mets held the first overall draft pick in 1994. Dating back to the Mets' championship successes of 1969 and 1986, the team had developed an identity that was focused on dominant pitching. From Tom Seaver, Jerry Koosman and Nolan Ryan to Dwight Gooden, Ron Darling and Sid Fernandez, pitching was the watchword for the Mets. It came as no surprise, therefore, that the Mets used their first pick to draft six-foot-five Florida State University ace Paul Wilson. Wilson's fastball flirted with triple digits on the radar guns. The expectations of greatness were understandable.

Like Dwight Gooden, Wilson hailed from Florida. Unlike Gooden, Wilson had spent three years pitching in college. In his junior season at Florida State, Wilson had a 13-5 won-loss record, with an earned run average of 2.08 and 161 strikeouts in 143 innings. Reporters and draft experts characterized Wilson as a savior for the Mets. Ron Hopkins, the area scout who signed Wilson for the Mets, attempted to keep the expectations at a realistic level. Hopkins explained, "he still needs to develop some consistency with his slider. There's no reason to put a timetable on him. He'll get there [to the majors] when the time is right. That is what's important – to get there and stay there."[137]

The expectations were also driven by the $1.55 million bonus the Mets shelled out for Wilson. The extraordinary bonus the Yankees had paid to Brien Taylor could no longer be seen as an anomaly; it was now the norm. Fans did not have to wait long to see Wilson in action. The Mets brought him to the big leagues in 1996 and immediately inserted him into the starting rotation. In his rookie season, Wilson posted a disappointing 5-12 won-loss record, with an earned run average of 5.38.

Nonetheless, hopes remained high that once Wilson harnessed his impressive repertoire of pitches, he would develop into an ace for the Mets. Unfortunately, due to a spate of injuries, he never pitched for the Mets in the Major Leagues after the 1996 season. When Wilson did return to the Major Leagues, it was in 2000 as a member of the Tampa Bay Devil Rays. In parts of seven years, Wilson won 40 games and lost 58, with an earned run average of 4.86. Like so many other number one picks before and after, he never came close to fulfilling the high expectations placed upon him.

The Oakland Athletics selected Texas prep school star Ben Grieve with the second pick of the draft.[138] For a few years, it appeared that the 1994 draft was unfolding in a way similar to the 1966 draft. In 1966, the Mets' overall number one pick, Steve Chilcott, incurred an injury that prematurely ended his career while the second overall pick, Reggie Jackson, took the baseball world by storm. For his first three years in the majors, Ben Grieve's performance was nearly on a level with that of Jackson. In 1998, his first full year in the big leagues, Grieve hit 18 home runs, drove in 89 runs and batted .288. His performance earned him the American League Rookie of the Year Award.

Over the next two seasons, Grieve slugged a total of 55 home runs. The comparison to Reggie Jackson was not far-fetched. Just before the start of the 2001 spring training, however, the Athletics traded Grieve to the Tampa Bay Devil Rays. Grieve's career arc took a noticeable decline in Tampa, and he never approached the greatness his early years suggested. He played for nine seasons in the Major Leagues. After slugging 76 home runs in a little more than three seasons with Oakland, Grieve hit only 42 homers during his final five seasons.

The best pick of the 1994 first round, and perhaps the entire draft, was the Boston Red Sox's selection of Georgia Tech shortstop prospect Nomar Garciaparra with the 12th pick. Garciaparra arrived in the majors in 1996 at the age of 23. By 1997, he was starting at shortstop for the Red Sox and hit .306 with 30 home runs, earning the Rookie of the Year Award in the American League. In 1999 and 2000, Garciaparra enjoyed the best years of his career, hitting .357 and .372, respectively.

Along with Derek Jeter and Álex Rodríguez, Garciaparra would complete the revolution at the shortstop position that Cal Ripken Jr. had begun. Like Ripken, all three provided stellar defense combined with middle-of-the-order power. For all of Ripken's storybook credentials and stature, Jeter, Rodríguez and Garciaparra took the position to an even greater level of celebrity. As sportswriter Josh Dubow noted, the three shortstops brought the game an excitement level and rivalry comparable to that surrounding the famous center field trio of Willie Mays, Mickey Mantle, and Duke Snider in the 1950s.[139] Individually and collectively, they transcended baseball and were considered A-list celebrities who dated Hollywood starlets and socialized with the likes of Michael Jordan. The emergence of the three shortstops could not have come at a better time for a sport that was still plagued with turbulence from the 1994 strike.

While the failure of a top prospect is often described in hyperbolic prose as an almost tragic event, the reality of real tragedy places the draft and the game in greater perspective. The Colorado Rockies selected left-handed high school pitcher Doug Million from Sarasota, Florida with the seventh overall pick. Million was generally considered to be the best high school pitching talent available. He signed with the Rockies for $905,000 but struggled mightily with his control in the minors. While playing for the Salem Avalanche in 1997, he suffered a severe asthma attack and passed away in September 1997 at the age of 21.

Feeling A Draft

Body Language

Texas Rangers broadcaster C.J. Nitkowski, a first-round pick of the Cincinnati Reds in 1994, pitched in the Major Leagues for ten seasons. He has seen plenty of baseball players come and go. Nitkowski has an ingrained preference for players such as Dustin Pedroia and Josh Harrison, players "who really love the game and get dirty all the time, guys who are not happy unless they are dirty."

On the other hand, Nitkowski says, there are plenty of other ballplayers whose body language may not be appealing at first sight but who, nonetheless, are really good talents. Nitkowski puts long-time Yankee second baseman Robinson Cano in this category.

"The mistake that I made in watching Robinson Cano was the body language," Nitkowski says. As a minor leaguer, he was exactly the same player that he became in the big leagues. He almost made it look like it was effortless. If you don't know him and you read it wrong, you think he doesn't care." Nitkowski is quick to point out that Cano, who made the American League All-Star team eight times, "turned out to be an unbelievable big leaguer."

For Nitkowski, it is the contrast in player styles that makes scouting amateur players "a really, really tough thing to do." It is not just Nitkowski who finds evaluating ballplayers to be difficult. Kip Fagg, the scouting director for the Texas Rangers, once sat down with Nitkowski in the broadcast booth during a Rangers game. Fagg told Nitkowski, "There are guys playing on this field right now whom I thought had no chance of getting to the big leagues."

The
Lineup

Scout Mike Toomey (right), shown with Kansas City Royals Hall of Fame third baseman George Brett. A center fielder during his playing days, Toomey was named the outstanding senior athlete at George Washington University for 1974. A year later, the 22-year-old Toomey was selected to be the head baseball coach at his alma mater, a position he held for five years. In 1980, the Pittsburgh Pirates named Toomey as manager of the Class A Alexandria Dukes in the Carolina League. He has scouted for six Major League organizations, most recently with the Kansas City Royals. From 2006 to 2018, Toomey worked for the Royals as a special assistant to the general manager.

Scout Ron Rizzi (right), shown with famed New York Yankees catcher Lawrence (Yogi) Berra. Rizzi grew up within walking distance of Yankee Stadium. As a student at Columbus High School in the Bronx, Rizzi excelled as both a pitcher and infielder. In 1964, he won the Public Schools Athletic League batting championship with a .444 average and was named the starting third baseman on the All-City team. Rizzi's dreams of playing professional baseball ended when he suffered a rotator cuff injury in college.

Ron Rizzi (right), pictured with actor Charlie Sheen on the set of the 1994 movie *Major League II*. Rizzi served as technical advisor for the movie. In preparation for filming, Rizzi recruited active and former professional players and umpires to play characters in the movie and worked with Sheen to improve his pitching form. Wearing uniform #52, Rizzi played the role of Cleveland's first base coach in the film.

Gilbert "Gib" Bodet, pictured with his wife, Jean. In 1969 Bodet got his start in scouting as a bird dog for the Boston Red Sox. In 1979 he joined the Los Angeles Dodgers as an area scout. He has worked with the Dodgers for 42 years as area scout, West Coast supervisor and national cross-checker. Says Bodet, "In any draft, the odds are 29 to 1 against a team. You're competing against a lot of very good evaluators who work for a lot of good clubs."

Ben McLure was a record-setting baseball coach at Lower Dauphin High School in Pennsylvania. Over a span of fourteen years, McLure's teams won more than 70% of their games and claimed seven league championships. McLure started working as a part-time scout for the St. Louis Cardinals in 1972. He spent 44 years as a scout, working for five Major League organizations. "For baseball players," McLure says, "confidence is a gift, just like hand-eye coordination. God taps you on the shoulder and says, 'Son, you're a hitter. Don't let them mess you up.'"

Billy Blitzer, pictured with former Chicago Cubs pitcher Jamie Moyer, was a standout ballplayer at Lincoln High School in Brooklyn, New York, where he was a teammate of future New York Mets star, Lee Mazzilli. An outfielder, Blitzer went on to play for Hunter College in Manhattan. By his own admission, he was "good hit, can't run." Blitzer has worked as an amateur scout for the Chicago Cubs for the past 40 years. He is one of only a handful of Major League scouts to be honored with his own baseball trading card.

Scout Matt Slater (right) is shown with former St. Louis Cardinals manager Tony La Russa. Slater began his scouting career with the Milwaukee Brewers. He joined the Cardinals in 2007 and, in 2012, was named the team's director of player personnel. He currently works as special assistant to the Cardinals general manager, with responsibility for player procurement. Before joining the Cardinals, Slater oversaw scouting operations for the Los Angeles Dodgers and Baltimore Orioles.

Feeling A Draft

Scout John Tumminia (holding radar gun) began in baseball as a bird dog for the California Angels in 1986. A year later, Tumminia took a scouting position with the Chicago White Sox. He has scouted for the White Sox for 33 years. Tumminia was named Scout of the Year by the New York Pro Baseball Scouts Association in 2007. He is the founder of Baseball Miracles, Inc., an organization that seeks to bring the game of baseball to children in underserved communities throughout the world.

As a high school student in Riverside, California, Darrell Miller developed a crush on classmate Cindy Cohenour. Three years later, Miller was playing baseball at California State Polytechnic University at Pomona and drawing attention from Major League scouts. In 1979, scout Lou Cohenour, the father of Miller's one-time crush, drafted and signed Miller for the California Angels. Miller spent five years in the Major Leagues, 1984-1988. After his playing days, Miller spent several years as an amateur scout for the Angels. He currently serves as Major League Baseball's Vice President for Youth and Facility Development, working to develop and promote Urban Youth Academies.

Scout Joe Caro (left), pictured with former New York Yankee general manager, Gene "Stick" Michael. A former high school coach, Caro began in scouting with the Kansas City Royals in 1989. He then spent three years as a part-time scout with the California Angels before moving on to the New York Yankees. He worked in various scouting capacities for the Yankees until 2018, when he was recruited by Derek Jeter to join the Miami Marlins as a special assignment scout. For Caro, predicting who will be able to hit in the Major Leagues is the hardest single thing to do in any sport. "Round ball, round bat, you've got to square it up," he says.

1995

It was 1995. I was filing reports and getting lunch for the scouts who were in the draft room. That was my job. I remember a pre-draft workout at Fenway Park. There was a player from Puerto Rico who came up for a workout. The Puerto Rican scout at the time for the Red Sox was Ray Blanco. He lived in south Florida. Ray really liked this kid. The kid was a relatively high-profile guy. He was going to get drafted high. Ray had spent a lot of time on the kid and believed in him. Back then, it wasn't as easy to get looks on kids from Puerto Rico, so three or four days before the draft, the team flew him up to Fenway to work out. I was only down there because I was the intern. My job was to make sure there was water down on the field, so I was on the field for this workout. This kid had trouble getting the ball out of the infield, never mind to the wall. He really struggled. I distinctly remember feeling this myself, walking off the field thinking there's no way this kid is a first-rounder. I walked up to the draft room and saw this kid's magnet had been moved down quite a bit. The kid was Carlos Beltrán.

– Ben Cherington, former general manager, Boston Red Sox; general manager, Pittsburgh Pirates

Going into the draft, baseball experts considered the 1995 talent pool to be perhaps as deep as the legendary 1985 class.[140] In retrospect, neither the talent at the top nor the depth of the draft were close to 1985.

The California Angels were in the driver's seat with the overall number one pick. It was the Angels' first overall number one pick since they selected Danny Goodwin in 1975. The Angels had a varied range of options to choose from with the number one pick. The choices included: (1) the most complete collegiate player in the draft; (2) a catcher considered to be the best high school position player in the draft; and (3) the best high school pitcher in the country.

The Angels went with the collegiate player, University of Nebraska outfielder Darin Erstad, passing on the high school catcher, Ben Davis, and the high school pitcher, Kerry Wood.

In many ways, Erstad was the safest choice for the Angels. He was from Jamestown, North Dakota, a city with a population of roughly 15,000. Jamestown is six hours from the closest Major League city, Minneapolis. Erstad's high school did not play baseball, so he played American Legion ball in and around Jamestown. Nonetheless, Erstad was no secret to the scouting community.[141] He had been drafted by the Mets in the 13th round of the 1992 draft but chose to play college ball at the University of Nebraska instead. In his final season at Nebraska, he hit .410 with nineteen homers and 76 runs batted in. During the summer before his junior year at Nebraska, he had been the preeminent star in the top collegiate summer baseball league, the Cape Cod League.

Sports Illustrated's Sally Jenkins speculated as early as April 1995 that Erstad would be the number one overall pick. Jenkins compared Erstad to North Dakota's only baseball legend, Roger Maris. Maris, of course, had broken Babe Ruth's single season home run record when he blasted 61 homers for the Yankees in 1961. The comparisons were obvious. Like Maris, Erstad was a left-handed hitter with a lightning bat. Like Maris, Erstad had starred in football in high school. Erstad was highly rated in all aspects of baseball, except for his subpar throwing arm. Scouts projected that his hitting would develop into his foremost skill but were divided over whether his tendency to hit line drives would produce power.[142]

While he was a safe pick for the Angels, Erstad may not have been the prototypical impact player that teams covet with the overall number one pick. Erstad made it to the big leagues by 1996. In his first full season, 1997, he hit .299 with 16 homers and 77 runs batted in. He followed up his 1997 season with an All-Star selection in 1998. In 2000, he made his second All-Star appearance and appeared to be emerging as a star, with 25 homers, 100 runs batted in, and a .355 batting average. From that point, however, Erstad's hitting slipped and his career stalled. Though he would play for nine more seasons, Erstad never again exceeded 10 home runs in a season and never made another All-Star Game. Erstad enjoyed a solid fourteen-year career. Yet the scouting reports that questioned his future power production were borne out. He hit only 124 homers in his 14 Major League seasons. While he was not a true impact player, Erstad clearly ranks in the top half of all number one overall selections.

The San Diego Padres, who perpetually seemed to be drafting high, sat right behind the Angels with the second pick. The Padres opted for hulking catcher Ben Davis from Malvern Prep in Pennsylvania. Mike Rooney, who coached Davis at Malvern Prep, called him "the total package."[143] Davis was a switch-hitter who had hit over .500 in his senior campaign at Malvern. He had power from both sides of the plate and was a superior receiver with a plus arm.[144] At Malvern, Davis was a leader on and off the field. Many scouts considered him the best high school position player available.

Off the field, Davis was an honors student and even read the morning news for the school's television station.

There were a few scouts who expressed concern about Davis having a long swing.[145] However, the Padres did not seem to have any doubts. Much as with high school pitchers, there is concern about taking a catcher high in the draft. Draft history is filled with stories of catchers who were drafted early in the first round and did not produce as expected. One of the most prominent busts was the Padres' own choice of Mike Ivie in 1970.

Nonetheless, the Padres were confident that Davis was the right choice. Their level of confidence was further underscored by the familiar options they turned down to draft Davis. San Diego had drafted both outfielder Geoff Jenkins and first sacker Todd Helton out of high school in 1992. Both Jenkins and Helton elected to go to college rather than turn pro. Both were available in 1995 when the Padres chose Davis. Moreover, two of the best high school prospects in the draft, outfielder Jaime Jones of Rancho Bernardo High school and pitcher Chad Hutchinson of Torrey Pines High School, played right in the Padres' backyard.

Davis played 76 games for the Padres in 1999 and was their primary backstop by 2001. San Diego traded him to the Seattle Mariners after the 2001 season. He played in the big leagues until 2004 but never came close to realizing the expectations that the Padres had for him.

In addition to Darin Erstad and Ben Davis, the 1995 draft featured Kerry Wood, an exceptional high school right-hander who appeared destined for greatness. Wood was a six-foot-five fireballer from Grand Prairie, Texas, who drew comparisons to Texas legends Nolan Ryan and Roger Clemens. Wood was notable for his "good old country fastball" and his demeanor on the mound. In his senior year of high school, he was 14-0 with a 0.77 earned run average and struck out 152 batters in 82 innings. Perhaps the foremost authority on Texas pitching, scout Red Murff, was uncharacteristically glowing in his praise for Wood: "I saw Bob Feller ... Sandy Koufax ... Roger Clemens ... and Nolan Ryan." In Murff's view, "Big ol' Kerry Wood has a chance to be right up there with them. He could pitch himself seven no-hitters, if everything stays right for him."[146]

The Chicago Cubs selected Wood with the fourth pick in 1995. Wood reached the Major Leagues with the Cubs in 1998. His arrival prompted great rejoicing on the Northside of Chicago; Wood would have the impact that teams dream about from number one selections. On May

6, 1998, at the age of 20 and pitching in only the fifth game of his career, Wood dominated the Houston Astros in a game at Wrigley Field. He struck out a record-tying 20 batters while allowing only one hit. Cubs Manager Jim Riggleman called it "the best [game] I've ever seen pitched by anybody."[147]

Wood won thirteen games against only 6 losses on his way to winning the National League Rookie of the Year Award. Wrigleyville's joy turned to concern, however, when Chicago had to shut Wood down in September due to elbow soreness. The concern soon gave way to despair when it was determined that the brilliant rookie would need Tommy John surgery and thus miss the entire 1999 season.

There were whispers. Wood had thrown 122 pitches in his 20-strikeout game. Many observers felt that the effort was too much for a young pitcher. Wood was able to return in 2000 and threw very hard again, but he never again was the dominating starter he had been in his rookie campaign. Despite the surgery and numerous other arm injuries during his career, Wood played as long as Erstad, yet managed only 86 career wins. In 2007, he made the difficult transition from starter to stopper for the Cubs. He saved 34 games in 2008 while striking out 84 batters over 66 innings.

Most players would have considered their careers to be very successful if they could match Wood's accomplishments. Nonetheless, the first thought most baseball people have of Wood is that of unfulfilled potential. He had arrived in the big leagues amid outsized expectations and came up short. His career trajectory may perhaps explain some of the trepidation surrounding the selection of high school pitchers early in the draft. There are some unique circumstances to Wood's case, however. In 1995, his high school coach let him throw a staggering 175 pitches in a game just two days after he was drafted. Understandably, Cubs general manager Ed Lynch, a former pitcher, called the workload "unfathomable."[148]

The Colorado Rockies selected Todd Helton with the eighth pick. He would develop into the best selection of all the top ten picks in the 1995 draft. Helton capably manned first base for the Rockies for 17 Major League seasons. In that time, he would become the face of the Colorado franchise, as he hit 369 home runs, drove in 1,406 runs and had a stellar .316 batting average for his career.

In retrospect, the best pitcher available in the 1995 draft was Roy Halladay. Halladay lasted until the 17th pick of the first round, when he was selected by the Toronto Blue Jays. Halladay was the ninth pitcher selected in the first round. It was not at all obvious that he would be the best of the lot. Prior to the draft, Halladay drew mixed reviews from scouts, but Toronto scout Tim Wilken spotted something special about him.

Wilken gave Halladay a 95 out of 100. Wilken's report noted that Halladay had a quick arm, loose and flexible delivery, "plus to plus-plus fastball with running life" and good rotation and spin on his knuckle curve.[149] Wilken was especially focused on Halladay's "repeatable delivery," which he described as a recipe for throwing strikes. Further, Wilken was impressed with Halladay's ability to adapt to the batter's approach at the plate.

Halladay's career was almost a mirror image of the career of Kerry Wood. Wood had a meteoric rise; Halladay had an inauspicious start. Wood dazzled Major League hitters early in his career; Halladay struggled early. Even after Halladay had experienced some success in the Major Leagues during the period 1998-2000, Toronto demoted him all the way to the Class A Dunedin Blue Jays in 2001 to reorient his delivery. Both Wood and Halladay would make the All-Star team in 2003. However, Halladay's career was ascending, while Wood would never again be the same dominating pitcher that he had been early in his career.

Blue Jays pitching coach Mel Queen helped Halladay change his delivery from an over-the-top approach to a three-quarter delivery. The change added more sink to Halladay's pitches. In July 2001, Halladay returned to the majors after his stint in Dunedin, armed with his new delivery. In 2002, he posted a 19-7 won-loss record and a 2.93 earned run average. He followed his breakout year with an even better season in 2003, in which he went 22-7 in 266 innings and won the American League Cy Young Award. Injuries limited his effectiveness and innings in 2004, but he returned to top form in 2005 and continued as a dominating ace for the Jays through the 2009 season.

Following the 2009 season, the Blue Jays traded Halladay to the Philadelphia Phillies. He didn't miss a beat in the National League, winning 21 games for the Phillies in 2010, with a 2.44 earned run average. His efforts earned him the National League Cy Young Award. He pitched a perfect game on May 29, 2010 and then, for good measure, a second no-hitter in the 2010 National League Division Series. Halladay won 19 games and finished second in the Cy Young voting in his second season with the Phillies. When he retired in 2013, Halladay had pitched 16 seasons in the majors and won 203 games with a career earned run average of 3.38. He was as dominating as any pitcher of his era and was elected to the Hall of Fame in 2019.

The best hitter of the entire 1995 draft, outfielder Carlos Beltrán, lasted until the second round before being selected. The Kansas City Royals took the Puerto Rican native with the 49th overall pick. Ironically, the Royals had used their first-round pick on another outfielder from Puerto Rico, Juan LeBron, who had drawn comparisons to Texas Rangers star Juan González. Lebron's career was derailed by injuries and he never reached the Major Leagues. Beltrán more than filled the void, hitting 22 home runs, driving in 108 runs, and winning Rookie of the Year honors in 1999. He would play in the Major Leagues for 20 seasons. In that time, he hit 435 homers, drove in 1,587 runs, stole 312 bases and played a stellar center field. Beltrán was elected to nine All-Star teams, won three gold gloves and crowned his career with a World Series ring while with the Houston Astros in 2017.

A Rookie in Awe

C.J. Nitkowski knew his place. As a 22-year-old rookie with the Cincinnati Reds in 1995, Nitkowski didn't talk much in the clubhouse. He tended not to speak unless someone spoke to him first. Cincinnati's second baseman, Bret Boone, passed by Nitkowski's locker one day and jokingly told him, "C.J., you need to shut up."

Nitkowski's first Major League appearance came on June 3, 1995 against the St. Louis Cardinals. He was wearing uniform number 49, the same number worn by his boyhood hero, New York Yankees pitcher Ron Guidry. Called on as a relief pitcher in the seventh inning, Nitkowski faced four batters, threw 17 pitches, and gave up one hit but no runs. Nitkowski vividly remembers walking off the mound after getting the third out. "I was sweating like crazy," he says, "and thinking, 'What just happened?'"

He had just thrown a shutout inning in the Major Leagues. Barry Larkin had caught the third out. A year earlier, Nitkowski was playing for the Chattanooga Lookouts in the Southern League and using Larkin on his video game.

When reflecting on the speed at which things happen at the Major League level, Nitkowski says, "It can go really fast. It's really helpful to be surrounded by good people who can talk you through that stuff."

1996

Now it's [1996] and I am draft eligible again. Scouts have followed me the last couple of years, trying to gauge how I stack up against the other pitchers available. Start after start, I go out there and audition in front of these guys I've never met, guys who could have a massive impact on my future. They have their notebooks and radar guns and organizational shirts and hats, and their task is to determine if you are worth spending a first-round pick, and a pile of money, on. It's the meat-market part of the business, and you find out about it early. If they like another cut of meat better than you, you are going to stay in the display case awhile longer. It all comes down to what they write up in their reports and how you grade out. Literally.

    –R.A. Dickey, former first-round draft pick of the Texas Rangers and 15-year Major League veteran, writing in his autobiography, *Wherever I Wind Up: My Quest for Truth, Authenticity and the Perfect Knuckleball*

D erek Jeter took over the starting shortstop role for the New York Yankees in 1996 and helped lead the Yankees back to the World Series. It would be the Yankees' first appearance in the World Series since 1981. In an exciting six-game Series, the Yankees defeated the favored Atlanta Braves, four games to two. The Braves were led by their number one overall selection in 1990, Chipper Jones, and their future Hall of Fame aces, Greg Maddux, Tom Glavine and John Smoltz.

The 1996 amateur draft was like no other draft before or after. Scott Boras introduced himself to the draft in 1983 and, with each succeeding year, he gained momentum as a force to be reckoned with. In 1996, he stood at center stage as he waged a full-frontal assault on the bonus structure. Boras identified and exploited an obscure clause in the collective bargaining agreement that required teams to tender draftees a contract within fifteen days from the draft.

In 1996, Boras identified a number of teams that failed to extend timely offers to their draftees. Multiple draftees filed grievances which led the Commissioner to declare them free agents. The four players who ultimately opted for free agency became known as the "loophole gang" – Travis Lee, John Patterson, Matt White, and Bobby Seay. Boras's gambit drove bonuses to lofty heights almost unimaginable when the draft was instituted in 1965. The total bonuses paid to the four free agents alone, $30 million, exceeded the bonuses of all the other first round picks combined!

Baseball quickly amended the bonus tender rule so it would not be a factor in future years. However, with the bonus amounts that teams offered to the four free agents, Boras was able to prove conclusively that, as he had long contended, the draft artificially deflated bonuses. In future years Boras would try more and more imaginative ways to have his clients declared free agents, so that others could feast on the owners' inability to restrain themselves in bidding wars. With all the attention paid to the free agent bonuses in 1996, the actual draft was somewhat overshadowed.

1996 was another Olympic year for baseball and a very special one. The Olympics were back on U.S. soil and situated in Atlanta. The USA baseball team battled gamely for the home fans but in the end could only manage the bronze medal, as they were again defeated by the Cuban and Japanese teams. As was the case in past years, however, the fanfare surrounding the Olympic team served to elevate the profile and popularity of players drafted in the first round. Seven of the first ten draft picks were members of the U.S. Olympic team. All 20 Olympians would be drafted.

Clemson University pitcher Kris Benson was the first Olympian off the board. The Pittsburgh Pirates selected Benson with the number one overall pick, primarily on the basis of his dominant junior season in which he was 14-0 with a 1.40 earned run average and 178 strikeouts. Benson's performance earned him *Baseball America*'s College Player of the Year Award. Few scouts considered Benson to be an ace in the mold of a Greg Maddux or Tom Glavine. Nonetheless, Benson enjoyed an elevated status in the draft because, although there were many solid players available, few of them were regarded as true impact players.

Benson's career started off well enough. He pitched full seasons in the majors in 1999 and 2000. However, just when he appeared to be hitting his stride, an injury necessitated Tommy John surgery. Benson would miss the entire 2001 season. He resumed pitching in 2002 and won 22 games for Pittsburgh in the stretch from 2002 to 2004, but his earned run average hovered near five. The Pirates traded him to the Mets in mid-season in 2004. He pitched well for the Mets for the remainder of 2004 and in 2005. Benson would spend nine seasons in the Major Leagues and finished his career with 70 wins and 75 losses.

The Houston Astros found a late-round gem in the 23rd round with Roy Oswalt of Holmes Community College in Mississippi, who turned out to be the best pitcher in the 1996 draft. Oswalt was a "draft and follow" pick. Under the "draft and follow" rule, a team was allowed to retain the rights to junior college players right up until the next draft. While Oswalt showed promise in 1996, he was undersized and had a number of mechanical flaws. By the time the Astros signed him in 1997, he had gained 20 pounds and increased his velocity from the low to high nineties.[150] Houston's high regard for Oswalt was evidenced by the fact that they signed him for a bonus of $435,000, which was approximately the same amount that a high second-round pick would have received in 1996; even at that it was a mere fraction of the loophole gang's bounty.

The Astros' confidence in Oswalt was well placed as he became a three-time All-Star and twice won 20 games in a season. He helped pitch the Astros to the World Series in 2005. Oswalt pitched for thirteen years, winning 163 games against 102 losses.

More Than A Footnote

Hitting had always been the strongest part of Jim Leyritz's game. When the Yankees signed him as a free agent in 1985, the front office asked Bill Livesey, then a Yankee scout, what position Leyritz should be listed at on the Yankees' depth chart. Livesey quipped, "Hitter."

Though Leyritz never hit more than 17 home runs in any of his eleven seasons in the Major Leagues, he has the distinction of hitting one of the most memorable home runs in franchise history.

Eighteen years removed from their last World Series championship, the 1996 Yankees won the American League pennant and took on the Atlanta Braves in the World Series. Entering Game 4, the Yankees trailed the Braves, two games to one. After five innings of the fourth game, the Yankees were behind 6-0. The Braves appeared to be on the verge of capturing the game and the series. However, the Yankees clawed back for three runs in the top of the sixth, putting the score at 6-3. In the top of the eighth inning, the Yankees mounted another rally, putting two men on base with one out. Leyritz strode to the plate to face the Braves' Mark Wohlers. As Leyritz was heading to the on-deck circle, he asked coach Don Zimmer, "What's this guy got?" Zimmer replied, "Jim, he throws 100 mph. Just get ready."

Leyritz had always preferred not to have too much information about a pitcher's repertoire. So, when he walked to the plate to face Wohlers, he knew that the pitcher's strength was his fastball but didn't know much else. Wohlers' first offering to Leyritz was a 98-mph fastball. Leyritz fouled it back. Leyritz looked down at his brand new bat – and saw that the imprint of the ball was right on the label. It meant that he was getting the head of the bat out in front of the ball. Wohlers' next two pitches were sliders, both missing the plate. With the count 2 and 1, Wohlers threw another fastball at 98 mph. Leyritz fouled it back. This time Leyritz was a little closer to the barrel but still not in a good spot. Wohlers' next pitch was a tough slider and Leyritz just barely got a piece of it, fouling it down the third base line.

The situation seemed to be calling for a fastball in on Leyritz's hands. In the broadcast booth, announcer Tim McCarver told his audience, "Wohlers will probably throw 100 mph this pitch." Leyritz took a half step off the plate. He looked for a fastball or slider out over the plate. Wohlers went back to the slider. He hung it just enough for Leyritz to put a charge on the ball. Leyritz recalled, "I was able to stay back. He had me leaning a little bit forward but my hands stayed back and I swung. I knew as soon as I hit it that it was going to carry." As Leyritz touched second base, he thought, "If we don't win this game, this home run – as good as it feels right now – is going to end up just a footnote." The Yankees held the Braves scoreless in the bottom of the eight and then scored two runs in the top of the 10th inning to win the game, 8-6.

The Yankees would go on to take the next two games and clinch the World Series, 4 games to 2. The victory ensured that Leyritz's Game 4 home run would endure as much more than a footnote.

1997

My third year in scouting, I was scouting the White Sox and Detroit was in there and Detroit brought in a guy who was throwing 100 to 102 mph. It was Matt Anderson. Being young like that, I remember thinking, 'This is some kind of velocity.' But Albert Belle and Frank Thomas were with the White Sox then and they were hitting Anderson's fastball like it was on a tee. Once they had seen the fastball and timed it up, it was easy. Anderson was just an arm strength guy. His fastball didn't have any movement. He didn't have a good secondary pitch. Belle and Thomas just sat on the fastball. As hard as Anderson was throwing, they just tore down the walls.

–Dave Jennings, scout, Baltimore Orioles

While each draft has its own unique tone and character, some also provide a faint yet distinct echo from the past. The 1997 draft provided subtle reminders of the 1992 draft, while setting its own course. There were whispers in 1992 that the number one overall pick, Phil Nevin, was a "signability" choice. There were even louder murmurs in 1997 that the number one overall pick, pitcher Matt Anderson, was likewise selected because he seemed willing to sign without contentious negotiations or exorbitant expense. Though the 1992 draft has become a narrative about one player – Derek Jeter – and his slippage to the sixth pick, the 1997 draft was at the time, and has become even more so, a story about one agent – Scott Boras – and his growing influence over the draft.

If Scott Boras was front and center for the 1996 draft, he took another step or two forward in 1997. His success in finding a "loophole" in 1996, and the resulting frenzied bidding on the four amateurs who were declared to be free agents, convinced Boras that free agency was a ticket to untold bonus remuneration. Major League Baseball's revision of its 15-day tender requirement would not deter Boras's search for the holy grail of free agency. The battle lines were drawn now more clearly than ever. Teams that once saw Boras as a nuisance were beginning to see him as the enemy.

Though "signability" had been part of the draft vocabulary for several years, it truly became a main current in 1997. In the past, a few teams would avoid drafting a player with inflated salary demands; now more teams were inclined to give greater weight to cost rather than talent. While a Derek Jeter might have fallen a few picks in the 1992 draft due to "signability" issues, elite talents in 1997 were sliding entirely out of the first round.

Of course, an agent's ability to influence the draft is only as potent as the talent he represents. In 1997, Boras represented the consensus best player and presumptive top pick in Florida State University out-fielder J.D. Drew. Draft experts considered Drew to be a once-in-a-gen-eration type player. He could hit for average, possessed power and could steal bases. At Florida State, Drew had become the first college player to hit 30 home runs and steal 30 bases in the same season. As a junior, he batted .455 with 31 home runs, 100 RBI's and 32 stolen bases in just 67 games. Some scouts compared him to Mickey Mantle.[151]

Drew's bonus demands were reported to be in the neighborhood of $10 million.[152] The Tigers owned the first pick in 1997 but steered away from Drew due to his salary demands. Instead, the Tigers selected Anderson, a tall right-handed pitcher out of Rice University. Anderson could reach triple digits on the radar gun with his fastball. Even with his extraordinary heater, however, Anderson was a curious pick because his secondary pitches and delivery raised concerns among the scouting community.[153]

The Tigers had high expectations for Matt Anderson and his pow-er arm in their bullpen. Anderson saved twenty-two games for Detroit in 2001 but, over the course of his career, turned out to be a major disap-pointment. He pitched for seven seasons in the big leagues and finished with a career record of 15 wins against seven losses, with an earned run average of 5.19.

The Philadelphia Phillies owned the second pick in the draft and gambled that they could sign Drew, even though Boras had warned them about Drew's extravagant salary demands. For the Phillies, draft-ing Drew was an egregious mistake. From the start, Boras attempted to have Drew declared a free agent. Boras claimed that the Phillies had mailed Drew's tender offer to an incorrect address. The Commission-er's Office concluded that the Phillies had sent the offer to the address that Drew had provided and rejected Drew's grievance.

The negotiations between Drew and the Phillies became heated and eventually broke off. The ever-creative Boras had Drew sign to play for the St. Paul Saints of the Northern League, an independent league team. Boras then tried, unsuccessfully, to argue that as a professional player, Drew was not subject to the draft and was therefore a free agent. Again, Major League Baseball rejected the attempt to liberate Drew from his draft ties to the Phillies. Further attempts to negotiate a deal were also futile. Drew never signed with the Phillies but, instead, waited a year and entered the 1998 draft.

The Anaheim Angels selected shortstop Troy Glaus with the third pick of the draft. Glaus was one of the featured amateur players available. He had starred for UCLA as well as for the 1996 U.S. Olympic team. Angels' scout Darrell Miller, a former catcher for the Angels, was extremely impressed with Glaus's demeanor and resiliency. Miller was present at a game in which Glaus was knocked down by a high and hard inside pitch. According to Miller, "Glaus dusted himself off, didn't say anything, calmly entered the batter's box and hit the next pitch out of the park." Miller says, "Right there I found everything I needed to know about his makeup." Miller and the Angels signed Glaus for a $2,225,000 bonus.

The Angels immediately shifted the six-foot-five, 225-pound Glaus to third base. By 1999, he was the Angels' regular third baseman and hit 29 homers with 79 runs batted in. The following year he truly broke out, belting 47 homers with 102 runs batted in and a .284 average. Glaus had a solid thirteen-year career in which he hit 320 home runs and collected 950 runs batted in while being named to four All-Star teams.

Another 14 pitchers would be selected in the first round, including Tim Drew, the younger brother of J.D. Drew. However, the most telling feature of the first round was that no team was willing to use a first-round pick on Boras's client, pitcher Rick Ankiel. In a manner similar to J.D. Drew, Ankiel had advised teams that unless he received a bonus of $5 million, he would decline to sign and would play for the University of Miami.

Ankiel was considered to be the best high school pitcher available. Some scouts evaluated him as the top pitcher available in the entire draft. During his senior year of high school in Port St. Lucie, Florida, Ankiel posted remarkable numbers, with an 11-1 won-lost record, an infinitesimal 0.47 earned run average and 162 strikeouts in 74 innings. He had thrown three no-hitters and four one-hitters. St. Louis Cardinals general manager Walt Jocketty rated Ankiel as a top ten talent.[154]

Cardinals scout John DiPuglia observed, "I've never seen a left-handed pitcher with his type of composure and stuff on the mound."[155] Nonetheless, Ankiel slid all the way out of the first round to the late second round. The Cardinals drafted Ankiel with the 72nd overall pick and signed him for a $2.5 million bonus. Ankiel's bonus was $1.85 million more than the Cardinals gave their first-round selection, second baseman Adam Kennedy.

Were it not true, the story of Ankiel's career would seem to border on fiction. In 2000, Ankiel's first full season with the Cardinals, he appeared to be on the way to justifying the Cardinals' investment. In 30 starts, he won 11 games and had 194 strikeouts in 175 innings. He finished second in the voting for the National League Rookie of the Year. Just when he appeared to be on the verge of breaking out as a top-of-the-line starter, he suffered a monumental meltdown. While pitching in the National League Divisional Series against the Atlanta Braves and Greg Maddux, he imploded in the first game of the series. He sailed through the first two innings but, in the third inning, he gave up four runs while walking four batters and throwing an improbable five wild pitches. In his very next start in the National League Championship Series, he was unable to last through the first inning. In two-thirds of an inning, Ankiel faced six batters and threw 33 pitches, five of which went straight to the backstop. After his debacle in the playoffs, Ankiel was never a dominating pitcher again and pitched only 34 more innings for the rest of his career.

Despite his pitching woes, Ankiel was far from finished in baseball. He followed Babe Ruth's career path, switching from the mound to the outfield. A dominant hitter in high school, Ankiel went back to the minors to reclaim his hitting stroke. He returned to the majors in 2007 and played in 47 games, hitting eleven homers and batting .285. In 2008, he had 413 at-bats and mashed 25 homers with 71 runs batted in. Ankiel continued for five more seasons but never regained the stroke he exhibited in 2007 and 2008.

Jeff Weaver, a large and dominant right-hander from Fresno State, possessed what many scouts believed to be first-round talent. However, Weaver also fell to the second round because he was yet another Boras client seeking a huge bonus. Weaver was one of the key members of the 1996 U.S. Olympic team. In 1997, he struck out 181 collegiate batters to lead the nation. He fell to the Chicago White Sox with the 62nd over-all pick in the 1997 draft. As a draft-eligible sophomore, he had much greater leverage than the average draftee. When he was unable to reach an agreement with the White Sox, Weaver returned to Fresno State to pitch another season in college ball.

In contrast to Weaver, Tim Hudson of Auburn University had almost no leverage in negotiations because he was drafted as a senior with no remaining eligibility. The Oakland Athletics selected Hudson in the sixth round. Hudson would turn out to be the best pitcher of the entire 1997 draft. In a year in which players were looking for million-dollar bonuses, the A's landed Hudson for only $22,000. Though one scout noted that Hudson was "intelligent and poised" with good "pitchability," teams shied away from him because his fastball topped out at 89 mph.[156] He turned out to be a superb investment for the Athletics, as he would become a four-time All-Star over an excellent 17-year Major League career in which he won 222 games.

With the 16th pick in the first round, the Houston Astros selected Lance Berkman of Rice University. Over the course of his Major League career, Berkman would prove to be the best position player in the entire 1997 draft. Berkman had been undrafted out of high school but caught the scouts' attention by hitting .431 with 41 homers and 134 runs batted in during his junior season at Rice. Berkman's scouting reports were mixed at best. There was no doubt about his hitting, but his lack of footspeed and defensive shortcomings appeared to limit him to first base.[157] Berkman enjoyed an excellent 15-year Major League career during which he hit .293 and earned six All-Star selections.

Outfielder Vernon Wells, the fifth overall pick, turned out to be the best high school player taken in the first round. The Toronto Blue Jays arranged a pre-draft deal for a below-market $1.6 million bonus with Wells. A five-tool outfielder, Wells was a steal for the Blue Jays. He became Toronto's starting center fielder in 2002 and hit 23 homers and drove in an even 100 runs. In 2003, Wells hit .317 for the Blue Jays, with 33 home runs, earning selection to the American League All-Star team. He retired following the 2013 season with a career batting average of .270.

Dancing In the Dugout

The Kansas City Royals drafted pitcher Jeremy Affeldt in the third round of the 1997 draft. Affeldt reached the Major Leagues with the Royals in 2002 and played for 14 years in the big leagues. While with the San Francisco Giants from 2009 to 2015, he became one of the most reliable relievers in baseball. He retired after the 2015 season with a record of 43 wins, 46 losses and a 3.97 earned run average.

By his own admission, there were times during Affeldt's teenage years in Spokane, Washington when he behaved as a "self-centered, hot-tempered high school athlete."* There were also times in Affeldt's high school years when, in the opinion of some scouts, he did not show sufficient dedication to baseball.

Greg Smith was the scout who signed Affeldt for the Royals. Smith started following Affeldt well before other scouts even knew of him. In May 1997, Affeldt attracted widespread attention when he led his high school, Northwest Christian, to a string of playoff victories.

There were scouts who viewed Affeldt as too casual and frivolous. According to Smith, "A lot of other scouts did not like how Jeremy would air-guitar between games of a doubleheader or do some Chubby Checker-style twist out by the dugout." Some scouts, Smith says, "look for something not to like."

In Smith's view, there was plenty to like about Affeldt. Smith remarked, "Sometimes the things that a player does are showing you that the guy is confident and doesn't care what you think. That was Jeremy."

* Jeremy Affeldt, *To Stir A Movement: Life, Justice, and Major League Baseball* (Kansas City, MO: Beacon Hill Press, 2013).

1998

[Drew Henson] was a young man who was on the cover of Sports Illustrated. One of the scouts who followed Drew told me, 'I thought he would be in the big leagues in 48 hours.' There was a rumor that George [Yankees owner George Steinbrenner III] wanted to get Drew signed with the Yankees simply so that he couldn't play quarterback against Ohio State. I was opposed to paying all that money – when it was all put together, it was about $12 million. To me, you play one sport or the other. Baseball is more difficult to master than football but both sports are difficult.

—Dick Groch, scout, New York Yankees

1998 was a year of rejuvenation for Major League Baseball – a timely and needed rejuvenation. Baseball's huge fan base had been showing significant foundational cracks since the 1994 labor conflict caused the cancellation of a substantial portion of the 1994 season. The World Series had become an expected part of the American calendar. When the month of October 1994 came and there were no World Series games, fans responded angrily. Many fans seemed to conclude that if billionaire owners and millionaire ballplayers could not rise above the greed, then they would stop attending and watching games. Lifelong fans renounced their allegiance. The game was reeling.

Then, in 1998, the New York Yankees had a season for the ages. New York was led by Hall of Fame manager Joe Torre and stars Derek Jeter, Andy Pettitte, Bernie Williams, Mariano Rivera, and Jorge Posada. The Yankees won 114 regular season games, an American League record. They dominated the postseason, culminating in a four-game sweep of the San Diego Padres in the World Series. While their past and future success would generate more animosity than admiration, the 1998 Yankees were generally respected throughout the game. The franchise's return to prominence served as a major boost to baseball in the late 1990s.

Much more significantly, 1998 became the year of the great home run chase, which generated intense fan interest. It had been thirty-seven years since Roger Maris broke Babe Ruth's seemingly untouchable single season mark of 60 home runs. Now there were multiple contenders to eclipse Maris's iconic record of 61 home runs. The three leading contenders were all familiar names: St. Louis Cardinals slugger Mark McGwire, Seattle Mariners superstar Ken Griffey Jr., and Chicago Cubs right fielder Sammy Sosa.

Griffey eventually fell far behind in the competition, although he would still end up with an impressive total of 56 home runs. McGwire and Sosa engaged in a compelling contest in which both players wound up breaking Maris's record. McGwire demolished the record by hitting 70 home runs. Sosa ended up with 66 home runs and won the National League Most Valuable Player Award. Their epic home run battle captivated the nation and gave the game a much-needed shot of attention and adrenaline. While the accomplishments of both McGwire and Sosa have since been diminished by evidence of steroid use, the chase for the home run record served to revitalize the game.

The 1998 draft appeared to be very similar to the 1997 draft. J.D. Drew was again acknowledged to be the best player. Again, due to "signability" issues, he would not be taken with the number one pick. Ironically, the Philadelphia Phillies, whom Drew had spurned the year before, had the number one overall pick. Drew had become public enemy number one in Philadelphia. In spite of the Phillies' continuing need for a Drew-like power-hitter, there was no chance they would select Drew. The mere mention of his name would prompt outrage in Philadelphia.

With the first pick, the Phillies selected Pat "the Bat" Burrell, who had compiled very impressive hitting numbers in his three years playing for the University of Miami Hurricanes. In the three years, he had a .442 average, with 61 homers and 187 runs batted in. The difficulty was that Burrell played third base, a position that was capably filled in Philadelphia by 1993 draftee Scott Rolen. Further, Burrell came with injury concerns. He had missed a significant portion of his 1998 season with the Hurricanes due to back problems. However, concerns over the injury were mitigated by Burrell's spectacular end-of-the-season return in the College World Series, when he smoked six home runs in only 22 at-bats. Despite the injury, Burrell still posted a .432 average with 17 homers in 118 at-bats in 1998.

The Phillies' director of scouting, Mike Arbuckle, compared Burrell's power potential to Mark McGwire.[158] With Rolen firmly ensconced at third, the Phillies planned to move Burrell to first base. Ultimately, Burrell found a home as Philadelphia's left fielder. In just two years, Burrell became a fixture in the Phillies' lineup and emerged as a reliable power source. In nine years in Philadelphia, he hit 251 home runs and drove in 827 runs.

The Oakland A's were next up with the second pick. Like Philadelphia, Oakland wanted no part of Scott Boras and J.D. Drew. The Athletics chose six-foot-six left-handed starter Mark Mulder of Michigan State University. Like Burrell, Mulder was already in the big leagues by 2000, and he became a big member of the starting rotation for the rising Athletics. In only his second big league season, Mulder dominated opponents with a 21-8 won-loss record, finishing second in the American League Cy Young Award voting. Mulder continued to pitch at an All-Star level for his next four seasons, but thereafter his career was derailed by rotator cuff injuries. He pitched for nine seasons in the big leagues.

The J.D. Drew draft day drama finally ended when the St. Louis Cardinals selected Drew with the fifth pick. The Cardinals reached agreement with Drew quickly for a relatively modest $3 million bonus. Drew's bonus was less than the amount that the Phillies would eventually pay to Pat Burrell, which was reported to be $3,150,000. Cardinals general manager Walt Jocketty trumpeted the signing of Drew, whom he called the best talent in the last two drafts. Addressing the Cardinals' high-risk embrace of Boras, Jocketty said, "We take risks because we have a high regard for talent." Boras was also glowing in his assessment of Jocketty and the Cardinals, saying, "They have a unique insight on talent." [159]

Understandably, the love fest between Drew and the Cardinals was not well received in Philadelphia, where general manager Ed Wade called Boras "the sports world's top-ranked terrorist."[160] Phillies fans saved up their anger for Drew's first appearance in Veterans Stadium, which the *Philadelphia Daily News* would term "Boo Drew Night."

Drew raced through the minors. He made his first appearance with the Cardinals on September 8, 1998, the same night that Mark McGwire broke Roger Maris's long-standing home run record. While Drew went 0 for 2 in his debut, he hit five homers in only 36 at-bats and batted .417 during his September call-up. Over the next five years, Drew was a solid contributor for St. Louis when he was in the lineup, but he was unable to avoid the injury bug. His best year in St. Louis was in 2001, when he slugged 27 homers and drove in 73 runs, with a .323 batting average in 109 games. Perhaps frustrated by Drew's inability to stay on the field, the Cardinals traded him to the Atlanta Braves after the

2003 season in a multi-player deal that netted the Cardinals three good pitchers. In his only season for the Braves, Drew managed to play in 145 games and post career-best numbers, hitting .305 with 31 homers and 93 runs batted in.

Despite his success with the Braves, Drew opted to move on via free agency in December 2004. He landed on the West Coast with the Los Angeles Dodgers, signing a 5-year, $55 million contract. Two years later, after two excellent seasons in a Dodgers' uniform, Drew and Boras choose to exercise an opt-out provision in his contract with the Dodgers. The move caught the Dodgers by surprise. Dodgers general manager Ned Colletti pretty well summed up his dashed expectations with Drew, saying "You learn in this business never to be surprised. I'm surprised how it (the decision to opt-out) came down. Everything we heard, everything that had been written led us to believe the player loved being here."[161] A free agent once again, Drew signed a five-year, $70 million contract with the Boston Red Sox. Drew would finish out the five years of his Red Sox contract and end his career in Boston.

The best player of the first round, if not the entire draft, was six-foot-six left-handed pitcher Carsten Charles Sabathia. Known as "CC," Sabathia slid down the draft board all the way to the Cleveland Indians, who were picking at number 20. Sabathia's fall was due to concerns about his weight. As a high schooler, Sabathia weighed 250 pounds. Many teams were worried that he would balloon up and would no longer be able to pitch effectively. However, the Cleveland scout who signed Sabathia, Paul Coogan, did not share those concerns.[162] Rather, Coogan saw CC as a large baseball player who was not hampered by his size at all. Coogan focused on the way Sabathia dominated the high school competition in Vallejo, California with his 95-mph fastball and excellent command. The first time that Coogan was ever on hand for a game in which Sabathia was pitching, Sabathia pitched a no-hitter and hit two 500-foot home runs. When asked by his supervisors what would happen if Sabathia put on more weight, Coogan provided the classic comment, "If he gets bigger, buy him bigger pants."[163]

No less an authority than former catcher and four-time All-Star Bob Boone was also enamored with Sabathia's ability. Boone, who is considered to be one of the best defensive catchers in baseball history, had been newly hired as an amateur scout for the Cincinnati Reds. In the Reds' draft huddle, Boone argued, forcefully but unsuccessfully, for the

Reds to take Sabathia with the seventh pick of the draft. Boone, later a scout for the Washington Nationals, described Sabathia as the best amateur player in the entire country.

Paul Coogan's faith in Sabathia was rewarded quickly. Sabathia won 17 games against only 5 losses in his first season in 2001, when he finished as the runner-up in the American League Rookie of the Year balloting. He recorded double-digit wins in his first seven seasons in Cleveland. In 2007, he won the American League Cy Young Award, with 19 wins and a 3.21 earned run average.

The Indians traded Sabathia to the Milwaukee Brewers in the middle of the 2008 season. Sabathia put the Brewers on his ample back and carried them to the postseason. In the latter three months of the season, Sabathia started 17 games for the Brewers, won eleven and had an earned run average of 1.65. In December 2008, Sabathia signed a lengthy and lucrative free-agent contract with the New York Yankees. Sabathia pitched for eleven seasons in New York, helping the Yankees to the 2009 World Series championship and being named to three All-Star Games.

Prospects on Divergent Paths

When the Oneonta Yankees took the field for opening day of the 1995 season, third baseman Mike Lowell was batting third in the order. Hitting in the cleanup spot was outfielder Shea Morenz.

In the view of the New York Yankee brain trust, Morenz was the far better prospect. Measured in terms of dollars, he was roughly $630,000 better than Lowell. That was the difference in their signing bonuses. Morenz, a first-round pick, commanded a bonus of $650,000. Lowell, taken in the 20th round, received $21,500.

There was a lot to like about Morenz. An all-around athlete, he had spent two years as the starting quarterback for the University of Texas Longhorns. At six-feet-two and 205 pounds, he had the look of an athlete. Lowell, on the other hand, weighed only 180 pounds. He possessed what scouts would derisively call "warning track power." The label "warning track power" suggested that Lowell possessed just enough power to drive balls to the dirt track located in front of the outfield fence, but not enough power to clear the fence. Over the next two years, Lowell packed 25 more pounds onto his six-foot-three-inch frame and blossomed into a legitimate power hitter. In 1997, at the age of 23, Lowell hit 30 home runs, 15 for the Double-A Norwich Navigators and 15 for the Triple-A Columbus Clippers. He was in the Major Leagues by the following September. Lowell would spend 13 years in the majors, leaving the game with a .279 batting average and 223 home runs.

Just as Lowell's career was taking off, Morenz was struggling to stay in baseball. His best year came in 1998, when he hit .256, with 16 home runs, in 129 games split between Double-A and Triple-A. He retired from baseball after the 1999 season, without ever playing a single game in the majors.

Not everybody missed on Lowell. In his second season of professional ball, Jimmy Johnson, the manager of the Class A Greensboro Bats, told Lowell that he would reach the Major Leagues. Johnson identified exactly how Lowell was going to get there. Johnson told Lowell, "You remind me a lot of Ken Caminiti when I had him in the minor leagues. He had a good baseball sense, like you, but he was so behind physically. ... That was all he lacked. You'll see. You're going to fill into your body, you're going to gain fifteen, twenty, twenty-five pounds in the next two years, and that's when you're going to be ready to play in the big leagues."*

As for Morenz, there was plenty of speculation regarding the factors that had held him back. Among other things, scouts pointed out that it is a difficult adjustment for an athlete to go from playing before a hundred thousand rabid fans at the University of Texas to playing in front of a crowd of 700 at a minor league baseball game.

* Mike Lowell, with Rob Bradford, *Deep Drive: A Long Journey to Find the Champion Within* (New York: Celebra, 2008), 114-15.

1999

Josh Hamilton was the All-American kid. He was the guy who, when the game started, would come out of the dugout and greet his grandmother and then he would have his turn at bat and they had a kid with Down syndrome in the dugout who was the batboy and Josh would help the kid retrieve bats for his teammates when he wasn't at bat. He was a true All-American kid in every aspect of the game.

    –Dan Jennings, former manager and general manager, Miami Marlins

It is hard to fathom how different the 1999 draft was from its immediate predecessors. The palpable tension from the protracted negotiations with J.D. Drew and other top players of the last few years seemed to evaporate in 1999. The focus of most of the pre-draft discussions had returned to finding the best baseball player available. The easy, partially accurate reason for the relative tranquility was the diminished role of agent Scott Boras. For the first time since his entrance in the draft in 1983, Boras did not have a first-round client. Yet, in fairness, first-round bonuses continued to rise substantially from the prior years. With or without Boras, negotiations would have been tense and combative if teams had tried to retrench on the size of bonuses in 1999.

The fledging Tampa Bay Devil Rays held the number one pick. The decision regarding whom to select fell to general manager Chuck LeMarr and scouting director Dan Jennings. Almost without exception, draft experts pegged the top two picks of the draft as a choice between two high school stars named Josh – slugger Josh Hamilton and pitcher Josh Beckett. The conventional wisdom, expressed by Dan Jennings, was that a team could not go wrong with either player because both "were fantastic baseball players, as equal as you could find." The Devil Rays spent a lot of time and effort trying to determine which Josh to bring to the Gulf Coast.

For Tampa Bay, Josh Hamilton would prove impossible to resist and he ultimately became the Devil Rays' choice. If J.D. Drew was often compared to Mickey Mantle, Hamilton's tools and make-up were so otherworldly he was more often compared to fictional heroes like "The Natural," Roy Hobbs, and radio hero Jack Armstrong – the All-American Boy. When Hamilton was compared to real-life players, it was usually to the absolute legends of the game. The Devil Rays once had Hamilton's eyes examined and the optician was amazed by his 20-10 vision. The only other player known for such visual acuity was the legendary Ted Williams, who allegedly could read the Commissioner's signature on the baseball as it approached the plate.

Another reasonable comparison was with Babe Ruth. Hamilton was a top-flight prospect as both a pitcher and a left-handed slugger. As a high school junior, he hit .636 with 12 home runs while compiling a 11-2 record on the mound with 159 strikeouts in 87 innings. As a senior, he was 7-1 with 91 strikeouts in 56 innings. Although most teams tried to pitch around him, Hamilton still hit .529 with 13 homers and 35 RBI's in 25 games. At six-foot-four and 220 pounds, and possessing a 97-mph fastball, Hamilton was an imposing figure on the mound at Athens Drive High School in Raleigh, North Carolina.

The consensus regarding Hamilton's pitching prowess, from both teammates and opponents, was that he was nearly unhittable. He possessed a nasty slider to complement his blazing fastball. As a hitter, Hamilton hit moon shots that could clear any fence. While no doubt apocryphal, according to local folklore, Hamilton once hit a 962-foot home run.[164]

The first time that Tampa Bay area scout Mark McKnight and scouting director Dan Jennings went to see Hamilton play in high school, he pitched the first five innings and was unhittable. Hamilton then moved to center field, where he made two spectacular plays and easily threw out a runner at home plate. At the plate, he hit a ball out of the high school stadium into the parking lot. McKnight and Jennings compared notes after the game. They each had assigned grades that equaled or exceeded the marks they had given to Ken Griffey Jr. and Álex Rodríguez during their senior seasons. McKnight, who had been scouting for nine years, called Hamilton "the best young player I have seen."[165]

While make-up or temperament is not an attribute that scouts measure or rate in a formal way, teams were becoming increasingly cognizant of the importance of drafting players of good character. Many high-round picks had come with red flags or, at the very least, an arrogance that might spell potential trouble in the clubhouse. Even the "other Josh," Josh Beckett, had a cockiness to his demeanor. But not Josh Hamilton. By all accounts, Hamilton was as unassuming and good natured as a human can be. Jennings remembers being more impressed by the person than by the player. Jennings took note when, during one game, Hamilton hit a blast out of the park and, after crossing home plate, headed to the stands to kiss his grandmother. Jennings was even more impressed when he saw Hamilton reach out to help a boy with Down syndrome.

McKnight started focusing on Hamilton as the 1999 draft drew near. McKnight noticed that Hamilton would rarely swing and miss, which is very unusual for a power hitter. While part of a scout's job is to unearth any negative information that may exist about a prospect, not a single person whom McKnight interviewed said anything remotely negative about Hamilton. To McKnight, Hamilton "was Jack Armstrong, All-American Boy."

With all the analysis and reports about the two Joshes, the task facing the Florida Marlins became simple once Tampa Bay chose Hamilton. The only realistic option was to take the other Josh – Josh Beckett. As Dan Jennings commented, "You pick one and the other is just as good."[166] Indeed, Beckett was nobody's consolation prize. Rather he was the latest in the seemingly endless line of dominating right-handed pitchers from the state of Texas. He stirred all the echoes of his noted predecessors but the most common comparison was with Nolan Ryan. In Beckett's senior season at Spring High School, the tall right-hander was nearly unhittable, with a 0.39 earned run average and two strikeouts per inning. *Sports Illustrated* writer Jeff Pearlman described Beckett as possessing a "J.R. Richard-caliber fastball and a knee-melting curve."

The Marlins handled Beckett's development with "kid gloves." In the low minors, Beckett was never allowed to throw over 100 pitches. Pitching for the Double-A Portland Sea Dogs, Beckett struck out 102 batters in only 74 innings. Stan Cliburn, manager of the New Britain Rock Cats, offered bountiful praise of Beckett: "He's a lot like Nolan Ryan but far more advanced than Nolan was with his breaking ball."[167]

Beckett made his eagerly awaited Major League debut in September 2001 and did not disappoint. He held the Chicago Cubs to one hit over six innings. His first few years were slowed by nagging injuries – a recurring blister on his finger and a sprained right elbow. However, in the 2003 playoffs, he carried the Marlins. In the 2003 World Series, Beckett struck out 19 New York Yankee hitters in sixteen innings and earned the

Most Valuable Player Award. Beckett drew universal respect by voluntarily pitching on only three days' rest. Through five years with Florida and seven years with the Red Sox, Beckett continued as a front-line pitcher. In 2007, he helped lead Boston to the World Series championship.

Josh Hamilton started his professional career by dominating the competition. In 2000, playing for the Charleston River Dogs, he was named the Most Valuable Player of the South Atlantic League All-Star game. Hamilton appeared to be on a trajectory straight to the Major Leagues. However, in the spring of 2001, he was involved in a serious auto accident while driving with his mother and father. Both his parents were hospitalized with serious injuries, but Josh seemed unharmed. Over time, Hamilton felt back pain but tried to play through it. He later described the pain as "someone stabbing you in the lower back with a knife." Playing for the Double-A Orlando Rays, Hamilton hit .180 in 23 games.

The decline in Hamilton's performance was evidence that something was very wrong. While it would have been reasonable to attribute his spotty performance to the accident, rumors of personal problems also surfaced. Before the accident, he reported to spring training with several body tattoos. The tattoos came as a shock to Hamilton's parents and to the Devil Rays organization as well. "What have you done to your beautiful body?" his mother asked. Jennings professed to have little understanding of the "tattoo culture" but thought it was strange that the All-American Boy would become an ink display.

In the spring of 2003, Hamilton's career seemed to be back on track. Tampa Bay manager Lou Piniella envisioned Hamilton as the possible opening-day right fielder. But then, in the clearest manifestation that Hamilton was no longer the clean-cut model of probity, Piniella cited him for several rule infractions and reassigned him to the minor league camp. Rumors were rampant that Hamilton had become a regular at late-night parties. In late March, the "other cleat" fell like a bomb as it was announced he was leaving the team for personal reasons. Speculation spread of illegal activities, including rumors that he was addicted to cocaine. After a series of failed drug tests, Hamilton was suspended for the entire 2004 season.

Instead of comparisons with baseball's immortals, Hamilton was now in danger of joining Steve Chilcott, Mark Merchant and Brien Taylor as "can't miss busts" or being compared with Darryl Strawberry for all his off-field problems. Sports reporter Jeff Pearlman matter-of-factly stated, "The Devil Rays had chosen the wrong Josh."[168] Unsure of Hamilton's future, the Devil Rays left him exposed in the December 2006 Rule 5 draft. The Chicago Cubs claimed Hamilton and then sold his rights immediately to the Cincinnati Reds.

On April 2, 2007, eight years after he was the number one overall pick, Hamilton played in his first Major League game. He was 25 years old. In testament to his struggle to persevere through hardship and addiction, the fans at the Great American Ball Park in Cincinnati gave him an ovation that lasted for 22 seconds. Hamilton played well for the Reds in an injury limited season, hitting 19 homers, with 47 runs batted in and a .292 batting average. He played alongside Ken Griffey Jr. in the Reds' outfield, making it the first time that two players who had been selected with the overall number one pick manned the same outfield. In spite of Hamilton's success in Cincinnati, the Reds traded him to the Texas Rangers after the 2007 season.

On opening day of 2008, Hamilton was the center fielder and batted third in the order for the Rangers. From the start, Hamilton played well for Texas. He went one for four in the opener and, the next day, was two for five with a home run. He was named the American League Player of the Month for both April and May. Hamilton made the 2008 All-Star team and, for the season, hit .304 with 32 home runs and a league-leading 130 runs batted in.

In 2009, Hamilton was just as lethal but was limited by injuries to only 89 games. Healthy again in 2010, he played in 133 games and led the league with a .359 batting average. He won the American League Most Valuable Player Award and carried the Rangers to the World Series. Hamilton had another stellar season in 2011, as he again led the Rangers to the World Series. In 2012, his last in Texas, he made his fifth straight appearance in the All-Star Game on his way to 43 home runs and 128 runs batted in. Baseball was fun again for Hamilton; once more, he was drawing comparisons to Babe Ruth. Reporters referred to him with a new moniker, "the Hambino."

Hamilton left the Rangers via free agency in December 2012 to sign a lucrative $125 million five-year deal with the Los Angeles Angels of Anaheim. His performance with the Angels never came close to matching his halcyon days in Texas. When it was revealed, in February 2015, that Hamilton had lapsed back into drug use, the Angels traded him back to Texas. The 2015 season would be his last year in the majors. Hamilton was able to demonstrate that, when physically and emotionally healthy, he could be as good as anyone in the game. From a larger perspective, his story represents the triumph of the human spirit over its ever-present demons and provides a stark reminder of how fleeting the victory can be.

In 1999, the Toronto Blue Jays, a team that once routinely paid bonuses above the market rate to lure top talent, was now a cash-strapped participant in the draft. Scouting director Tim Wilken tells of the day that his boss, Toronto general manager Gord Ash, told him that the team only had $2.5 million available for the entire draft. Toronto's first pick, the 19th overall, was expected to demand $1.7 million alone. Wilken needed to find a needle in a haystack, a player they could sign for a below-market bonus who would still be an impact player.

Wilken was raised in scouting. His father, Karl, covered the Midwest for the Phillies. Foremost among Karl Wilken's signees was Phillies' legend Robin Roberts. Now the younger Wilken needed to find the best player "affordable" or else the Blue Jays would end their draft day very early. Wilken retreated to the darkened office of Blue Jays executive Paul Beeston and reflected on his predicament. He thought of a young and slightly-built Puerto Rican outfielder, Álex Ríos, who stood six-feet-five but weighed only 160 pounds. Even so, Ríos had strong, quick wrists.

Wilken envisioned that Ríos would eventually grow into his frame and develop power. Wilken's excitement grew when he learned that his national cross-checkers, Chris Buckley and Mark Smith, were thinking along the same lines. Wilken instructed Buckley to try to reach a pre-draft bonus agreement with Ríos. Buckley learned that Ríos was amenable to accepting a below-market bonus. Ultimately, Ríos accepted a stunningly low $845,000 bonus. The amount was lower than the bonus for any other first-rounder. Due to Wilken's ingenuity, the Blue Jays not only got Ríos but also drafted and signed future major leaguers Reed Johnson, Brandon Lyon and Matt Ford in later rounds without exceeding their limit of $2.5 million.

In his first four seasons of minor league ball, Ríos hit only seven home runs. However, in 2005, Ríos' first full season in the majors, he hit ten home runs. The potential that excited Tim Wilken began to emerge. In 2006 and 2007, he hit 17 and 24 home runs, respectively, and was named to the All-Star team each year. Ríos played 12 seasons in the Major Leagues and finished his career with 169 home runs and a .277 batting average.

In the 13th round, the St. Louis Cardinals drafted Albert Pujols. Of the 401 players drafted in 1999 before Pujols, none was better. The Pujols draft story is told in greater detail in the chapter, "Diamonds in the Rough."

Scouting Heartbreak

Heartbreak comes in many forms in baseball. There is heartbreak that derives from injuries, personal demons, or just plain bad luck. There is individual heartbreak, as when the career of a prized prospect is derailed by injury. There is team-wide heartbreak, when injuries decimate a collection of promising pitchers just as they appear poised to make their mark.

Mickey White, director of scouting for the Pittsburgh Pirates from 1998 to 2001, is something of an expert on heartbreak. White came to the Pirates in November 1998 with the intent of beefing up Pittsburgh's pitching. He drafted talented right-hander Bobby Bradley with the eighth overall pick in the 1999 draft. The next year, White took pitcher Sean Burnett with the 19th pick in the first round and selected hurlers Chris Young and Ian Snell in later rounds. In 2001, White drafted another potential front-line pitcher, John Van Benschoten, with the eighth overall pick.

White and the Pirates envisioned that the quintet of pitchers would form the nucleus of their starting rotation for years to come. The hope was not unfounded. By the end of the 2003 season, Bradley, Burnett, Young, Snell, and Van Benschoten had compiled a cumulative record of 138 wins and 65 losses in the minor leagues – an impressive .680 winning percentage.

The first sign of trouble came when Bradley required arthroscopic surgery in June 2001. Later that same year, he underwent Tommy John surgery, followed by a third surgery in 2003. Van Benschoten missed the latter part of 2004 with what was diagnosed as shoulder fatigue. In November 2004, the right-hander had rotator cuff surgery on his left arm and then underwent surgery for a torn labrum in his right shoulder in 2005.

Burnett, Young and Snell all had respectable big league careers. Burnett spent nine seasons at the Major League level, mostly as a reliever, and finished with 15 wins and a 3.52 earned run average. Young pitched for 13 seasons and won 79 games. Snell recorded 38 wins over seven seasons. However, the two most highly regarded prospects, Bradley and Van Benschoten, never made an impact. Bradley retired from baseball in 2006 without ever reaching the majors. Van Benschoten left baseball after the 2011 season, having won two games in the majors and posting a 9.20 earned run average.

More than 20 years after taking over as the Pirates' director of scouting, Mickey White still feels the heartbreak. "I thought we had drafted a complete rotation," he says.

2000

If you saw [Chase Utley] in high school, you would say 'this little guy can't hit.' His approach, it wasn't going to work. But Chase had something in his swing that was different from anything I have ever seen. His swing was really short, quick and boom! When you saw him play and saw him hit the ball, you would say, 'This can't be right.' He was too skinny and too small. You would think, 'How can he hit the ball so hard with his size?' [Fellow scout Gib Bodet] and I went out and saw him and told the front office, 'We love this guy.' To us, Chase was a second-rounder. Almost everybody else chuckled at us. They asked, 'How can you draft this guy in the second round?' He went to UCLA and, two years later, everybody in the world was saying, 'Oh wow!'

–Bobby Darwin, scout, Los Angeles Dodgers, and former Major League outfielder

The 2000 baseball draft ended the brief tranquility of 1999. Once again, signability issues came to the forefront of the draft. Prior to the draft, Major League Baseball, led by Director of Baseball Operations Sandy Alderson, made a concerted effort to educate teams on negotiating tactics. Alderson's purpose was to tamp down what Major League Baseball considered to be the alarming escalation of bonuses for high school and college players.

Fresh off its draft of Josh Beckett in 1999, the Florida Marlins selected Adrián González, a first baseman, with the overall number one pick. *Baseball America*'s scouting report called González the best pure hitter in the draft and compared him to Mark Grace and Rafael Palmeiro. Other draft experts, including some Marlins personnel, believed González was at best a middle first-round pick and not worthy of the number one overall pick.[169] Al Avila, the Marlins' scouting director, flatly denied economics had a role in the signing. Avila asserted that González "was the most complete player in the draft."[170]

Despite vehement denials from the Marlins brass, doubts about the pick lingered because González and the Marlins had agreed to a deal, four days before the draft, for a $3 million bonus. González's bonus was almost a million dollars less than the Devil Rays had paid Hamilton the year before and considerably less than the amount that the Marlins paid Beckett. Alderson's efforts seemed to be bearing fruit. In the case of

González and some of the other high picks in 2000, the bonuses the players received were significantly lower than the bonus amounts in 1999.

González's agent, John Boggs, confirmed that the pre-draft negotiations were cordial and that both sides desired to avoid a protracted and acrimonious negotiation. Boggs poignantly noted the González family is "not looking at robbing the bank today." The parents recognized that their son would need considerable time in the minor leagues before he was ready to make an impact in the big leagues. Boggs went on to affirm that "money is not the driving factor here."[171]

Even Scott Boras seemed more accommodating in 2000. To assist the cash-strapped Cincinnati Reds, Boras negotiated deals with the Reds for both their first pick, shortstop David Espinosa, and second round pick, catcher Dane Sardinha, that did not involve any bonus money. In each case, Boras's clients received Major League deals, which guaranteed Espinosa $2.95 million and Sardinha $1.95 million, spread over time. In Boras's own words, "We had to get creative to get these deals done."[172]

Adrián González had a slow start to his career. He labored in the minors for the next six years and was traded twice, once by the Marlins and then again by the Texas Rangers, before he had even played a full season in the Major Leagues. The perception began to grow that the Marlins had made a mistake in drafting González as number one. For González, his third team, the hometown Padres, proved to be the charm. He blossomed in 2006 with 24 homers and 82 runs batted in while hitting .304. In 2007, his power numbers rose to 30 homers and 100 runs batted in. González continued to put up big power numbers in San Diego for the next three seasons while making the National League All-Star team each year.

In 2010, San Diego traded González to the Boston Red Sox. In two seasons as a member of the Red Sox, González hit a combined .321 and slugged 42 home runs. In the latter part of his career, González spent five productive seasons with the Los Angeles Dodgers. He finished his career in 2018 as a member of the New York Mets. Due in part, perhaps, to the fact that González was traded five times in his career, he never seemed to get the acclaim that was warranted. A lifetime .287 hitter and five-time All-Star, González enjoyed an exceptional big-league career.

The draft story of Matt Harrington is another of the many cautionary tales of "can't miss prospects who missed." Harrington, a stud pitcher from Palmdale High School in Palmdale, California, had actually been under consideration by the Marlins as the number one pick of the draft. Many scouts believed Harrington to be the top arm, if not the top prospect, in the draft. Standing six-foot-three, Harrington threw in the mid to upper-nineties with impeccable command. In his senior season of high school, he was 10-0 with a 0.59 earned run average. His strikeout ratio was nearly two batters per inning. Both *Baseball America* and *USA Today* named him High School Player of the Year. Despite his impressive credentials, Harrington fell dramatically on the Marlins' draft board after his agent, Tommy Tanzer, warned teams not to draft him unless they were willing to pay a $4.9 million signing bonus.

Ultimately, the Colorado Rockies selected Harrington with the seventh overall pick. The subsequent negotiations became extremely acrimonious, making even Scott Boras's more testy negotiations seem almost cordial. Each side accused the other of lying. Tanzer maintained the Rockies had offered, and then reneged on, a pre-draft $4.95 million deal. Colorado vehemently denied the claim, admitting only that they had promised that, "Harrington would not get by their pick." The players drafted immediately before and after Harrington were signing for bonuses in the low $2 million range, providing the Rockies with little incentive to break the bank on Harrington. In an effort to end the stalemate, the Rockies progressively increased their initial offer of $2.2 million all the way to $4.9 million, only to have Tanzer summarily reject it.

When Harrington could not reach agreement with the Rockies, he chose to join J.D. Drew's old team, the St. Paul Saints of the Independent Northern League. His plan was to reenter the draft in 2001. However, the decision to play for the Saints proved catastrophic. Over nineteen innings, Harrington's velocity plummeted and his earned run average climbed steadily to 9.47. In spite of Harrington's rocky stint in independent ball, the San Diego Padres and general manager Kevin Tower were only too happy to draft Harrington with their second round pick in 2001. In hopes of signing, Harrington fired Tanzer and hired Scott Boras.

When Boras was unable to reach agreement with the Padres, Harrington retained his eligibility for future drafts. He would be drafted three more times in the three subsequent drafts – only to not sign again, and again, and again. Harrington eventually fired Boras. He finally signed with the Chicago Cubs in 2006 as a free agent for $1,000. The Cubs released him the following spring. Harrington retired from baseball in 2007 and took a job with Costco Wholesale Corporation. Harrington's saga remains one of the saddest draft stories of all time.

With the 12th pick of the draft, the Chicago White Sox selected outfielder Joe Borchard from Stanford University. In three years at Stanford, the switch-hitting Borchard smashed 40 home runs, drove in 187 runs and hit .346. The White Sox were enamored of his tape-measure home runs. White Sox scouting director Duane Shaffer compared Borchard to slugger Mark McGwire.[173]

Borchard was a quarterback of considerable talent for the Stanford University football team. In 1999, he came on in relief of Stanford's starting quarterback and threw five touchdown passes against UCLA, earning national player of the week honors from *USA Today*. Borchard was slated to be the starting quarterback in Palo Alto in 2000. As a two-sport star, he had significant leverage in negotiating with the White Sox. Chicago paid Borchard a $5.3 million bonus to sign. Aside from the four prospects who had been granted free agency in 1996, Borchard's bonus was the largest in draft history. Sandy Alderson offered one of the draft's all time understatements, saying, "in my judgment, it isn't a good signing."[174]

The White Sox brass were enthralled with Borchard's potential. Some in the organization described him as having "Mickey Mantle" potential.[175] However, other members of the staff questioned whether Borchard would be able to hit Major League pitching. Long-time White Sox scout John Tumminia recounts he almost "fell out of his chair" when he heard the comparison to Mantle. Tumminia's concerns proved to be well-founded. Borchard would only play parts of four seasons for the Sox and was never able to make consistent contact. The projected power that had White Sox executives drooling never materialized; he managed to hit only twelve home runs during his four seasons with Chicago. Borchard retired after a six-year Major League career with a dismal .205 batting average. He turned out to be a poor investment and a disappointment. His draft story is another installment in a long line of "reaches" from Major League teams when drafting football stars.

Three picks after the White Sox chose Borchard, the Philadelphia Phillies hit it big with UCLA second baseman Chase Utley. *Baseball America* ranked Utley as the best pure hitter in college baseball. At UCLA, he had hit .342 and had 53 homers.[176] The Los Angeles Dodgers had draft-ed Utley out of high school in 1997. Even though he was a slight 155 pounds, Dodger scouts Gib Bodet and Bobby Darwin were fascinated with his bat. After finishing his high school career, Utley was amenable to signing with the Dodgers. After his senior classes ended, Utley em-barked on a vacation trip with classmates. Instead of signing Utley be-fore the trip, the Dodgers chose to wait until he returned. When Utley came back from his travels, however, he changed his mind and enrolled at UCLA. "We fumbled it with Utley," Bodet says.

While Utley was still on the smallish side in 2000, the Phillies scout-ing director Mike Arbuckle was very impressed with his work ethic and bat speed. Arbuckle described him as a combination of All-Star Jeff Kent and former St. Louis first-rounder Adam Kennedy.[177] Arbuckle was pro-phetic, as Utley turned out to be better than both Kent and Kennedy and everyone in the 2000 draft class. He became a six-time All-Star and helped lead the Phillies to the 2008 World Series championship. In his 16-year Major League career, Utley hit 259 homers and drove in 1,025 runs.

Much of the uncertainty of the 2000 draft involved Scott Boras's clients. As was typically the case, most teams shied away from Boras's clients due to the agent's exorbitant demands. In all, Boras had nine clients in the 2000 draft. Most had fallen out of the first round due to Boras's monetary demands.[178] One of the most intriguing Boras clients was outfielder Xavier Nady of the University of California. A superior power hitter, he had been considered an early first-round talent but fell all the way to the San Diego Padres at the 49th pick. Even though Nady fell out of the first round, Boras was able to negotiate a $1.1 million bonus with the Padres. Nady cobbled together a 12-year big league career but never developed the middle-of-the-order power that San Diego had expected.

The Montreal Expos selected University of Arkansas left-handed pitcher Cliff Lee in the fourth round. Lee's numbers at Arkansas were unimpressive. During the 2000 college season, he had a 4.45 earned run average and walked 52 batters in only 65 innings. However, Phil-lies scout Joe Jordan observed a special competitiveness about Lee.[179] As Lee matured, the competitiveness served him well. He went on to win 143 games during his 13-year Major League career, which included four All-Star appearances. Lee won the 2008 American League Cy Young Award, winning 22 games against only three losses, with a 2.54 earned run average.

What Scouting Is All About

Sam Hughes, an area scout for the Chicago Cubs, liked outfielder Buck Coats from the start. Coats played for Valdosta High School in Valdosta, Georgia. He was not a known commodity; only Hughes had shown any interest. But, at six-foot-three and almost 200 pounds, Coats was athletic and well-built. In the days leading up to the 2000 draft, Hughes visited Coats and his mother in their home. Coats told Hughes that he was planning to attend Valdosta State College.

Hughes could see that Coats and his mother did not have an easy life. He tried to be helpful. Hughes told Coats that if he enrolled at Valdosta State, the Cubs would follow his progress and keep him in mind for the draft after his junior year. Another option, the scout suggested, was for Coats to play for a junior college team coached by a friend of Hughes. Hughes also mentioned a third option – if Coats wanted to turn pro, the Cubs could draft him, but Hughes would not be able to offer any more than $37,000.

After meeting with Coats, Hughes drove from Valdosta back to Atlanta. When Hughes got back to Atlanta, he found that Coats had left a voice mail message on Hughes's landline phone. The message said, "Mr. Hughes, call me as soon as you get this message." Hughes returned the call. Coats told Hughes, "I want to sign. I wanted to hurry up and call you because I didn't want you to change your mind. I really wanted to run you down in the parking lot of my apartment."

The Cubs selected Coats in the 18th round of the 2000 draft. Four days after the draft, he signed for $37,000. Coats made it to the Major Leagues in 2006. Though never a household name, he spent parts of three seasons in the majors with the Cubs, Reds and Blue Jays. He hit his only Major League home run in his rookie season off Aaron Harang.

Hughes has always felt a special affinity for Coats. He says, "That's what it is all about – to get a phone call from a kid who didn't have much in Valdosta, Georgia and who didn't sign for much and yet grinded his way through our system and then you get that phone call from him and he tells you that he's been called up to the big leagues. That's what scouting is all about, finding those diamonds in the rough, the ones who aren't as sexy as others but you saw something in them and you feel like you, as the scout, are in the same boat with the player and then they make it all the way up."

2001

I came up with David Wright. There were times that he struggled, but he had some great mentors. You look at guys such as Howard Johnson. Howard was David's coach in A ball. People assume that David had the confidence that he could perform at the Major League level his entire career. I would say, 'No, he didn't.' There were times when David needed that push, needed his confidence bolstered, and he got that support from some excellent coaches such as Howard.

–Bobby Keppel, former Major League pitcher

In the fall of 2001, the Arizona Diamondbacks unseated the New York Yankees as World Champions. Sports journalist Buster Olney proclaimed that the defeat marked the end of the Yankees' dynasty.

In the 2001 draft, the Minnesota Twins were hoping to turn around their fortunes as they held the first overall pick for the first time since 1983. Not only did the Twins finish with the worst record in the American League in 2000, but their draft history with early first-round picks was spotty at best. In 1983 the Twins drafted pitcher Tim Belcher but could not reach agreement on a contract. In fact, the Twins led all of baseball with the dubious record of having been unable to sign six of their first-round draft picks since the inception of the draft.[180] Consequently, the Twins were understandably concerned with getting the first overall pick right in 2001.

The most noteworthy feature of the 2001 draft was the exceptional level of available talent. Contract demands and signability issues took a backseat. The Twins were laser-focused on finding the right player. As draft day approached, the Twins narrowed their choice to two players, University of Southern California pitcher Mark Prior and local high school catching prospect Joe Mauer.

Both Prior and Mauer were sculpted six-foot-five athletes. Both seemed to fit the part of a leading man ready to turn around the fortunes of a flagging franchise. Prior boasted "all the pitches," plus the intangibles that separate staff aces from back-of-the-rotation hurlers. In some quarters, Prior was labeled as "the best college pitcher ever."[181] In his junior campaign at USC, he had compiled a 15-1 record with a 1.69 earned run average and led the nation with 202 strikeouts.

Twins area scout Mark Wilson had been following Joe Mauer since Mauer was in the ninth grade. Wilson had the feeling that Mauer was special from the first time he laid eyes upon him.[182] Mauer had hit .605 with 15 homers in his senior season of high school and received solid grades for his catching ability. Wilson and the Twins considered Mauer the best high school player in the nation, a player with true five-tool potential.[183]

Twins scouting director Mike Radcliffe was enamored with Mauer's sweet swing. Radcliffe commented, "The swing. It's the best swing I've ever seen by an amateur. Smooth, technical, balanced – an almost perfect baseball swing. I didn't see Ted Williams, but I've never seen anybody square the ball up every time he swung, like Joe did. On top of that, he was athletic and a catcher with a double-plus arm, double-plus glove. Álex Rodríguez [received] the highest number I've ever put on a high school guy overall, but Joe's swing graded higher."[184]

Despite all the praise for Mauer, Twins scout Joe McIlvaine, who had played such a large role in building the stellar Mets teams of the 1980s, revealed that the Twins were seriously considering drafting Prior. However, as the draft neared, the Twins backed away from Prior. Minnesota's discussions with Prior's father, Jerry, had become acrimonious because the Twins suggested that they were also considering the possibility of taking Mauer with the first choice.

Former Twins assistant general manager Wayne Krivsky recalls that, when the senior Prior realized the Twins were not going to pay his son anywhere near the $20 million he was demanding, an angry shouting match broke out. Prior's father yelled into the phone, "You don't have enough money to sign us! Don't take us! If you pick us, you are going to regret it."[185] For McIlvaine, Mr. Prior's tone was all too reminiscent of the last-minute problems the Mets had encountered with another USC star, Mark McGwire, and his father in 1984.

Jerry Prior's warning to the Twins was not just a shot across the bow, but a chilling reminder to the organization that the team could not afford to miss with this choice. When Radcliffe and the Twins opted for Mauer, they went to great lengths to emphasize that they considered Mauer the best player available and that he was not a signability choice by any stretch. While explaining that four of his scouts rated Mauer as the number one player, Radcliffe reiterated that the Twins could not afford to have another mishap with the pick.

Despite their efforts to proactively promote the Mauer selection, Radcliffe and the Twins were heavily criticized in the media and in the baseball industry. *Star Tribune* columnist Dan Barreiro wrote, "Please don't pretend the Twins took the player they thought to be the best player. ... Understand that money is the one and only reason the Twins went the direction they did."[186] Radcliffe remembers being besieged by scouts from other teams who questioned the Mauer selection, or more correctly, the non-selection of Prior. Few of the detractors would believe that Mauer was the player the Twins really wanted.

Ironically, most teams also saw Mauer as a signing risk because he was a two-sport star. Mauer had what teams feared most – legitimate options beyond baseball. A quarterback in football, Mauer had been named the national high school football Player of the Year. He had a scholarship to play for the powerhouse Florida State University team. McIlvaine and the Twins were confident they would be able to lure Mauer away from the gridiron because, upon visiting Mauer's home, the Twins' scouting team had seen that all the posters in his bedroom were of baseball players. Of course, the local connection that would one day allow him to play for his hometown Twins – only seven miles from his high school field – didn't hurt either. Mauer signed quickly but hardly at a hometown discount. He received the largest bonus ever for a high school player at $5.15 million. Despite all the post-draft criticism, Mauer turned out to be the right choice.

Mauer made his Major League debut in 2004 and hit .308 in his first exposure to big league pitching. In 2006, he led the league with a .347 batting average. He made his first All-Star team that season and hit 13 home runs with 84 runs batted in. Criticism of the Mauer selection vanished. He would be selected to five more All-Star teams. In his career year of 2009, Mauer won the American League Most Valuable Player Award with a season for the ages: a .365 batting average, 28 home runs and 96 runs batted in. Mauer played his entire 15-year career for the Twins.

The Chicago Cubs and scouting director John Stockstill were happy to use the second overall pick on Mark Prior. Prior did not get the $20 million that his father was demanding from the Twins but ultimately agreed to a

$10.5 million guaranteed Major League contract. Prior was the first player in his draft class to reach the big leagues, making his debut on May 22, 2002.

In his inaugural season, Prior won six games, lost six, and struck out 147 batters in only 117 innings. The following year Prior truly introduced himself to the game, with an 18-6 won-loss record, a 2.43 earned run average and 245 strikeouts in 211 innings. He made the 2003 National League All-Star team and finished third in the Cy Young balloting. Prior and fellow starter Kerry Wood led the Cubs to the National League Central title and a first-round victory over the Atlanta Braves in the Division Series.

As the sixth game of the Cubs' National League Championship Series against the Florida Marlins began on October 14, 2003, the Cubs were seemingly cruising to their first World Series since 1945. Chicago led the series, three games to two, and needed only one more victory to advance to the World Series. Prior started the game for the Cubs and had given up only three hits through seven innings. He retired the first batter in the top of the eighth inning and gave up a double to the second. The Marlins' third hitter of the inning, Luis Castillo, lofted a fly ball to left field. As the Cubs left fielder, Moises Alou, jumped to make the catch, a fan named Steve Bartman deflected the ball. Alou was unable to make the catch, giving new life to Castillo. He drew a walk and the Marlins came from behind to win the game, 8 to 3. The Marlins won the next day as well and went on to win the 2003 World Series.

Unfortunately for Prior, his career also seemed to decline in a relative instant. In 2004, he was slowed by injuries and posted a 6-4 mark in 119 innings. He was never again the same dominating pitcher. Prior attributes his rapid decline to two serious injuries, a collision with Marcus Giles in 2003 and a broken elbow suffered on a line drive in 2005.[187] Despite the abrupt end to his career, Prior still managed to compile a Wins Above Replacement value of 16.6 for his five Major League seasons.

Infielder Mark Teixeira, a product of Annapolis, Maryland, was considered to be the best hitter available in the 2001 draft and a possible first overall pick.[188] Teixeira fell to the Texas Rangers with the fifth overall pick. He had hired Scott Boras as his agent. It appeared that neither the Devil Rays, picking at number three, nor the Phillies, who held the fourth pick, wanted to deal with Boras.

Teixeira joined the Rangers in 2003 and immediately established himself as a middle-of-the-order presence, with 26 homers and 84 runs batted in. Over his next three seasons in Texas, Teixeira averaged 35 homers and 122 RBI's while playing a Gold Glove-caliber first base. Just as he was hitting his stride in 2007, the Rangers shipped him to the Atlanta Braves for a package of young prospects that included the future shortstop for the Rangers, Elvis Andrus.

Teixeira played the final eight years of his career with the New York Yankees and established himself as a fan favorite by maintaining reliable power production and Gold Glove defense. In 2009, he led the American League in home runs, with 39, and runs batted in, with 122, and finished second to Joe Mauer in the American League Most Valuable Player voting.

Another of the top players from the 2001 draft, third baseman David Wright, hailed from Chesapeake, Virginia. The New York Mets selected Wright with the 38th overall pick. Wright had starred at Hickory High School in Chesapeake. As a high school senior, he attracted the attention of Mets scout and former Major League first baseman, Randy Milligan. Milligan pushed for the Mets to draft Wright.[189] In July 2004, Wright made his Major League debut and hit .293 in 69 games, with 14 home runs. Wright was one of the first in what would become a steady stream of solid Major League players from the Tidewater, Virginia area.

Standing a touch under six feet, Wright was on the smaller side for a third baseman but became a franchise icon for the Mets. By 2005, he was a rising star as he hit 27 homers, drove in 102 runs and hit .306. "Captain America," as he became known, would become a fixture at third base in the National League All-Star Game. At age 30, Wright was the unquestioned leader of the Mets. He appeared to be on his way to breaking almost every batting record for the Mets franchise when injuries struck. In 2018, after 14 Major League seasons, Wright retired from baseball. At the time of his retirement, he held the Mets' career records for runs batted in, doubles, runs scored, walks, hits and extra base hits.

In the fifth round, the Philadelphia Phillies drafted another corner infielder, six-foot-four, 220-pound Ryan Howard of Missouri State University. The power hitting left-handed first baseman turned out to be one of the steals of the draft. He would team with 2000 first-rounder Chase Utley to form a dynamic right side of the infield and a potent duo for the Phillies for more than a decade. Howard played in 88 games in 2005, a year in which he belted 22 homers, drove in 63 runs, and was named the National League Rookie of the Year. The next year, he won the National League Most Valuable Player Award, as he smashed a league-leading 58 homers, drove in 149 runs and hit .313.

For the next five seasons, Howard continued to be near the top of the league in all of the power categories and in the Most Valuable Player voting. The three-time All-Star combined with Utley and former Montreal Expos draftee Cliff Lee to lead the Phillies to a World Series victory in 2008. While Howard was the regular first baseman for Philadelphia for most of his thirteen-year career, his performance declined precipitously over his last five seasons. He appeared to be on an arc toward Cooperstown in his early years, but his later performance tarnished his legacy.

The Oakland Athletics used the 26th pick in the 2001 draft to select high school pitcher Jeremy Bonderman of Pasco, Washington. The selection was newsworthy because Bonderman was the first high school junior ever selected in the first round. Bonderman had passed his General Equivalency Diploma exam and successfully petitioned for permission to enter the 2001 draft. While Bonderman went on to have a nine-year Major League career, he became more celebrated for his incidental role in the 2001 draft-day tirade of Oakland Athletics general manager Billy Beane. The incident, reported in *Moneyball: The Art of Winning An Unfair Game*, would serve as a visual exclamation point on Beane's drafting philosophy. In particular, Beane's philosophy placed extreme emphasis on avoiding high school pitchers in the draft.[190] Beane would have little use for Bonderman and shipped him to the Detroit Tigers in an August 2002 trade.

Another pillar of Beane's philosophy is the use of on-base percentage as a tool for evaluating hitters, rather than the more traditional reliance on batting average. The 2001 draft yielded the "walking embodiment" of Beane's philosophy in third baseman Kevin Youkilis, who was selected by the Boston Red Sox in the 8th round. Youkilis, referred to as the "Greek God of Walks" in *Moneyball*, had become Beane's ideal of the prototypical hitter. Youkilis proved to be an excellent draft pick for the Red Sox. He spent most of his ten-year Major League career with Boston, where he was a significant contributor to the Red Sox' World Series championships in 2004 and 2007.

"Great Anticipation, Great Player"

The 2001 American League Division Series featured a dramatic play in the 7th inning of the third game. The Oakland Athletics had defeated the New York Yankees in the first two games of the series and needed one more win to move on to the American League Championship Series.

Entering the bottom of the 7th inning in Game 3, the Yankees were leading, 1-0. With the Athletics' Jeremy Giambi on first base, A's left fielder Terrence Long hit a sharp ground ball past first base that caromed into the right-field corner. Giambi advanced to second base and then headed for third, intent on scoring. As Giambi approached third, the Yankees' right fielder, Shane Spencer, fielded the ball and threw in the direction of home plate.

Spencer overthrew the cutoff man but Yankee shortstop Derek Jeter fielded the throw near the first-base line and in a single fluid motion flipped the ball to catcher Jorge Posada to nail Giambi at home and preserve the Yankees' lead. It was one of the signature plays in Jeter's career, helping to cement his reputation as a clutch player.

The Yankees held on to win the game and then took each of the next two contests, ending the Athletics' pennant hopes.

In the aftermath of Game 3, reporters and fans marveled that Jeter was in position to corral Spencer's errant throw. Even Spencer was mystified. "How?" he asked. Clearly, the first-base line was not the obvious spot for a shortstop to cover.

A's second baseman Frank Menechino was among those who were curious. Sometime after the game, Menechino caught up with Jeter and asked why he had been hovering near the first-base line. Jeter told Menechino that Spencer tended to overthrow the cutoff man. According to Menechino, Jeter had watched it happen all year. Said Menechino, "It was just anticipation by a great player."

The "Moneyball" Era of the Amateur Draft (2002 – 2014)

The one constant through all the years, Ray, has been baseball. America has rolled by like an army of steamrollers. It has been erased like a blackboard, rebuilt and erased again. But baseball has marked the time. This field, this game: it's a part of our past, Ray. It reminds us of all that once was good and it could be again.

—Author Terence Mann in *Field of Dreams*[191]

Baseball analyst and author Jeff Passan has described the changes heralded by *Moneyball* as the most significant in the game since Jackie Robinson and the Brooklyn Dodgers integrated baseball in 1947.[192] Passan goes on to present the *Moneyball* epiphany as a straightforward and stark challenge to the old guard of the game. "Adapt or die," Passan warns.[193]

The iconic 1989 blockbuster *Field of Dreams* explained that baseball's timeless appeal is found in its relative lack of change. Ironically, baseball's continued popularity has transformed it from an idyllic game to a multi-billion dollar business. Inevitably, this change would percolate down to the management and operation of the game. *Moneyball* primarily chronicles the captivating story of the Oakland Athletics charismatic general manager Billy Beane and his on-field success in spite of the immense financial disparities between the "haves" and the "have nots" of baseball.

However, the more historically significant contribution of *Moneyball* may be to herald the changing of the guard in the management of baseball teams. In a relatively short time, Beane and his progeny of Ivy League educated general managers would introduce empirical analysis as a replacement for the time-honored intuitive approach of the old-time "baseball men." The effect would be to overwhelm and displace many of the rough-hewed individuals who had populated the scouting ranks.

By 2012, just a decade after the historic 2002 "Moneyball" draft, the Houston Astros became the poster child for embracing sabermetrics. Under the leadership of general manager Jeff Luhnow, Houston implemented sabermetrics in a way that transformed Moneyball's evolution into a full-blown revolution. Baseball commentator Brian Kenny described Luhnow's commitment as "ballsy and brilliant." Kenney wrote, "The Astros were going to be a pure, data-driven, logical organization."[194] Houston would do a full rebuild, to include employing former NASA scientists who would complete the "Moneyball" vision.

The Astros' march to the 2017 World Series championship appeared to be a pivotal point in baseball history. In some quarters, Houston's success appeared to affirm both the wisdom of sabermetrics and the logic of relegating the scouting community to the ashbin of baseball history. Subsequent developments, however, have at least slowed the march to sabermetric supremacy. First, the "old school" Washington Nationals defeated the sabermetrically advanced Astros in the 2019 World Series. Then, like a thunderclap from on high, substantial revelations in *The Athletic* about extensive electronic cheating in 2017 led to an investigation by Major League Baseball. When the allegations of cheating were confirmed, the Commissioner imposed draconian penalties, including the suspension and subsequent dismissal of Luhnow and Astros manager A.J. Hinch. It is left to baseball historians to evaluate the significance of these developments and their relevance, if any, to the continuing sabermetric revolution.

Returning to 2002 and the start of the "Moneyball" era, a few basic explanations and observations are in order. First, Billy Beane's experience as a promising high school baseball prospect and player seemed to inordinately shape his rather jaundiced view of baseball scouting. The hulking six-foot-four, 195-pound Beane was the quintessential five-tool player over whom scouts would drool.

In fact, the Mets' Harry Minor, one of the most respected scouts in the game, preferred Beane over Darryl Strawberry, whom the Mets ultimately chose as the number one overall pick in the 1980 draft. After drafting Strawberry, the Mets did draft and sign Beane with a later pick in the first round. However, Beane's tools never translated into Major League success. Minor, who passed away in January 2017, consistently maintained that Beane would have been successful as a player if he had not chosen to retire at the age of 27. A persuasive consensus has formed around the thesis that Beane was done in by the elusive "sixth tool" – confidence.

As confidence is fraught with subjectivity, Beane's lack of success is best explained by way of comparison with his Mets' minor league colleague Lenny Dykstra, another player whom Harry Minor signed. In stark contrast to Beane's hulking physique, Dykstra stood five-foot-ten and weighed 160 pounds. When Dykstra showed up for a Mets tryout, Minor mistakenly identified him as the batboy. Unlike Beane, Dykstra spent little time dwelling on failure. From all accounts, Dykstra put little effort into analyzing his at-bats, he just strode up to the plate and started swinging.

Former pitcher Jeff Bittiger, an Oakland scout and confidante of Beane, was a teammate of both Beane and Dykstra. Bittiger has a vivid recollection that explains the contrast in make-up between Beane and Dykstra as simply and as well as is possible. One day, as the Mets prepared to face Philadelphia's four-time Cy Young winner, Steve Carlton, Beane agonized over the matchup and worried aloud if he would be able to lay off Carlton's legendary slider. Dykstra, in contrast, didn't even know Carlton's name. Regardless of who was on the mound, Dykstra was confident that he would get two hits. In a twelve-year career, Dykstra compiled a 42.4 Wins Above Replacement value and made three All-Star appearances; Beane struggled to a negative 1.6 WAR value during his six years in the Major Leagues.

Beane's struggles led him to a sincere desire to redesign Oakland's amateur scouting system to take advantage of the inherent inefficiency of the process. Beane believed, fervently, that the baseball community did not appreciate the benefit of using on-base percentage to evaluate players. Oakland is a small market franchise that lacks the resources to compete with wealthier organizations in signing expensive free agent stars. Beane attempted to compensate for the disparity in wealth by replacing free agent stars who departed Oakland with undervalued players who excelled at getting on base.

Beane's starting point, and ending point, was to focus exclusively on the college talent pool and ignore the pool of talent at the high school level. To Beane, the approach made sense, especially because, as a high school prospect himself, he had struggled so mightily at the professional level. Beane's approach was inherently logical. To his mind, players in the collegiate pool are three or more years older than high school athletes and have already overcome the daunting challenge of leaving the comforts of home. Moreover, college players are more physically mature, so the challenge of projecting teen growth is eliminated. Further, collegiate statistics, especially from the more respected NCAA conferences, are much more reliable guides of future performance than the high school statistics that are compiled from games between vastly differing talents.

Over time, there have been distinct periods when it appeared that college talent would be the wave of the future. However, there is one major drawback to the otherwise logical focus on drafting solely collegiate players. There will always be certain high school teenagers who are special talents – touched by the hand of God, as it were.

The "God players," as long-time Major League scout Ron Rizzi calls them, are preternaturally equipped to overcome the rigors of Major League Baseball and join the ranks of baseball's immortals. As a prime example, the Seattle Mariners changed the history of their franchise by opting for high school phenom Ken Griffey Jr. in 1987 over the "safe" college choice, pitcher Mike Harkey. Like the Mariners in 1987, many teams will recognize the risk in selecting an Álex Rodríguez or a Mike Trout out of high school and will nonetheless embrace that risk. The payoff, of course, lies in the hope of acquiring high school talents who will prove capable of joining Ron Rizzi's pantheon of "God players."

The more controversial aspect of the "Moneyball" approach to the draft was the belief that, properly analyzed, statistics could largely replace scouts and eliminate possible biases that would favor tools (i.e., potential) over performance. Historically, it had been accepted that scouts need to see players and have their eyes evaluate the talent. However, the radical approach that began with "Moneyball" and culminated with the Houston Astros' revolution explicitly advocated, "do not trust your eyes, trust the instruments (or stats)."[195]

As Michael Lewis made clear in *Moneyball*, Billy Beane did not trust scouts, as "[he] had come to believe that baseball scouting was at roughly the same stage of development in the twenty-first century as professional medicine had been in the eighteenth."[196] The narratives that follow will review the "Moneyball" years with an eye toward identifying the influences of the "Moneyball" philosophy on the draft and evaluating its successes and failures.

Distinguishing Between A Slider and A Curveball

Matthew Burns is an associate scout for the Pittsburgh Pirates. His job is to scout ballplayers at the high school and collegiate levels. Burns has a unique background for a scout. Before starting to work for the Pirates in 2017, he operated the TrackMan Baseball data system at FNB Park, home to the Harrisburg (Pennsylvania) Senators in the Eastern League.

The TrackMan system is a technology that captures comprehensive ball-tracking data and is used by professional and some college teams during games and practices. TrackMan records approximately twelve different attributes of baseballs that are thrown from the pitching mound, including the velocity, the rate at which the baseball is spinning, and the vertical and horizontal movement of the ball.

For balls that are hit by a batter, TrackMan captures roughly eight other attributes, including the exact point of impact, the launch angle, and the velocity of the baseball immediately after the bat makes contact with the ball.

The TrackMan data can be helpful in evaluating players, especially in situations where a scout is trying to identify whether a pitcher possesses a slider or a curveball. According to Burns, the task of distinguishing between a slider and a curveball can be difficult because many pitchers throw a pitch that may have attributes of both a slider and a curveball.

The TrackMan data is helpful because it depicts the point at which the pitcher releases the ball and the break angle of the pitch. The data allows scouts to see which way the ball is breaking and whether it has more horizontal break or more vertical break.

Burns find that even pitchers may be confused as to whether the pitch they are throwing is a slider or a curve. "Some guys," he says, "will call their slider a curveball even when it looks like a slider (i.e., breaks horizontally) to everybody."

The larger question is whether a pitcher is able to get batters out with his pitch, whether it be a slider or a curve. However, when pitchers throw a pitch that is between a curveball look and a slider look, it is useful for scouts to specifically identify the pitch in order to present the most accurate information possible in their reports.

2002

I didn't have a beef with Oakland selecting Jeremy Brown. Everybody sees players differently. My beef is with pretending that Oakland was so smart because they picked Jeremy Brown.

– Gib Bodet, long-time Los Angeles Dodgers scout

The 2002 draft received more scrutiny than any other draft in baseball history. Michael Lewis' best-selling book, *Moneyball*, devotes a whole chapter to an analysis of the draft through the fascinating prism of the Oakland Athletics' draft room discussions.

Oakland's failure to draft Kevin Youkilis in 2001 would haunt general manager Billy Beane for years. In 2002, Beane would become more involved in the draft process in an effort to extend his "Moneyball" innovations to the scouting world. The Athletics were ideally positioned to make some noise in the 2002 draft; they possessed seven first-round and supplemental first-round choices. Beane's strategy was to focus on collegiate players to the exclusion of high school players.

In view of the financial handicaps that had driven Beane to search for competitive advantages in undervalued talents, it is understandable that he would extend the strategy to the draft. Drafting collegiate players is less expensive for an organization than drafting their high school counterparts because college players are older and more Major League ready and therefore require less development time and expense. Simply stated, college players are poised to fill Major League roster positions sooner than high school players.

Major League readiness was an especially important attribute for the cash-strapped Athletics, who were repeatedly in need of replacements for veteran free agents whom they could not afford to retain. As such, Beane's strategy was eminently reasonable and noncontroversial. However, *Moneyball* goes on to say, unequivocally, that Beane preferred collegiate players to high school players even if all things, including payroll, were even. Michael Lewis then proceeds to document how the Athletics' approach to the 2002 draft demonstrated Beane's commitment to this radical proposition.

Moneyball meticulously details the Athletics' draft room discussions in 2002 and provides Beane's actual "Top 20 Player Draft List." Significantly, all of the players on Oakland's Top 20 List were collegiate players. Most tellingly, *Moneyball* describes Beane pumping his fist in apparent victory as opposing teams would select high school players in the first round of 2002, thus leaving his target list of collegiate talent undisturbed.

The intense focus on *Moneyball* has obscured the most significant fact about the 2002 draft: it was a very good and very deep draft.[197] The first round was the most prolific in the history of the draft as a record eighty percent (24 out of 30) of the first-rounders made the Major Leagues. Not only did 24 first-rounders make the majors, but most had very long and successful careers. Fourteen of the first-round selections played at least ten seasons in the Major Leagues. Despite the historical depth of the talent in the 2002 draft, there was little clarity as to who would be the overall number one pick. There were no consensus picks such as there had been in 2001 with Mark Prior and Joe Mauer.

The Pittsburgh Pirates held the first overall selection for the first time since they had picked Clemson right-hander Kris Benson six years earlier. This time the Pirates opted for another tall right-handed college pitcher in six-foot-five Bryan Bullington of Ball State University. In his final season at Ball State, Bullington had dominated opposing teams with a 2.86 earned run average and had struck out 139 batters while issuing only 18 walks.[198] Bullington was clocked at 96 mph on the radar gun. Increased velocity is an irresistible siren's song for most scouts. That was certainly the case for the Pirates in 2002. While there were concerns about the level of competition that Bullington had faced in the Mid-American Conference, no one could argue with the speed of his fastball.

The Bullington selection was widely criticized as a "signability pick," even though it took months of contentious negotiations to come to agreement. Bullington ultimately signed for a $4 million bonus, twenty percent less than Mauer had received in 2001. The selection of Bullington turned out to be one of the worst "number one, number one" picks in the history of the draft. Bullington did not win a single game for Pittsburgh and only managed to win one game during his entire career, which consisted of only 81 innings over five years.

Dan Jennings and the Tampa Bay Devil Rays were up next with the second pick. True to his draft philosophy of selecting potential "impact players" early in the draft, Jennings selected a high school phenom in five-tool shortstop B.J. Upton of Greenbrier Christian Academy in Chesapeake, Virginia.[199] Upton was a teammate of David Wright in youth baseball and was as close to a consensus pick as there was in 2002. Nonetheless, though Upton possessed tools in ample supply and hit an eye-catching .641 at Greenbrier, there was considerable doubt regarding his ability to hit Major League pitching.[200] The Rays signed him to a $4.6 million bonus, which exceeded the bonus paid to Bullington and everyone else in the 2002 class.

Upton made it to Tampa for a 45-game stint in 2004 at the age of 19. As a 22-year-old, he had a breakout season for the Devil Rays in 2007, hitting 24 homers with 82 runs batted in and 22 stolen bases. Despite striking out 154 times, Upton batted an even .300. Jennings and the Rays seemed to have their "impact player" and then some. Chuck LaMar, general manager of the Devil Rays, opined that "the sky was the limit" for Upton. However, his performance over the next few seasons raised concerns. For four consecutive years, 2009 through 2012, Upton's batting average was at .246 or lower. Pitchers seemed to exploit the holes in his swing with each successive season. He retired after the 2016 season with a career average of .243.

The Kansas City Royals' selection of Florida high school pitcher Zack Greinke with the sixth pick would change the narrative of the 2002 draft dramatically, in time. While Beane no doubt pumped his fist in the air when Greinke's name was announced, Greinke would prove to be the best player selected in the entire 2002 draft. Nonetheless, despite his impressive high school credentials, Greinke was anything but an overnight success.

Greinke had been a dual threat at Apopka High School in Orlando, Florida, on the mound and at shortstop. Draft experts reported that Greinke "does just about everything other than run at the Major League level. He can hit, hit with power, field and has one of the best arms in high school baseball.[201] Royals scout Cliff Pastornicky stated that Greinke "could have been a shortstop, third baseman, catcher or pitcher."[202] While it was Greinke's bat that first caught the attention of the scouting community, it was his 97-mph fastball and his advanced pitching instincts that fascinated Royals scouting director Deric Ladnier.[203] Royals general manager Allard Baird had instructed Ladnier and his team to draft a college pitcher with their pick. In response,

Ladnier assured his boss that Greinke was as polished as any collegiate pitcher in the nation and closer to the majors than any other pitcher.[204]

As the Royals had hoped, Greinke shot through their farm system. He was already up with the big club by 2004. However, initially, he struggled mightily in the big leagues. Part of Greinke's problems resulted from a severe social anxiety disorder. The Royals proved to be as patient with Greinke's disorder as they were with his learning curve. Greinke rewarded the patience with 13 wins in 2008 and a breakout year in 2009, when he led the American League with a sterling 2.16 earned run average and won the American League Cy Young Award.

In December 2010, the Royals traded Greinke to the Milwaukee Brewers and received in return key prospects, including Lorenzo Cain and Alcides Escobar. Cain and Escobar would both play significant roles in the Royals' 2015 World Series victory over the New York Mets. Greinke continued to perform as an ace pitcher while pitching for six different teams – making six All-Star teams and pitching for the Astros in the 2019 World Series. He will no doubt receive serious Hall of Fame consideration in future years.

With the seventh overall pick, the Milwaukee Brewers selected high school slugger Prince Fielder. Once again, Beane was pleased with the pick because Fielder was another high school talent in whom Beane had no interest. However, Fielder would turn out to be one of the ten best picks in the draft. The son of former Detroit Tigers slugger Cecil Fielder, Prince Fielder was a standout at Eau Gallie High School in Melbourne, Florida. *Baseball America* described him as a "polarizing prospect" because of both undeniable power and his girth. Fielder was five-feet-eleven; his weight fluctuated between 250 and 300 pounds.

Michael Lewis described Fielder as "too fat even for the Oakland A's." The weight issue aside, Fielder was, of course, undraftable for the A's because he was a high school player. Playing in 157 games for the Brewers in 2006, he hit 28 home runs and drove in 81 runs. He truly broke out in 2007, as he led the American League with 50 homers. When healthy, Fielder served as a big bat in the middle of the order for the rest of his 12-year Major League career. He closed out his career with two years in Detroit and three years with Texas. He hit 319 lifetime home runs.

The New York Mets selected left-handed pitcher Scott Kazmir from Houston, Texas at number 15. The Mets' selection of Kazmir assured that Ohio State outfielder Nick Swisher would be available for the Athletics at number 16. Swisher sat first in line on Billy Beane's Top 20 List. Swisher had caught Beane's attention precisely because he was the laid-back antithesis of Beane himself. Swisher would go on to have a very solid twelve-year Major League career. His lifetime Wins Above Replacement value of 21.5 ranks him among the top 20 players of the 2002 draft.

The Philadelphia Phillies selected left-handed high school pitcher Cole Hamels with the 17th overall pick. Aside from Greinke, Hamels would have the best career of any player in the 2002 draft. Like Greinke, Hamels was viewed as a complete pitcher with mound presence and maturity beyond his years. He remained available at the 17th pick because he had broken his humerus during his sophomore season and missed all of his junior season. Hamels was a key component of Philadelphia's World Series team in 2008, winning the Most Valuable Player Awards for both the National League Championship Series and the World Series.

The Athletics' second first-round pick, number 24 overall, was University of Kentucky starter Joe Blanton. Blanton had established himself as a first-round choice in March 2002 when he outdueled the eventual overall number one choice, Bryan Bullington, in a game. In that contest, Blanton registered 95 miles an hour on the radar gun and recorded 16 strikeouts. Blanton would go on to have a 13-year Major League career, playing for three full seasons with Oakland and, thereafter, with six other clubs.

The Giants selected right-handed pitcher Matt Cain from Houston High School in Germantown, Tennessee with the 25th pick. The Giants area scout, Lee Elder, had turned in a glowing recommendation on Cain. Elder was particularly impressed by Cain's repeatable delivery, command and pitch movement. "I think ... unlike most high school kids or even college pitchers, he got a little bit better every time out. He has a chance, with his delivery being so repetitive, to go a long way."[205] Cain proved Elder to be prophetic as he would star in the Bay Area for 13 years, which included three All-Star Game selections and two World Series championships.

With the 26th pick, the Athletics selected shortstop John McCurdy of the University of Maryland. Most teams had ranked McCurdy lower because he only had one solid college season. Additionally, McCurdy's defense was suspect. Beane saw him as another Jeff Kent who could move to second base. While the A's may have reached a little for McCurdy, he was genuinely a borderline first-round pick. The same could be said for Fresno State pitcher Ben Fritz, whom Beane selected with the 30th overall pick. In college, Fritz was both a pitcher and a catcher but the Athletics projected him as a pitcher. In fact, Beane's draft guru, Paul DePodesta, considered Fritz to be the third best pitcher in the entire draft.[206] Fritz underwent Tommy John surgery in 2004. He pitched for seven years in the minor leagues, advancing as high as Triple-A, but never reached the Major Leagues.

In a very real sense, the true "Moneyball" revolution did not begin until the supplemental first round. The first four Oakland selections in the first round, arguably, were drafted at or near their pre-draft rankings. Writing in *Moneyball*, Michael Lewis noted that with the supplemental round, everyone in the draft room was about to learn "how new and different is the Oakland A's *scientific* selection of amateur baseball players."[207] With the 35th pick of the draft, the A's shocked the baseball world by selecting Alabama catcher Jeremy Brown. Brown is described in *Moneyball* as an overweight catcher whom Beane was fixated on drafting because of his high on-base percentage.

Most teams did not expect Brown to be drafted in the first thirty rounds. The consensus was that he lacked traditional baseball skills. In terms of the traditional five-tool analysis, it was not readily apparent what Brown's tools were. Nonetheless, he became the litmus test for the Athletics' new philosophy. Brown's performance in the minor leagues was undistinguished. In six minor league seasons, he hit .268 with 68 home runs. In 2006, he joined Oakland in the majors for what baseball people call a "cup of coffee." His career statistics read: five games, 10 at-bats, 3 hits and no runs batted in. Like so many others before him, Brown became a blip on the radar screen of Major League Baseball but will be forever immortalized by *Moneyball*.

In the second round of the draft, the Athletics downsized. With the 67th pick, they chose diminutive University of Notre Dame outfielder Steve Stanley. Stanley was generously listed at five-feet-eight and 160 pounds. Again, Billy Beane was sticking his finger in the proverbial eye of established scouting wisdom. Stanley was a very solid college outfielder blessed with great speed and a solid work ethic. Other Major League teams, however, had advised Stanley that he would not likely hear his name called until at least the 15th round.

Overall, Stanley's small stature and lack of superior hitting skills made him a dubious choice by the traditional standards of scouting. Stanley played five years in the minors and never made it to the Major Leagues for even a "cup of coffee." Though Stanley never had any highlights at the Major League level, there was one stretch in his minor league career where he truly sparkled at the plate. In 2004, playing in 36 games for the Midland RockHounds, Stanley had 62 hits in 148 at-bats, good for a .419 batting average.

Some of the best players of the 2002 draft lasted until the second round. None of them were better than Joey Votto, a catcher from the Richview Collegiate Institute in Toronto. The Cincinnati Reds took Votto with the 44th overall pick. Votto's catching skills were suspect, causing the Reds to move him to first base. However, his left-handed swing and hitting skills were never in doubt. It took Votto until 2008 to make it to the majors for a full season but his impact was immediate. He finished second in the National League Rookie of the Year voting in 2008, with 24 homers, 84 runs batted in, and a .297 average. The next year his power numbers were almost identical, yet he raised his average to .322. The best was yet to come. In 2010, he won the National League Most Valuable Player Award, with 37 homers, 113 runs batted in, and a .324 average. Votto has accumulated six All-Star appearances in his career.

The Boston Red Sox also struck second-round gold when they selected left-handed pitcher Jon Lester of Tacoma, Washington. Lester was yet another two-way player who impressed scouts with his bat and his work on the mound. The Sox viewed him as a first-round pitching talent. To entice him away from Arizona State University, Boston paid him first-round bonus money in the neighborhood of $1 million. Lester made it to Fenway Park by 2006 and was almost an immediate success. He has been selected to five All-Star teams and has been a key member of three World Series championship teams.

The second round continued to provide star power as the Atlanta Braves used the 64th pick of the draft to select a local product, high school catcher Brian McCann. In 2006, McCann's first full year in Atlanta, he started with a bang, slugging 24 home runs and driving in 93 runs while hitting .333. McCann became a key part of the Braves' lineup and a seven-time National League All-Star.

In the 7th round, Oakland selected another player on its Top 20 List, Brant Colamarino of the University of Pittsburgh. Colamarino was described by Paul DePodesta as perhaps "the best hitter in the country." DePodesta added correctly, "No one else in baseball will agree."[208] Unfortunately for Billy Beane and the Athletics, their contrarian approach again failed. In six minor league seasons, Colamarino hit .273 with 91 home runs but never advanced to the Major Leagues.

At the end of the 2002 draft, Billy Beane was ecstatic. He proclaimed, "This is the best draft I have ever been part of. We got everything we wanted and more."[209] With the benefit of hindsight, the Athletics' overall performance in the 2002 draft was fair at best. Oakland drafted two solid major leaguers in the first round – Swisher and Blanton. By the usual standards, gaining two productive players from any one draft is an accomplishment. However, 2002 proved to be a very deep draft for high school talent. Seventy percent of the top ten achievers of the draft, as judged by Wins Above Replacement values, were high school players. Thus, in choosing to avoid high school players, Oakland shunned the deepest part of the talent pool.

Any evaluation of Oakland's 2002 draft must be tempered by the outsized expectations that "Moneyball" had created. The unorthodox choices that emerged from the central thesis of the revolution were disappointing. The approach of using statistics to replace the judgment and observation of scouts did not prove tenable.

In the words of former New York Yankees scouting director Bill Livesey,

I have seen a million kids who could turn stuff into stats but … you can't turn stats into stuff without tools. That's what happened with Billy Beane's draft. The guys they drafted had stats but no tools.

The Signing of Jim Leyritz

In August 1985, New York Yankees scout Bill Livesey was attending the National Baseball Congress World Series, a tournament that takes place each summer in Wichita, Kansas. As is customary, there were roughly 30 amateur teams from across the country participating in the tournament, involving approximately 800 players.

Livesey was drawn to a third baseman playing for one of the teams. After one of the games, Livesey asked the team's coach, "Who is your third baseman?" The coach responded, "It's a kid from the University of Kentucky."

Livesey learned that the player's name was Jim Leyritz and that he had not been selected in that year's June draft. Livesey asked Leyritz if he was interested in turning pro. Leyritz said he was. Leyritz told Livesey that he was already talking with the director of scouting from another Major League team. The team had made a preliminary overture to Leyritz but had not yet offered any money.

On the spot, Livesey offered Leyritz a signing bonus. "If I'm going to a tournament in the heat in the middle of Kansas," Livesey says, "I'm going to sign somebody."

Leyritz hedged on the offer. He wanted to see how high the other team might go. Livesey told Leyritz that if the team intended to give him a signing bonus, it would have done so already.

Still not persuaded, Leyritz told Livesey, "Come back and see me tomorrow." Livesey then said, "Jimmy, I'm leaving tomorrow morning. When I jump on the plane, the offer goes with me."

Unwilling to pass on the Yankees' offer, Leyritz signed.

Leyritz spent 11 seasons in the Major Leagues as a utility infielder, outfielder, catcher and designated hitter. He is best remembered for his dramatic home run in the fourth game of the 1996 World Series that helped to propel the Yankees to a come-from-behind victory and, ultimately, to the World Championship.

2003

[Nick Markakis] was probably one of the toughest kids that I have ever scouted. He just had no desire to give up on anything. In any part of the game, there was no give whatsoever. He was very determined, a very hard worker, quiet. Some of the guys you notice just because of their antics. Nick was just a quiet, go-at-it type who did everything he needed to do. I think he could have been a first-round pitcher. He was just determined to make it. There was no quit in that kid.

—Dave Jennings, scout, Baltimore Orioles

In 2003, the New York Yankees again won the American League pennant and represented the junior circuit in the World Series. It was the Yankees' sixth appearance in the World Series since 1995. The Yankees' dominance was close to an end, however. They lost the 2003 Series to the upstart Florida Marlins and would only make one other World Series appearance in the next sixteen years.

The Marlins, in only their eleventh season, beat the heavily favored Yankees in six games. While 72-year-old Marlins manager Jack McKeon made history by becoming the oldest manager to ever win a World Series, they relied on twenty-three-year-old Josh Beckett to shut down the powerful Yankees in the decisive sixth game at Yankee Stadium. It was only four years earlier that the Marlins had selected Beckett with the number two overall pick in the famous "two Joshes" draft.

The Tampa Bay Devil Rays were back again with the number one overall draft pick in 2003. Losers of 106 games in 2002, the Devil Rays were desperate to turn their fortunes around. In the first five years of Tampa Bay's existence, the franchise had finished last in the American League East each season, with losses approaching or exceeding 100 every year. Although the Devil Rays had drafted some excellent young talent since their inaugural draft in 1996, their on-field performance was beginning to resemble the futility of the early years of the New York Mets.

Tampa Bay used its number one overall pick to take high school outfielder and slugger Delmon Young from Camarillo, California. Young was pretty much the consensus number one pick in what was considered to be a shallow draft class. Some scouts considered Rickie Weeks of Southern University to be a contender for the number one overall pick. However, Tampa Bay general manager Chuck LeMar and scouting director Cam Bonifay focused on Young and salivated over his plus-plus power potential. Bonifay described Young as "the kind of guy that you don't want to get out of your seat and go buy a hot dog when you know he's coming to the plate."[210]

Young had good Major League bloodlines. His older brother, Dmitri, was the fourth overall pick in 1991. The older Young, nicknamed "Da Meat Hook," had a productive 13-year career in which he appeared in two All-Star Games. Delmon was expected to easily exceed his brother's production. When Delmon was drafted, he mentioned Ken Griffey Jr. and Álex Rodríguez as his measuring sticks for quick and sustained Major League success. Young's hitting numbers in the minor leagues seemed to support his expectations. In three minor league seasons, he hit .318 with 59 homers and 273 runs batted in.

With Delmon Young, however, there always seemed to be "other issues" that undermined his potential for stardom. In Double-A, playing for the Montgomery Biscuits, he was named *Baseball America*'s minor league Player of the Year but was also suspended three games for bumping an umpire. In 2006, Young played for the Triple-A Durham Bulls, the franchise made famous in Kevin Costner's hit movie, *Bull Durham*. In one game with Durham, Young argued over a called strike and then flung his bat at the home plate umpire, hitting him in the chest. For this behavior, Young was suspended a record 50 games. It was not, of course, the type of record the Rays were expecting him to set. Even with the behavioral issues, Young made it to Tampa Bay for 30 games at the end of the 2006 season and hit three home runs while batting .317. In his rookie season of 2007, he played all 162 game for the Rays and finished second in the Rookie of the Year voting.

While it seemed that Young was on the precipice of realizing his immense potential, the Rays traded him to the Minnesota Twins in the 2007 off-season for pitcher Matt Garza and infielder Jason Bartlett. Young joined Joe Mauer in Minnesota and had three good seasons for the Twins offensively. However, his long-anticipated power did not manifest itself until 2010, when he hit 21 homers, with 112 runs batted in, and batted .298. The next season, the Twins traded him to their division rivals, the Detroit Tigers, and received two minor leaguers in return.

Young paid almost immediate dividends for the Tigers, hitting three home runs in the 2011 American League Division Series against the Yankees. In the 2012 Championship Series against the Yankees, Young was even better, hitting .353 with two home runs and being named the Most Valuable Player in the series. Nonetheless, the Tigers declined to re-sign him after the 2012 season. Off-field trouble hastened Young's departure from Detroit. He had been arrested outside a Manhattan hotel for allegedly accosting pedestrians with anti-Semitic epithets. Young would go on to play for ten Major League seasons and three more teams but he never was able to duplicate his career year of 2010. With a career Wins Above Replacement value of 3.2, Young was one of the worst overall number one picks of all time.

With the second overall pick in the draft, the Milwaukee Brewers chose Rickie Weeks. Weeks had a stellar season for Southern University in 2003 and was named *Baseball America*'s College Player of the Year. Weeks was a consummate hitter, having led the NCAA in batting in both 2002 and 2003.

In an interesting coincidence, the top two selections of the 2003 draft were the polar opposites of each other on many of the key "Moneyball" criteria. Weeks was older than Delmon Young, had three years of college experience and, in the all-important category of on-base percentage, he approached the divine status of the "Greek God of Walks," Kevin Youkilis. Conversely, the "Moneyball" draft philosophy would have properly raised red flags on Delmon Young's propensity for swinging and missing. In the end, however, Weeks' Major League career was almost as disappointing as the career of Delmon Young. Weeks played for 14 seasons in the Major Leagues and was a lifetime .246 hitter. During his career, Weeks hit 161 home runs, compared with 109 home runs for Delmon Young.

The Baltimore Orioles made the best selection of the entire first round when they used the seventh overall pick to take Nick Markakis of Young Harris Junior College in Georgia. The hard-nosed, competitive Markakis was no secret to scouts. He had played travel baseball in the talent-rich Atlanta area with future major leaguers Jeff Francoeur, Jeremy Hermida and Kyle Davies. In each of the two seasons immediately prior to the 2003 draft, *Baseball America* had named Markakis the Junior College Player of the Year.

When Baltimore drafted Markakis, the only source of controversy was the Orioles' decision to designate him as an outfielder. In junior college, Markakis threw 96 miles an hour, so most teams had projected him as a pitcher.[211] Orioles area scout Dave Jennings scouted and signed Markakis. Baltimore's East Coast cross-checker, Mickey White, had also seen Markakis and told Jennings that Markakis had the best bat on the whole East Coast and that he wanted to start him as an outfielder. Jennings asked Markakis if he wanted to be introduced in Camden Yards as a pitcher or an outfielder. True to his no-nonsense and ultra-competitive nature, Markakis simply responded, "I don't care, I just want to be introduced in Camden Yards."[212]

The Orioles' decision to start Markakis in right field was proven correct in short order. He progressed directly from Double-A to Baltimore in 2006 and finished sixth in the American League Rookie of the Year voting. Markakis became a fixture in right field at Camden Yards for the next nine years. He was consistently one of the Orioles' best hitters and played a stellar right field, earning two Gold Glove Awards. In December 2014, Markakis signed as a free agent with the Atlanta Braves and became a fixture in the Braves' lineup. In 2018 he posted perhaps his best year to date when, at age 34, he played all 162 games and was voted to his first All-Star Game while winning the Silver Slugger Award and a Gold Glove Award.

As a junior college player, Markakis did not fit neatly into the dichotomy drawn in "Moneyball" between high school and four-year college players. Though his lifetime on-base percentage of nearly .360 fits the "Moneyball" template nicely, his intense competitiveness and refusal to give away at-bats would appeal to any traditional scout. Markakis can simply be thought of as a baseball player in that he plays all aspects of the game well but did not project as a superstar. Players like Markakis are usually overlooked and undervalued in the early part of the draft. The Orioles were proven correct in using a top-ten pick on him. However, in agreeing to a "below slot" bonus of $1.85 million, it seems that both the Orioles and Markakis tacitly acknowledged that he was drafted higher than his skills might otherwise have warranted. By way of comparison, the seventh pick of the draft in 2002 received a $2.4 million bonus and the seventh pick of the 2004 draft would receive a $2.3 million bonus.

The Texas Rangers drafted second baseman Ian Kinsler in the 17th round. Kinsler went on to become the best player of the entire 2003 draft.

Rangers scout Mike Grouse scouted Kinsler and really liked him but surmised that no other team was interested. Consequently, the Rangers drafted him later than they believed his talent warranted. Perhaps because he was largely overlooked in the draft, Kinsler seemed to play with a chip on his shoulder. He reached the Major Leagues in 2006. In his fourteen-year career, he was named to the All-Star team four times and twice won the Gold Glove Award at second base. For his career, he had over 250 homers and almost 250 steals.

The Importance of Velocity

Oakland Athletics scout Jeff Bittiger pitched for four seasons in the Major Leagues and for another fifteen seasons in the minors. "I pitched so long," he says, "I was all of the labels. I was prospect. I was suspect. I was a minor league free agent. I spent time in every category."

When Bittiger came out of high school, his fastball touched 94 miles per hour. In the pro ranks, however, Bittiger's fastball lost some of its zip. For most of his time in the big leagues, his velocity hovered around 90 mph.

Bittiger found that teams were constantly in search of pitchers who could throw harder. "No matter how good I would pitch," he says, "they would still be striving to replace my style with someone who could light up a consistent *plus velocity* fastball."

Bittiger candidly admits that, as a player, he didn't like the emphasis that scouts placed on velocity. At the end of his playing career, Bittiger turned to scouting. He vowed that, when scouting, he wouldn't attach so much importance to the speed of a pitcher's fastball.

Even so, Bittiger says, "I find myself doing it – all those things that I didn't like as a player." He recognizes that there is a distinct advantage for a team to have pitchers with great velocity. "Velocity adds room for error," he says, "the margin for error increases exponentially with velocity."

2004

Justin Upton, for example, you could see him one time in batting practice and you say, 'Okay, that's the Number One pick in the draft.' There's not going to be much else that you need to see. There are other guys like Dustin Pedroia, you could walk up on him and you are probably not going to be impressed because he is a short-stature guy. He doesn't have a real live body. He doesn't have quick feet. He runs with effort. His swing is a big man's swing on a little man's body. You think, 'No chance that this is going to work.' But those guys can do it because they have that mentality that separates them from the rest of the pack. A scout is not going to keep his job very long if he drafts a bunch of Dustin Pedroias. But if you find the one Dustin Pedroia, you are going to be golden in this game for a long time.

– Russ Ardolina, scout, Texas Rangers

The 2004 season was the year of redemption for the Boston Red Sox and their long-suffering fans. For the first time since 1918, Boston advanced to and won the World Series. To reach the World Series, Boston had to get past their archrival, the New York Yankees, in the American League Championship Series. The Red Sox did so in dramatic fashion, coming back after the Yankees had jumped out to a 3-0 lead in games.

The 2004 draft is noteworthy from a variety of perspectives. First and foremost, it stands out for one of the worst number one overall choices of all time. Second, it presents one of the starkest disparities between the number one and number two choices. It also represents a high-water mark for first-round success, as ninety percent of the players drafted in the first round reached the big leagues. Aside from two pitchers, however, few of the first-rounders had an impactful Major League career.

The 2004 draft also presented a sharp contrast from the 2003 draft. In 2003, teams invested heavily in hitters in the first round. In 2004, nineteen of the 30 players selected in the first round were pitchers. The 2004 draft also represented the return of Scott Boras to prominence. Boras represented two high-profile prospects in the draft, pitcher Jered Weaver and shortstop Stephen Drew. Boras's demands would dictate the cadence and timing of player signings even more than in prior years. Both Weaver and Drew were victims of the "Boras slide," as many teams were wary of having to negotiate contracts with Boras. Weaver slid to the 12th spot in the first round, Drew to the 15th.

In 2004, the "Moneyball" approach seemed to have taken hold. Teams drafted a record number of college players. Especially in terms of drafting philosophy, teams are often inclined to try to imitate successful franchises, and Michael Lewis' *Moneyball* had reinforced the view that no one was as successful in exploiting market inefficiencies as Billy Beane.

In 2004, the San Diego Padres held the first overall draft choice. It would be the fifth time in the 36-year existence of the Padres that they would pick first among all other teams. The Padres' record with their prior overall number one picks was spotty at best. Only Andy Benes, whom San Diego drafted in 1988, is considered a fully successful choice. Their previous picks of Mike Ivie, Bill Almon, and Dave Roberts were much less successful. In some very tangible ways, none of their earlier "misses" would compare to the futility of their choice of shortstop Matt Bush in 2004. Bush would eventually make it to the Major Leagues – but as a pitcher and not a shortstop – and long after the Padres had given up on him.

The Padres' mistake in taking Bush was made all the more painful by the success of Justin Verlander, who was selected by the Tigers with the second overall pick. Not since 1966, when the New York Mets selected Steve Chilcott at number one instead of Reggie Jackson, had there been such a striking disparity between the performance of the two top draft picks. In a cosmic justice sense, the Tigers deserved the first choice. Detroit had lost 119 games in 2003 and yet were picking behind the Padres, losers of 98 games, because it was the National League's turn to draft first.

San Diego had identified three college players as possible number one picks, Fresno State's Jered Weaver, Arizona State's Stephen Drew and Rice University's Jeff Niemann. Shortly before the draft, Padres owner John Moores instructed his general manager, Kevin Towers, to avoid all three of the players that Towers and his staff had identified.[213] Moores was not interested in dealing with Scott Boras, who was the agent for Weaver and Drew. Moores also ruled out Niemann due to his history of injuries.

Matt Bush was a convenient alternative to Weaver, Drew and Niemann. He had starred at San Diego's Mission Bay High School, which was less than ten miles from the Padres' Petco Park Stadium. Bush had taken the nearly unprecedented step of contacting the Padres area scout, Tim McWilliams, to urge that the Padres draft him with the number one pick. Bush had hit .447 with 11 homers in his senior year of high school and had played a stellar shortstop. When not playing in the field, he pitched for Mission Bay and compiled a 5-1 record with an 0.73 earned run average. His lobbying efforts, coupled with the Padres' favorable evaluation of his skills, led San Diego to take Bush with the number one pick.

Bush signed for $3,150,000. The pick was immediately criticized as a cost-savings maneuver. Critics also found fault because, at 5 feet, 9 inches and 180 pounds, Bush was the smallest number one pick in history. While "Moneyball" may have been taking hold with other franchises, the Padres blithely ignored the most basic tenet of Billy Beane's philosophy – avoid high school players in the early rounds.

Bush began his career inauspiciously, both on and off the field. He was suspended for a bar fight in spring training before he ever played a single inning of professional baseball. When he did get on the field in 2004, playing primarily for the Padres' Rookie League team, he hit an anemic .192. In 2005, with the Class A Fort Wayne Wizards, his hitting improved only marginally to .221. In the spring of 2006, Bush broke his ankle and missed much of the season.

Bush's hitting struggles continued in 2007. As a pitcher, however, Bush was registering 98 mph on the Juggs gun, leading the Padres to convert him to full-time pitcher. Just as he seemed to be on the verge of success as a pitcher, he suffered another injury–a torn ligament in his pitching elbow. The injury led to Tommy John surgery, causing Bush to miss both the 2007 and 2008 seasons. After a highly publicized public intoxication incident at a high school in which Bush allegedly assaulted two students, the Padres sold him to the Toronto Blue Jays in 2009. The change of scenery did not improve either Bush's behavior or judgment. While at spring training with the Blue Jays in 2009, he threw a baseball at a woman while at a party. The Blue Jays promptly released him, and he remained out of the game for all of 2009.

In 2010, the Tampa Bay Rays added credence to the old maxim that hope often triumphs over experience, signing Bush to a minor league contract. For two years, he pitched with some effectiveness for the Rays in the minors. Expectations were high that Bush would soon be promoted to the parent club. He was slated to start the 2012 season with the Triple-A Durham Bulls. However, after he was arrested for driving his car over a 72-year-old man during spring training, the Rays suspended him. Bush pled guilty to the charges and was sentenced to 51 months in prison. In what was becoming a familiar story, Tampa Bay released him on October 5, 2012. Bush reported to prison and served his time. His next release – from Florida's Mayo Correctional Institution – came on October 30, 2015.

From that point, Bush made a remarkable turnabout in his career. His story harkens back to pre-draft days when scouts scoured the country looking to find undiscovered talent in remote locations. Bush, then 29 years old, worked out for the Rangers in the parking lot of the Golden Corral restaurant where he worked. His velocity and movement impressed the Rangers and, on December 18, 2015, the team signed him to a minor league contract.

With Texas, Bush's luck and behavior both began to turn around. He pitched well in a short minor league stint, leading the Rangers to call him up on May 13, 2016. Bush deserves plaudits for resuscitating his career with the Rangers. As of the beginning of the 2021 season, he has appeared in 136 Major League games and is considered a mainstay of the Rangers' bullpen.

The Detroit Tigers found almost immediate success with their selection of six-foot-five right-handed pitcher Justin Verlander as the second overall pick. *Baseball America*'s pre-draft scouting report described Verlander as having the "best pure arm in the draft with a 99-mph fastball with run and sink."[214]

As a high school pitcher in Goochland, Virginia, Verlander went largely unnoticed by the scouts. Even though his fastball was clocked in the 90's, he was unable to play when the scouts came to town due to a bout with strep throat and was not drafted. Following high school, Verlander played at Old Dominion University in Norfolk, Virginia, where he increased his velocity and once struck out 17 batters in a game against James Madison University. Verlander signed with the Tigers in October 2004. Less than a year later, he was in the Major Leagues and made his debut for the Tigers on July 4, 2005. Verlander's path to the Major Leagues was unique in that, unlike most college players who are drafted in the first round, he went undrafted out of high school.

By 2006, Verlander was a true diamond, winning the American League Rookie of the Year Award with a 17-9 record and a 3.63 earned run average. The very next year he was even better at 18-6 and made the American

League All-Star team. He would make five more All-Star teams for the Tigers. In 2011, Verlander had a truly dominating season with a 24-5 record and a league-leading 2.40 earned run average, winning both the Cy Young Award and the American League Most Valuable Player Award. In 2017, the Tigers traded Verlander to Houston, where he was instrumental in leading the Astros to the 2017 World Series championship. Verlander's 71.8 Wins Above Replacement value ranks him as the best player in the 2004 draft and as a potential Hall of Fame candidate.

The Angels ended the slide for Jered Weaver, selecting him with the 12th pick of the draft. Weaver's dominating career at Long Beach State drew comparisons to former University of Southern California star Mark Prior. Angels owner Arte Moreno was eager to spend his wealth to improve the fortunes of the Angels. Moreno was not intimidated by either Boras's reputation or the prospect of exorbitant bonus demands. Nonetheless, negotiations were painful and lengthy. Weaver did not reach agreement with the Angels until May 31, 2005, when they settled on a $4 million bonus. The price tag seemed worth it as the long and lanky Weaver went on to become the Angels' ace from 2006 through 2016 and was a three-time All-Star. Weaver retired in 2017 with an even 150 wins for his career.

The Arizona Diamondbacks selected shortstop Stephen Drew with the 15th pick in the draft. Drew became the third member of the family to be drafted in the first round; brothers J.D. and Tim were both drafted in the first round of 1997. Like his brother J.D., Stephen played at Florida State University. However, Stephen was not quite as dominant in college as J.D. had been. Nonetheless, the fact that he could hit well and played a premium position had teams viewing him as a possible number one selection. After protracted negotiations, Drew signed with the Diamondbacks one week after Jered Weaver signed with the Angels and for the same $4 million bonus that the Angels paid Weaver. Stephen Drew had a credible 12-year Major League career. However, by the end of his career, he was regarded as little more than a solid utility player.

The Boston Red Sox selected second baseman Dustin Pedroia with the 65th overall pick. Scouts viewed the five-foot-nine Pedroia as a steady, albeit undersized performer. No one could have fully anticipated how well Pedroia would perform in the Major Leagues. He was already in a Red Sox uniform by 2006. In 2007, he won the American League Rookie of the Year Award and was a key contributor to Boston's World Series championship. In 2008, he was even better, slugging 17 home runs and batting .326 while winning the American League Most Valuable Player Award. Pedroia has been selected to four American League All-Star teams.

A Ready Resource

If you see a turtle sitting on the fence post, you know it didn't get there by itself. And I certainly didn't get here by myself.

– Former pitcher Phil Niekro, speaking at his Hall of Fame induction ceremony, August 3, 1997.

Phil Niekro used the occasion of his induction into the Baseball Hall of Fame to pay tribute to his first manager in the minor leagues, Harry Minor, and to others in the Braves organization who had played a role in his development.

Long-time pitcher, Jeff Suppan, feels a similar indebtedness to one of his former coaches, Al Nipper. In Suppan's first three years in the minor leagues, 1993-1995, Nipper served as his pitching coach. "I was blessed to have Al Nipper," Suppan says.

In 1994, Nipper fought for Suppan to remain with the Sarasota Red Sox, even after Suppan lost five consecutive games to start the season. Thinking the young pitcher was overmatched, Boston wanted to send him back to rookie ball. Nipper proved persuasive. Suppan stayed with Sarasota and then went on a tear, winning 13 of his next 15 starts. He finished the season with a record of 13 wins and 7 losses.

In July 1995, while Suppan, then 20 years old, was playing for the Trenton Thunder in the Eastern League, Boston called him up to the majors. Nipper accompanied him to Boston and served as a ready resource for Suppan as he settled in at the big-league level.

Suppan is unstinting in his praise. "He taught me more in one year than I probably would have learned in four years of college," Suppan says. "He taught me how to prepare for the entire season, how to keep track of my life so that I would be ready to perform at my best. He taught me a lot about the mental side of the game and my whole career I made sure to give him all the credit. He was a very good developer."

2005

He's become more than I ever thought he'd be. If I thought he'd turn into an All-Star, I wouldn't have waited until the third round to take him.

— Damon Oppenheimer, New York Yankees vice president for amateur scouting, commenting on how the Yankees "missed" on Brett Gardner. [215]

In the 2005 season, the Chicago White Sox won the World Series, sweeping the Houston Astros in four games. It had been eighty-eight years since the White Sox had last won the World Series. In the American League, the overall number one pick in 1993, Álex Rodríguez, won the 2005 Most Valuable Player Award. In the National League, the late-round 1999 draft choice, Albert Pujols, captured the MVP Award. After four decades without baseball, the nation's capital finally had a team again as the Montreal Expos moved to Washington, D.C. The Anaheim Angels stayed put but changed the team's name to the Los Angeles Angels of Anaheim.

The 2005 draft class was full of exceptional prospects. The talent level reminded some draft experts of the historic 1985 class, widely considered to be the best draft class of all time. Like the 1985 class, 2005 was front-loaded with collegiate prospects; eight of the first ten picks were from the college ranks. Logic would suggest that the focus on collegiate talent resulted from the growing acceptance of the "Moneyball" philosophy. However, for context, it should be noted that in 1985, when Billy Beane was still toiling as a spare outfielder for the New York Mets, eleven of the first twelve picks were college players.

The 2005 class got off to an excellent start. Many draft observers were ready to anoint it as historically great. Yet, as is often the case, many players put together exceptional seasons early but saw their careers tumble unexpectedly as the years progressed. The 2005 draft class saw many players rise like rockets only to fall like shooting stars. While 2005 will still be judged as one of the better draft classes of all time, in the end the 2005 class lacked the Hall of Fame credentials that makes the 1985 draft class so compelling.

The Arizona Diamondbacks held the first pick. After selecting the third and final Drew brother in the first round of 2004, the Diamondbacks selected muscular shortstop Justin Upton, the younger brother of B.J. (soon to be "Melvin") Upton. With the drafting of Justin, the Upton brothers became the first brother duo drafted at either number one or number two in the history of the draft. Justin Upton's selection as number one overall would also represent the high-water mark for the Tidewater, Virginia area and its historic run of stellar draft picks, from David Wright and B.J. Upton to Justin Upton and Ryan Zimmerman.

Commenting on the selection of Justin Upton, Arizona's scouting director, Mike Rizzo, said, "I [had] watched Justin grow up playing baseball and dominating the competition at all levels. He's exceeded all age groups and time frames and everything else. ... I've always personally leaned towards Justin going as far back as when we, I guess you would say, 'clinched,' the first pick in the draft last year."[216] The younger Upton was a five-tool player, just like his brother, and an even safer choice because he projected as a better hitter. For good measure, Justin had a .519 batting average, with 12 home runs, in only 64 at-bats in his senior season at Great Bridge High School in Chesapeake, Virginia.

The Diamondbacks general manager, Joe Garagiola Jr., fully concurred with Mike Rizzo's assessment, noting that Justin Upton "had a maturity about him that is unbelievable for a seventeen-year-old."[217] Such great potential did not come cheaply; the Diamondbacks reached an agreement with Justin on a record $6.1 million bonus. Having drafted their shortstop of the future in Stephen Drew the year before, the Diamondbacks planned to convert Justin to the outfield. Justin made his debut with the Diamondbacks in 2007 at the age of 19. In his six years in Arizona, Upton fulfilled much of the early expectations. Twice he was named to the National League All-Star team. However, in six years with the Diamondbacks, he had only one season with more than 30 home runs.

In January 2013, the Diamondbacks traded Upton to the Atlanta Braves for five players. He was a consistent force in the middle of the Braves' lineup during his two seasons in Atlanta. In December 2014, the Braves traded him to San Diego, where he enjoyed another All-Star season, with 26 home runs and 81 runs batted in.

With the second pick of 2005, the Kansas City Royals selected left-handed hitting third baseman Alex Gordon from the University of

Nebraska. Gordon was *Baseball America*'s College Player of the Year in 2005 as he hit .372 with 19 home runs and drove in 66 runs. In his first four seasons in the Major Leagues, 2007 to 2010, Gordon struggled to make consistent contact at the plate. In 2010, he hit .215 in 74 games. Gordon's paltry batting average had some observers wondering if he would ever fulfill his potential.

In 2011, the Royals made Gordon their full-time left fielder. The change worked wonders. Gordon became a Gold Glove caliber fielder and emerged as a productive hitter, with a .303 batting average and 23 home runs. From 2013 to 2015, Gordon made the American League All-Star team each season. His development mirrored that of other young Royals as they won the American League championship in 2014 and the World Series in 2015.

The newly minted Washington Nationals franchise owned the fourth pick in 2005 and selected Ryan Zimmerman, a third baseman who had starred at the University of Virginia. Zimmerman was yet another product of the Tidewater, Virginia area and had grown up playing AAU ball against David Wright and the Upton brothers. It was clear from Zimmerman's college career that he was a superior fielding third baseman with an above average bat. However, there was considerable concern about the lack of power when he was playing at Virginia. Texas Rangers Mid-Atlantic scout Russ Ardolina had seen a lot of Zimmerman and correctly predicted that he would develop power as he matured. Ardolina said, "Ryan had great eye-hand coordination ... and he could leverage the baseball very well, so I expected the power to come."

The Nationals brought Zimmerman to the big leagues late in his first year of pro ball. He played in 20 games for the Nationals at the end of 2005 and, with a .397 batting average, he gave a glimpse of what was to come. In 2006, Zimmerman's power manifested itself when he hit 20 home runs, drove in 110 runs, and hit .287. Zimmerman's biggest obstacle to stardom would be the challenge of staying healthy. In 2009, Zimmerman fully established himself as the face of the new franchise as he was selected to the National League All-Star team and won his first Gold Glove for his work at third base.

For almost an entire decade, Zimmerman appeared destined for continued success and greatness but, in 2014, the injury bug bit him in a big way. Shoulder problems and other ailments caused him to miss major parts of four seasons. The shoulder injury hindered his ability to throw across the diamond and forced him to move to first base. In 2017, Zimmerman was fully healthy and again displayed his superior skills, batting .303 with 36 home runs and earning a spot on the National League All-Star team. After his renaissance in 2017, he experienced two more injury-riddled seasons.

The Milwaukee Brewers took Ryan Braun of the University of Miami with the next pick, making it three third sackers among the top five. Braun was a five-tool talent at Miami with good speed. Unlike with Ryan Zimmerman, it was clear at Miami that Braun possessed significant power. While it took him a few years longer than Zimmerman to make it to the majors, Braun had an even more impressive debut, winning the National League Rookie of the Year Award in 2007. Like Alex Gordon, Braun moved off third base and found a home in the outfield. From 2008 to 2012, Braun was named to the National League All-Star team every year. He won the league's Most Valuable Player Award in 2011 after hitting .332 with 33 home runs and 111 runs batted in.

Braun clearly had the best start to his career of any 2005 draftee and appeared to be on a trajectory for enshrinement in Cooperstown. However, he was implicated in a major performance-enhancing drug scandal and was suspended for 65 games in 2013. Braun continues to play at a high level for the Brewers but, since 2013, he has earned only one selection to the National League All-Star team.

The Colorado Rockies drafted Long Beach State shortstop Troy Tulowitzki with the seventh overall pick. Although Tulowitzki was not drafted out of high school, his skills developed at Long Beach State to the point that he was considered a five-tool prospect. He became the Rockies' starting shortstop in 2007 and clubbed 24 home runs with 99 runs batted in. Injuries limited him to 101 games in 2008, but he rebounded in 2009 to finish fifth in the National League Most Valuable Player voting.

From 2013 to 2015, Tulowitzki was a fixture at shortstop for the National League All-Star team. As both a multiple Gold Glove and Silver Slugger recipient, Tulowitzki was on his way to joining the very best shortstops of all time. However, much like Ryan Zimmerman, Tulowitzki suffered a series of injuries that made it difficult for him to stay on the field.

Ever since selecting Barry Bonds with the sixth pick in 1985, the Pittsburgh Pirates have experienced an abundance of misses in the draft. The Pirates and the city of Pittsburgh were due, if not desperate, for some good news in 2005. The good news came in the person of five-tool high school outfielder Andrew McCutchen, a product of Fort Meade, Florida. McCutchen would create the most enthusiasm in Pittsburgh since 1992, when Bonds was patrolling left field at Three Rivers Stadium. McCutchen batted an astounding .709 with 16 home runs in his senior season at Fort Meade High School. Pirates scouting director Ed Creech noted that, beyond his athleticism, he had "a big-league bat."

The man known as "Cutch" arrived in Pittsburgh in 2009. In short order, he revived hope among the moribund Pirates fan base. By 2012, it was clear that McCutchen was the best Pirates player since Bonds. He represented Pittsburgh in five straight All-Star Games and, in 2013, won the National League Most Valuable Player Award. McCutchen played nine seasons in Pittsburgh until the Pirates traded him to San Francisco in 2018. McCutchen clearly restored hope and, for a brief period, a winning tradition in Pittsburgh. With Cutch in the lineup, the Pirates enjoyed winning records in 2013, 2014 and 2015.

If one were to evaluate the 2005 draft class based on its trajectory as of 2012, one might conclude that the 2005 class was primed to displace the mighty 1985 class as the preeminent class in the history of the draft. With the benefit of several additional years of observation, the stature of the 2005 class has clearly dimmed. Nonetheless, the 2005 class remains one of the more accomplished classes in draft history.

A Study in Contrasts

Brett Gardner and his teammate of several years, Jacoby Ellsbury, provide an interesting study in contrasts. Both players were drafted in 2005, Ellsbury by the Red Sox in the first round, Gardner by the Yankees in the third round. As speedy leadoff hitters who cover a lot of outfield real estate, they are ostensibly quite similar. Yet, their differences are also quite profound. Ellsbury was a top talent coming out of Oregon State. The smaller Gardner was not even drafted out of the College of Charleston in 2004, when he first became eligible for the draft as a collegian.

Gardner and the Yankees agreed to terms on June 12, 2005. The Yankees had offered a relatively meager signing bonus of $210,000. Lacking the option of returning to campus for another year, Gardner possessed little leverage in the negotiations. Meanwhile, with one year of college eligibility remaining, Ellsbury negotiated a $1.4 million bonus with the Red Sox. He signed less than a month after Gardner.

In 2013, Gardner became the Yankees' everyday center fielder, manning the position for 138 games. In addition to playing excellent defense, Gardner put together a respectable year at the plate, with 10 triples, eight home runs, and a .273 average. As solid as Gardner's performance was, it was not enough to dissuade the Yankees from offering a free agent contract to Ellsbury. In December 2013, the Yankees opened their vault to sign Ellsbury to a $153 million contract for seven years. When the 2014 season started, Gardner had been moved to left field, leaving the center field position for Ellsbury.

Yet, it was the hard-working Gardner who was selected to the All-Star team in 2015, not the high-priced Ellsbury. Since 2015, Gardner has continued to outperform Ellsbury in nearly every offensive category. Injuries complicate the comparison; Ellsbury would spend the entire 2018 and 2019 seasons on the disabled list. In Ellsbury's absence, Gardner has continued to serve as a mainstay in the Yankee outfield. While his batting average has fallen in recent years, Gardner has emerged as a more consistent home run threat. And unlike the injury-prone Ellsbury, Gardner has been a ubiquitous presence on the field.

2006

Some players don't want to be great; they are content to be good. Being great takes a lot more work. It's tougher to maintain that level and persist in the pursuit of greatness. [Clayton] Kershaw, however, always had that extra gear and an inquisitiveness about learning how to pitch and then a competitiveness that is as strong as anybody I have ever been around in my 40 years. He competes against the other team but he also competes against the craft of what he does. He competes against the lack of perfection inside a baseball game – to see how close he can get to perfection in a game. That's how he competes – against the other team but also against the game itself.

    –Ned Colletti, former general manager, Los Angeles Dodgers

The Kansas City Royals lost 106 games in 2005. The Royals' horrific season gave them the first pick in the 2006 draft. In most years, having the first pick is a reason for organizational optimism. However, in 2006, the Royals bemoaned the perceived lack of impact players eligible to be drafted. Royals cross-checker Brian Murphy summed up the mood of the organization, saying "this is not a great year to have a top pick. I can think of at least eight players last year who were more attractive than any of the players in this year's draft."[218]

Pitchers were the cream of the crop in 2006. Eighteen out of the first 30 picks were pitchers. Three of them – Clayton Kershaw, Max Scherzer and Tim Lincecum – would become major impact players, each winning multiple Cy Young Awards.

In the days before the draft, many experts considered six-foot-seven left-hander Andrew Miller of the University of North Carolina to be the most dominant pitcher available. However, the Royals shied away from Miller due to concerns about the amount of bonus money he was likely to demand. The Royals opted instead for another collegiate hurler, Luke Hochevar of the University of Tennessee. It was a curious decision because Hochevar was represented by Scott Boras. Teams normally did not pivot *toward* Boras clients for signability reasons.

The availability of Hochevar in the 2006 draft was a story in itself. He was actually eligible for the 2005 draft. He had dominated the competition at the University of Tennessee that year and was widely considered to be at least the second-best arm available in 2005.[219] The Dodgers chose Hochevar with the 40th overall pick in 2005 but encountered difficulty in signing him. Both sides remained far apart as classes were about to begin at Tennessee. Hochevar appeared headed back to school for another season but surprisingly veered in a different direction, dismissing Boras and hiring agent Matt Sosnick. Sosnick and the Dodgers came to an agreement on terms. However, instead of following through and signing the contract, Hochevar weaved his way back to Boras and reneged on the deal. Both sides remained at a stalemate and Boras elected to have Hochevar pitch in the independent American Association.

The Dodgers' failure to reach agreement with Hochevar appeared to be good fortune for Kansas City. As a result of not signing in 2005, Hochevar was available for the Royals with the first pick in 2006. Moreover, Boras had made uncharacteristic pre-draft overtures to the Royals. Boras suggested that his client would accept a below-market bonus if drafted by the Royals. The overture encouraged Royals general manager Dayton Moore and scouting director Deric Ladnier to take Hochevar with the overall number one pick. He became the first Boras client to be selected with the overall number one pick since Álex Rodríguez in 1993. Hochevar ultimately signed with the Royals for a $3,500,000 bonus, a little more than half of what the Diamondbacks had given Justin Upton as the number one overall pick in 2005.

Hochevar was already in the big leagues by the next year. However, in six years as a starter for the Royals, he never posted a winning record. After an 8-16 record with a 5.73 earned run average in 2012, Kansas City moved him to the bullpen. The change was therapeutic. In 2013, he pitched 70 innings in relief and recorded an earned run average of 1.92. Just as he was hitting his stride in the bullpen, however, Hochevar suffered an elbow injury and required Tommy John surgery. He missed all of the 2014 season but was able to return and make 49 appearances for the Royals out of the bullpen in 2015. Hochevar would pitch one more season for the Royals in 2016 before retiring.

The Los Angeles Dodgers held the seventh pick in the draft. All along, the Dodgers' brain trust had been focused on one player and one player alone, Clayton Kershaw from Highland Park High School in Dallas, Texas. Dodgers general manager Ned Colletti, scouting director Logan White and area scout Calvin Jones held their collective breaths as the first six teams made their selections. When the Detroit Tigers picked Andrew Miller with the sixth pick, Colletti and his team knew Kershaw would be a Dodger. They let out a sigh of relief and rejoiced as they submitted Kershaw's name. Ned Colletti immediately saw the big picture as it unfolded. Miller had been the presumptive number one pick of the draft and might well have been taken by the Royals if Hochevar was not available to them. The Hochevar saga at once appeared as a blessing rather than a debacle. If the Dodgers had been successful in signing Hochevar in 2005, Clayton Kershaw may never have become a Dodger.

Kershaw was the latest in a long line of stud high school pitching prospects from Texas. His numbers at Highland Park were otherworldly – a 13-0 record and more than two strikeouts per inning. Logan White made sure to have at least one Dodgers scout at each of Kershaw's outings. In one game, Kershaw struck out every batter he faced. As Kershaw became increasingly dominant, White openly worried that he would not be available to the Dodgers at number seven. Colletti would say later, "You want the guy you are focusing on to do well but you don't want him to be so dominant as to strike out 15 out of 15." Shortly thereafter, in a park packed with scouts for a playoff game in Frisco, Kershaw had his first and only mediocre outing of the season. The first batter hit a home run off him; his breaking ball and command were all over the place. Kershaw gutted it out to win the game, but it was his worst performance of the season. The Dodgers were quietly pleased, hoping that the outing might throw some teams off the scent.

Internally the Dodgers were pretty much in agreement with selecting Kershaw. Even so, Tommy Lasorda, then a special advisor to the Dodgers chairman, asked Calvin Jones why he was so certain about drafting the high school lefty with the seventh pick. Jones responded with a spirited defense of Kershaw: "I've played with Randy Johnson, I've seen Nolan Ryan, I've seen Roger Clemens, I've seen Greg Maddux … and, Tommy, this is the best arm I've seen."[220]

Kershaw reached the Major Leagues in 2008 and pitched 107 innings for Los Angeles at the age of twenty. In 2011, he blossomed in a big way, leading the National League in wins, earned run average and strikeouts and taking home the Cy Young Award. Since his breakout year of 2011, Kershaw has dominated the National League. He has been selected to eight All-Star squads, while winning two more Cy Young Awards. In 13 Major League seasons, he has won 175 games and has racked up more than 2,500 strikeouts, with an earned run average of 2.43.

The San Francisco Giants were lying in wait with the tenth pick. Much like the Dodgers at number seven, the Giants were hoping that no team ahead of them would beat them to University of Washington pitcher Tim Lincecum. Lincecum was on the short side, standing only five-foot-eleven. However, he had dominated opponents in his final season of college, striking out 199 batters in 125 innings with a fastball that touched triple digits. The Royals considered taking Lincecum at number one. Fortunately for the Giants, most teams ahead of them were concerned about using a top-ten pick on a smaller right-handed pitcher whose delivery was described by some as resembling a pinwheel. As Baltimore Orioles general manager Jim Duquette noted, "There was a feeling ... he was going to break down."[221]

The Giants were as solidly committed to Lincecum as the Dodgers had been to Kershaw. When Lincecum remained available at number ten, the Giants jumped. With Lincecum safely in the fold, Dick Tidrow, the Giants vice-president of player personnel, admitted, "We're kind of shocked he got to us at number ten."[222] Giants general manager Brian Sabean added, "He should have been gone before we picked, so by the time we got him it was an easy, easy call."[223] Matt Woodward was the San Francisco scout who brought Lincecum to Tidrow's attention. Tidrow, who pitched for five different clubs over a period of thirteen years, is widely regarded as one of the preeminent experts on pitching talent. "I love the stuff and love the athletic ability. I love everything about him but his size," Tidrow said.[224] Tidrow ceased worrying about Lincecum's size and durability when he saw that Lincecum had the uncanny ability to repeat his unconventional delivery without putting undue stress on his arm.

Many years before the 2006 draft, Kansas City Royals scout Greg Smith had stumbled upon Lincecum when he stopped to watch a tournament in Richland, Washington. Smith was struck by the pitcher, who despite his diminutive size, was striking everyone out. Smith did not bother to find out the name of the pitcher at the tournament because the kid was only four-feet-eleven inches tall. Smith surmised that the pitcher was still in grade school. A few years later, Smith came across the kid again when he saw him pitch during his senior year of high school. Smith knew immediately that it was the same pitcher he had seen at the Richland tournament. This time, Smith found out the pitcher's name. It was Lincecum. "I loved this kid," Smith recalled.

Lincecum went on to play at the University of Washington and started to routinely hit 97 miles an hour on the Juggs gun with a plus slider, a good change-up and an above average curve. Smith advocated as aggressively as he could for the Royals to draft Lincecum. In response, Kansas City scouting director Deric Ladnier moved Lincecum to the second round on the Royals' draft board. Smith persisted, arguing that Lincecum should be the Royals' first pick. It was a tough sell because there was great concern that Lincecum's delivery was too violent. To rebut the concerns, Smith brought in a video of a young Greg Maddux and made a side-by-side comparison with Lincecum. To Smith, Lincecum's delivery looked very much like Maddux's delivery. Smith's argument was persuasive; the front office moved Lincecum to the top spot on the draft board. The next day, however, when Smith returned to the draft room, he saw that the 6'5" Hochevar had replaced Lincecum as number one. Long after the draft, Royals scouting legend Art Stewart pulled Smith aside and told him that he wished the Royals had listened to Smith.

By May 2007, Lincecum was already pitching for the Giants in San Francisco. In his first season, he won seven games, lost five and averaged more than a strikeout per inning. The next year, Lincecum's first full season in the majors, he had a record of 18 wins and five losses, struck out a league-leading 265 hitters, and won the Cy Young Award. In 2009, Lincecum had an earned run average of 2.48, again led the league in strikeouts, and won his second Cy Young Award.

Lincecum led the Giants' pitching staff again in both 2010 and 2011. In each of his four full seasons with the Giants, he had been elected to the National League All-Star team. Further, he had helped the Giants win three World Series championships. Few pitchers in history have had such a meteoric start to their careers. Lincecum was so dominant that a 2011 Bleacher Report argued that Lincecum should have been "the hands down" number one pick of the whole draft.[225]

As of the end of the 2011 season, Lincecum, then 27 years old, had won 69 games in the Major Leagues. Cooperstown seemed within his reach. But, from that point, his career took a rapid turn downward. He lost 15 games in 2012 and gave up more than five runs per nine innings. Three more mediocre seasons followed. The most obvious reason for Lincecum's rapid decline was a sudden lack of command. He walked batters at an alarming rate.

Lincecum experienced periodic flashes of his old dominating self. He pitched no-hit games in 2013 and 2014, both against the San Diego Padres.

His occasional successes made his inability to recover the old magic all the more mystifying. He spent time with various pitching gurus, including Tidrow, but was unable to rectify the problem. Eventually, injuries played a role in his decline, including a back injury in 2014 and a more consequential degenerative hip injury in 2015. When he proved unable to compete effectively, the Giants allowed him to become a free agent after the 2015 season.[226]

The Arizona Diamondbacks selected Missouri right-handed starter Max Scherzer with the 11th pick of the draft. At one point, Scherzer was considered a possible top-five pick because his heater often exceeded the mid-nineties. He slid in the draft because he developed a case of bicep tendinitis and perhaps, also, because he was represented by Scott Boras. While not as heralded as Lincecum or as coveted as Kershaw, Scherzer was very highly regarded and, in time, would earn the moniker "Mad Max" for his ultra-competitive nature.

Scherzer reached the majors with the Diamondbacks in 2008 but was traded to the Tigers after the 2009 season. He flourished immediately and found his groove in Motown. In 2013 he won the American League Cy Young Award with 21 wins against three losses with a 2.90 earned run average. In 2014, Scherzer had another excellent year, winning 18 games and losing only five. Following the 2014 season, he signed as a free agent with the Washington Nationals. In Washington, Scherzer hit his zenith as he would win back-to-back Cy Young Awards and was a key player for the 2019 World Champion Nationals team. He has been named to the All-Star team each year for seven consecutive seasons, 2013 to 2019.

Feeling A Draft

Landing Kershaw

The 2005 amateur draft can only be regarded as a disaster for the Los Angeles Dodgers. The two most notable players taken by the Dodgers were pitcher Luke Hochevar, selected in the first round, and infielder Jordy Mercer, drafted in the 26th round. Neither Hochevar nor Mercer ever spent a day in a Dodgers uniform. Hochevar was unable to come to terms with Los Angeles after the draft. Mercer, a high schooler, elected to enroll at Oklahoma State University rather than turn pro.

The only other notable Los Angeles draftee in 2005, outfielder Scott Van Slyke, signed with the Dodgers and spent six years with the team (2012-2017), hitting .242 with 29 home runs.

When the time came for the 2006 draft, the Dodgers and their new general manager, Ned Colletti, had their sights set on high school pitcher Clayton Kershaw from Highland Park High School in Texas.

The Dodgers' draft misfortunes of the previous year boosted the team's chances of landing Kershaw. With Hochevar available for the 2006 draft, the pool of pitching talent – a group that included Brandon Morrow, Andrew Miller, Tim Lincecum, and Max Scherzer, among others – became even deeper. Hochevar was certain to be picked in the top five, potentially dropping Kershaw to a lower spot in the draft.

As the draft played out, Hochevar went to the Kansas City Royals with the first pick. Four of the next five picks were also pitchers, Greg Reynolds (Colorado Rockies), Brad Lincoln (Pittsburgh Pirates), Morrow (Seattle Mariners), and Miller (Detroit Tigers). To Colletti's relief, when it came time for the Dodgers to select at Number 7, Kershaw was still on the board.

In essence, the Dodgers traded Hochevar and his 46 career wins for Kershaw and his 175 career wins.

2007

I loved [Giancarlo] Stanton. I was doing big league scouting, but I probably saw him as much as our area scout because when I would go to cover the Dodgers, I'd stop at Notre Dame High School first, see the game, see what scouts were there. People were afraid because he was such a good athlete and excelled at football. Everyone thought he was going to go to USC to play football. That's always a tough thing to overcome. I kept pushing the Marlins to take him in the first round. I would have died if we didn't get Stanton. He was too good to lose, such a great athlete. He could run, throw, hit for power. I played with Dave Kingman at USC. I hadn't seen anybody hit a ball like Stanton since Kingman.

> – Orrin Freeman, former special assistant to the general manager, Miami Marlins

The 2007 draft had a new and yet very familiar feeling to it. For the first time in history, the first round of the draft was televised live on ESPN. The familiar feeling came in the form of the Tampa Bay Devil Rays. In 2006, the Devil Rays had again lost over one hundred games, thereby reclaiming their grip on last place in the American League East and gaining the overall number one pick for 2007. So, for the third time in a stretch of eight years, Tampa Bay held the overall number one pick.

In the 1960s, the New York Mets had been historically bad, routinely losing over one hundred games a season. With their losing ways, the Mets earned both a reputation for losing and two overall number one picks in the first decade of their existence. Tampa Bay's early futility surpassed even the lovable Mets as the standard bearer for failure. Despite all the jokes and jabs the Mets endured in their early years, they had cleverly built a solid pitching foundation under manager Gil Hodges. In 1969, the Mets would stun the baseball world by winning the World Series in only the eighth year of existence.

If the Devil Rays' early history was a second-generation reincarnation of the losing Mets, it was appropriate that their scouting director, R.J. Harrison, was a second-generation baseball executive who possessed extensive experience with the number one overall pick. As the son of long-time Seattle Mariners scout Bob Harrison, R.J. had literally grown up watching his father navigate the often treacherous waters of the draft, fishing for the best player available. R.J. had a front-row seat to observe his father's significant involvement in the scouting and drafting of four overall number picks, including arguably the best of all time – Ken Griffey Jr.

In his college days, R.J. Harrison was a big left-handed pitcher for Arizona State University. At ASU, he roomed with the overall number one pick of 1976, Floyd Bannister. As national cross-checker for the Devil Rays, R.J. was intimately involved in the number one selections of Josh Hamilton in 1999 and Delmon Young in 2003.[227] Including 2007, Harrison was directly involved in or associated with eight overall number one picks.

In 2007, the Devil Rays drafted six-foot-five left-handed pitcher David Price from Vanderbilt with the first overall pick. Price was at the top of Tampa Bay's draft board before his junior season and remained there all year as he led the nation with 194 strikeouts. Price was clearly the consensus number one pick in the nation, garnering both the Golden Spikes Award and *Baseball America*'s Player of the Year Award. Unlike the debate surrounding the choice between the "two Joshes" in 1999, the choice confronting the Devil Rays in 2007 was much easier. Prior to the draft, Harrison revealed, "[Price] is the standard by which we're measuring everyone."[228]

In 2008, the Rays would win the American League East title. In doing so, Tampa Bay won 97 games, a total of 31 games more than the Rays had won in 2007. The reasons for the dramatic turnaround were manifold. Foremost among them was the clever drafting of Dan Jennings, R.J. Harrison and the Rays' scouting team during the previous years. Tampa Bay's recent draft haul included Carl Crawford, B. J. Upton, Rocco Baldelli, Evan Longoria, and pitchers James Shields, Scott Kazmir, Jason Hammel, and Andy Sonnastine. Another prime factor in the turn-about was the inspired hiring, in 2006, of manager Joe Maddon, who was instrumental in changing the team's losing culture.

Maddon's calming yet definitive leadership was the key to unlocking the potential of the young Rays, just as Gil Hodges had inspired the Miracle Mets some forty years earlier. Those inclined to seek a more spiritual basis for the turnabout will no doubt point to the team giving Satan the boot in 2008, as they officially dropped the "Devil" from their name and became simply "the Rays." In 2008, the Rays not only won their division for the first time ever, but also defeated both the White Sox and the

Red Sox to win the American League championship. The Rays' 2008 fairy tale season was stopped one step short of equaling the 1969 Mets, as they lost the World Series in five games to the Philadelphia Phillies. Nonetheless, their 2008 season was, at the very least, a minor miracle in Tampa.

After drafting Price, the Rays opened their vault to pay him a $5.6 million bonus, far exceeding what the Royals had paid Luke Hochevar in 2006. For the Rays, it would be money well-spent, as Price became the top-of-the-rotation ace pitcher the Rays had been seeking. Price would join the Rays for the entire season in 2009 and anchor the team's stellar pitching staff. By 2010, Price made his first of five All-Star appearances and won 19 games against only 6 losses. Two years later, he won 20 games and captured the Cy Young Award.

Over time, teams had become wary of using high first-round picks on catchers because the selections have frequently led to disappointment. Nonetheless, the Baltimore Orioles rolled the dice with the number five pick and selected Matt Wieters, a six-foot-five backstop from Georgia Tech. Matt Wieters hit from both sides of the plate and boasted a power bat and superior catching skills. Based on a strong recommendation from area scout Dave Jennings, the Orioles gave Wieters a $6 million bonus to sign. It would be the largest bonus received by any draft pick in 2007. Jennings liked both Wieters' ability to switch hit and the strength of his arm. Jennings noted, "He had power from both sides, a chance to hit for [batting] average and a plus arm with a quick release."

Wieters started his career in an impressive fashion. He made the American League All-Star team in both 2011 and 2012 and became a potent middle-of-the-order run producer while also winning two Gold Gloves. A significant injury to his throwing elbow led to Tommy John surgery in 2014. The injury seemed to have sapped Wieters of his impressive power. Before the injury, Wieters consistently hit more than 20 home runs each season. After the injury, he averaged less than 10 home runs per year.

The 2007 draft class was loaded with excellent pitching prospects, most of them tall. Picking at number 10, the Giants nabbed a six-foot-four, 220-pound left-hander with a big fastball in Madison Bumgarner. The Detroit Tigers selected six-foot-five Seton Hall Prep star Rick Porcello with the 27th pick. Many considered Porcello to be the best high school pitcher in the nation. Bumgarner had fallen in the draft because of concerns about his secondary pitches. Porcello nearly fell completely out of the first round due to concerns about the likely demands of his agent, Scott Boras.

In the fourth round, the San Diego Padres drafted another large right-handed starter in six-foot-four Texas-born Corey Kluber of Stetson University. Kluber spent the years from 2007 to 2010 in the minor leagues, without making much of an impression. The Padres traded him to the Cleveland Indians in 2010. Kluber spent parts of the next two seasons in the minors before finally sticking with Cleveland in 2013. He became a bona fide star in 2014, a season in which he started slowly but came on with a rush at the tail end. In the month of September alone, he won five games. Kluber would finish the season with 18 wins and a 2.44 earned run average. In an oddity, having started slowly, Kluber was not selected for the 2014 All-Star Game in July but led the American League in wins and won the American League Cy Young Award. Kluber continued to dominate the American League competition and won another Cy Young Award in 2017.

In the fifth round, the Orioles drafted a late bloomer in Jake Arrieta from Texas Christian University. Arrieta received a $1.1 million bonus from the Orioles, the largest payment to a fifth-rounder in the history of the draft. Prior to the 2007 collegiate season, Arrieta projected to be a possible first-rounder. However, he had a mediocre season for TCU in 2007 and, in addition, he was represented by Scott Boras. The two factors likely caused Arrieta to drop in the draft. In 2010, Arietta made it to the Orioles and showed flashes of promise but was maddeningly inconsistent.

In 2013, the Orioles traded Arrieta to the Cubs, and it was in Chicago that he truly shined. During a stretch of five seasons with the Cubs, he won 68 games and lost 31. In his career year of 2015, Arrieta won 22 games with a 1.77 earned run average, winning the National League Cy Young Award. In a strange coincidence, as was the case with Corey Kluber in 2014, Arrieta was not selected as an All-Star in 2015, yet won the Cy Young Award. Like Kluber in 2014, Arrieta had a dominating second half of the season in 2015.

In addition to big power pitchers, the 2007 draft boasted big power hitters. The biggest and most intimidating hitter in the draft was a six-foot-six, 220-pound high schooler with light tower power named Mike Stanton. Stanton played for Notre Dame High School in Sherman Oaks, California, which is only 17 miles from Dodger Stadium. In a fortuitous coincidence, Florida Marlins pro scout Orrin Freeman had grown up near Sherman Oaks and had been recruited to play at Notre Dame High School. After high school, Freeman would star in baseball for the powerhouse University of Southern California Trojans.

When scouting at Dodger Stadium, Freeman would stop at Notre Dame High School whenever he could to watch the youngster with light tower power. In every conversation with Marlins scouting director Stan Meek, Freeman would urge Meek to take Stanton with the Marlins' first-round pick. Freeman viewed Stanton as a generational talent whose rare combination of power, bat speed, and athleticism were impossible to resist.

Stanton put on a display in batting practice for all the scouts at the Area Code Games – a national showcase event for high school talent. However, scouts lost interest when they noticed that Stanton rarely made contact in his at-bats during games. The consensus was that Stanton was not able to hit curveballs. Further, Stanton was a football player and, with his prototypical middle linebacker physique, it was widely assumed that he would accept a scholarship offer to play football at Southern California. However, in discussions with Stanton, Marlins scout Tim McDonnell learned that baseball was Stanton's first love.

McDonnell and Freeman were thrilled that other teams were "off the scent." However, they were still worried about persuading their own front office. Stan Meek had made his name as one of the best in baseball at gauging the proper round in which to draft a player. Freeman's protestations notwithstanding, Meek was confident that the Marlins could wait until the second round to take Stanton. Meek reasoned that other scouts had only recently begun to follow Stanton after the Area Code Games and were not heavily invested in him. Meek's judgment proved accurate; the Marlins were able to get Stanton in the second round with the 76th overall pick.

Stanton powered his way through the Marlins' farm system and joined the Marlins in 2010. During the course of eight seasons in Miami, 2010-2017, Stanton became known for hitting mammoth home runs. For Freeman, Stanton's power displays rivaled what he was used to seeing from slugger Dave Kingman. Freeman spoke of Stanton's home runs in almost reverential tones and compared Stanton to Kingman. Freeman recalled, "I once watched my USC teammate, Dave Kingman, hit a homer during batting practice prior to an annual exhibition game with the Dodgers [that went] clear out of Dodger Stadium. I thought Dodger manager Walter Alston was going to have a heart attack. No one had ever hit one out of Dodger Stadium before. After Mike made it to the Marlins, I was in the stands one night at Dodger Stadium and I saw him also hit one as far or farther than Kingman."

For Stanton, the home runs and runs batted in came in bunches, as did the acclaim. Stanton was elected to four National League All-Star teams. In his career year of 2017, he led the league in home runs with 59, and in RBI's with 132. He learned how to handle curveballs and, for his eight seasons with the Marlins, had a batting average of .268. Stanton no longer played using the name of "Mike" but, instead, reverted to the use of his given first name, Giancarlo. In 2014, the Marlins gave Stanton a 13-year contract worth $325 million, presumably intending to keep the superstar in south Florida for his entire career.

However, in October 2017, the ownership of the Marlins changed. The new owners chose to introduce a cost-cutting regime. The owners deemed Stanton to be too expensive and, in December 2017, stunned the baseball world by trading him to the New York Yankees. As a member of the Yankees, Stanton batted .266 and hit 38 home runs during the 2018 season. He missed most of the 2019 season due to injuries to his shoulder, biceps and knee.

With the 14th pick in the draft, the Atlanta Braves also found a big power hitter in six-foot-five high school outfielder Jason Heyward. A graduate of Henry County High School in McDonough, Georgia, Heyward had drawn comparisons to Fred McGriff, Willie McCovey and Frank Thomas. The Braves believed Heyward was the best player in the draft behind David Price. Heyward spent three seasons in the minor leagues and then made his debut with the Braves on opening day of 2010. In his rookie season, he made the National League All-Star team, hit .277 and had 18 home runs. He displayed power, plate discipline and stellar outfield defense and it appeared he might be on his way to stardom. Atlanta traded him to the St. Louis Cardinals in 2014 and, in 2015, he signed with the Chicago Cubs as a free agent. During Heyward's career, his batting average has ranged from a high of .293 to a low of .227. His power production has generally ebbed since his early years in Atlanta and the expectations of long-term stardom have been dampened by his later years.

The Braves struck it doubly rich in the 2007 draft with left-handed power-hitting first baseman Freddie Freeman, whom they selected in the second round. Freeman graduated from El Modena High School in Orange, California. Like Heyward, Freeman advanced quickly through the Braves' farm system and made his debut with the Braves in 2010. He has since become a fixture at first base and in the middle of the Braves' lineup and has been named to four National League All-Star teams.

The Chicago Cubs drafted another power-hitter in third baseman Josh Donaldson from Auburn University with the 48th overall pick. Donaldson has become a consistent candidate for the Most Valuable Player Award and has made three All-Star appearances. In 2015 he won the American League Most Valuable Player Award, leading the league in runs scored, runs driven in, and total bases while belting 41 home runs. Despite being limited by injuries in 2018, he rebounded in 2019 to have a big season with the Braves.

The Boston Red Sox drafted first baseman Anthony Rizzo in the sixth round of 2007. Rizzo was out of Stoneman Douglas High School in Parkland, Florida. In December 2010, the Red Sox traded Rizzo to the San Diego Padres. After only 128 at-bats in San Diego, the Padres gave up on Rizzo and dealt him to the Cubs. In Chicago, Rizzo has flourished, emerging as a three-time All-Star and one of the key components in the Cubs' 2016 World Series championship.

The 2007 draft class was anticipated to be the best high school draft class in years. The performances of Stanton, Bumgarner, Porcello, Heyward, Freeman, and Rizzo have served to confirm that expectation. In fact, 2007 was the first draft since the seminal 2002 "Moneyball" draft in which the number of high school players drafted in the first round exceeded the number of college players.

Powered By Cresse

Over the course of four years at Louisiana State University, Brad Cresse developed into one of the most feared power hitters in the college ranks. In 2000, Cresse's senior season, he received the Johnny Bench Award, which is given to the nation's best collegiate catcher.

Cresse, the son of long-time Los Angeles Dodgers coach Mark Cresse, once hit a home run in the College World Series that was measured at 530 feet. The home run was a nice addition to Cresse's résumé but not so good for his bat manufacturer, Easton Bats. No college hitter was supposed to hit a home run that far. The National Collegiate Athletic Association (NCAA) quickly imposed new rules to reduce the "trampoline effect" of metal baseball bats. With the new rules in place, Easton had to re-tool all its bats. Easton also had to discard thousands of bats that were already in its inventory. An Easton official told Mark Cresse, "Your son's home run killed me."

The Arizona Diamondbacks drafted Cresse in the fifth round of the 2000 draft. In his first season in the minor leagues, he hit .312 with 18 home runs. Over time, the Diamondbacks attempted to change Cresse's swing, convinced that it was too long. In subsequent years, both Cresse's batting average and home run totals progressively declined.

Cresse spent seven years in the minor leagues, advancing as high as Triple-A. He retired from baseball following the 2006 season without reaching the Major Leagues.

2008

When someone like John Barr says he had a gut feeling on Buster Posey, what they are talking about are the intangibles. They mean that this guy will do whatever it takes to win a game. This guy is not going to be denied. Those are things that really can't be measured.

– Chris Buckley, scouting director, Cincinnati Reds (2006-2018)

The Tampa Bay Rays held the first overall pick in the 2008 draft. It was the first time in the forty-four years of the Major League Draft that the same team owned the first overall pick in back-to-back years. While this dubious distinction would normally be a reflection of lean times at the Major League level, the Rays were riding high. The team was starting play to its potential and, under the leadership of manager Joe Maddon, would actually finish the 2008 season in first place in the American League East. Being both in first place in the standings in June of 2008 and having the first pick of the draft was a rapid change of fortune for the Rays.

After getting it right with the selection of David Price in 2007, there was considerable discussion in Tampa Bay's scouting department about picking another college player. Their focus was on Florida State catcher Buster Posey. While Price and Posey could have combined to form a formidable battery in the future, the Rays instead used the first pick on a Georgia high school star, shortstop Tim Beckham. Beckham was a five-tool player from Griffin, Georgia who was named *Baseball America*'s High School Player of the Year. Scouting director R.J. Harrison saw Beckham as a combination of the Upton brothers, Gary Sheffield, Orlando Hudson and Brandon Phillips.[229] Beckham signed quickly for $6.15 million, which exceeded the princely bonus given to David Price the year before.

Beckham has never come close to providing a level of production commensurate with his draft position and outsized bonus. He struggled in the minor leagues for parts of five seasons. Some of his troubles have been self-inflicted. In 2012, he was suspended for 50 games for use of banned drugs. When he did play in 2012, he hit .256 in 72 games with six home runs for the Triple-A Durham Bulls. He spent the 2013 season with Durham as well, hitting .276 in 122 games with four home runs.

Beckham missed most of the 2014 season with a torn anterior cruciate ligament. He played in 82 games for Tampa Bay in 2015 and hit .222. It was not the production expected from a five-tool player. Eventually the Rays decided to cut their losses and traded Beckham to Baltimore in exchange for a minor leaguer. In January 2019, Beckham signed a free agent contract with the Mariners. Playing in 88 games with Seattle in 2019, he hit .237 with 15 home runs.

With the third pick, the Kansas City Royals reached into the high school ranks and selected first baseman Eric Hosmer from American Heritage High School in Plantation, Florida. In his last two minor league seasons, 2010 and 2011, Hosmer went from Class A to Triple-A, hitting a combined .354. Promoted to the majors in May 2011, Hosmer hit .293 with 19 home runs in 128 games. From 2011 to 2017, Hosmer teamed with third baseman Mike Moustakas, the second overall pick in 2007, to provide power and smooth fielding for Kansas City at the corner positions. Along with Alex Gordon, the second overall pick in 2005, Hosmer and Moustakas created a formidable middle-of-the-order presence in the Royals' lineup.

Moustakas and Hosmer were drafted under the watchful eye of Kansas City general manager Dayton Moore. Moore joined the Royals in 2006 after serving as assistant general manager for the Atlanta Braves. In Kansas City, Moore's first order of business was to change the Royals' losing culture through solid drafting, excellent international free agent signings, and other clever player acquisitions. By 2013, Moore's new look Royals finished ten games above the .500 mark. By 2014, they were the American League champions. The next year the Royals completed their return to glory as they defeated the New York Mets to win the World Series.

The Royals' renaissance provides a useful blueprint for rebuilding a team through the draft. In addition to Gordon, Moustaukas and Hosmer, the Royals' selection of Zack Greinke in the 2002 draft was an important key to their future success. Greinke was long gone when the Royals began to see the fruits of their rebuilding efforts, having been traded to Milwaukee. However, the Greinke trade was significant because the Brewers sent prospects Lorenzo Cain and Alcides Escobar to Kansas City in the transaction. Cain and Escobar became two of the most important parts of Kansas City's 2015 championship team.

In 2008, scouting director John Barr was conducting his first draft for the San Francisco Giants. Buster Posey, a catcher from Florida State University, had been on Barr's radar for years. Barr had first met Posey and his family during a high school showcase event. After seeing Posey excel at the showcase tournament, Barr followed him closely while Posey was at Florida State. All the while, Barr was working for the Los Angeles Dodgers. The Dodgers held the 15th overall pick in the 2008 draft. On one occasion when Posey and Barr met, Posey asked if Barr was going to consider drafting him. Barr responded, "Of course, I would, but you are going to be taken long before the Dodgers get to pick."

When Barr took over as scouting director for the Giants, he realized that the Giants had the fifth pick in 2008. At the beginning of spring in 2008, Barr went to see Florida State play. He met Posey and told him, "Hey, I've got a chance to get you now." Posey laughed and said, "Wow!" Of the teams ahead of the Giants, only the Tampa Bay Rays and the Royals had closely scouted Posey. Once Dayton Moore picked Hosmer for the Royals with the third pick, Barr knew that Posey would be headed to San Francisco.

During his time at Florida State, Posey had made himself into the best defensive catcher in college baseball and the best all-around player.[230] In his junior season, Posey led the NCAA in batting average, on-base percentage, slugging percentage, total bases and runs batted in. He fell two homers shy of the lead in home runs. Barr was convinced Posey was the best player in the draft. "What I liked about him was the way he played the game," Barr commented, "you knew he was the guy you want up in key situations."[231]

The Giants paid Posey a $6.2 million bonus. In 2009, his first full season in the minor leagues, he hit .325. He arrived in San Francisco to stay in May 2010 and won the National League Rookie of the Year Award. Posey handled the Giants' pitching staff like a proven veteran as San Francisco stormed its way to the 2010 World Championship. It was the Giants' first World Series victory since 1954, when the franchise was located in New York and Willie Mays was roaming center field at the Polo Grounds.

A gruesome home plate collision limited Posey to 45 games in 2011. However, he rebounded in a big way in 2012, hitting a league-leading .336, winning the National League Most Valuable Player Award and leading the Giants to another world championship. Posey became the first catcher to lead the league in batting, win the MVP Award, and win the World Series in the same season. In 2014, Posey again led the Giants to the World Series championship. He has been selected to six All-Star teams during his career.

It was apparent from the beginning that Posey would be a different personality and a quieter star than typically populated the game. In spite of his success and fame, he has remained close to his humble country roots on Turkey Farm Road in Leesburg, Georgia. Posey's country simplicity is reminiscent of the late Hall of Fame pitcher Catfish Hunter, who never left or forgot his simple Hereford, North Carolina roots.

With Posey leading the way, the Giants won three World Series championships in five years. Their success was the result of insightful drafting. Giants general manager Brian Sabean built San Francisco's team around dominating starting pitching, led by the magnificent trio of Matt Cain, Tim Lincecum, and Madison Bumgarner. The Giants and the Royals matched up in the 2014 Series. The Giants won a thrilling and hotly contested seven-game series in which Madison Bumgarner had one of the most dominating World Series ever by a pitcher. He won the first and fifth games and saved the finale, recording a 0.43 earned run average over 21 innings. Bumgarner took home the Most Valuable Player Award for the Series. *Sports Illustrated* ranked his performance in the World Series on a par with the heroics of baseball's immortals like Christy Mathewson, Lew Burdette and Bob Gibson.[232]

Inevitably, the match-up between the Royals and the Giants called into question the decision by Dayton Moore to choose Eric Hosmer over Posey in the 2008 draft. Moore explained that the Royals had seriously considered drafting Posey but ultimately opted for Hosmer. Moore said he thought Hosmer was a better fit for the Royals because they were building the team around defense and Hosmer was a "plus, plus defender."[233] Over the years, Hosmer proved Moore to be a keen judge of talent, winning four Gold Gloves for his sterling defense at first base. Fittingly, the Royals succeeded the Giants as World Champions in 2015, and Hosmer was a very key contributor.

In 2008, John Barr may have had the best inaugural draft of any scouting director. In addition to Buster Posey, Barr also drafted UCLA shortstop Brandon Crawford. Crawford joined the Giants in 2011 and provided stellar defense at shortstop for both the 2012 and 2014 World Series champions. Exceeding expectations, Crawford has developed into a solid hitter. In 2015, he slugged 21 homers and drove in 84 runs while making his first All-Star team. Crawford returned to the mid-summer classic in 2018 and has continued to provide big hits for the Giants to complement his exceptional fielding.

Statistically, the 2008 draft proved to be quite successful. For the first round, 27 out of the 30 picks reached the Major Leagues. Additionally, a record 140 of the players drafted in the first ten rounds reached the Major Leagues. A total of 275 players selected in the draft reached the Major Leagues. By these metrics, 2008 was the best draft ever. However, it can be argued that only one true superstar, Buster Posey, has come out of the draft. From that perspective, the 2008 draft falls far short of the vaunted 1985 draft.

How Does A Scout Know?

When it comes to prospects, there are no guarantees. There are signs, however, which suggest that a prospect may be a good risk. In some cases, the sign may come in the form of insightful words from a grandmother. When the New York Yankees finally acceded to Andy Pettitte's demand for an $80,000 bonus in May 1991, Pettitte's grandmother assured scout Joe Robison, "You just spent your money wisely, young man." (Ian O'Connor, ESPN.com, 4 February 2011.) History would, of course, prove Pettitte's grandmother to be correct.

Sometimes the sign comes in the form of a player's unmistakable inner confidence. The Baltimore Orioles drafted catcher Gregg Zaun in the 17th round in 1989. Zaun had a scholarship offer from the University of Texas. He told the Orioles scout, Paul Fryer, "I really want to sign but I think I am worth $40,000. If you guys come watch me play, you will realize that is a bargain, but I am staying at $40,000." John Barr, then the scouting director for the Orioles, said, "When Zaunnie was behind home plate, that was his life. It was where he loved to be."

The San Francisco Giants gained key insights about infielder Joe Panik as the result of a snowstorm. The Giants area scout, Johnny DeCarlo, was scheduled to meet with Panik at Panik's home in Hopewell Junction, New York. There was a big snowstorm on the day of the meeting. Concerned about missing the meeting, DeCarlo called Panik to assure him that he would be there. Panik was most gracious. His primary concern was to make sure that DeCarlo stayed safe, even if it meant postponing the meeting. Panik's concern for DeCarlo's safety left a lasting impression. Panik came across as both sincere and authentic. When touting Panik, DeCarlo often included the story of how gracious Panik was on the day of the snowstorm.

Barr, who served as San Francisco's assistant general manager for scouting and international operations, looks for players who are relaxed and comfortable in the batter's box and in the field. He says of Gary Sheffield, "No matter what he was doing, when he walked into that batter's box, there was no other place that he was more comfortable. When he was in the batter's box, he knew he was good and he knew he could do some damage."

Barr sees the same attributes in Buster Posey and Brandon Crawford. According to Barr, "When you watch Buster walk up to the plate, you can see the confidence level. When you watch Brandon at shortstop, even though there are 50,000 people in the stands for Game 7 of the World Series, there's no place else that he would rather be than right there at shortstop. That's a comfort factor that I look for in a player."

2009

One of the issues that teams ran into when trying to scout Mike Trout was that he was a man among boys when he was playing high school baseball and competing against New Jersey pitching. There was just not the depth of really competitive arms to get a real gauge of who Mike Trout was. Mike ended up getting drafted 25th overall because of it. And even though that was a really good draft in 2009, it's pretty easy to say now that he was the best player available and will surely be regarded as the best player to come out of that draft.

– C.J. Nitkowski, Texas Rangers broadcaster; former Major League pitcher

The 2009 draft was perhaps the most hyped draft ever. Forty-five years had passed since the inaugural draft of 1965. Never had there been hysteria and anticipation on a level that surrounded pitcher Stephen Strasburg of San Diego State.[234] While hyperbole is commonplace for high first-round phenoms, the Strasburg hype reached a rare fevered pitch. One scout went well beyond the standard pre-draft adulation to label Strasburg "a once in a lifetime talent."[235]

The six-foot-five, 225-pound Strasburg had dominated college baseball in 2009, going 13-1 with a 1.32 earned run average and 195 strikeouts. His stuff was even more impressive than his statistics. He possessed an electric fastball that touched 103 miles per hour and a Doc Gooden-like knee-buckling curve. Even more, Strasburg possessed the ability to locate his pitches with almost pinpoint precision.[236] The Washington Nationals held the first overall pick in 2009 and were primed to take Strasburg.

In 2005, Major League Baseball relocated the Montreal Expos to Washington, D.C. The team was renamed the Washington Nationals. The Nationals had a respectable season in 2005, winning exactly half of their games. Over the next three seasons, however, Washington finished with losing records. In 2008, the team was horrid, finishing with 102 losses and thereby earning the first pick in the 2009 draft.

Changes were underway. In 2008, the Nationals had moved into a new stadium, Nationals Park, located adjacent to the Anacostia River. Just before the 2009 draft, Washington elevated long-time scout and executive Mike Rizzo to the general manager position. Rizzo had been the scout most responsible for drafting Hall of Fame first baseman Frank Thomas for the Chicago White Sox. More recently, as scouting director for the Arizona Diamondbacks, he had helped build the Diamondbacks into a World Series winner. For Rizzo and his staff, it was an easy call to take Strasburg, but they still had much work ahead of them to rebuild the team they inherited from Montreal.

Scott Boras represented Strasburg. Boras had floated trial balloons suggesting that Strasburg would not sign for less than $50 million. The Nationals were able to come to terms with Strasburg and Boras right at the signing deadline for a $15.1 million contract, which included a record $7.5 million signing bonus. After signing, Strasburg made eleven starts in the minor leagues and held opponents to 1.30 runs per nine innings. He made his Major League debut before a sellout crowd at Nationals Park on June 8, 2010. Baseball's newest wunderkind did not disappoint, allowing only two earned runs over seven innings and striking out 14 batters.

Strasburg was similarly dominant in his next two starts. Strasburg mania acquired its own name – "Strasmas." Baseball announcer Bob Costas labeled the debut as "one of my personal top ten games."[237] Strasburg pitched a total of 68 innings in 2010 and struck out 92 batters. However, the "Strasmas" phenomenon was short-lived. In August 2010, the Nationals announced that Strasburg had suffered a torn ulnar collateral ligament in his right elbow and would undergo Tommy John surgery. The ligament was successfully repaired but the surgery kept Strasburg out of action for most of the 2011 season. In 2012, Strasburg picked up where he left off, winning 15 games, striking out 197 batters in 159 innings, and making his first All-Star team.

With Strasburg's return to dominance, the Nationals made their first post-season appearance in 2012. Based on the advice of the Nationals' medical team, however, Rizzo shut Strasburg down for the post-season. The decision generated a storm of media criticism and disappointed many Nationals fans. Although Strasburg returned to form in 2014, leading the National League in starts and strikeouts, minor injuries limited his effectiveness in 2015. However, he pitched well enough in 2016 and 2017 to be elected to the All-Star team both years.

By 2017, along with Strasburg's reputation for striking out opponents, there was a growing perception that he succumbed too easily to minor injuries, discomforts and perceived slights. Strasburg silenced the criticism with a dazzling elimination game performance against the Chicago Cubs in the 2017 National League Division Series. Despite suffering from severe flu symptoms, he dominated the potent Cubs lineup. The performance dramatically changed Strasburg's reputation. In the eyes of many fans and observers, Strasburg was now a warrior.

In 2019, Strasburg had a stellar 18-6 regular season. He further shed any lingering concerns about his competitive spirit, leading the National League in innings pitched and helping the Nationals reach their first-ever World Series. Strasburg won a record five post-season games and was named the Most Valuable Player in the World Series.

In 2009, to capitalize on the Strasburg hype and attract more viewership, baseball moved the draft headquarters from New York City to Secaucus, New Jersey, the home of the Major League Baseball Network. There was an expectation that some of the draft eligible players would travel to Secaucus to view the proceedings in person. Ironically, the prime time event attracted only one draft eligible player, a somewhat obscure high school outfielder from Millville, New Jersey. The player's name was Mike Trout.

In the first 45 years of the draft, there had never been a first overall pick who hailed from New Jersey. Further, only ten players from New Jersey were ever drafted in the first round. By comparison, eleven overall number one picks hailed from California. Nine California players were drafted in the first round of 1980 alone. Prior to 2009, none of the prospects from New Jersey who were drafted in the first round had achieved much success.

The most famous major leaguer with New Jersey ties is no doubt the late New York Yankee legend, Yogi Berra. However, Berra was a transplant who was born and raised in St. Louis, Missouri. Berra moved to Montclair, New Jersey during his days with the Yankees and became a beloved resident of the Garden State. Though he ranks as one of the greatest baseball players of all time, the Hall of Fame catcher serves as an appropriate archetype for the underappreciated state; he is more remembered for his unforgettable malapropisms than for his sterling playing career.

Scout Ron Rizzi grew up in New York City and knew Berra well. As Rizzi tells the story, writer Dick Young of the *New York Daily News* once encountered an irate Yogi in the Yankee clubhouse. Berra was looking at the boxscore printed in the *Daily News* for the game played the previous day. The boxscore showed Berra as having three hits in four at-bats. In fact, he had hit safely in all four times at the plate. Berra bellowed, "Dick, I went four for four yesterday." Young tried to calm Berra, saying, "Yog, it's a typographical error." Berra responded with increasing agitation, "No it wasn't, Dick. I swear it was a clean hit."

Trout, the 17-year-old outfielder who had traveled from Millville to Secaucus to witness the 2009 draft proceedings, would become the biggest story of the draft. Trout is the best baseball player ever to come from New Jersey and it seems likely that, in due time, he will become New Jersey's first true Hall of Famer.

The fact that Trout lasted until the 25th pick in the 2009 draft is a story in itself. Clearly, the scouting community failed to realize and appreciate Trout's potential. Scouts themselves often ask, "How the hell did we miss this guy?" Noted baseball journalist Tom Verducci conducted an inquiry into that very question.[238] The most obvious answer is "East Coast bias." Ironically, it's a phrase normally used to describe the sports media's tendency to overrate and excessively cover Eastern sports teams as compared with their West Coast counterparts.

In scouting, the term "East Coast bias" actually describes an opposite phenomenon that leads scouts to underrate prospects from the East Coast. The 2009 draft may remain, for all time, the most prominent example of East Coast bias. As Oakland A's scouting director Eric Kubota explained, "There is a shorter season to see a player in the East." Kubota says, "If you happened to go in and [Trout] had a bad day, which all guys do, you might not have had the opportunity to get in and see him again. In Florida and California and Texas, you have plenty of time. It's a lot harder when they are up in the northeast."

With regard to Trout, Kubota's analysis was not idle speculation. Oakland general manager Billy Beane and San Francisco Giants general manager Brian Sabean both went to New Jersey to observe Trout. Neither came away with a sufficiently favorable impression to justify using a first-round pick on Trout. Beane and his data analyst, Farhan Zaidi, saw Trout on a day on which he did not get the ball out of the infield.[239] As a result, Oakland, which was picking at number 13, chose Grant Green from the University of Southern California instead of Trout.

Beane, in a bit of self-deprecating humor, refers to his failure to see the potential in Trout as an example of the business axiom known as the Peter

Principle.[240] In addition to Oakland and San Francisco, nineteen other teams passed on Trout, including the Washington Nationals and the Arizona Diamondbacks twice; Washington and Arizona each held two picks among the top 20 draft positions. *Baseball America*'s draft preview compared Trout to Aaron Rowand, a .273 career hitter, noting that Trout's bat "is not a sure thing."[241]

The Angels might have missed also but for the aggressive advocacy of Northeast area scout Greg Morhardt, who had played together in the Twins' organization with Trout's father, Jeff.[242] From the first time he laid eyes on Mike Trout as a sixteen-year-old, Morhardt was certain that Trout was going to be a Major League player.[243] Morhardt's infatuation with Trout continued to grow with each observation. Morhardt would write comments in his reports such as "best athlete, best player in the world – period, best player on the planet." His praise reached such a fulsome level that many in the Angels organization considered Morhardt to have fallen victim to the common trap of losing perspective on a player.

One day the Angels scouting director, Eddie Bane, along with his cross-checker, Jeff Malinoff, came to Millville to watch Trout. Morhardt was also in attendance. Malinoff commented on Trout's awkward grip on the bat, but Morhardt would hear nothing of it. Morhardt said to Malinoff, "Jeff, he's a Hall of Famer. Leave him alone."[244] The area scout continued to compare Trout to the legends of the game. Most often, Morhardt compared "Mikey" as he called him, to New York Yankee legend Mickey Mantle, a comparison that always made Bane shudder.[245]

Bane was an excellent assessor of talent in his own right, having drafted Paul Konerko for the Dodgers and having played a role in the Angels' drafting of Jered Weaver. By the time the draft rolled around, Morhardt's obsession with Trout was a source of amusement in the Angels' front office. In the war room, Bane asked his scouts to write down the four best players in the draft. All but Morhardt began with Stephen Strasburg, the pitcher from San Diego State. Bane read Morhardt's list out loud, "Trouter, Trouter, Trouter, and Trouter." Everybody in the room laughed.[246] The Angels possessed both the 24th and 25th picks in the draft. With the 24th pick, the Angels selected Texas high school outfielder Randal Grichuk. Then, to the great delight of Greg Morhardt, the Angels took Mike Trout with the 25th pick. Thus the Angels have the distinction of both passing on "Trouter" *and* taking "Trouter" in the first round.

Feeling A Draft

After ten seasons in the Major Leagues, Trout has already established himself as the greatest player in the history of the Angels' franchise. He won the Rookie of the Year Award in 2012 and Most Valuable Player Awards in 2014, 2016 and 2019. He has been named to eight consecutive All-Star teams and, for his career, has amassed 302 homers and 201 stolen bases while batting .304. Billy Beane provided perhaps the most apt description of Trout's unique talents when he said, "I swear he is the only Major League player in which I become an eight-year-old kid."[247] By 2019, Trout would be considered one of the best draft picks of all time, on a par with Ken Griffey Jr., Barry Bonds and Álex Rodríguez, and on his way to joining Mantle, Willie Mays and Henry Aaron as a baseball immortal.

The 2009 draft yielded another perennial All-Star and Most Valuable Player candidate in the eighth round. The Arizona Diamondbacks may have whiffed twice on Mike Trout, but they struck it rich with first baseman Paul Goldschmidt from Texas State University in San Marcos. Tripp Couch, a scout for the Diamondbacks, turned in a third-round grade on Goldschmidt. In hindsight, Couch's assessment of the six-foot-three, 225-pound first sacker was too timid. Like Trout, Goldschmidt possesses both power and speed. In ten Major Leagues seasons, Goldschmidt has hit 249 home runs and stolen 128 bases. The six-time National League All-Star has won three Gold Glove Awards.

If Trout, Strasburg, and Goldschmidt were not enough talent for one draft, 2009 also provided some other stud players. The Colorado Rockies drafted third baseman Nolan Arenado from Lake Forest, California in the second round. In his eight Major League seasons, Arenado has captured eight Gold Gloves Awards and four Silver Slugger Awards and has been named to five All-Star teams. Arenado was anything but a surefire pick coming out of high school. Colorado scout Jon Lukens, who signed Arenado, had mild reservations about recommending him. Lukens considered Arenado to be "too fat, too slow, too angry, and too quiet."[248] Nonetheless, Lukens did see something special in Arenado's abilities. However, Lukens admits he had no clue that Arenado would work so hard to make himself into a perennial All-Star third baseman.[249] In recognition of Arenado's work ethic and achievements, the Rockies rewarded him with a $260 million contract extension in 2019.

The Invisible Ball

Pitcher Bartolo Colon retired from professional baseball in 2018 at the age of 45. For the better part of 21 seasons, Colon confounded Major League hitters. He left baseball with a record of 247 wins and 188 losses.

When asked to comment on the reasons for Colon's success, scout John Tumminia seemed to shake his head. "I've been watching him for years and years," he said. "The only thing I write on my report is that he throws an invisible ball."

Former Major League pitcher C.J. Nitkowski has seen the "invisible ball" up close. "I played with guys who had what we called the 'invisible fastball'," Nitkowski says. "They wouldn't light up the radar gun, they might throw 88 to 90 miles an hour. A hitter would come back to the dugout and say, 'I have no idea how I missed that pitch."

Nitkowski says that Chris Young, the six-foot-ten right-hander from Princeton University, was a good example of a pitcher with an invisible fastball. According to Nitkowski, Young was "a high spin-rate guy who could throw 88 mph up in the zone and get away with it in the Major Leagues because he was spinning the baseball more than most."

Nitkowski concludes that when a hitter says, "I can't get to his fastball," chances are that the pitcher has a really high spin rate.

2010

I never saw [J.T. Realmuto] mentioned in any publications. No one knew about him. Our people had him evaluated in the first round. When we got to the draft, I said, 'Guys, Realmuto hasn't been written about. We go to the park and there's not many scouts there.' We got to the third round in the draft and I said, 'I think I'm going to wait one more round and we can take another guy in the third round.' I said, 'I think I'm going to wait until the fourth round.' One of our smart regional guys said, 'If you lose this guy, you're going to shoot yourself. Are you sure you want to wait another round?'

    –Stan Meek, former scouting director, Miami Marlins

In June of 2010, all eyes were focused on a baseball prodigy in Las Vegas, Nevada. The buzz actually began in June of 2009 when *Sports Illustrated* featured 16-year-old Bryce Harper in a cover story titled "Chosen One."[250]

The Washington Nationals again owned the number one pick in 2010, having finished with the worst record in baseball in 2009. With the number one spot came the right to draft the "Chosen One." The 2010 class was perceived to be deeper and more talented than the previous year. Leading up to the draft, Washington's general manager, Mike Rizzo, and his veteran scouting staff had scoured the nation to do their due diligence. By May 2010, the members of the Nationals' scouting department were in agreement that Harper would be the pick.

Like Strasburg, Harper was represented by Scott Boras. The Nationals knew that signing Harper would be neither easy nor inexpensive. Negotiations dragged on until just before the signing deadline. Tension was in the air. Just seconds before the signing period expired, Harper signed his contract and became a member of the Nationals. The team agreed to pay a bonus of $6.25 million. The amount was less than Strasburg's bonus and less than the second pick of 2010 would receive, but still a record amount for a position player.

Both Strasburg and Harper were number one overall picks; both were drafted by the Nationals; and both were represented by Scott Boras. Yet, they were significantly different in age and persona. Strasburg was almost 21 years old when he was drafted. Harper was only

17 when he was selected. In the words of writer Tom Verducci, Harper was a prodigy.[251] Strasburg was a relatively late bloomer. He was so unheralded that he was not even drafted out of high school. Conversely, Harper and Boras were cleverly weighing options for Harper to leave high school after only two years in order to accelerate his draft eligibility.

The ultra-creative Boras maneuvered to have Harper eligible for the 2010 draft by arranging for him to graduate high school early with a General Education Diploma and then enroll at a junior college. After one year of domination at the junior college, the College of Southern Nevada – where he hit .443, with 31 homers and 98 runs batted in – Harper became eligible for the draft and a very large payday.

Strasburg was not even considered much of a collegiate prospect when San Diego State University's head coach, Tony Gwynn, first laid eyes upon him. In fact, the team's strength coach, Dave Ohton, and many others on the team viewed Stephen as soft and out of shape. Ohton pushed Strasburg to improve, but also burdened him with the unfortunate nickname of "Slothburg."[252]

Soon thereafter, Strasburg began to work out like a fiend, changing both his physique and his perspective on hard work. While he started his collegiate career in the bullpen, it all clicked for him when he was converted to a starter in his sophomore season. Major League scouts began flocking to see him register triple-digit readings with his fastball. Over the next two college seasons, he was nearly unhittable.

Another stark difference between "Harp" and "Stras," as Rizzo would affectionately call them, was their level of comfort with the spotlight. Strasburg had only two seasons in the limelight in college before he was thrust into national prominence in Washington. He was not comfortable with all the attention and media scrutiny. By contrast, Harper seemed to have been born for the spotlight. Starting at the age of six, and at every step along the way up to college, Harper played against older kids and usually dominated the competition. Through all types of tournaments and showcases, he not only thrived but excelled. While only sixteen, he played at a showcase at Tropicana Field, home of the Tampa Bay Rays, and hit a ball more than 500 feet – the longest ball ever hit at "the Trop." Even Harper's batting practices were crowd-pleasers. It was easy to understand why Harper was in a hurry to get to the big leagues; at every level, the competition provided little challenge.

Much like Boras, Harper was not at all shy about self-promotion. Nor was he one to tamper down the expectations. His future goals went way beyond merely reaching the Major Leagues at an early age. He elaborated on his goals in a *Sports Illustrated* article: "Be in the Hall of Fame, definitely. Play in Yankee Stadium. Play in the Pinstripes. Be considered the greatest player of all time."[253] Given his accomplishments as an amateur, the goals did not seem particularly outlandish. His tools were hard to beat: speed, size, hitting, hitting for power, a missile-launcher for an arm, and great baseball aptitude. The whole package was so impressive that *Sports Illustrated* pegged him as "the next LeBron."[254] The suggestion seemed to be that there wasn't even an appropriate baseball comparison for Harper unless one looked to the fictional hero in *The Natural*, Roy Hobbs.

After less than a full season of games in the minors, Harper began mashing in the big leagues in 2012. He delivered on his much-promised potential by winning the National League Rookie of the Year Award and making the first of his appearances at the All-Star Game. After injuries limited his 2014 season, he bounced back in 2015 with 42 home runs, 99 runs batted in, and a .330 batting average. Harper would spend three more All-Star seasons in Washington, but none of them approached his 2015 achievements.

Strasburg and Harper would share a clubhouse for seven seasons in Washington. Though sharing the same agent, they approached their second professional contract in a very different manner. While other prominent baseball agents such as Ron Shapiro, who represented notable clients like Kirby Puckett and Cal Ripken, believed it benefits players to make long-standing associations with a team and a city, Boras zealously believes in the "hired gun" approach, because of his earnest belief in the inequities of baseball's pay structure.[255]

After a long winter of protracted negotiations following the 2018 season between Boras and numerous suitors, Harper brought his talents to Philadelphia, signing a record $330 million, 13-year contract with the Phillies. In 2016, however, Strasburg became one of the few Boras clients to sign a second contract with his existing team rather than explore free agency. Strasburg's contract called for $175 million over seven years but allowed him to opt out of the contract after the 2019 season. Following the Nationals' victory over Houston in the 2019 World Series, Strasburg opted out of his contract and, two months later, accepted a seven-year, $245 million deal to remain with Washington.

Unlike 2009, when Strasburg was the consensus number one choice, the 2010 draft had two players, in addition to Harper, whose talents warranted consideration as the first overall pick. One, Jameson Taillon, was the 2010 version of the seemingly endless supply of special Texas right-handers. Taillon's dominating high school portfolio and his 97-mph heater had scouts dreaming again of Ryan, Clemens and Beckett. The Pittsburgh Pirates chose Taillon with the second pick. The 2010 draft made it 45 consecutive years that right-handed high school pitchers would be passed over for the number one pick in the draft. So far in Taillon's career, persistent and serious injuries, including two major arm surgeries, have significantly limited his development.

High school shortstop Manny Machado was the third player who was on the short list of choices for the first pick. Scouts compared Machado to Álex Rodríguez. The Baltimore Orioles had the third pick in the draft and claimed Machado. Like Harper, Machado was already raking in the big leagues by 2012. Machado quickly became a luminous star in "Charm City." In seven years in Baltimore, Machado was named to four All-Star teams and recognized with two Gold Gloves for his stellar defense. He also slugged 162 home runs for the Orioles. Like Harper, Machado became a free agent following the 2019 season. Like Harper, Machado is represented by Scott Boras. In 2019, Machado signed a ten-year, $300 million contract to play for San Diego.

Notwithstanding all the accolades showered upon Harper, Taillon and Machado prior to the draft, lanky left-hander Chris Sale of Florida Gulf Coast University may have been the best player available in 2010. The Chicago White Sox selected Sale with the thirteenth pick. In his junior year of college, Sale had a record of 11 wins and no losses with nearly 150 strikeouts. He lasted until the 13th pick because some teams believed his three-quarters delivery made him more suited for the bullpen rather than starting. Others feared his herky-jerky motion might lead to future injury.

Sale was the first in the 2010 draft class to make it to the Major Leagues, joining the White Sox in August 2010. Sale spent the 2010 and

2011 seasons exclusively as a relief pitcher. In 2012, the White Sox put him in the starting rotation, a role in which he thrived. He made the American League All-Star team for seven consecutive seasons and established himself as one of the premier starters in baseball and a perennial Cy Young contender. The White Sox traded him to the Red Sox in December 2016 and he helped lead the Red Sox to the 2018 World Series championship.

The Florida Marlins scored a major coup when they landed Westlake High School prospect Christian Yelich with the 23rd pick of the first round. Yelich was much less heralded than the players selected at the top of the first round, in part because he played the infield in high school, a role in which his defensive ability was suspect.

Tim McDonnell was the Florida Marlins area scout who followed and signed Yelich. It was the second time in four years that McDonnell managed to identify a future star in the Los Angeles area who was under the radar. McDonnell had followed and signed Giancarlo Stanton in 2007. It is rare for an area scout to find one MVP-caliber player in his whole scouting career. To find two players with the potential to be designated as the Most Valuable Player borders on the incredible.

McDonnell, in classic scout speak, remembers Yelich as always having the "hit tool." McDonnell went further out on the limb when he predicted that the slightly built Yelich would hit with power.[256] McDonnell had been confident in the "power tool" ever since he had seen Yelich, as a high schooler, hit a bomb to dead-center off future big leaguer Tyler Skaggs.[257] To boot, Yelich had speed and a great make-up.[258] Once the Marlins moved Yelich to the outfield, the concerns about his fielding evaporated. In 2014, playing primarily in left field, Yelich won a Gold Glove.

Marlins general manager Dan Jennings strongly shared McDonnell's assessment of "the hit tool." In 2015, Jennings predicted that Yelich's ability to use the whole field would eventually lead to a batting title. The batting title would come three years later but, unfortunately for the Marlins, it came after Miami had traded Yelich to the Milwaukee Brewers in a fire sale after the 2017 season. Yelich has fulfilled McDonnell's prediction that he would hit with power, slugging 36 home runs in 2018 and 44 more in 2019. Yelich won the 2018 National League MVP Award and finished second in the MVP voting in 2019.

If Yelich was overshadowed by the big names of the 2010 draft, catcher J.T. Realmuto was thoroughly obscured. The advent of the draft and advances in scouting have largely eliminated the captivating stories of scouts finding unknown talents in the corn fields and coal mines of rural America. However, every now and then, a genuine prospect still goes undetected.

Realmuto was not unknown in Oklahoma. Rather, he was quite well-known for his talent in football. As the starting quarterback for Carl Albert High School, Realmuto had led his team to the state's coveted football title. Marlins scouting director and Oklahoma native Stan Meek witnessed Realmuto's heroics that day and learned that the quarterback intended to attend Oklahoma State University on a baseball scholarship. Meek made a note to pay Realmuto a visit in the spring when baseball season arrived.

When Meek returned in the spring, he brought along Marlins area scout Steve Taylor. The two had expected to see Realmuto playing shortstop. However, due to an injury to one of Realmuto's teammates, the high school coach had to insert Realmuto at catcher. The coach apologized to Meek, expressing regret that Meek could not see him at shortstop. For the Marlins, it was a blessing. With one throw by Realmuto to second base, Meek realized that Realmuto had the arm to catch at the Major League level. Meek was sufficiently impressed with Realmuto's work behind the plate that he placed him on the Marlins' draft list and highlighted his name with a star. Realmuto also hit a home run in the presence of Meek and Taylor, solidifying the impression. Amazingly, it was the only game that season where Realmuto was the catcher, and Meek and Taylor were the only scouts on hand to see it.

Steve Taylor continued to monitor Realmuto for the Marlins. Taylor informed Meek that "no one was coming to see him." As had been the case with Giancarlo Stanton, Meek thought the Marlins could "steal" Realmuto in a round later than his scouting grade would warrant. Again as with Stanton, Meek was persuaded by his scouts not to risk losing out on a potential star, so the Marlins picked Realmuto in the third round. Realmuto became the Marlins' starting catcher in 2015 and improved each subsequent season to the point of becoming an All-Star in 2018. Unfortunately for the Marlins' fans, Realmuto was another casualty of the payroll-cutting initiative in Miami. The Marlins traded Realmuto to the Phillies prior to the 2019 season. Once in Philadelphia, Realmuto would earn his second All-Star selection.

The New York Mets had the seventh pick in the draft and chose hard-throwing right-handed starter Matt Harvey from the University of North Carolina. In the ninth round, the Mets chose right-hander Jacob deGrom from Stetson University. Harvey and deGrom became pillars of the Mets' rotation and led the team to the 2015 National League pennant.

Harvey made his first splash in the Big Apple in 2013. He started for the National League in the 2013 All-Star Game and finished the season with a sterling earned run average of 2.27. For a time, Harvey was the toast of the town. Former Mets manager Bobby Valentine opined that Harvey might become the best Mets pitcher of all time.[259] *Sports Illustrated* dubbed him the "Dark Knight of Gotham."[260]

Harvey encountered elbow problems that short-circuited his 2013 breakout season and led to Tommy John surgery. He missed all of the 2014 season but came back in 2015 to win the National League Comeback Player of the Year Award. It appeared that Harvey's career was back on track but he experienced more injuries in 2016 and 2017 that kept him out of the rotation. In May 2018, the Mets traded Harvey to the Cincinnati Reds.

Jacob deGrom arrived in New York in 2014 and promptly won the Rookie of the Year Award. By 2017, deGrom had overtaken Harvey as the undeniable ace of the Mets' staff. In 2018, he won the National League Cy Young Award, pitching to a microscopic 1.70 earned run average. In 2019, deGrom led the National League in strikeouts and won his second straight Cy Young Award. If he continues to progress at his current pace, deGrom may be considered one of the best later round choices of all time and will join the conversation for best player of the 2010 draft.

The Emergence of "Joey Bats"

It is not clear when veteran outfielder José Bautista acquired the nickname "Joey Bats," but the moniker was certainly not in common usage in the years prior to 2010. Bautista made the Baltimore Orioles' roster out of spring training in 2004. His Major League debut came on April 4, 2004 as a pinch runner. From that point on, Bautista's rookie season was a succession of limited appearances with five different teams in two different leagues. The Tampa Bay Rays selected Bautista off waivers from Baltimore on June 3. The Rays then sold Bautista to the Royals on June 28. On July 30th, he was traded twice within 24 hours, first from the Royals to the Mets and then from the Mets to the Pirates.

For the 2004 season, Bautista played in 16 games for Baltimore, 12 for Tampa Bay, 13 for Kansas City, and 23 for Pittsburgh. His season-ending statistics were dismal, a combined batting average of .205 with no home runs and only two runs batted in. Bautista spent most of 2006-2008 with Pittsburgh, playing third base and second base as well as all three outfield positions, all without distinction. Traded to Toronto in August 2008, "Joey Bats" had clearly arrived by 2010, when he clubbed 54 home runs and drove in 124 runs. Between 2010 and 2015, he was named to the American League All-Star team every year. In that span, he averaged 38 home runs and 97 runs batted in per year, to go with a .268 batting average. Not surprisingly, J.P. Ricciardi, the Toronto general manager who traded for Bautista, considers it one of the best trades he ever made.

Bautista was originally drafted by the Pirates in the 20th round of the 2000 amateur draft. Mickey White was the scouting director for Pittsburgh at the time. He had seen Bautista play for Chipola College in Florida and was in the stands when Bautista hit a ball over a light tower at Chipola. White always thought that Bautista held great potential. When Bautista signed to play pro ball with the Pirates in May 2001, White gave him a bonus of $560,000, second round money for a 20th round pick. White left his position with the Pirates in February 2002, joined Baltimore, and was instrumental in convincing the Orioles to claim Bautista in the December 2003 Rule 5 draft.

When asked why it took so long for Bautista to emerge as "Joey Bats," White offers a few theories. He believes the Pirates never gave Bautista the time to settle in during his first stint with the organization. A new regime had taken over in Pittsburgh and Bautista was left exposed to Rule 5. White thinks the new regime did not place great value on Bautista and other players that the Pirates had drafted during White's tenure. That tends to happen with regime changes, White says. During Bautista's minor league years with the Pirates, 2001-2003 and 2005, and even during his Major League seasons with the Pirates, from 2006 to 2008, Pittsburgh used Bautista as a utility player. In White's view, "when you are a utility guy but you are kind of a thoroughbred, you can lose the edge on your skills quickly."

When Bautista landed with the Blue Jays, Dwayne Murphy was the hitting coach. Murphy worked with him to tone down his leg kick so that he could get his front foot planted sooner. White is of the opinion that, once Bautista started getting his foot down sooner, all of the torque that Pittsburgh scouts Jack Powell and Mark McKnight had seen from Bautista in college again became a factor.

2011

He had a personality that was very rare in sports. Getting to see it over the years, it was a personality you got drawn to. He was always smiling and always having fun. He loved playing the game of baseball. Every time he got on that mound, he brought the best out of you. It's not only a loss for baseball, but this whole country really, Cuba and everything.

–Freddie Freeman, first baseman for the Atlanta Braves, reflecting on the passing of José Fernández, who died on September 25, 2016 in a boating accident[261]

The 2011 draft did not have the hype of its two predecessors. However, the draft more than made up for what it lacked in name recognition with quality and quantity. It was one of the deepest drafts in recent history. The 2011 draft will also be remembered for record bonus amounts that were driven by significant changes to the collective bargaining agreement.

The year 2011 would be the last year before significant penalties would kick in that would effectively create a slotting system that Major League teams had desired for years. Not surprisingly, therefore, 2011 saw teams spend like drunken sailors in an effort to have one last unrestricted spending spree.

The Pittsburgh Pirates would again hold the first overall pick in the draft. It would be the fourth time in the 47-year history of the draft that Pittsburgh would lead off. Pittsburgh's record with their earlier three number one picks was rather mediocre. The Pirates had twice opted for starting pitching, selecting Kris Benson in 1996 and Bryan Bullington in 2002. In 2011, Pittsburgh again went for starting pitching, and the third time was the charm. The Pirates selected UCLA's stud right-hander Gerrit Cole. The six-foot-four, 225-pound Cole clearly was one of the handful of prospects worthy of the first pick.

As a high schooler, Cole had spurned the New York Yankees three years earlier when they drafted him in the first round. Instead of signing with the Yankees, he chose to attend UCLA. In his three years with the Bruins, he demonstrated a fastball in the high nineties, a dominant slider and a plus change-up, all with superb command and composure beyond his years. Perhaps the only red flag may have been that he was a client of Scott Boras. However, even the sometimes parsimonious Pirates jumped into the 2011 spending jamboree with both feet and signed Cole for a bonus of $8 million.

After turning pro, Cole met and even exceeded expectations. He was in the Steel City by 2013 and won 21 games for the Pirates over his first two seasons, with excellent corresponding statistics. In 2015, Cole had a breakout year, making the All-Star team and winning 19 games against 8 losses, with an earned run average of 2.60. Cole's 2016 season was limited by a triceps injury that put him on the disabled list. He returned to start 33 games for Pittsburgh in 2017, winning 12 and losing 12.

Prior to the start of the 2018 season, the Pirates dealt Cole to the Houston Astros for four players. In Houston, under the tutelage of pitching coach Brent Strom, Cole ratcheted his fastball up to 102 miles per hour and improved his secondary pitches. Strom helped Cole develop his four-seam fastball and taught him the concept of "tunneling," a pitching technique which makes Cole's fastball, slider and change-up more difficult for a hitter to distinguish.[262] The results have been exceptional.

In two seasons with the Astros, Cole made the All-Star team each year, winning 15 games in 2018 and 20 in 2019. He led the Astros to the World Series in 2019, with Houston facing the Washington Nationals. Cole and Stephen Strasburg squared off as the respective aces of their teams. After the World Series, Cole signed a nine-year, $324 million free agent contract with the New York Yankees, a deal that made him the highest paid pitcher in baseball.

The next three picks after Cole were also pitchers, marking the first time in the history of the draft that a position player was not among the first four picks. With the second pick, the Seattle Mariners selected University of Virginia left-hander Danny Hultzen. The pick came as a surprise to many observers because the Mariners had been linked to Rice University third-sacker Anthony Rendon. The Arizona Diamondbacks used the third pick to take Cole's teammate at UCLA, pitcher Trevor Bauer. Then the Baltimore Orioles, picking fourth, chose the High School Player of the Year in right-handed pitcher Dylan Bundy from Owasso, Oklahoma.

Hultzen had been dominant during his career at the University of Virginia, winning 32 games and losing only five. However, after signing with the Mariners, he fell victim to serious shoulder injuries. He has made only a brief appearance in the big leagues. Bauer became the first member of the 2011 draft class to reach the big leagues when he debuted with Arizona in June of 2012. After Bauer had pitched only 16 innings for Arizona, however, the Diamondbacks traded him to the Cleveland Indians in a deal that brought shortstop Didi Gregorius to Arizona.

In each of his first three seasons in Cleveland, Bauer posted losing records. However, he began to figure it out in 2016, winning 12 games for the Tribe in 2016 and another 17 games in 2017. In 2018, Bauer made the All-Star team and caught the attention of baseball with a 2.21 earned run average. He was one of the front runners to win the 2018 Cy Young Award until his season ended prematurely when a line drive fractured his leg.

While Bauer's talent and dedication are beyond dispute, his manic and unusual training techniques and his painfully honest and sometimes egotistical quotes often do not sit well with teammates or management. Bauer's antics have created the perception that he is a selfish teammate.[263] The Indians traded Bauer to the Cincinnati Reds in July 2019. In his two months as a member of the Reds, Bauer started ten games and won only two, with a 6.39 earned run average.

Bundy had acquired almost legendary status at Owasso High School, where he pitched to a 0.25 earned run average and averaged more than two strikeouts per inning. At the high school level, his combination of fastball, curve and cutter proved nearly unhittable. Bundy's high school catcher, Drew Stiner, compared him to "a machine" for the way he could repeat his delivery and dominate opposing hitters.[264] Most scouts considered Bundy to be a "can't miss" number one starter. Long-time Tampa Bay Rays executive R.J. Harrison compared him favorably to Josh Beckett.

Bundy pitched well in the minor leagues, recording a 2.59 earned run average over three seasons. In 2013, he suffered an elbow injury that required Tommy John surgery. As a result, Bundy did not start for Baltimore until 2016. Hope was rekindled when he had a strong start to the 2018 season, posting a 1.42 earned run average through his first five starts. From that point, however, Bundy faltered. For the season, he led the American League in the dubious categories of losses, with 16, and home runs allowed. In his four big league seasons, Bundy held a 38-45 won-lost record and a disappointing 4.67 earned run average. The

Orioles traded him to the Los Angeles Angels in December 2019 in exchange for four minor league prospects.

The Kansas City Royals surprised some draft observers when they used the fifth overall pick to take five-tool outfielder Bubba Starling out of Gardner-Edgerton High School in Gardner, Kansas. Starling had committed to play football for the powerhouse Nebraska Cornhuskers. The Royals persuaded Starling to forgo football with a $7.5 million signing bonus. At the time, Art Stewart and the Royal hierarchy were elated to have Starling in the fold. To date, however, he has not realized his potential and has spent only a short stint with the Major League club.

The selections of Bundy and Starling meant that Rice University's All-American third baseman, Anthony Rendon, was still available when the Washington Nationals were set to pick at number six. *Baseball America* had rated Rendon as the best prospect in the whole draft, touting his hitting, power, arm strength and superior defense at third base.[265] However, significant injuries, including a shoulder injury and a broken ankle, had caused Rendon's draft stock to slip. Washington's physicians examined Rendon's medical records and were fully confident that he had recovered from the injuries. The Nationals wasted no time in calling Rendon's name and signed him to $6 million contract. With the addition of Rendon in 2011, the Nationals' draft haul of Strasburg, Harper and Rendon in consecutive years arguably ranks as the greatest three-year coup in draft history.

Strasburg, Harper and Rendon were all represented by Scott Boras. Though many teams were averse to dealing with the agent whom the *New Yorker* had labeled the "extortionist," the Nationals had no such aversion. In fact, they also selected two more Boras clients, pitcher Alex Meyer and outfielder Brian Goodwin, in the later part of the 2011 first round.

While Harper gravitated to the spotlight and Strasburg avoided it, Rendon appeared totally indifferent to the attention. The preternaturally laid-back Rendon turned out to be as good as advertised and was already in the big leagues by 2013. With all the hype surrounding Strasburg and Harper, the nonchalant Rendon managed to fly under the radar during his time with the Nationals. Washington's hitting coach, Kevin Long, noted "even his swing is quiet."[266] The results of that swing are often deadly to opposing pitchers. In 2014, Rendon's first full season, he finished fifth in the National League's Most Valuable Player voting.

Other than 2015, when Rendon was limited by an injury, he has been a model of consistency. His most successful season came in 2019, when he led the National League in runs batted in and provided clutch hitting throughout the Nationals' run to their first-ever World Series championship. In December 2019, Rendon signed a free agent contract to play for the Los Angeles Angels.

Each draft has its own story; each draft has interesting subtexts and coincidences. In 2011, for example, three players surnamed Bradley were taken in the first and supplemental first round.[267] The most interesting subplot of 2011 involved the intersecting stories of two shortstops, Francisco Lindor and Javier Báez. Both were Puerto Rican natives whose families had settled in Florida early in their childhoods. Both were dynamic shortstops with potent bats and a true zest for the game. They were drafted one after the other in the first round of 2011, Lindor by the Cleveland Indians with the eighth pick and and Báez by the Chicago Cubs with the ninth pick. Both have become rising superstars for their teams, and the two faced off against each other in the 2016 World Series.

The Indians selected Lindor based on the scouting and advocacy of area scout Mike Soper, who had zeroed in on him at a baseball showcase in Lindor's sophomore year of high school. Soper was impressed by the natural ability of the five-foot-eleven shortstop and, particularly, his advanced footwork, work ethic and pure joy when playing.[268] Lindor's infectious smile and personality, combined with his All-Star talent, have captured the hearts and affections of Cleveland fans. In his first five seasons, Lindor has been selected to four All-Star teams and received two Gold Glove Awards and two Silver Slugger Awards.

Sometimes a scouting director identifies a player whom he covets and is going to take the player, if available, no matter the circumstance. Such was the case with Chicago Cubs scouting director Tim Wilken and Javier Báez. Wilken admits he would have had to call a time-out in the unlikely event that either Rendon or Cole slipped to the ninth pick, but otherwise he fully intended to draft Báez with the pick. Wilken loved Báez's explosive bat, exceptional glove and the fact that he had an "innate sense how to play the game that you cannot teach."

Baseball America's pre-draft discussion of Báez alluded to make-up concerns, emotional outbursts and aloofness. Wilken dismissed these worries after conferring with his area scout, Tom Clark, who assured him that *Baseball America*'s sources were misinterpreting Báez's passion and natural shyness.

Wilken and Clark both realized that Báez's swing-from-the-heels approach would lead to some "swing and miss" but they considered it a small price to pay for all the other skills that Báez brought to the baseball field. Most especially, they were taken by Báez's subtle strengths, such as sliding, deft tagging and "off-the-charts instincts."[269] Báez has been nicknamed "El Mago," meaning "the Magician." The nickname is in recognition of Báez's well-honed skills – the type of skills, Wilken says, that a player develops "in the backyard through years of practice."

Báez did have some growing pains at the start of his Major League career, the sort of growing pains that the Cubs had anticipated. In 2014, Báez's first season with Chicago, he batted only .169 in 52 games. However, with each succeeding year, Báez has consistently made more contact and evidenced more power. In 2018 he finished second in the National League Most Valuable Player voting after hitting .290 with 34 home runs and leading the league in runs batted in. He had another excellent season in 2019 and appears poised to become one of the best players in the game. Even Báez's staunchest advocate, Tim Wilken, admits, "I didn't even think he would be this good."

The Houston Astros chose six-foot-three University of Connecticut outfielder George Springer with the 11th pick. The five-tool center fielder would become another one of the true impact players that were so plentiful in the 2011 draft. Springer reached the Major Leagues in 2014. Initially, he struggled with contact but, through hard work, has improved his batting average greatly. In Houston, Springer consistently provides the power and defensive excellence he displayed at the University of Connecticut. He is an atypical leadoff hitter but has been successful in that capacity for the powerhouse Astros. He routinely exceeds one hundred runs scored each season and has been selected to three American League All-Star teams.

Three picks after the Astros took Springer, the Marlins selected high school pitcher José Fernández of Braulio Alonso High School in Tampa, Florida. Fernández came to the United States as a 15-year-old. A native of Cuba, he possessed a relentless desire to defect to the States. Fernández's efforts to covertly leave Cuba included three failed attempts, each attempt resulting in imprisonment in Cuba. On his fourth attempt,

Fernández, his mother and sister reached Mexico and later settled in Tampa. Once in Florida, Fernández quickly became a stud pitcher at Alonso High. He had grown into a muscular six-foot-three, 220-pound specimen; his pitching arsenal featured a 98-mph fastball. His unquenchable will to win made him a hot commodity in the scouting community. Marlins scouting director Stan Meek fell in love with Fernández, both for his pitching skills and his enthusiastic approach to the game.

From the first day that Marlins general manager Dan Jennings saw Fernández play, Jennings was greatly impressed with the pitcher's enormous talent. Jennings became even more impressed when he had the opportunity to speak with Fernández. Aside from his pitching ability, Fernández possessed a dynamic "light up the room" personality that was infectious. Along with Lindor and Báez, Fernández was another 2011 draftee who brought great joy to the game.

Fernández rocketed through the Marlins' minor league system and was starring in the majors for the Marlins in 2013. At the age of 20, Fernández dominated Major League hitters with a 2.19 earned run average. For his efforts, he captured both an All-Star birth and the National League Rookie of the Year Award. Fernández injured his arm in 2014 and required elbow surgery. The surgery shut him down until July 2015. During the latter three months of 2015, Fernández won six games, losing only one and showed the same overpowering repertoire as he had before the surgery. In 2016, Fernández was back to full All-Star form, with a 16-8 won-loss record and a 2.86 earned run average.

Hall of Fame baseball writer Jayson Stark dug deeper into Fernández's numbers to demonstrate the truly extraordinary scale of Fernández's achievements. Stark found that, since World War II, no right-handed pitcher under the age of 25 had posted a lower career earned run average than Fernández. Further, Fernández's home record at Marlins Park – 29 wins and two losses and a 1.49 earned run average – was the best home record for any pitcher in modern history. Remarkably, right-handed hitters could manage only a .180 batting average against Fernández.[270]

Not surprisingly, Fernández became a fan favorite in Miami and especially among its large Cuban-American population. He filled the stands with fans and instilled excitement and joy in the city of Miami. Jennings, who regarded Fernández as a surrogate son, called him the brightest light among the bright lights of a vibrant city. The pitcher was affectionately referred to as "El Nino." In Jennings's words, Fernández was "the puppy dog with the big ears."[271]

Of course, with the vigor and high-spirited energy of boundless youth often comes reckless abandon. For José, that recklessness led him to take unfathomable risks. Before dawn on September 25, 2016, Fernández was operating his high-powered speed boat off Miami Beach at an estimated speed of 65 miles an hour. The boat struck a jetty and crashed, killing Fernández and his two male companions. It was later determined that Fernández, then 24 years old, was under the influence of cocaine and alcohol.

News of Fernández's tragic death cast a pall over all of baseball. The game had suffered a terrible loss. Jennings and members of the Miami Marlins organization, and others who knew and loved Fernández, felt an ineffable void. For baseball historians, Fernández's premature death leaves them with only the ability to speculate on his future greatness and his place in the game. His former pitching coach, Chuck Hernandez, and many others in baseball fully believed that Fernández was destined for Cooperstown.[272]

With the 18th pick of the first round, Billy Beane and the Oakland Athletics nabbed another impact player in Vanderbilt University ace Sonny Gray. Gray had a stellar career at Vanderbilt, going 27-10. He possessed a mid-nineties heater and a knee-buckling curveball. Gray was a victim of the long-standing bias against undersized right-handed pitchers. He was slightly under six feet in height. Almost assuredly, had Gray been taller, he would have been drafted much earlier in the first round. Gray rewarded the Athletics in short order, as he was already the staff ace by 2013 and was an All-Star in 2015.

The Boston Red Sox had a draft for the ages in 2011. The Sox collected seven major leaguers in the first five rounds, including two starting outfielders of the future, right fielder Mookie Betts and center fielder Jackie Bradley Jr.

Betts, who was selected in the fifth round, would turn out to be the steal of the draft. The first time that Red Sox area scout Danny Watkins saw Betts play, he had one of those "gut feelings" that are so cherished by scouts and ridiculed by sabermetric gurus.[273] Betts's consistent play and his calm demeanor reinforced Watkins's gut feel.[274] Former Boston general manager Theo Epstein, with his Ivy League pedigree, is the ideal embodiment of the sabermetrics-guided baseball executive. When considering Betts, Epstein needed something more persuasive than the "gut feel" of a scout. The Red Sox employed the cutting-edge technology of "neuroscouting" – the science of measuring how fast a baseball brain works on pitch recognition and decision-making – to evaluate Betts. Mookie scored off the charts, and the Sox began to realize they had found a hidden gem.[275]

Betts quickly rose through the Sox's minor league ranks and was already with the parent club by 2014. After a solid 2015 season, Betts truly hit his stride the next year, his first of four consecutive selections to the American League All-Star team. He played Gold Glove defense in the outfield, and his offensive numbers ranked at the top of the league. He stole bases with ease. Writer Tom Verducci aptly captured Betts's production when he said, "Betts fills up a stat line like a bingo card."[276] In 2018 Betts had a season for the ages, leading the Red Sox to a World Series victory and running away with the American League Most Valuable Player Award. Betts's 42.0 Wins Above Replacement value far exceeds the production of the most successful of his 2011 draft mates, including Francisco Lindor, Javier Báez, Anthony Rendon, George Springer, and Gerrit Cole.

Theo Epstein compares Betts's talents to those of former Pirates' first-rounder Andrew McCutchen. To Epstein, Betts has a comparable "combination of a short swing, bat speed, superior hand-eye coordination and athleticism." For Boston's famed designated hitter, David Ortiz, it is Betts's plate discipline that stands out. Ortiz says that Betts "knows exactly what he's doing at the plate."[277] In the lingo of today's game, Betts "controls the zone," meaning that he knows the strike zone and swings only at pitches that he can drive with authority.

At the end of the day, the 2011 draft class appears to be on a trajectory to surpass its more heralded predecessors. However, all draft predictions are fraught with peril. Extrapolation of early career production is especially perilous. The investment advisor's standard disclaimer – past performance is not a guarantee of future results – applies in spades. Nonetheless, in ten years or so, baseball scribes may well speak of the 2011 draft class in reverential tones.

A Tale of Two Quarterbacks

The San Diego Padres had a notably poor draft in 1992. Of the first 22 players that the Padres selected, only three – first baseman Todd Helton and pitchers Brett Laxton and Todd Erdos – would make it to the Major Leagues. Of the three, only Erdos signed with San Diego. Both Helton and Laxton passed up offers from the Padres and, instead, enrolled in college. For Padres general manager, Joe McIlvaine, the selection of Helton in the second round was particularly unsettling.

Helton had starred in both baseball and football at Central High School in his hometown of Knoxville, Tennessee. As a senior, Helton, a quarterback, accounted for 2,772 combined yards passing and rushing. He was even better in baseball, hitting 12 home runs and posting a batting average of .655. McIlvaine had always been wary of drafting high school players from the South who had played football. "Football is just so dominant in the South," he says, "there is so much that goes along with being a football star in the South."

Before the Padres made the decision to draft Helton, McIlvaine grilled Reggie Waller, the Padres director of scouting. Waller assured McIlvaine that Helton would forego college and sign with the Padres. Three times McIlvaine asked Waller, "Are you sure?" Each time, Waller assured McIlvaine that Helton was going to sign. After the draft, when the Padres attempted to negotiate with Helton, he turned the team down. His heart was set on playing football for the University of Tennessee. In McIlvaine's view, it was as if Helton didn't have a choice. "He felt like he had an obligation," McIlvaine concluded, "that he had to go to the University." Years later, when reflecting on Helton's decision, McIlvaine remarked, "It was all because of the mentality of Southern boys about football."

At the college level, Helton proved to be better in baseball than football. He never gained the starting quarterback position at Tennessee. He served as the backup to Heath Shuler for two seasons and then as second string to Peyton Manning for one year. Helton spent three years at Tennessee before being drafted by the Colorado Rockies in the first round in 1995. He went on to play 17 seasons in the majors, all with the Rockies.

By 2001, McIlvaine had moved on to the Minnesota Twins as a special assistant to general manager Terry Ryan. The Twins had the first overall pick in the draft that year. Early on, the Twins identified high school catcher Joe Mauer as the player they wanted. Mauer was a hometown kid, born and raised in St. Paul, Minnesota. Like Helton, Mauer had been an outstanding football player in high school. According to McIlvaine, Mauer might have been the best high school quarterback in the country. Unlike Helton, however, McIlvaine had no doubt that Mauer intended to play pro baseball.

In the days before the 2001 draft, a scout for the Twins had visited Mauer at his home. During the visit, Mauer and the scout talked in Mauer's bedroom. After the visit, the scout reported back to the Twins that all of the pictures on Mauer's bedroom wall were baseball pictures. "This is the difference between a Northern kid and a Southern kid," McIlvaine says. "A Southern kid would have all football pictures on his bedroom wall. A Northern kid tends to be much more open to baseball."

2012

When we took [Corey] Seager, my national guy at the time, Paul Fryer, a terrific scout, called me and said, 'Hey, I just saw the best hitter in the draft.' I said, 'Really?' He said, 'Yeah, you have got to get in there and see him.' It was Seager. However, Paul said, 'But I don't think he's going to play shortstop.' So, I went to see Seager. I called Paul during the game and said, 'I think you are right. I think this guy is the best hitter in the draft but I think you are wrong about the position, I think he can stay at short.' We laughed about it. We still laugh about it to this day.

    –Ned Colletti, former general manager, Los Angeles Dodgers

The island of Puerto Rico's most famous exports are rum and baseball players. The godfather of Puerto Rican baseball, of course, is the Hall of Fame legend, Roberto Clemente.[278] In addition to Clemente, the Caribbean island has also produced baseball greats Roberto Alomar, Orlando Cepeda, Carlos Delgado, Juan González, Edgar Martinez, and Bernie Williams. None of those legendary players was subject to the draft. Until 1989, Puerto Rican players were not subject to the draft and could be signed as free agents.

As of 2012, there were only eleven players of Puerto Rican heritage playing in the Major Leagues. However, a new resurgence of interest in baseball on the island was generated by the 2012 draft and its number one overall pick, shortstop Carlos Correa, a native of the municipality of Santa Isabel in Puerto Rico.

The Houston Astros held the number one pick in the draft, having finished last in all of baseball in 2011 with 106 losses. However, 2012 would mark a new era for the franchise with a new owner in Jim Crane and a new general manager in Jeff Luhnow. The Astros selected Correa with the number one pick, expecting that he would become the marquee player in Houston. Following the successful sabermetric models of the Oakland Athletics and the Boston Red Sox, the Astros turned around their sinking ship in record time. Luhnow and the Astros would go beyond all other franchises in embracing analytics as its lodestar. Their new approach would lead to a World Series title in 2017.

The 2012 season was the year for which the owners of Major League teams had been longing. "Fiscal restraint" was returned to the draft. When Correa signed, it was for a $4.8 million bonus. Correa's bonus was forty percent below the bonus that the 2011 number one choice, pitcher Gerrit Cole, had received. Even though the second overall choice, Byron Buxton, signed with the Minnesota Twins for a $6 million bonus, the overall first-round bonus money dropped by 6.7 percent.[279] There was speculation that spending concerns had led the Astros toward Correa and away from Buxton. However, in retrospect, Correa appears to have been the best choice in the first round and perhaps of the entire draft class.

At six-foot-four and 185 pounds, Correa projected to be a middle-of-the-order hitter, with good running speed and power at the plate. Astros area scout Joey Sola was particularly taken with Correa. "I had never scouted and seen a player like this," he said, "his maturity was off the charts."[280] At his introductory press conference with the Astros, Correa chose to wear uniform number 12, both to denote that he was the first player chosen in the 2012 draft and to pay homage to his childhood hero, Roberto Alomar, who had worn number 12 during his career.[281]

Correa has more than fulfilled expectations. He reached the Major Leagues in 2015 at the age of 20 and won the American League Rookie of the Year Award. Though hindered by injuries in 2018 and 2019, when Correa has been healthy, he has consistently provided middle-of-the-order pop, base stealing and superb shortstop play. In 2017, he was named to the American League All-Star team and was a key component in Houston's improbable World Series victory.

The 2012 draft may have also produced the best Puerto Rican pitcher of the draft era in José Berríos. The Minnesota Twins drafted Berríos with the second pick of the supplemental first round. Berríos features a fastball that reaches the upper nineties and excellent complementary pitches. He made it to the Major Leagues in 2016 and was selected to the American League All-Star team in both 2018 and 2019.

In the third round, the Seattle Mariners selected another Puerto Rican right-handed fireballer in pitcher Edwin Días. By the time he joined the Mariners in 2016, Días had added a wipeout slider to his almost triple-digit heater. The results were impressive. By 2018 Días was widely considered to be the best closer in baseball, as he recorded 57 saves, made the All-Star team and finished eighth in the Cy Young Award voting.[282]

In addition to the resurgence of Puerto Rican baseball, 2012 had another major story line: Billy Beane and the Oakland Athletics drafted a high school player in the first round. Actually, counting the supplemental first round, they drafted three high school players in the first round. It was a dramatic reversal of their recent past drafting preferences and contrary to one of the most basic tenets of "Moneyball." The 2012 draft was the first time the A's had drafted a high school player in the first round in over a decade. The last high school player whom the Athletics had selected in the first round was pitcher Jeremy Bonderman in 2001. Of course, as all "Moneyball" aficionados know, the selection of Bonderman prompted Beane's infamous chair-throwing tirade. While the wall in the draft room was the first casualty of Beane's war on drafting high school talent in the early rounds, the man responsible for choosing Bonderman, scouting director Grady Fuson, was shown the door in relatively short order.

Not only did the Athletics draft three high school players in the first round of 2012, but the players selected all turned out to be good choices. With the 11th pick, the A's drafted shortstop Addison Russell from Pace High School in Florida. The A's traded Russell to the Cubs in 2014. He soon became a key component of Chicago's infield and was the starting shortstop on the Cubs' 2016 World Series championship team. The Athletics drafted another high school shortstop, Daniel Robertson, with the 34th pick. Oakland traded Robertson to the Tampa Bay Rays while he was still in the minors. He has played parts of four seasons in the majors and appears poised to have a solid career as a utility player in the big leagues.

The Athletics saved the best for last, selecting first baseman Matt Olson from Parkview High School in the Atlanta area with the 47th pick. The A's have not been tempted to trade Olson. Rather, he has become a star for Oakland at first base. He won the Gold Glove Award in both 2018 and 2019 and has slugged 89 home runs in his three seasons as a regular for the Athletics.

The Washington Nationals drafted Lucas Giolito with the 16th overall pick in 2012. Giolito had starred at Harvard-Westlake High School in Los Angeles, where he dominated hitters with a fast ball in the high nineties and what *Baseball America* described as a "plus-plus curve." He was still available to the Nationals at number 16 because he had previously suffered a serious elbow injury. Wahington general manager Mike

Rizzo rolled the dice on Giolito nonetheless. After Tommy John surgery and a lengthy rehabilitation process, Giolito was throwing as hard as ever. In December 2016, Rizzo sent Giolito and two other young hurlers to the White Sox in a trade for outfielder Adam Eaton. Eaton would become an important contributor on the Nationals' 2019 World Series championship team.

The Los Angeles Dodgers and scouting director Logan White nervously waited for their opportunity to pick at number 18. In White's words, "I was more nervous about 2012 than 2006 when we drafted Kershaw because I feared Corey would be gone." "Corey" was six-foot-four shortstop Corey Seager from Concord, North Carolina. Seager profiled as a pure left-handed power hitter. Seager's swing impressed the Dodgers national scout, Paul Fryer, so much that he described Seager as the best hitter in the draft. Many scouts were of the opinion that Seager was too big to play shortstop and would have to play third base in the majors.[283] Dodgers scouting director Logan White disagreed, concluding that Seager would be able to remain at shortstop.

To the delight of White and the Dodgers, Corey Seager remained available when the 18th pick came around. They immediately snapped him up. White has proved to be right on both counts: Seager has been good enough defensively to play shortstop for the Dodgers and his bat has been really good. Seager played 155 games at shortstop for the Dodgers in 2016, his first full year in the big leagues. He was named to the National League All-Star team, won the Rookie of the Year Award and finished third in the Most Valuable Player voting. Seager's success has put him on a par with Carlos Correa as the best players to come out of the 2012 draft.

Picking immediately after the Dodgers, the St. Louis Cardinals selected six-foot-six Texas A&M pitcher Michael Wacha. Wacha burned through the minor leagues and was already pitching in St. Louis early in 2013. He was dominant in the 2013 post-season for the Cardinals. Facing the Dodgers in the National League Championship Series, he won two games and didn't allow a run in 14 innings. The Cardinals defeated the Dodgers in the Championship Series, four games to two, to advance to the World Series.

Following Los Angeles' loss to the Cardinals in the Championship Series, Dodgers general manager Ned Colletti asked Logan White why the Dodgers didn't draft Wacha instead of Seager. White assured Colletti that, soon enough, he would understand why the scouting department preferred Seager. By the end of the 2019 season – a full four years into Seager's Major League career, the evidence is clear. After Wacha's meteoric start with the Cardinals in 2013, his pitching has ebbed and flowed. Wacha made the National League All-Star team in 2015, when he won 17 games and had an earned run average of 3.38. In the years since then, however, his earned run average has fluctuated from a low of 3.20 to a high of 6.62. In contrast, Seager's career has been on a consistent upward arc.

A Renewed Determination

Like many scouts, Pat Murtaugh has a soft spot for stories about players who seem to come out of nowhere and find success. Murtaugh talks fondly of pitcher Zack Godley. A 10th round pick of the Chicago Cubs in 2013, Godley spent 2013 and 2014 in the minor leagues. He was nowhere close to the majors. Godley was a hard thrower but had done nothing to distinguish himself.

Murtaugh saw something appealing in the way that Godley pitched. "I really liked his focus," Murtaugh says. "He would come in to relieve in tough situations and get the outs. I thought if he could improve his breaking ball, he had a chance."

In December 2014, the Diamondbacks' front office called Murtaugh and posed a question. The front office told Murtaugh that the team was planning to trade catcher Miguel Montero to the Cubs in a salary dump. Arizona needed to know the name of a player in the Cubs' farm system whom it could ask for in exchange for Montero. "Just give us the name of a player we can get back who has a chance," the caller said. Murtaugh recommended Godley. Shortly afterward, the trade was announced.

Godley, then 25, started the 2015 season with Arizona's high Class A team in Visalia, California. He pitched well in Visalia and was promoted to the Double-A Mobile BayBears on July 1, 2015. Within a month, he was in the big leagues, making his debut on July 23. Godley started six games for Arizona in 2015 and compiled a 5-1 won-lost record. He played for five seasons in Arizona, from 2015 to 2019. His best year came in 2018 when he won 15 games.

Murtaugh explains Godley's success in very simple terms. "He saw that somebody wanted him and he took that as renewed determination," Murtaugh says.

2013

There are a lot of people who will try to tell you that they can predict who will be able to handle failure and who will not, but I don't believe in that. If you look at the history of the draft, if we knew all those things, then why was Mike Trout the 25th overall pick in 2009? Why was Mark Appel the first pick overall in 2013 and not Kris Bryant? Anybody who tells you they can predict with certainty whether a player will be able to handle failure is deluding themselves. You go to see a high school kid and he's always been the star, you almost never see him under pressure because he is pretty much dominating everybody he plays against. When do you see him fail, when do you see him against any competition that he is buckled? Look at the kids who have had great college careers and then they get to pro ball and they can't seem to get over the hump.

–J.P. Ricciardi, former general manager, Toronto Blue Jays

Twenty-three years after the Yankees selected Brien Taylor, the Houston Astros used the first overall pick in the 2013 draft to take another "can't miss" pitcher, Mark Appel of Stanford University. Appel had been named the National Pitcher of the Year for his 2012 season at Stanford and then was drafted number eight overall by the Pirates in the 2012 draft. He chose to return to Stanford, however, when he and his agent, Scott Boras, could not reach agreement with Pittsburgh.

Appel endured a torturous road after he was drafted. He pitched well in Class A in 2013 but struggled mightily the following season. Playing for the high Class A Lancaster JetHawks during the first half of the 2014 season, he started 12 games and yielded more than nine runs for each nine innings. Despite his difficulties, the Astros promoted him to Double-A Corpus Christi where, in six starts, he significantly lowered his earned run average. Appel started the 2015 season with Corpus Christi and compiled a 5-1 won-loss record in 13 starts. His performance earned him a spot as the Astros' representative at the 2015 minor league All-Star Futures Game.

The appearance in the Futures Game represented a high-watermark for Appel. The Astros promoted him to the Triple-A Fresno Grizzlies for the remainder of the 2015 season. Though he compiled a 5-2 record in 12 starts for the Grizzlies, Appel gave up an unsightly 34 earned runs in 68 innings. Following the 2015 season, the Astros parted ways with Appel, trading him to the Philadelphia Phillies. An appendectomy had slowed Appel's progress in the Houston organization but, even when healthy, he did not show the dominating pitches that had been his trademark in college.

Appel's tenure in the Phillies organization was hindered by a shoulder injury and Philadelphia released him in November 2017. Finally, in February 2018, Appel announced that he was taking a break from baseball.

In 1999 Nike produced an entertaining commercial, titled "Chicks Dig the Long Ball," that featured Mark McGwire, Tom Glavine, Greg Maddux and actress Heather Locklear. The 2013 draft illustrates that scouts also dig the long ball or, in scout-speak, "the power tool." Power is considered to be perhaps the most difficult of the five tools to scout because it involves: (1) projecting the physical development of youngsters in their teens; (2) discerning whether "light tower power" will translate to the majors against elite pitching; and (3) predicting whether development coaches will be able to make tweaks to a swing that will add power.[284]

Just three years after the hoopla surrounding the drafting of Bryce Harper, Las Vegas produced another power-hitting star, Kris Bryant, who had starred at the University of San Diego. Bryant was *Baseball America*'s College Player of the Year in 2013. He had generated Ruthian-like power in college, blasting 31 home runs in his junior season. For comparison, his home run total in his junior year exceeded the total number of home runs hit by 223 college teams in Division I of the NCAA.[285] To the delight of scouts and front office executives, Bryant exhibited extraordinary plate discipline and was able to make contact on a consistent basis. Further, he possessed an above-average throwing arm that would allow him to play third base or right field in the majors. Lastly, he scored high on the all-important issue of player make-up. Teams were impressed by Bryant's maturity and his interests beyond the game of baseball.

The Chicago Cubs had the second pick of the draft and they were focused on pitching, which they desperately needed. General manager Theo Epstein, who had come over from the Red Sox, and senior vice president for scouting and player development Jason McLeod acknowledged that their top targets were Appel and Jon Gray of the University of Oklahoma. The Cubs anticipated that the Astros would use the number one pick on Appel and so had pretty much settled on Jon Gray early in April. At the team's "mid-point organizational meetings," scout Sam Hughes suggested that the Cubs give further consideration to drafting Bryant. Other powerful voices joined in.

Despite the Cubs' glaring weaknesses on the mound, they ended up using the second overall pick on Bryant. He arrived in Chicago in 2015 and proceeded to win the National League Rookie of the Year Award, with a .275 average, 26 home runs and 99 runs batted in. Bryant's sophomore season, 2016, was even better, as he hit .292 with 39 home runs and won the National League Most Valuable Player Award. More importantly for the team's long-suffering fans, Bryant led the 2016 Cubs to the franchise's first World Series championship in 108 years. Injuries slowed Bryant during the 2018 season, but he returned to All-Star form in 2019.

Thirty picks after the Cubs selected Bryant, the New York Yankees took Fresno State outfielder Aaron Judge. At six-foot-five and 230 pounds, Kris Bryant is large and dominating. At six-feet-seven and 280 pounds, Aaron Judge seems to be a real-life Paul Bunyan. Taller hitters are saddled with the inherent disadvantage of a very large strike zone. For that reason, there have been very few players in the history of the game who possess the height of an Aaron Judge and are able to make consistent contact. Frank Howard and Dave Winfield were two notable exceptions. Aaron Judge is an exception as well.

The Yankees national cross-checker at the time, Brian Barber, had followed Judge at Fresno State. Barber explained, "His strike zone is so large you have to ask 'can he reach the pitch outside? Can he get the bat on the inside pitch?'"[286] To overcome the disadvantage, it takes great athleticism, an attribute that most extraordinarily large players lack. Judge had been a three-sport star in high school. When settling on Judge as their first-round pick, the Yankees concluded that he was blessed with the necessary athleticism in abundance.

The Yankees assistant general manager, Billy Eppler, was impressed by Judge's speed and agility and the "wow factor" to his game.[287] Scouting director Damon Oppenheimer noted that the Yankees had nine scouts following Judge and they all had given him a first-round grade.[288] The Yankee brain trust was especially taken by the speed at which the ball came off his bat.

Judge made his Yankees debut in 2016 in auspicious fashion, homering in his first at-bat. However, he then went into a slump, collecting only 14 hits in 83 at-bats, with 42 strikeouts. Draft-day sceptics appeared to be justified in questioning whether the behemoth from Northern California would be able to make consistent contact to justify his majestic home runs. The sceptics received their answer the very next year, as Judge led the American League in home runs, with 52, and in runs and in walks. He was voted the American League Rookie of the Year, made the All-Star team and finished second in the Most Valuable Player voting.

As impressive as Judge's numbers have been, his temperament has been equally impressive. The expectations and demands that accompany playing for the Yankees in the pressure-cooker environment of New York present an imposing challenge for players. Judge's calm and humble demeanor allows him to thrive where others have wilted. Judge's former manager, Joe Girardi, compared Judge's media skills to those of Yankee legend Derek Jeter.[289] Further, while Jeter was always guarded, Judge displays genuine interest in and affection for fans, teammates, opponents and even, at times, the hardened New York media. His unaffected approach to life allows him to take things in stride and with good humor. As an example, a passerby taken by Judge's size but unfamiliar with his baseball success once asked him what sport he played. Responding with good humor and a smile and an element of truth, Judge responded, "fantasy football."[290]

Improbably, Logan White and the Dodgers appear to have found a third power hitter in the fourth round, Cody Bellinger of Hamilton High School in Chandler, Arizona, who may eclipse both Bryant and Judge. In many significant ways, Bellinger was the antithesis of Bryant and Judge. Most obviously, as a high school player, Bellinger was younger and less physically developed. While Bryant and Judge came to the big leagues with tape-measure credentials from their college years, scouts legitimately wondered if the tall but rail-thin Bellinger would develop power as he matured. As a high school senior, Bellinger had only hit one home run. He presented a textbook example of the challenge facing scouts when they attempt to project the power potential of a young, physically undeveloped teenager. Adding to the puzzle, Bellinger's father, Clay, had spent three seasons with the Yankees but was never noted for home runs.

Logan White had worked with Bellinger in White's backyard hitting cages since Bellinger was 12 years old. White was confident that Bellinger's strong wrists and quick swing would generate power down the road, but he faced skepticism from others in the Dodgers organization, especially among the sabermetrics staff. White was not dissuaded in the least. The Dodgers area scout, Dustin Yount, agreed with White's assessment. Further, White is a big believer in bloodlines. He knew Bellinger's father well and was confident that the younger Bellinger would work as hard as his father had worked.

While the Dodgers would have drafted Bellinger much higher, they were confident they could wait until the fourth round because no other scouting directors had seen him play. By 2017, the rest of the baseball world would find out about Bellinger, as he hit 39 home runs, won the National League Rookie of the Year Award and made the All-Star team.

Bellinger truly broke out in 2019. He hit over .400 well into May and finished the season with a .305 average, 47 home runs and 115 runs batted in. As he became more disciplined and more selective at the plate, he began to hit left-handers well. In his first three seasons, Bellinger hit 111 homers. Even Logan White was surprised by Bellinger's power. White remarked, "I thought he'd hit .275 to .280 and ... between 18 and 25 homers a year. I'd be lying to you if I said I thought he would have this kind of power."

Like Father, Like Son

The Chicago Cubs possessed the second overall pick in the 2013 draft. When the Cubs' scouting department assembled in mid-April for pre-draft discussions, the focus was on trying to fill the organization's need for pitching. Two college pitchers, Jon Gray and Mark Appel, had separated themselves from other prospects. All other things being equal, the Cubs intended to take either Gray or Appel.

As the pre-draft meeting proceeded, the scouts were asked for input. Most everyone was comfortable with either of the two pitchers under consideration. As a follow-up, the group was asked if anyone wanted to put any other player in the mix. Sam Hughes raised his hand. "Kris Bryant," he said. Hughes mentioned all the reasons why he thought the organization should consider Bryant. "Too good to ignore," he offered in conclusion.

Hughes would recall, "I at least had a hand in doing the uncomfortable, knowing that we wanted a pitcher. So we sort of took the road less traveled and doubled back on Bryant – which we ended up all being pretty happy about."

Thirty-two years earlier, Sam Hughes' father, Gary, had experienced a similar level of discomfort. At the time, Gary Hughes was in his third year as a scout for the New York Yankees, a relative newcomer. The 1981 draft was approaching. The Yankees had relinquished their first-round pick as compensation for signing free agent Dave Winfield. The scouting department was meeting to consider, among other things, which player the team would select in the second round. Yankee owner George M. Steinbrenner III was participating by telephone. It was widely known that Steinbrenner was enamored with Stanford University outfielder/ quarterback, John Elway.

Of all the scouts in the meeting, Hughes had the most information on Elway. The general manager and the scouting director pushed Hughes to the speakerphone. Steinbrenner asked about Elway. Hughes replied that the Yankees did not have to take Elway in the second round because he was going to play pro football anyway. Undeterred, Steinbrenner expressed concern that another team might claim Elway if the Yankees passed him up in the second round.

Hughes was in the position of having to tell Steinbrenner news that he did not want to hear. "If we take him," Hughes said, "he's going to have to play baseball." Hughes could hear the scouts behind him murmuring, "Uh-oh!" Hughes then said to Steinbrenner, "I love this job. I don't think he's going to play baseball. I think he's going to play football." Steinbrenner responded, "Duly noted."

Events unfolded much as Gary Hughes had expected. The Yankees did select Elway in the second round, but he chose to play pro football. The Yankees lost Elway; Hughes kept his job.

Like Father, Like Daughter

The Seattle Mariners hired Amanda Hopkins as an area scout in 2015. At the time, Hopkins was still living at the family home in Seattle. Her father, Ron Hopkins, was a special assistant to the general manager of the Pittsburgh Pirates. Needing her space, Amanda placed a warning for her father on her bedroom door. The warning read, "Stay out, we're opponents."*

Tom McNamara, previously the scouting director for the Mariners, is the individual most responsible for placing Hopkins in a scouting position. Prior to being hired as a scout, Hopkins had worked for the Mariners as an intern in the scouting department. McNamara had sat with Hopkins at a couple of games and was fascinated as he listened to her break down the players. McNamara thought to himself, "Man, she has a really good feel and breaks down a player like a veteran scout."**

In short order, the Mariners sent Hopkins to the two-week Major League scouting development program. She received top grades and rave reviews at the school, prompting the Mariners to hire her as a scout.

Hopkins came by her talent naturally. As a youngster, she had traveled with her father to watch games in the Alaskan and Cape Cod Summer Leagues. During her childhood, Hopkins dabbled in soccer and participated in Irish dancing. However, when she was in the sixth grade, she began playing softball and the sport soon became her primary focus. After high school, Hopkins spent four years at Central Washington University, where she captained the women's softball team in her junior and senior years.

When asked what advice her father had given her when she started out in scouting, she responds, "He always told me we're wrong more than we are right anyway, so you might as well be wrong with your opinion rather than the opinion of someone else."

* Tracy Ringolsby, "Mariners Female Scout Hopkins Blazing Trail," 18 January 2018, mlb.com/news/scout-amanda-hopkins-making-name-for-herself/c-264872782.

** Greg Johns, "Mariners Hire Woman Area Scout," 8 December 2015, mlb.com/news/amanda-hopkins-hired-by-mariners-as-scout/c-159132908.

2014

Baseball is so hard. It has so much failure in it. When I coach kids, I tell them it is not simply a case of whether you reached first base or not, you have to figure out whether you won the at-bat. A hitter who hits the ball relatively hard has won the at-bat. Once a hitter hits the ball, he doesn't have a lot of control over what happens.

   –Jeff Bittiger, former Major League pitcher and current scout for the Oakland Athletics

For the first time in the 50-year history of the draft, the same team would hold the first overall pick in the draft for three consecutive years. The team was the Houston Astros, who were then in the process of an ambitious rebuild that would become a model of sabermetric redesign of a franchise. The Astros even hired a former engineer for the National Aeronautics and Space Administration, Sig Mejdal, to ensure they were in the forefront of the analytics movement.

One of the more traditional aspects of the redesign was an emphasis on building from the draft. However, even this time-honored tradition was recast in a manner that made it seem different, if not foreign. There were somewhat overt intimations from the Astros organization that losing big was the price that had to be paid for eventually winning big. Thus, the Astros and their fans endured three consecutive 100-loss seasons. The losses were portrayed as a steep but necessary short-term price to pay for building a championship team for the long haul.[291] Houston's 2017 World Championship brought more attention to the value of sabermetrics than perhaps even Michael Lewis's *Moneyball* had. Interestingly, just a few weeks after the 2014 draft, *Sport Illustrated* baseball writer Ben Reiter had predicted that the Astros would win the World Series in 2017.[292] It was a stunning prediction at the time, but Reiter was truly prophetic.

Of course, the amateur draft has a nasty habit of undermining the best laid plans. The 2014 draft added an exclamation point to that nasty habit. The Astros were sitting pretty as the June draft approached, with their cornerstone shortstop on hand in Carlos Correa and their future ace right-hander on the way in Mark Appel. They were poised to grab another stud and, just as the Nationals had been able to do with the addition of Strasburg, Harper and Rendon, rise to the top of the standings in short order.

The pre-draft wisdom considered 2014 as the year of the pitcher, with almost all the top prospects on the board being hurlers. The analytics movement was reconsidering some of the game's time-honored precepts. However, the maxim that a team can never have too much pitching remained an article of faith; the available statistics seemed to support the adage.

The task for Astros general manager Jeff Luhnow was to determine which pitcher was the best fit for their rising team. Three pitchers were at the top of most of the draft boards – North Carolina State lefty Carlos Rodon and two high school stars in left-handed Brady Aiken from Cathedral Catholic High School in San Diego, California, and right-handed Tyler Kolek from Shepherd High School in Shepherd, Texas. The Astros ultimately chose Aiken over both Rodon and Kolek.

Aiken stood six-feet-four. His fastball touched the mid-nineties. He had a plus curve and a plus changeup and had struck out almost two batters per inning in his senior season.[293] His potential proved irresistible to the Astros even though they knew full well that drafting a high school pitcher with the overall number one pick was a high-risk maneuver. The only two occasions on which teams had taken a high school pitcher with the overall number one pick – David Clyde (Texas Rangers, 1973) and Brien Taylor (New York Yankees, 1991) – were colossal disappointments. Yet the Astros found Aiken's command, delivery, and make-up so enticing they took the risk. "In the category of high school pitchers," Luhnow said, "[Aiken] is about as safe a player as you can have."[294] Ben Reiter referenced an Astros scout who believed that Aiken not only had Hall of Fame potential but could be "one of the best pitchers of all time."[295]

The enthusiasm for selecting Aiken was tempered when a routine examination revealed abnormalities in his pitching elbow. Both Aiken and the Astros had already agreed in principle to a $6.5 million signing bonus, but the Astros significantly reduced their offer after learning of the medical evaluation. Aiken rejected the revised offer and became the first number one overall pick since Tim Belcher in 1983 to go unsigned. Aiken went on to pitch at IMG's post-graduate academy to showcase his tools for the 2015 draft. Unfortunately, the looming elbow injury surfaced in his very first start and required Tommy John surgery. He was redrafted in 2015 by the Cleveland Indians with the 17th overall pick. However, Aiken was unable to recreate his pre-surgery success. In two seasons at the lower levels of the Indians' system, 2016 and 2017, he allowed over five runs per game in 179 innings. In 2019, he announced he was taking a leave of absence from the game.

The Astros were harshly criticized by the Major League players union for rescinding their initial offer to Aiken. However, under new draft rules, Houston would be compensated with the number two overall pick in the next draft if the team was unable to sign Aiken. The Astros used the compensation pick in 2015 to take star third baseman Alex Bregman from Louisiana State University. Bregman was already in Houston by 2016 and made a large and immediate impact for the Astros in 2017, swatting 19 homers and driving in 71 runs. His 2018 and 2019 seasons were even better, as he made the American League All-Star team each season.

Theo Epstein and the Chicago Cubs surprised the baseball world when they selected Indiana University catcher Kyle Schwarber with the fourth pick of the draft. Schwarber had slugged 14 homers in his junior season at Indiana. Cubs scout Stan Zielinski viewed Schwarber as the best player in the draft and was ready to "pound the table" for him.[296] Zielinski had been scouting the Midwest for 35 seasons. Cliff Floyd and Jeff Samardzija were among the many Major League players he had signed. Zielinski viewed Schwarber as perhaps the best he had ever seen.

Schwarber rewarded Zielinski's faith in him by making it to the majors in 2015 and hitting 16 homers in only 232 at-bats. However, just as he was anticipating a truly breakout season in 2016, he sustained a serious knee injury in only the second game of the season. Schwarber worked hard to return in time to join the Cubs in their magical 2016 World Series season. Almost miraculously, he made it back to serve as the designated hitter for the Cubs in the World Series. In addition to the emotional lift he provided, Schwarber collected seven hits and batted .412 during the Series. Zielinski watched Schwarber's heroics like a proud papa. General manager Theo Epstein graciously gave the veteran scout credit for the team's success. "Without Stan we certainly would not have won the World Series," Epstein said.[297] Zielinski would pass away just a few months after the Series.

The Philadelphia Phillies drafted Louisiana State University star Aaron Nola with the seventh pick. In the "year of the pitcher," Philadelphia may have landed the best hurler of them all. In his final two years at LSU, Nola went 23-2 with a 1.52 earned run average. With the ability to command a mid-nineties fastball, he was considered the "most polished pitcher" in the draft by *Baseball America.*[298] Nola reached the Major Leagues in 2015. In his five big league seasons, he has established himself as the ace of the Phillies' staff with a 53-35 record.

In all, twenty pitchers were selected in the first round in 2014. The twentieth, Cardinals' right-hander Jack Flaherty of Harvard-Westlake High School in Los Angeles, had one of the best seasons of any pitcher in baseball in 2019. Flaherty was practically unhittable after the All-Star break and finished the year with an 11-8 won-loss record and a stellar 2.75 earned run average.

Picking in the tenth spot in the draft, the New York Mets selected outfielder Michael Conforto from Oregon State University. In his first year of professional ball, Conforto hit .331 for the Brooklyn Cyclones in low Class A in 2014. He followed that up with a .312 average in 45 games at Double-A Binghamton in 2015. By July 2015, he was in the Major Leagues. Conforto has emerged as a solid Major League hitter with increasing power, slugging 28 home runs for the Mets in 2018 and 33 homers in 2019.

The San Diego Padres used the 13th overall pick to select shortstop Trea Turner of North Carolina State. In December 2014, the Padres engineered a three-team trade with the Washington Nationals and the Tampa Bay Rays. Turner was a key part of the transaction for the Nationals. He was included in the trade as "a player to be named later" because the rules in effect at the time did not allow for a draftee to be traded until the first anniversary of his signing.

In Washington, Turner has displayed excellent defensive skills, occasional pop with the bat, and blazing speed. He stole 33 bases in less than a half season in 2016 and took over as the full-time shortstop in Washington in 2017. Despite missing over a month of the season in 2019 with a hand injury, Turner clubbed 19 homers while hitting .298 and stealing 35 bases. He played a pivotal role with the Nationals as they defeated the Astros in the 2019 World Series.

Billy Beane's Oakland A's snagged another star player when they selected Cal State Fullerton third baseman Matt Chapman with the 25th pick of the first round. Chapman's stellar defense at third featured a rocket-launcher for an arm. At bat, Chapman possesses the ability to make consistent contact to all fields. In his first two full seasons in the big leagues, 2018 and 2019, he has displayed a sparkling gold glove at the hot corner while developing into a consistent home run hitter.

Hoop Dreams

The Baltimore Orioles selected right-handed University of Notre Dame pitcher Pat Connaughton in the fourth round of the 2014 draft. The pick was especially critical for the Orioles because Baltimore had previously surrendered its first and second round picks in 2014 as compensation for signing free agent players.

When the Orioles were giving thought to using the fourth round pick on Connaughton, there was undoubtedly more than the usual level of anxiety. The six-foot-five pitcher was also a highly regarded guard for Mike Brey's Fighting Irish basketball team. For Connaughton, a career in pro basketball was a distinct possibility.

Thirteen years earlier, when the Minnesota Twins were fretting that catching prospect Joe Mauer might choose to attend Florida State University on a football scholarship, the Twins drew comfort from the fact that posters of baseball players – not football players – dominated the walls of Mauer's bedroom. Events following the 2014 draft suggest that it would have been prudent for Baltimore to sneak a peak at the posters in Connaughton's bedroom before making its pick.

In the days after the draft, the Orioles signed Connaughton for a bonus of $428,100 and assigned him to the short-season Aberdeen IronBirds, where he showcased a 96-mph fastball and recorded a 2.45 earned run average in six games. By agreement with the Orioles, however, when the 2014-15 college hoops season began, Connaughton returned to Notre Dame to play his senior season of basketball.

Months later, the Brooklyn Nets selected Connaughton with the 41st overall pick in the NBA draft. To the Orioles' dismay, Connaughton hasn't thrown a pitch in pro baseball since, save for throwing out the ceremonial first pitch before a Milwaukee Brewers-Colorado Rockies game in May 2019.

Now a reserve shooting guard for the Milwaukee Bucks, Connaughton has become a dependable member of All-Star Giannis Antetokounmpo's supporting cast and a fan favorite in Wisconsin. In comments to reporters over the past few years, Connaughton has hinted that he might someday resume his baseball career. Speaking with Eduardo Encine of *The Baltimore Sun* in 2016, he said, "In my mind, I will pitch in Major League Baseball, and I want to achieve that." In 2019, he told a Brewers' on-field reporter, "I'm not saying there may not be a day when I play baseball."

Nonetheless, with Connaughton approaching 30 years of age, the window for embarking on a career in baseball is rapidly closing. Additionally, now that Connaughton's basketball image adorns the bedrooms of teenagers in Milwaukee and elsewhere, there is likely to be a strong incentive to continue on the path that has brought him success. Regardless of how the future unfolds, any hope in Baltimore that Connaughton would help to shore up the Orioles' starting rotation was dashed long ago.

The New York Yankee Dynasty
and the Unsung Role of Scouts

If you look at the way the [Yankee] teams of the 1990s were put together, it was amazing. We traded to get Chuck Knoblauch, Tino Martinez, David Cone. So, while you had the Core Four, you needed other guys to fit in around them. We were able to get these other players to fit in around the Core Four because of the work our scouts did.

–Bill Livesey, scout and former director of player personnel, New York Yankees

Numbers alone tell a convincing story of the New York Yankees' dominance in baseball: 27 World Championships, 40 American League pennants, and 27 inductees in the Hall of Fame. The story becomes even more compelling when the names of the players most responsible for the championships are listed: Ruth, Gehrig, DiMaggio, Mantle, Ford, Berra, Jeter, and Rivera, to name but a few. Unfortunately, the names of the unsung heroes who discovered the players are rarely mentioned and no scouts are even enshrined in Cooperstown – a sore point in the scouting world.

For one baseball scout to discover a single Hall of Fame player is the scouting equivalent of catching lightning in a bottle. Long-time New York Yankees scout Paul Krichell signed four Hall of Famers – Lou Gehrig, Tony Lazzeri, Phil Rizzuto, and Whitey Ford. In fact, Krichell came very close to inking a fifth Hall of Famer for the Yankees in slugging first baseman Hank Greenberg, a product of James Monroe High School in the Bronx. Greenberg declined Krichell's offer. Fearful of being buried on the Yankee bench behind Gehrig, who was then only 27 years old, Greenberg opted to sign with the Detroit Tigers. Perhaps even more astounding than Krichell's Hall of Fame discoveries is the fact that the Yankees had at least one of Krichell's signees on every one of its championship teams from 1923 to 1964 – twenty World Series championships in all.

Ironically, Krichell came to the Yankees from the Boston Red Sox with another Yankee legend, Ed Barrow. While Boston's infamous sale of Babe Ruth to the Yankees in 1919 is one of the most well-chronicled stories in all of baseball, the departures of Barrow and Krichell have received much less attention. With Barrow as manager in 1918, the Red Sox won the World Series. When the Boston franchise began to sell off its star players, Babe Ruth among them, Barrow joined the Yankees as chief of baseball operations and took Krichell to be his chief scout. While Ruth quickly became the so-called "architect" of the new Yankee Stadium, Krichell played a largely anonymous role in laying the foundation for "the House that Ruth built." Krichell quickly proved his worth by adding some of the key components of the team that featured the famed "Murderers' Row."

Scouts typically need to "beat the bushes" in backwater locales. However, Krichell was able to find many of his most significant signings right in the Yankees' backyard. Krichell found his most notable discovery, Henry Louis Gehrig, just a few miles from Yankee Stadium at Baker Field in Manhattan. In 1923 Krichell first laid eyes on the Columbia University slugger, who hit two mighty home runs in three at-bats during a game against Rutgers University. "I knew then," Krichell said, "that I would never have another moment like that for the rest of my life."

Gehrig had previously worked out for the New York Giants' Hall of Fame manager, John McGraw. Although Gehrig hit seven pitches into the stands, McGraw still passed on signing him. After taking his cuts at the plate, Gehrig went to field balls at first base. On one of his first fielding attempts, he let a ground ball go through his legs. Shortly thereafter, McGraw announced that he had seen enough.[299] In McGraw's mind, Gehrig's power display was not sufficient to compensate for his lapse on defense. The Giants' decision to pass on Gehrig might also have stemmed from McGraw's failure to fully appreciate – or his unwillingness to accept – the way the game was changing. With 54 home runs in 1920 and another 59 in 1921, Babe Ruth had already introduced his prodigious power to the Big Apple. Even so, McGraw seemed to regard Gehrig as a liability in the "old-school" game of bunt and steal that had brought the Giants their success.[300]

After seeing Gehrig's home run clouts against Rutgers, Krichell enthusiastically reported back to Barrow. Barrow instructed Krichell to watch Gehrig in another game. In that game, playing against New York University, Gehrig reportedly hit a ball clear out of the stadium. Krichell quickly persuaded Barrow to sign Gehrig. In addition to finding "the next Babe Ruth," Krichell was also involved in signing Tony

Lazzeri and Mark Koenig. Together, Lazzeri and Koenig comprised the middle infield combination for the famous 1927 Yankees World Series team.

During the course of his scouting career, Krichell organized many tryout camps in New York City for the Yankees, one of which yielded Hall of Fame shortstop, Phil "Scooter" Rizzuto. As had happened with Gehrig, Krichell and the Yankees benefited from a stroke of good fortune. The Yankees' cross-town rivals, the Giants and the Brooklyn Dodgers, both had the opportunity to sign Rizzuto before the shortstop showed up at Krichell's tryout camp. Both teams passed. Folklore records that one misguided Dodgers scout told the five-foot-six inch Rizzuto not to sell his shoeshine kit.

Amazingly, the story largely repeated itself again in 1947. A smallish left-handed first baseman, Edward Charles Ford, attended Krichell's tryout camp. Krichell was impressed by how hard the five-foot-six-inch Ford threw and showed him how to throw a curveball. Playing semi-pro ball in New York City, Ford grew about four inches and perfected the curveball that Krichell had taught him. Again, the rival Giants and Dodgers had ample opportunity to see and sign Ford, but neither team pursued him in earnest until after Krichell had ingratiated himself with Ford and his family.

Krichell signed Ford for the Yankees in 1947 for $7,000. Ford, of course, who would become better known as "Whitey," became perhaps the most accomplished Yankee pitcher of all time, winning 236 games along with six World Series championships and one Cy Young Award. Ford was named to ten American League All-Star teams and was inducted into the Hall of Fame in 1974.

Krichell served as the Yankees' lead scout from 1920 until the mid-1950s. In addition to Gehrig, Rizzuto and Ford, he signed over 200 other players for the Yankees, including future stars Red Rolfe, Vic Raschi, Johnny Murphy, Charlie "King Kong" Keller, and George "Snuffy" Stirnweiss. Moreover, Krichell hired many of the other scouts who made significant contributions to the Yankees' dynasty. From 1926 to 1964, the Yankees dominated their American League opponents year after year. Throughout that stretch, Krichell's scouting acumen provided the foundation.

While Krichell's greatest scouting finds were only a token ride away from Yankee Stadium, he oversaw the development of a national scouting organization that was second to none. In fact, it would be the Yankees' West Coast scouting operation that would identify and sign some of the most significant players in the 1940s and 1950s. Two excellent scouts in particular, Joe Devine and Bill Essick, led the way. The two scouts each played a role in signing the future Yankee superstar who would eventually take the mantle from Lou Gehrig – Joe DiMaggio, the "Yankee Clipper."

By the time Joe Devine joined the Yankees, he was already a legend in scouting. He had signed three future Hall of Famers for the Pirates, shortstop Joe Cronin, and brothers Lloyd Waner and Paul Waner. In 1932, Krichell brought Devine over to the Yankees to head the team's West Coast scouting. Bill Essick, a former major leaguer, was the Yankees' key scout in California and had already signed future Hall of Famer Lefty Gomez and shortstop Frankie Crosetti from the San Francisco Seals. However, Joe DiMaggio would become Essick's crown jewel.

Long before the New York Giants even contemplated leaving the Polo Grounds to relocate to San Francisco, the "City by the Bay" was home to some quality baseball. The San Francisco Seals had been a dominant team in the Pacific Coast League since their founding in 1903. The Seals had won 14 Pacific Coast League championships and sent many stars to the majors. Of course, DiMaggio had captured the attention of every Major League team. His stellar play for the Seals included a remarkable 61-game hitting streak in 1933.

Teams were lining up to acquire "Joltin' Joe." The speculation was that DiMaggio would command a purchase price of $100,000, even against the backdrop of the Great Depression. However, a career-threatening knee injury scared almost every team away. Essick persevered in spite of the injury concern. He had received medical advice indicating that ample rest would allow DiMaggio's knee to fully heal. Essick trusted the medical advice. He was able to convince Joe Devine and the Yankee brass, including newly hired farm director George Weiss, to pay the Seals $25,000 for DiMaggio. In addition to the cash, the Yankees assigned the contracts of five players to the Seals. The purchase price was still a princely sum in 1934 but also only twenty-five percent of what had been the perceived going rate for the Seals' star a few months earlier.[301] "Vinegar Bill," as Essick was known, had a keen eye for talent, but it was his willingness to put his job and career on the line for DiMaggio that would be his scouting legacy.

The Yankees pilfered another legendary scout, Tom Greenwade, from the Brooklyn Dodgers. In the late 1940s, Greenwade signed DiMaggio's eventual replacement in center field, Mickey Mantle, for a bonus of $1,400. Greenwade famously offered, "Now I know how Paul Krichell felt when he first saw Lou Gehrig."[302] In addition to Krichell and Devine, long-time scouts Lou Maguolo, Pat Patterson and Eddie Taylor worked tirelessly to scout and sign promising young players. Maguolo signed Bill "Moose" Skowron in 1950, outfielder Norm Siebern in 1951, and versatile Tony Kubek in 1954. Taylor signed pitcher Mel Stottlemyre in 1961 and laid the groundwork for selecting another pitcher, Steve Kline, in the 1966 draft. Patterson signed Tom Tresh out of Michigan in 1958. Tresh went on to become the American League Rookie of the Year in 1962, but his promising career was derailed by injuries.

In January 1955, Krichell signed former Notre Dame infielder Tom Carroll. It would be his last signing for the Yankees. Krichell retired soon afterwards and passed away less than three years later. Despite the work of Maguolo, Taylor and other scouts, the Yankees of the 1960s were unable to maintain their lengthy dominance of the American League. The 1964 season was the last truly stellar year of Mantle's Hall of Fame career. He hit .303 that year and clubbed 35 home runs. He would never again come close to the magical .300 mark.

For years, the Yankees had been in search of "the next Mickey Mantle." The list of pretenders to the throne was long. Each contender came equipped with outstanding schoolboy accomplishments. The list included Roger Repoz, signed in 1960; Steve Whitaker, signed in 1962; Bobby Murcer and Jerry Kenney, both signed in 1964; and Bill Robinson, acquired in a trade for Cletis Boyer in 1966. All proved to be capable ballplayers but none came close to the heights that Mantle had reached. Of the five, only Murcer enjoyed an extended tenure with the Yankees. Murcer, like Mantle, hailed from Oklahoma and was signed by Tom Greenwade.

As Mantle aged and his health declined in the mid-1960s, there were no truly gifted ballplayers to help preserve the Yankees' standing atop the American League. The Yankees of 1965 finished in sixth place in the league, ending a run of five consecutive pennants. Author David Halberstam attributes the collapse to deficiencies in the Yankee farm system. For Halberstam, the farm system was no longer "the majestic organization" that Krichell, Greenwade, and their successors had helped to build. More particularly, Halberstam points to the Yankees' reluctance to dip into the pool of African-American talent. In the stretch from 1950 until the early 1960s, Elston Howard had been the only notable black player signed by the Yankees. Halberstam writes, "Sure of their success, sure of their past, and sure of their own racial attitudes, they had essentially sat on the sidelines in the fifties as a number of National League teams had signed the best of these young, supremely gifted and determined athletes."[303]

The depletion of the Yankees' once vaunted farm system caused the Yankees to fall on hard times. The team failed to win any titles from 1965 through 1975. Successful Yankee owners of the past had consistently allowed their "baseball people" to determine personnel decisions. Most recently, owners Del Webb and Dan Topping had led the team to success in the 1950s and early 1960s by allowing the tandem of general manager George Weiss and field manager Casey Stengel to make personnel decisions. In November 1964, Webb and Topping sold the team to the Columbia Broadcasting System (CBS). Changes came quickly. CBS and its hand-picked leader, Mike Burke, imposed financial restraints that, among other effects, led to a dramatic reduction in the scouting system.

By 1972, CBS had reached the conclusion that owning a baseball team was not a good fit for the corporation. Burke found a willing buyer for the team in Cleveland businessman, George M. Steinbrenner III. The sale to Steinbrenner was announced in January 1973. Steinbrenner, soon to be known as "the Boss," was a markedly different owner. He interjected himself into every decision, as significant as the selection of baseball players and as trivial as the pricing of hot dogs at the concession stands. In short order, Steinbrenner injected hope and promise into an organization that had become moribund. Steinbrenner had great plans for restoring the luster of the Yankees, plans that were enhanced by the advent of free agency in 1975.[304]

Popular belief holds that Steinbrenner used free agency to construct his championship teams of the late 1970s. As a result of his lavish spending and imperial manner, Steinbrenner succeeded in doing the near-impossible: making the Yankees even more detested by their peers throughout baseball than they were when they consistently won world championship after world championship. The Steinbrenner Yankees are commonly portrayed as having purchased their championships.

There is some truth to that assertion, as the Yankees in the early Steinbrenner years acquired big-dollar free agents such as outfielder Reggie Jackson and pitchers Don Gullett, Rich "Goose" Gossage, and Catfish Hunter. However, the Yankees were able to assemble the championship rosters of 1977 and 1978 primarily because the team made stellar decisions when selecting prospects in the draft and then trading its young talent for established veterans.

The heart and soul of the 1977-78 championship teams – catcher Thurman Munson and pitcher Ron Guidry – were acquired through the draft. Munson was selected with the fourth pick in the 1968 amateur draft. Yankee scout Gene Woodling, a former Major League outfielder, followed Munson closely during his junior year at Kent State and pushed the Yankees to make him their first pick in the 1968 draft. After only one full year of minor league training, Munson captured the American League Rookie of the Year Award in 1970 and was voted the Most Valuable Player of the American League in 1976.

Yankees scout Atley Donald, a protégé of Paul Krichell, was instrumental in the selection of left-handed Cajun fireballer Ron Guidry from Louisiana Lafayette College. The Yankees took Guidry in the third round of the 1971 draft. While Hall of Famer Catfish Hunter had a better overall career than Guidry, it was clearly Guidry's left arm that propelled the Yankees to their championships in 1977 and 1978. "Louisiana Lightning," as Guidry was known, would remain the cornerstone of the Yankees' rotation for the decade to come.

Like many such draft "success stories," Guidry's rise to stardom almost never happened. After his selection in the 1971 draft, Guidry advanced rapidly through the Yankees' farm system. However, Guidry found it difficult to secure a spot on the Major League roster. He had a brief fling with the parent club in 1975 and pitched well in spots. The following year, however, he endured a particularly shaky outing in a spring training game, prompting Steinbrenner to remark, "He'll never be more than a Triple-A pitcher."[305] Guidry overheard the comment and decided he was through with baseball. He and his wife, Bonnie, immediately packed up their car and began driving home to Lafayette, Louisiana. Mid-trip, during an extended discussion, Bonnie persuaded her husband to give baseball one more shot, and Guidry turned the car around.

Guidry spent the bulk of 1976 with the Yankees' Triple-A club in Syracuse and pitched in 22 games, exclusively in relief. With five wins against one loss, nine saves, and a 0.68 earned run average, Guidry's numbers earned him redemption. The next season, 1977, Guidry made the Major League roster out of spring training and started 25 games for the Yankees. He recorded 16 wins against 7 losses, with a 2.82 earned run average. In 1978, he posted one of the most dominant pitching years in the history of baseball. His 25 and 3 record propelled the Yankees to a razor thin one-game playoff victory over rival Boston. Guidry won the Cy Young Award while sporting a microscopic 1.74 earned run average, with 248 strikeouts and nine shutouts.

While Munson and Guidry were the only two stars of the 1977 and 1978 New York teams acquired through the draft, the Yankees had acquired stalwarts Graig Nettles, Chris Chambliss, Mickey Rivers, Willie Randolph, Bucky Dent, Ed Figueroa, and Dick Tidrow through a series of clever trades using players acquired in the draft. Therefore, it is somewhat hyperbolic, if not misleading, to claim that the Steinbrenner-driven Yankees of 1977 and 1978 were primarily the by-product of free agency. Their success, more correctly considered, represents a combination of good drafting, clever trade acquisitions, and well-spent free agent dollars.

Unlike earlier Yankee championship runs, the dominance of the 1977-1978 teams was short-lived. Two major factors curtailed the Yankees' success: first, the departure of general manager Gabe Paul in January 1978; and, second, Munson's premature death in a plane crash in 1979. Without Gabe Paul to rein in the Boss's extravagances and lacking Munson's timely hitting, the Yankees eventually slipped back into relative mediocrity.

While Steinbrenner appeared to have purchased the "goose that laid the golden egg" for the Yankees, he also appeared to have killed it. After their winning ways in the years 1976-1981, the Yankees did not win anything for the next fourteen years. Some pundits openly wondered whether the Yankees would again win as long as Steinbrenner owned the team. Under Steinbrenner, there could be no such thing as a youth movement, for "the Yankees of the seventies and eighties seldom if ever trusted anyone under 30."[306] In many of the years prior to 1994, the Yankees were hopeless also-rans, finishing 20 or more games out of first place. Even when they finished with the best record in the American League in 1994, a labor strike prematurely ended their chances of post-season play.

Steinbrenner had apparently learned the wrong lessons from the Yankees' successes in the late 1970s. Instead of crediting the baseball acumen of Gabe Paul and the Yankees' scouting apparatus, he attributed the success to his own "wisdom" in acquiring free agents. A baseball wag once said that to accuse Steinbrenner of spending like a drunken sailor would be a serious affront to drunken sailors. The Yankee organization paid a real price for its expensive free agent signings, as Major League Baseball rules required the franchise to forfeit a draft pick as compensation to the team losing each free agent. Eventually, the continuing loss of high-round draft picks would hamstring the Yankees' baseball operation to the point that the team could no longer be competitive.

While Yankee fans were initially forgiving because they appreciated Steinbrenner's all-consuming passion to win, they belatedly came to understand that his lack of baseball judgment and overbearing personality appeared to consign the Yankees to unending failure. However, just as optimism for returning to sustained glory appeared to have been extinguished, hope arrived from the most unlikely of quarters. In January 1989, Yankees outfielder Dave Winfield had filed suit against George Steinbrenner for failing to make a required $300,000 annual contribution to Winfield's charitable foundation. Steinbrenner retaliated by countersuing Winfield. Steinbrenner then added to the intrigue by paying $40,000 to an admitted gambler and con man to dig up defamatory information about Winfield. On July 30, 1990, baseball commissioner Fay Vincent permanently banned the Boss from day-to-day management of the Yankees for his effort to purchase "dirt" on Winfield.[307]

Although the "permanent ban" was lifted in March of 1993 – less than three years after it was imposed – Steinbrenner's absence gave the Yankee organizational brass vital breathing room and an opportunity to draft and develop the building blocks for the future Yankee dynasty. Surprisingly, even Steinbrenner appeared to recognize the excellent job that general manager Gene Michael and his team were doing in rebuilding the Yankees' farm system. Even more surprising, Michael was able to dissuade Steinbrenner from following his naturally impatient instincts that stifled the development of younger talent.

Of course with Steinbrenner, patience and restraint were present only in limited degree: if he was more patient and less impulsive than the pre-suspension "Boss," he was still more impatient and intrusive than any other owner in baseball. Although Michael had a keen eye for baseball talent and assembled a stellar group of executives and scouts during his tenure, his most significant contribution to the Yankees was his ability to rein in Steinbrenner. Despite his easy-going manner and sly wit, Michael was, at times, less than candid with Steinbrenner, an approach that allowed the Yankees to retain the crown jewels of their farm system. When Steinbrenner once directed Michael to trade outfield prospect Bernie Williams, who would hold down center field for the Yankees from 1993 to 2005, Michael reported back to Steinbrenner that he had called all 27 other teams and could not find any takers. In fact, Michael had called all of the teams but never once mentioned that Williams was available.

Michael hailed from Ohio, as did Steinbrenner. He was widely known as "Stick" in baseball circles for his tall and slender appearance, much more than for his batting prowess. In his days as a player, his lifetime average was .229. To say he had a complicated and convoluted relationship with Steinbrenner was an understatement. Of course, every relationship with Steinbrenner was complicated, but very few of his subordinates had the temerity to contradict the Boss. Those who did rarely survived long with the Yankees, yet Michael worked for the Yankees for over 40 years as a player, coach, general manager and super scout. As with most Steinbrenner employees, Michael was fired at least three times over that period and was threatened with dismissal countless other times. Yet his easy-going demeanor, quick Irish wit, steadfast self-assurance and baseball acumen somehow calmed Steinbrenner and earned his trust to the point of deference to his judgments. At various times, Stick was able to protect not only Williams but also Derek Jeter, Mariano Rivera, and Andy Pettitte from being dispatched by the Boss before they were able to mature into keystones of a new Yankee dynasty.

It is not always as easy as it may seem to assign beginning and end points for a baseball dynasty. Yankee beat writers Joel Sherman and Buster Olney provide assistance in this case by authoring books about the birth and end of the Yankees' last dynasty. With that assistance, we will examine the Yankee drafts leading to their on-field success in 1996 and beyond. In addition to the draft, an increasing number of Major League players are from foreign countries not covered by the draft, or acquired apart from the draft as unsigned free agents. The Yankees used all three methods of talent acquisition – judicious drafting, signing foreign players, and spending for veteran free agent players – to build the dynasty that stretched from the late 1990s to 2009.

Fortunately for Steinbrenner and the Yankees, during the Boss's three-year exile, Michael assembled a corps of first-rate talent evaluators and development personnel who guided the team back to prominence. The scouting department consisted of a virtual All-Star team of talent evaluators, including stellar scouts Bill Livesey, George Bradley, Mark Newman, Doug Melvin, Dick Groch, Joe Robison, Roberto Rivera, Fred Ferreria, Herb Raybourn, Brian Sabean, Greg Orr, and Mark Batchko.

In 1990, the Yankees came up with three "diamonds in the rough" when they signed Mariano Rivera, Andy Pettitte, and Jorge Posada. Rivera, Pettitte, and Posada, along with Derek Jeter, would comprise the vaunted "Core Four" that propelled the Yankees to success. Rivera, then a scrawny teenager, was signed to a free agent contract in February 1990. Five months later, the Yankees selected Pettitte in the 22nd round of the draft and Posada in the 24th round.

The signing of Rivera would become one of the Yankees' most important signings of all time. Herb Raybourn, the Yankees' Panamanian scout, first saw Rivera playing shortstop in Panama in 1988. At the time, Rivera made little impression. A year later, Rivera had converted to pitcher; the Yankees invited him to a tryout camp, where he showed off a fastball that reached 87 mph. Rivera was inexperienced on the mound but displayed an effortless pitching motion that enticed Raybourn. When the Yankees dangled a bonus of $2,500, Rivera signed immediately.

When the 155-pound Rivera signed, no one in the Yankees organization could have imagined that he would go on to become the greatest closer in Major League history, with an astounding 652 saves. Rivera would help the "Core Four" bring five World Series championships to New York, the first in 1996 and the last in 2009.

The Yankees' Panamanian pipeline had started with third baseman-outfielder Héctor López, who had played on the Yankees' pennant winning teams of the 1960s. In 1982, the pipeline yielded outfielder Roberto Kelly. Kelly spent four productive seasons in New York, from 1989 to 1992, but his biggest contribution to the Yankees' glory years came when he was traded in November 1992 for outfielder Paul O'Neill. O'Neill would become another pillar in the dynasty of the late 1990s. The pipeline also produced Ramiro Mendoza, who would be a vital middle inning relief cog from 1997 to 2002, and Mariano Rivera's cousin, Rubén Rivera, who was once considered one of the top prospects in baseball. In fact, in 1996, Rubén was considered to be a far more important talent to the Yankees than his cousin or any other prospect in the system.

The Yankees drafted Pettitte, a tall left-handed Texan, in the 22nd round as a "draft and follow" prospect.[308] Pettitte was playing at San Jacinto Junior College. His coach, Wayne Graham, compared him to Roger Clemens, who had also played for Graham. After "following" Pettitte for a year, the Yankees decided to make him an offer of $60,000 to sign. Yankees scout Joe Robison had first seen Pettitte in high school at Deer Park, Texas. Robison had gone to Deer Park along with dozens of other scouts to observe right-handed pitcher Kirk Dressendorfer, who would soon become a first-round selection of the Oakland Athletics.

In May 1991, the Yankees sent Robison to the Baton Rouge home of Pettitte's grandmother to convey the team's offer. Robison knew Pettitte had significant potential. He also knew he was only authorized to offer a maximum signing bonus of $60,000. Time was running out; Robison's visit came only hours before the Yankees' exclusive window to sign the left-hander would close. Pettitte was adamant that he would not sign for less than $80,000. Many years later, Bill Livesey, who was the Yankees scouting director from 1991 to 1996, recalled that Andy was stubborn then and always has been. For Livesey, it was one of the qualities that made Pettitte a great pitcher. "When he said he wouldn't sign for a penny less than $80,000, he meant it," Livesey remarked long after the fact.

Livesey authorized the additional $20,000 in signing bonus and curtly told Robison not to come back if he couldn't get the kid signed. Pettitte signed at his grandmother's kitchen table for $80,000. Pettitte's grandmother then brought Robison a cup of coffee along with some comforting words. "You just spent your money wisely, young man," she told him.[309] Pettitte's grandmother proved to be prophetic; her grandson went on to win 256 Major League games, five World Series titles and eight pennants. Pettitte was a winner, pitching in the playoffs for fourteen of his eighteen Major League seasons and compiling more post-season wins than any other Major League pitcher in history.

Two rounds after selecting Pettitte in 1990, the Yankees pulled the same trick with "draft and follow" candidate Jorge Posada. Posada was of Cuban-Dominican heritage. Although born in Puerto Rico, Posada was eligible for the Major League Draft because he was playing college baseball at Calhoun Community College in Decatur, Alabama. Yankees scout Leon Wurth saw the switch-hitting Posada at Calhoun and liked his bat. At the time, Posada was playing shortstop and, according to Yankees cross-checker Jack Giles, playing it very poorly. Wurth was able to sign Posada for less than $30,000.

Once Posada signed, the Yankees played him at second base in the minor leagues until they realized that his complete lack of footspeed would preclude a career as a middle infielder. Scouts joked that Posada's "speed" could be measured with a sundial. Posada was soon moved to catcher in order to find a home for his potent bat and strong arm. Posada went on to win four world championships with the Yankees, appeared in five All-Star Games, slugged 275 home runs, and drove in over 1,000 runs during his Major League career.[310]

The 1992 June draft provided another very key member for the Yankees' looming dynasty. In the first round, at pick number six, the Yankees drafted Kalamazoo, Michigan high school standout Derek Jeter. The tall and lanky Jeter would grow physically and baseball-wise into the mainstay of the Yankees for twenty seasons in the Bronx. In that time, he would lead the Yankees to five World Series championships. So significant was Jeter to these teams and the franchise that he inherited the role of Yankee "Captain."

All drafts have a certain drama and gamesmanship. The 1992 draft was akin to a soap opera, replete with pre-draft era scouting shenanigans. Many scouts believed Jeter was committed to playing college baseball or else would use the college option as leverage to demand an outrageous signing bonus. Yankee scout Dick Groch had been sold on Jeter for a long time. The problem for the Yankees was that they could not envision Jeter being available when their pick came along at number six. Groch, with the support and direction of the Yankee brass, engaged in a "disinformation campaign" to prompt other Major League teams, especially the five teams picking before New York, to think the Yankees were not sold on Jeter or, alternatively, to promote the perception that Jeter intended to accept a scholarship to the University of Michigan.

In reality, Groch was convinced that Jeter preferred to turn pro rather than play college ball but did harbor some concerns that Jeter's girlfriend, who would be enrolling at Michigan, might entice him to accept the Wolverines' scholarship offer. Groch's efforts to conceal the Yankees' interest in Jeter called to mind some of the artful tactics of scouts in the pre-draft era. Even when going to see Jeter in high school games, Groch would only watch Jeter from his car outside the ballpark, for fear of being detected by rival scouts. Privately, Groch assured his bosses that Jeter would sign with the Yankees and rebutted concerns that he was headed to Michigan with the now famous line, "the only place this kid is going is Cooperstown."

The Houston Astros owned the first pick in the 1992 draft. Former star pitcher Hal Newhouser, then a scout for the Astros, was a zealous advocate for using the "number one, number one" to take Jeter. Instead, the Astros selected Cal State Fullerton outfielder Phil Nevin with the first pick. After the draft, Newhouser was livid. According to some accounts, Newhouser felt so strongly about Jeter's potential that he resigned in protest.[311]

The Cleveland Indians chose University of North Carolina pitcher Paul Shuey with the second overall pick of 1992. Former Indians scouting director Mickey White, who had also signed Manny Ramírez and Rob Dibble, recalls that Shuey was a "need" pick. Pitching was the Indians' most pressing need at the time. White also had the misfortune of observing Jeter after he had hurt his ankle badly. Over twenty years later, White wistfully commented, "I wish I had seen Derek healthy." Livesey and the Yankees were able to exhale again after the Expos took another college pitcher, B.J. Wallace, with the third pick. Dan Duquette, who was then general manager of the Expos, noted retrospectively, "Obviously, we didn't give it enough consideration."[312]

The Yankees again dodged a bullet when the Orioles took Stanford star Jeffrey Hammonds, a player in whom the Yankees had little interest, at number four. Orioles scouting director Gary Nichols noted, "Jeter was our highest [rated] high school player at the time, but we liked Jeffrey Hammonds." Ironically, Hammonds, like Jeter, had grown up as a fan of the Yankees and was hoping to be selected by New York. At that juncture in the draft, Livesey and the Yankees were very concerned that the Cincinnati Reds, sitting ahead of them with the fifth pick, would ruin their day by taking Jeter. Livesey described the mood in the Yankee draft room as one of "cautious pessimism." Their concern was apparently well-placed because Reds scout Gene Bennett – the Reds' draft guru – argued vociferously for the Reds to draft Jeter and no one else.[313] Bennett had worked Jeter out as an outfielder prior to the draft and was very impressed. "I'm telling you," Bennett would say later, "he looked like Willie Mays going after the ball."[314]

With Barry Larkin ensconced at shortstop for the Reds, general manager Bob Quinn and scouting director Julian Mock were focused on the selection of an outfielder with the fifth pick. Unpersuaded by Bennett's high praise for Jeter as an outfielder, Quinn opted for collegian Chad Mottola with the fifth pick. "I felt like I was going to have a heart attack," Bennett said. "I was shocked when we didn't take [Jeter]."[315]

Conversely, according to Livesey, in the Yankee draft room in Tampa, "we were an awfully happy room." No longer needing to hold their breath, the Yankee draft room erupted into loud cheering when the Mottola pick was announced. The Yankees immediately pounced on Jeter with the sixth pick. According to Livesey, "I had already convinced George we would take Jeter if he was there, which wasn't easy because George preferred college players." The impatient owner asked when Jeter would be in the majors. Livesey replied, "1996." It was a wild guess, but it turned out to be on the mark. The Yankees signed Jeter for $700,000, which was $300,000 more than the Reds gave their pick at number five, Chad Mottola.

Unsure that Jeter would fall to them, the Yankees had a contingency plan in place. If they could not get Jeter, New York was poised to take pitcher Jim Pittsley. In fact, the Yankees had scout Johnny DeCarlo sitting in the driveway of Pittsley's home as a way of sealing the deal. When the Yankees landed Jeter, DeCarlo's efforts were no longer needed, so he left without even speaking to Pittsley.

With the tenth pick of the first round, the Kansas City Royals and their super scout Art Stewart, formerly of the Yankees, had been eagerly waiting to select Jeter and were disappointed when the Yankees chose him. The Royals drafted Michael Tucker with the tenth pick and then later selected the Yankees' backup choice, Jim Pittsley, with the 17th pick in the first round.

In his first full season in the minor leagues, Jeter looked to be an unlikely candidate for Cooperstown. Playing for the Class A Greensboro Hornets in 1993, Jeter set a record for errors with 56. It also became clear that he had to make some adjustments at the plate. Nonetheless, the Yankees never wavered in their belief that Jeter would be their short-stop of the future. Livesey recounts, "Jeter never doubted himself, so we never doubted him either."

By 1994, every member of the "Core Four" had reached the Triple-A Columbus Clippers, the Yankees' top farm club. By 1996, Jeter, Pettitte, and Mariano Rivera were all on the Major League roster. Posada would join them in 1997.

While much has been written about the "Core Four"and their foun-dational importance to the Yankees of the late 1990s and 2000s, the sig-nificant on-field contributions of low-key switch-hitting center fielder Bernie Williams are often overlooked. The story underlying the signing of Williams incorporated aspects of the pre-draft scouting era in base-ball, a time when finding ways to hide a talented prospect could be just as critical as discovering the talent in the first place. Williams was born as Bernabé Williams Figueroa in 1968 in San Juan, Puerto Rico. Fifteen years later, he attracted international notice as a world-class track star in Puerto Rico. At the same time, the late Yankee scout Roberto Rive-ra noticed Williams on the baseball fields of Puerto Rico, along with his friend, future Texas Rangers star Juan González. Roberto Rivera immediately recognized Williams's potential in baseball but, under Major League Baseball's rules, the Yankees could not sign him until he reached the age of 17.

With the permission of Williams's parents, Rivera brought the pros-pect to the United States and "stashed" him at a baseball camp near the Connecticut home of the Yankees scouting director, Doug Melvin. Iron-ically, Williams wanted to bring Juan González to Connecticut with him for company but Steinbrenner vetoed spending the additional money. No other scouts picked up the scent, and the Yankees' ploy was suc-cessful. On September 13, 1985, Williams celebrated his 17th birthday by signing with the Yankees. Williams regularly patrolled center field for the Yankees from 1993 until 2005 and retired in 2006. His unique personality, combined with his speed and power hitting, made him a mainstay of the Yankee dynasty. During his sixteen-year career, Williams accumulated a batting average of .297 with 287 home runs. He was named to the American League All-Star team for five consecutive years, 1997 through 2001. During the prime years of his career, 1995 to 2002, Williams never hit below .305 and, in 1998, he led the league in batting with an average of .339. His contributions are every bit on a par with those of the "Core Four."

Catcher and outfielder Jim Leyritz was one of the complementary pieces that every great team needs. Leyritz had been a highly regarded prospect while in high school in Cincinnati. In 1982, Barry Larkin was regarded as the best schoolboy player in the Cincinnati area. According to some sources, Leyritz was the second or third best prospect in the area behind Larkin. In the 1982 draft, the Cincinnati Reds selected Larkin in the second round.[317] The Atlanta Braves were looking to draft Leyritz but, two days before the draft, he broke his leg while playing tennis. Concerns about the severity of the injury resulted in Leyritz not being drafted at all. He went to play in junior college and then at the University of Kentucky.

When the 1985 draft came, there was again little interest in Leyritz. During the summer of 1985, Leyritz played in the highly respected Jayhawk League, where he caught the attention of Yankee scout Doug Melvin. Melvin liked Leyritz as a catcher and brought in Bill Livesey to meet Jim and his father. The Yankees signed Leyritz as a free agent in August 1985. After Leyritz signed, Yankee brass asked Livesey what position Leyritz should be listed under on the team's depth chart. The expected answer was either catcher or third base. In response, Livesey presciently quipped, "hitter."

Aside from Williams, Leyritz and the "Core Four," most of the other key players of the Yankee dynasty were acquired by trades involving talent amassed by Gene Michael and scouting director Bill Livesey during the period 1991 to 1996. As Livesey recalls, "If you look at the way the teams of the 1990s were put together, it was amazing. We traded to get Chuck Knoblauch, Tino Martinez, David Cone, Paul O'Neill, Graeme Lloyd, and Jeff Nelson. So, while you had the 'Core Four,' you needed other guys to fit in around them. We were able to get these other players to fit in around the 'Core Four' because of the work our scouts did."

While the Yankees were initially criticized for trading Roberto Kelly in exchange for Paul O'Neill, the trade proved to be a steal. O'Neill became one of the most reliable Yankee power hitters and played a stellar right field. First baseman Tino Martinez, who anchored the middle of the Yankee lineup, was acquired with key relief pitcher Jeff Nelson from the Seattle Mariners for top Yankee prospects Sterling Hitchcock and Russ Davis. Staff ace David Cone came from the Toronto Blue Jays for pitching prospect Marty Janzen. Lloyd, a left-handed relief specialist, was acquired in a trade with the Brewers for outfielder Gerald Williams and pitcher Bob Wickman. The speedy leadoff batter Knoblauch was acquired from the Twins for a king's ransom of organizational talent: first-round picks Brian Buchanan (1994) and Eric Milton (1996) and highly acclaimed international prospect Cristian Guzmán. Finally, the Yankees landed slugger Cecil Fielder from the Tigers in a deal for 1993 first-round pick Matt Drews.

By the time the Yankees popped open the champagne bottles in 1996, Gene Michael, the primary architect of the championship team, was no longer the general manager. The impetuous Steinbrenner had replaced him with Bob Watson in 1995. Nonetheless, Michael's imprint on the team was clear. Leyritz, for one, insists that Michael didn't get enough credit for opening the door for the "Core Four" when they were all merely prospects. In Leyritz's view, "Those guys got the opportunity because, in 1990, Gene Michael said, 'I've got the power and I'm going to do it this way.'" For Leyritz, giving Michael free rein to run the team during Steinbrenner's three-year ban "was probably the best decision the Yankees ever made."

Under the leadership of Michael and with the insights of his corps of scouts, the Yankees had demonstrated that judicious use of the amateur draft, coupled with savvy trading, confidence in youthful prospects, and a dose of luck, formed the most reliable way to reinvigorate a dynasty.

The Most Successful Yankee Scout

Maybe Paul Krichell was not destined for a long and prosperous career as a Major League catcher. Maybe his career batting average of .222, accumulated over two seasons, would have caused him to wash out of the Major Leagues anyway. But when Ty Cobb leapt, feet-first, at Krichell while the catcher was blocking home plate in a game late in the 1912 season, the ensuing collision all but guaranteed that Krichell would never spend another season in the Major Leagues.

In Cobb's telling of the incident, Krichell often tried to hook Cobb's leg and flip the speedster over when Cobb slid into home. Cobb was said to have warned Krichell, "Don't ever do that again." When Krichell tried the tactic again, Cobb recalled, "I scissored my legs, caught him under an arm and almost detached it."

Krichell was able to hang on for a few years in the minor leagues and would even achieve a small dose of fame in 1914 when, playing for the International League Buffalo Bisons, he singled and doubled against George Herman Ruth – not yet known as "the Babe" – in Ruth's professional pitching debut for the minor league Baltimore Orioles.

Notwithstanding his success against Ruth, Krichell was soon looking for a job away from the dugout. He tried running a saloon in the Bronx, but the advent of Prohibition in January 1920 ended that venture. Krichell returned to the profession he knew best – baseball. Over the next four decades, he made his mark as the most successful Yankees scout of all time.

Diamonds in the Rough:
Hidden Gems Uncovered in the Draft

Most of the guys who are taken down low and then reach the majors have great tenacity. They are guys who totally believe in what they do. They have enough ability that, combined with what's inside, helps them to succeed. They all seem to have a chip on their shoulder.

–Stan Meek, former director of scouting, Miami Marlins

The draft confounds even baseball experts with its maddening unpredictability. While the "misses" still greatly outnumber the hits, there has been a slow and steady improvement over time in early round success. As frustrating as the countless "misses" are, perhaps even more confounding are the late-round finds that were missed by almost every scout.

While these late round "diamonds" are almost as rare as appearances by Haley's Comet, the stories of these players stand as a testament to their dedication, perseverance and ability to believe in themselves when few others did. In this chapter we will look primarily at the late-round draft stories of Albert Pujols, Don Mattingly, Mark Buehrle, Keith Hernandez, and the biggest miss in draft history, Hall of Famer Mike Piazza.

The San Diego Padres held the first pick in the 1988 draft. San Diego used that pick to select pitcher Andy Benes. One thousand three hundred and eighty-nine picks later – in the 62nd round – the Los Angeles Dodgers selected Mike Piazza. Benes turned out to be a creditable major leaguer, the winner of 155 games during a fourteen-year career. Piazza turned out to be a Hall of Famer.

Even as a teenager, Piazza was not an unknown talent. In 1984, when he was 15 years old, Piazza spent time in his backyard batting cage hitting under the watchful eye of one of the greatest hitters in history, Boston Red Sox legend Ted Williams. Williams was impressed. "I guarantee you," Williams told Piazza's father, "this kid will hit." Williams was effusive. "I never saw anyone who looked better at his age," he said.[317]

Piazza clearly ranks as the "Big Miss" of the first 50 years of baseball's amateur draft. For context, the Dodgers drafted 61 players prior to taking Piazza – and they took him only as a favor to Dodgers' legend Tommy Lasorda, a friend of the Piazza family.

As Lasorda recounts it, "I did the Dodgers a favor." Indeed, he did. How did it happen? According to Lasorda, he sent five scouts from five different organizations to take a look at Piazza. None of the five saw any big league potential in the future National League Rookie of the Year and twelve-time All-Star. Only one scout, Brad Kohler of the Major League Scouting Bureau, even turned in a report on him. Kohler's report advised scouts to "follow" Piazza, based on the prodigious power and bat speed he possessed even then.

Amazingly, no scouts picked up on the advice to follow Piazza, laying the foundation for the biggest blunder in the history of the draft. Piazza lacked both footspeed and a natural position, the most common reasons cited for the scouts' lack of interest. He had played first base in high school and college – and, by his own admission, not very well. Yet the annals of the draft are dotted with selections of players who were slower than Piazza and much less adept in the field.

In Piazza's autobiography, *Long Shot*, he states,

> *There has been a misconception I materialized out of nowhere as a baseball player. The fact is I had two exceptional years as a high school player [at Phoenixville High School, outside of Philadelphia] and was not unknown to the area scouts. My junior year, by some accounts, was one of the greatest high school seasons in the history of Pennsylvania. The rap was that we played in a weak league, but I don't know about that."*[318]

Piazza's attitude may also have been an impediment. He confesses to being a bit of a "wise ass" and a very poor student. However, these factors do not really explain the lack of interest in Piazza by the scouts; scores of first-round picks have been neither good students nor good citizens. While it is now part of baseball's draft lore that Piazza was drafted in the 62nd round and only as "a favor," it is largely overlooked that he was not drafted at all out of high school. Rather, it was after playing one year at the University of Miami and then a second year at Miami Dade Community College that the Dodgers drafted him in 1988. Thus the story becomes even more remarkable, for Miami is hardly a remote outpost of baseball obscurity. In other words, the Major League scouting apparatus actually missed on Piazza twice, once upon his graduation from high school and the second "miss" in 1988.

Even after Piazza was drafted, it still took the active intervention of Lasorda to get the Dodgers to give him a legitimate shot. According to a widely circulated myth, Lasorda was Piazza's baptismal godfather. In reality, Lasorda was a close friend of Piazza's father, Vince, and godfather of Mike Piazza's brother, Tommy. Piazza refers to Lasorda as a "goombah," an Italian term of endearment for a close friend and advisor.[319] The Dodgers viewed the drafting of Piazza as a "courtesy pick" for Lasorda and were not even intending to sign him.

Vince Piazza lobbied hard to convince Dodgers scouting director Ben Wade to give his son a tryout. Wade reluctantly arranged a tryout at Dodgers Stadium, with Lasorda and Dodgers scouts Gib Bodet and Bobby Darwin in attendance. Mike took batting practice and routinely smoked balls out of the park, some almost out of the stadium entirely. This was nothing new for Piazza, as he frequently put on such batting practice heroics while at Phoenixville High. However, the scouts typically derided such displays as "five o'clock power."

Bodet and Darwin watched Piazza's prodigious power display in open-mouthed awe, occasionally uttering an "oh, wow" or "holy shit" to the other. In Piazza's telling, Darwin and Bodet were looking at each other like, "How did everybody miss this guy?" Darwin remembers the sound of the ball flying off the bat and thinking of the great power hitter, Dick Allen of the Phillies. "He kept hitting the ball so hard, all I could think of was this is the next Dick Allen," Darwin said. "Even the ground balls were smoked." Darwin asked the batting practice pitcher, Mark Cresse, to start throwing lower in the zone because it was clear Pizza could clobber the high pitch. "To my amazement, he hit the lower pitches even harder," Darwin recounted. "One went out of the stadium to right center that I think is still traveling."

Bodet remembers Piazza putting on "the best hitting exhibition of any I have seen in years." Bodet felt Piazza had "every prerequisite to be a good hitter ... a lightning quick bat and the ball jumped off his bat. Those things are not teachable."[320] Darwin and Bodet needed no more convincing and were already salivating at the prospect of Piazza wearing Dodger blue. Bodet was so impressed by Piazza's hitting display, he urged Wade to offer Piazza $25,000 to sign him right then and there. Darwin, a former power hitter himself, felt Piazza should be offered $40,000. To provide some context, the Dodgers had just *signed* sixth-round selection Eric Karros for $35,000. Karros would go on to win the National League Rookie of the Year Award in 1992.

Wade, though also impressed by Piazza's hitting, was still not inclined to sign him until he had the opportunity to observe him in a game. If not for quick thinking by Lasorda, Piazza would have left Los Angeles still unsigned. Aware that Piazza had been working out as a catcher, Lasorda presented Wade with a hypothetical. Lasorda asked, "If I brought a catcher in here and he hit the stuffing out of the ball like Mike just did, would you sign him or want to see more?" Wade answered, "I'd sign him." "Well, then sign him," Lasorda countered, "he's a catcher now. Sign him!"

Wade then had Piazza throw from behind the plate. The Dodgers personnel were sufficiently impressed by his arm to envision him making the transition to catcher. Wade offered Piazza a signing bonus of $15,000 and a trip to the Instructional League to learn to catch. Piazza, who would have signed for 15 cents, jumped at the opportunity. The rest is history.

How did almost all the other scouts miss on Piazza's immense talent? Even Piazza's biggest supporters – a very limited group – explain that his game had many flaws. Darwin describes him as having had a terribly weird and awkward swing, with the bat held way up by his head. Most scouts all assumed this flaw would be exposed by good pitching and was not capable of being fixed. Additionally, as Darwin noted, "He had no position ... No position! Even projecting him as a catcher took a bit of a leap of faith." Moreover, many scouts felt Piazza had an oversized ego from his relatively privileged upbringing and his special relationship with Tommy Lasorda. Even Piazza comments, in his autobiography, "I am not sure if Tommy's support was a positive or a negative for my career."

Beyond the simple but true explanation that sometimes everyone gets it wrong, Gib Bodet offers perhaps the most telling explanation. "Scouts have a strong independent streak and once they make up their mind on someone, they don't like to admit they made a mistake," Bodet says. "Even the testimony of Ted Williams would not sway them, if they have made up their minds." This strong streak of independence, combined with the real yet inadmissible notion that even scouts can succumb to "group think," seems to have created a perfect storm against Piazza. The more Tommy Lasorda pushed his candidacy, the more scouts ignored his attributes.

Even Bobby Darwin believed that Piazza would have to make some changes in his swing to be a successful Major League hitter. Piazza and nearly everyone else involved in his draft history credit Dodgers hitting instructor Reggie Smith with making adjustments. Smith, a very good hitter in his own right, was able to recognize Piazza's potential as clearly as had Bodet and Darwin. "Mike always had great power and you cannot teach power," Smith opined. "Baseball people have a tendency to make hitting too complicated. I just worked with him to shorten his swing through the zone, which eliminated the loop he had in his swing."

As a member of the Boston Red Sox and a contemporary of the great Ted Williams, Smith had participated in numerous discussions on hitting with Williams. Smith recalled, "[Williams] did not try to change my stance or approach. We both agreed that it doesn't matter if you stand on your head if you can get the bat to the ball and through the zone on the right plane."

While Mike Piazza's case is the most egregious example of talented players being overlooked in the draft, there are other significant "misses" worth reviewing. Keith Hernandez, a five-time All-Star and the National League's Most Valuable Player in 1979, was not drafted until the St. Louis Cardinals took him in the 42nd round of the 1971 draft. In 17 big league seasons, the smooth-fielding first baseman won eleven Gold Gloves and drove in over 1,000 runs with a .296 batting average. Hernandez's drop resulted from considerations that were unrelated to talent. He had left his high school team due to a dispute with the coach, leading scouts to believe that he may have been a prima donna.

The Cardinals also "stole" perennial All-Star first baseman Albert Pujols in the 13th round of the 1999 draft. A total of 401 players were selected in 1999 before the Cardinals took Pujols. A near-certain first-ballot Hall of Fame inductee, Pujols is not only much better than the 401 players drafted before him but may be better than many of the players already enshrined in Cooperstown. In his 20-year Major League career, Pujols has amassed 662 home runs, more than every first baseman in the Hall of Fame. Of the nineteen first basemen in the Hall, Pujols also has more runs batted in – 2,100 – than all of them.

As a high school player in Independence, Missouri, Pujols showed enough promise to play in the Area Code Games baseball showcase and make *Baseball America*'s list of the top 100 prospects. However, most scouts discounted his chances of making an impact in baseball due to what was termed a "bad body." Though Pujols had played shortstop in college, the consensus was that his body was too thick to play that position in the pros. Some scouts also felt that he had an excessively long swing. Not everyone missed on Pujols, however. Fernando Arango, an area scout in the late 90s for the Tampa Bay Devil Rays, was enamored with Pujols from the very start. Arango saw him play in a tournament in Missouri when Pujols was still a junior in high school. Then a third baseman, Pujols smacked line drives all over the park.

Arango saw Pujols play again the next year and reported that, when Pujols hit a baseball, it "sounded like a cannon went off." Arango quickly turned in a glowing scouting report to the Devil Rays' (renamed the Rays in 2008) scouting director, Dan Jennings.[321] To Arango's dismay, other Tampa Bay scouts did not share his enthusiasm. Tampa Bay cross-checker Stan Meek had seen a game in which Pujols struck out multiple times. Meek was skeptical. He told Jennings, "I don't know what position he'd play, I can't do anything with him. I can't write him up." In rebuttal, Arango told Jennings, "All I want to say about this guy is that someday he'll hit 40 home runs in the big leagues." The Devil Rays national cross-checker, R.J. Harrison, took a look at Pujols and echoed Meek's assessment. "I can't do anything with this guy," Harrison told Jennings.

Jennings sought to give Pujols one last shot and so invited him to a pre-draft workout in the spring of 1999. Jennings wasn't impressed with Pujols' performance at the workout. "Where's the power?" he asked Arango. Arango communicated the concern to Pujols, telling his prospect, "they'd like you to hit it a little farther." On the very next pitch, Pujols crushed the ball off the top of the left-field foul pole. It was all to no avail. Up and down the Devil Rays' hierarchy, Arango was unable to find any supporters. When the draft came, Tampa Bay had the opportunity to select Pujols in each of the first thirteen rounds. Each time, the team passed him over.[322] When St. Louis claimed Pujols with its pick in the 13th round, Arango was livid. Shortly thereafter, he quit his job with the Devil Rays.[323]

The Cardinals, and specifically area scout Dave Karaff, saw untapped potential in Pujols. After seeing him tear up the summer Jayhawk League, the team signed him for a bonus of $60,000. In his second instructional league at-bat with the Cardinals in Jupiter, Florida, Pujols crushed a homer off the roof of a building beyond the left-field fence. As eyebrows arched and jaws dropped, farm director Mike Jorgensen nudged St. Louis scouting director John Mozeliak in the ribs and asked, "What do we have here?" Ten All-Star appearances and 662 home runs later, the Cardinals have their answer: a first-ballot Hall of Famer in waiting. Pujols' long-time manager, Tony La Russa, ranks him a close second to Barry Bonds as the greatest player he has ever seen.

When scouts miss on a player, whether it's a miss of major proportions as in the case of Mike Piazza or a miss on a more modest scale, the tendency is to review the scouting reports to see where the analyses went wrong. Some of the "misses" in the scouting business can be traced to the fact that not all scouts are as perceptive as a Fernando Arango. In other instances, the "misses" can be traced to unfortunate timing or plain bad luck.

Veteran scout Carl Loewenstine readily admits that he missed in his evaluation of Don Mattingly. Loewenstine happened to scout the left-handed Mattingly on a day when Mattingly seemed to line everything to left field. Loewenstine's impression was that Mattingly had trouble getting around on pitches. "Late on fastballs," Loewenstine noted. Years later, after Mattingly had proven Loewenstine and several other scouts wrong, Loewenstine asked the Yankee first baseman about the game in which he had hit everything to left. Mattingly remembered the day well. He told Loewenstine that he was intentionally working on taking pitches to the opposite field.

Loewenstine's experience underscores the importance of observing prospects on more than one occasion. When Mattingly was still a student at Reitz Memorial High School in Evansville, Indiana, Jax Robertson was an area scout for the New York Yankees. It was largely at Robertson's urging that the Yankees drafted Mattingly in the 19th round in 1979. Before the start of the draft, Robertson had seen Mattingly play on three separate occasions. Robertson also observed Mattingly in three games after the draft, at a time when Reitz Memorial was still competing in the Indiana State high school baseball tournament. Each time Robertson watched Mattingly play, Robertson's enthusiasm grew.

Mattingly's running and throwing tools did not grade out particularly well. However, one of the tricks that Robertson had learned from a highly respected mentor, Tony Lucadello, was to watch players from the waist down. When Robertson watched Mattingly from the waist down, he liked what he saw. What Robertson saw was that Mattingly "had very good balance, body control, good feet and, beyond that, his hands were the real separator." At the plate, Mattingly "was able to manipulate the bat, always squared the ball up, and rarely swung through the ball."

In a nutshell, Robertson saw the skills that would propel Mattingly to a fourteen-year career with the Yankees and six consecutive appearances in the Major League All-Star Game. Robertson saw what Carl Loewenstine, also a protégé of Tony Lucadello, would likely have seen if he had observed Mattingly for more than a single game. Having seen Mattingly on only one occasion, Loewenstine missed big.

Other "misses" are not so easily explained. Over the period from 2000 to 2015, pitcher Mark Buehrle proved to be one of the most dominant pitchers in baseball. Coming out of college, however, few scouts were impressed. The White Sox took Buehrle in the 38th round of the 1998 draft. As befitting such a late-round pick, the expectations were underwhelming.

The knocks on Buehrle were numerous. Draft experts took issue with the fact that he came from a school, Jefferson College in Hillsboro, Missouri, that was virtually unknown. They said that his fastball, which rarely hit 90 mph, was far from intimidating and that his other pitches were lackluster. Scouts and writers faulted him for not striking out enough hitters. In 2001, Buehrle's first full season in the majors, he won 16 games while losing only 8 and posted an earned run average of 3.29. Even after that performance, however, the doubters were unimpressed. Rany Jazayerli, one of the founders of *Baseball Prospectus*, wrote in 2014, "Everyone makes mistakes. One of mine is that it took me a long time to appreciate Mark Buehrle."[324]

John Sickels, author of the *Baseball Prospect Book*, had doubted Buehrle as well. Sickels rated Buehrle's arsenal of pitches as "nothing special." Sickels wrote, "I remember thinking that Buehrle was a fluke of some kind and that in the long run he would be an average pitcher, at best." For a long time, Sickels remained convinced that the hitters would eventually catch up with Buehrle and figure out how to beat him.

Except, as Sickels concluded, "They never did."[325] Though few have been able to explain Buehrle's success, no one can deny that Buehrle knows how to pitch. When Buehrle retired after the 2015 season, with 16 years in the Major Leagues under his belt, his record stood at 214-160 with an earned run average of 3.81.

Like Mark Buehrle, infielder Rich Aurilia was a long shot to make it in the Major Leagues. Aurilia played his high school ball at Xaverian High School in Brooklyn, roughly a block or so from the home of Chicago Cubs scout Billy Blitzer. Blitzer saw Aurilia play on several occasions. "For me," Blitzer says, "he never hit." Blitzer evaluated Aurilia as a classic "good field, no hit" player. Texas Rangers scouts Brian Lamb and Omar Minaya thought otherwise. Based on favorable words from Lamb and Minaya, the Rangers selected Aurilia in the 24th round in 1992. In 1995, Aurilia made it to the Major Leagues with the San Francisco Giants. Fifteen years later, he closed out his big league career with 186 home runs and an overall batting average of .275. Years after Aurilia had proven him wrong, Blitzer had a chance encounter with Brian Lamb and Omar Minaya. "What did you do," Blitzer asked, "sprinkle fairy dust on this kid?"

At the end of day, it is impossible to fully explain how talents like Don Mattingly, Albert Pujols, and Mike Piazza fell so far in the draft. The most obvious reason is the short sample size a scout might have had, as was the case when Carl Loewenstine scouted Don Mattingly. Another explanation is the enduring scout bias against "bad bodies," which affected the evaluations of both Pujols and Piazza. Ironically, Oakland Athletics general manager Billy Beane was particularly irritated by this bias and accused scouts of looking for "apparel models" instead of baseball players. Additionally, while a scout's livelihood depends on the ability to project a player's development, it is next to impossible to know if a player has the "burning desire" to work continuously to improve his skills.

The White Sox Draft A Fisherman

In June 1993, Frank Menechino found himself in Marathon, Florida, a baseball player disguised in fisherman's gear. To that point, Menechino had experienced success at every level of his baseball career. He had parlayed two seasons with Florida's Gulf Coast Community College into a scholarship to the University of Alabama. In his first season at Alabama, he led the Crimson Tide in batting average, triples and stolen bases.

Even so, the first three days of the 1993 amateur draft had passed, some 40 rounds had unfolded, and no Major League team had called. For the first time in Menechino's memory, there appeared to be no demand for his talents on the diamond. Rather than endure yet another day of disappointment, Menechino chose to go fishing; the bountiful reefs of Marathon seemed an ideal refuge. Early during Menechino's first day in Florida, his mother left a frantic telephone message: "Tell my son he got drafted by the Chicago Red Sox or the Boston White Sox or some team. He needs to come home, he needs to come home."

For Menechino, "home" was Staten Island. He arrived the next day. Waiting for him was a scout named Warren Hughes, a cross-checker for the Chicago White Sox. Hughes had been in Alabama early during Menechino's senior year to watch the Crimson Tide play its in-state rival, the University of South Alabama. That day, Menechino was stellar, hitting for the cycle and leading Alabama to victory. In the best of coincidences, he had experienced his most productive day in baseball on the same day that Warren Hughes happened to be in the stands.

With Hughes' backing, the White Sox selected Menechino in the 45th round. As delighted as he was to be drafted, Menechino was well aware that he had been labeled a "non-prospect." The Sox had drafted him only after squandering a pick, two rounds earlier, on an 18-year-old female softball player, Carey Schueler, the daughter of Chicago's general manager. Jokes and juvenile attempts at humor followed.

For Menechino, being drafted after a softball player was no reason to be offended. "Didn't bother me at all," he says. "I was so happy that I got drafted." He recalls, "They gave me $800 after taxes. They gave me a free glove that was half broken in. I didn't care. I just wanted a shot to play because I knew that once I got there I would show them what I could do. Some people before me didn't like it too much. Someone put a bra and panties in Todd Hall's locker. (The White Sox drafted Hall, a shortstop-third baseman, one round after Carey Schueler.) Me, I didn't care."

Menechino hit well at every level of the minors, capped by a .309 average with the Vancouver Canadians in 1999. The parent Oakland A's beckoned. At the age of 28, Menechino made it to the majors. He would spend seven solid seasons in the big leagues. Menechino's career stands as a testament to his hard work, patience, and refusal to quit. In Menechino's words, "I worked my butt off at every level and made them want me."

The Sixth Tool: Confidence

People don't understand – the degree of difficulty of the game itself. Over the years, I have had this debate with some fans who say that these guys are playing a boys' game. I answer them, 'No, no, cops and robbers is a boys' game. This is much harder than that.'

–Phil Wood, baseball historian and broadcaster

While the vast majority of scouting reports are focused on the analysis and projection of a prospect's physical tools, there has always been a subtle recognition that the mental aspects of a player's game may be of equal or even greater significance. Yogi Berra's famous observation that "ninety percent of the game is half mental" has been in circulation for over sixty years. Yet baseball people have always approached the subject with caution, if not loathing.

An "old school" attitude has long held that even discussing the mental side of the game was an admission of weakness. Fortunately, today almost all teams have mental coaches on staff and openly encourage discussion of this underexplored aspect of the game. As former Nationals reliever Sean Doolittle explains, "It's stupid that there is [a stigma]. I think it's the reverse. I think there's actually strength in asking for help."[326]

Though projecting the development of a player's physical "tools" is a challenging task for a scout, the task pales in comparison to predicting the player's mental "durability." The perpetual question is how a player will respond to failure. A scout needs to have at least an "educated guess" on the issue. This is the reason why scouts pay such careful attention to a player's love for the game, his work habits, and, above all, his innate confidence in his abilities. As Marlins scout Jim Fleming emphatically stated, "You have to be in love with the game!" When a player encounters failure for the first time, his love for the game is often the incentive to refocus that gets him past the struggles.

Carter Kieboom of the Washington Nationals knows the experience of having to refocus after encountering failure. He entered the 2020 spring training as the leading candidate to fill the Nationals' vacancy at third base. Throughout his minor league career, Kieboom has shown promise. He has consistently been rated as Washington's top prospect. Yet, the 2020 spring training brought questions and doubt. Kieboom had played shortstop for the Nationals in ten games in 2019. The experience did not go well. In his brief stint in the majors, Kieboom made four errors, struck out 16 times in 39 official at-bats, and had a batting average of .128.

Less than two weeks after being called up to Washington, Kieboom was on a plane to Sacramento to rejoin the Triple-A Fresno Grizzlies. "When I returned to the minors in May," Kieboom says, "it was like: 'my life is not over. This is okay.'" "I had to take a minute to breathe," Kieboom adds. He says, "I remember standing at shortstop in Sacramento, feeling a little tired from it all, and just breathing. It was a relief."[327]

Few players in the history of the game ever loved playing more than Hall of Famer Willie Mays, the "Say Hey Kid." Similarly, few players struggled more at the beginning of their Major League careers. When Mays joined the New York Giants in 1951, he was one of the top prospects in the game. He had "torn through the American Association like buckshot through tissue paper," hitting almost .500 in 35 games at Triple-A.[328] Yet, when he first was called up to New York, he suffered through an historic slump, managing only *one* hit in his first 25 at-bats. Neither Mays nor the Giants lost confidence in him and he went on to win the National League Rookie of the Year Award. For his career, he would slug 660 homers and garner 3,283 hits. Mays was not at all deterred by his initial struggles. To the chagrin of scouts, however, the history of the game is littered with other top prospects who never overcame their first bout with failure.

Another Hall of Fame example of handling and overcoming failure comes from New York Yankee legend, Derek Jeter. Jeter was a talented yet very raw prospect when he was signed by Yankee scout Dick Groch out of high school. Although the Yankee organization had an expressed preference for selecting collegians over less mature high school talents, Groch was adamant that Jeter would have the ability to handle failure, based on Jeter's attitude, family history and unshakable confidence. Indeed, Jeter struggled almost immediately in his first taste of minor league ball. He started his professional career in 1992 by striking out five times in seven at-bats in his very first game. In 47 games in the Gulf

Coast League, he hit .202. In his next stop, Greensboro, North Carolina, Jeter made nine errors in only 48 chances. The next year, he set a South Atlantic League record with 56 errors in a season. However, neither Jeter nor the Yankees ever doubted that he would turn it around. By 1996, he was the starting shortstop and a leader on the Yankees' first World Championship team since 1978.

Jeter's close friend and Yankee teammate Jorge Posada explained that even when Jeter was in his rookie season in the Major Leagues, he was a team leader who always kept things positive. He never seemed to even acknowledge the possibility of failure. According to Posada, Jeter set the tone for the team. Posada was in constant amazement as Jeter would return to the dugout after striking out against a dominating pitcher such as Randy Johnson and loudly proclaim, "This guy sucks!" Like many other legends, Jeter never seemed to entertain the thought that he might not succeed.

Willie Mays had the confidence to overcome his horrific start to his career with the Giants, but perhaps the most telling example of unbounded self-confidence comes from Willie's godson, Barry Bonds. Bonds's former Pittsburgh Pirates teammate Mike Brown vividly remembers a game in which Bonds struck out in his first three at-bats. Each time after striking out, Bonds came back to the dugout and told his teammates, "the pitcher has nothing, absolutely nothing." As one-time big league catcher and former scout Darrell Miller picks up the story, "Wouldn't you know, he got to face the pitcher a fourth time and he promptly hit a bomb way out of the park." Says Miller, "I think most players, myself included, would have been hoping to avoid that fourth at-bat. The great ones, however, always believe they will get you the next time."

Giants' scout J.P. Ricciardi, a former teammate and close friend of Billy Beane, says, "You can never predict how a player will handle failure." Ricciardi remembers the times that Beane was greatly distressed by failure. Beane and Darryl Strawberry were teammates on the Jackson Mets in 1982. Both players were 20 years old. Both had been drafted in the first round of 1980. While Strawberry was en route to winning the league's Most Valuable Player Award, Beane was struggling to stay above "the Mendoza Line."[329] Beane agonized over his inability to keep pace with Strawberry. More troubling for Beane were the comparisons between himself and the indefatigable Lenny Dykstra. Beane and Dykstra were teammates on the 1984 Jackson Mets. Beane lamented, "Lenny was so perfectly designed, emotionally, to play the game of baseball. He was able to instantly forget any failure and draw strength from every success. He had no concept of failure." Beane concluded, "I was the opposite."[330] Ricciardi went on to explain that "Billy, who is widely acknowledged to possess a brilliant baseball mind, might have been too smart for his own good. Guys who are too cerebral can over-think things. But if a player is not as aware, he might just go up and hit."

Beane's inability to handle failure has become legendary due to the *Moneyball* book and film. In contrast, most top prospects who are unable to handle failure simply fade from the game. That was the case with Augie Schmidt, the Toronto Blue Jays' first-round pick in 1982. Schmidt was a star shortstop at the University of New Orleans and the 1982 Golden Spikes Award winner as the best collegiate player in America. In the eyes of Toronto's front office, Schmidt was another "can't miss" player. Almost from his first day with the Blue Jays, however, Schmidt felt inordinate pressure. He was trying to compete with shortstops Tony Fernandez and Alfredo Griffin. According to Schmidt, "baseball is totally about dealing with failure. If you don't know how to deal with failure, it can crush you . ... The pressure I put on myself being Toronto's first pick just mounted and mounted."

Blue Jays scout Al LaMacchia referred to Schmidt as the biggest disappointment in his scouting career. LaMacchia openly criticized Schmidt for being "lazy." However, LaMacchia was missing the point. He failed to understand that though Schmidt was expending maximum effort to succeed, his overwhelming fear of failing was counterproductive. Like Beane, Schmidt continually fretted over his ability to play baseball at the professional level. Schmidt says, "I lost half of a head of hair. It was coming out in clumps. There were nights I couldn't sleep. I was swinging a bat at night right in the bedroom."

Schmidt tried to overcompensate for his failure and swing for the fences in each at-bat. The effort made things even worse. After five minor league seasons, Schmidt was out of professional baseball without having even spent a day in the Major Leagues. The Blue Jays Hall of Fame general manager Pat Gillick was surprised and disappointed that Schmidt did not thrive. Perhaps unaware of the enormous pressure that

Schmidt placed on himself, Gillick chalks up Schmidt's experience to the fact that predicting Major League success remains a scout's greatest challenge. "I really don't know what went wrong with Augie," Gillick says, "from a talent standpoint, he had all the talent."

Schmidt has served as the head baseball coach at Carthage College in Kenosha, Wisconsin since 1988. He has come to grips with his failure in professional baseball but it took time. He says, "It used to be the draft would come around and my name would pop up in articles. For a long time, it hurt." In a wonderful story of baseball redemption, Schmidt has closely mentored his nephew, Gavin Lux, who was the first-round pick of the Los Angeles Dodgers in the 2016 draft. Lux is considered one of the top prospects in baseball.

Entering the 2020 season, Lux already had 23 Major League games under his belt. Schmidt is thrilled with his nephew's success. He knows he has had an influence on Lux. "The lessons I taught my nephew were way more about the mental side," Schmidt says. "I look at that and say baseball didn't work out for me, but I learned a lot and now I'm just going to pass it on. It's been fun." Schmidt adds, "The lesson for anyone who wants to listen is that baseball is totally about dealing with failure. The number one thing a player has to learn is that some days baseball just wins. So you wake up the next day and try to make it your day."

National Football League Hall of Fame cornerback Lem Barney has commented that, "What a cornerback truly needs is a short memory."[331] Texas Rangers scout Greg Smith would agree with Barney. "A short memory is a baseball player's best friend," Smith says. "A hitter can't develop an image in his head that he failed if he goes 0 for 4, but rather has to believe tomorrow is another day and he will come out on top."

New York Yankees scout Pat Murtaugh believes the successful players have an innate confidence that allows them to triumph over failure. Murtaugh offers a favorite example, veteran Yankees outfielder Brett Gardner. Gardner has "overachieved" to carve out an impressive and ongoing career in the majors. Murtaugh recalled that, "Brett once struck out twice in a row in a playoff game. In his third at-bat, he was determined not to strike out and fouled off 12 or 13 pitches until he got a hit." For Murtaugh and his colleagues, the big challenge in amateur scouting is that a scout often only sees a player a few times and might miss the key at-bat or play that allows the scout to make an educated guess on the player's inherent confidence. If a scout is lucky enough to be present on a day when he can gain some insight into a player's confidence, it makes the scout more inclined to pound the table for the player in the draft room.

Maintaining confidence is just as important on the pitching side of the equation as for a hitter. Hall of Fame pitcher Jim "Catfish" Hunter allowed 374 home runs in his career. Some were of the tape measure variety. It is said that Mets slugger Dave Kingman once hit a 600-foot bomb off Hunter.[332] Largely unfazed by the homers and the moon shots, Hunter was the glue for Oakland's three consecutive World Series championships from 1972 to 1974. As teammate and friend Sal Bando remembered, nothing bothered Catfish. He was a "down home" North Carolina farm boy at heart, and nothing that happened on the field ever stayed with him. "He had an innate confidence he would get the next batter or the key batter out, and he almost always did," Bando said. Regardless of Hunter's success or failure on the mound, nothing ever changed Catfish; his focus was on keeping the game contained in his mind and, sooner or later, returning to his farm.

From the humble and low-key Catfish Hunter to the flamboyant hurler José Lima, pitching personalities vary greatly. Lima's career earned run average of 5.26 suggests that he had experienced many more struggles than Hunter ever encountered. However, Lima, like Hunter, wasn't one to let failure get him down. Lima and fellow pitcher C.J. Nitkowski were teammates for three years with the Detroit Tigers. Nitkowski was fond of Lima and especially admired how he was able to shrug off bad performances. Nitkowski says,

> *[Lima] could give it up in a heartbeat because he threw a lot of strikes. His fastball didn't move, his changeup was not yet what it would become. He would get lit up badly, three or four games in a row, and you would never know he was having a rough time. Then he would go out there and pitch a good game, and he would act like he does it all the time. Four out of five starts would be horrific, but then he would throw six shutout innings and he'd be dancing and having a blast and be full of confidence. He'd have a party. I envied that about him.*

While Hunter and Lima seemed naturally capable of ignoring the pressure of a poor performance, former Dodgers pitcher Orel Hershiser learned to use the pressure to his advantage. As a scrawny 17th round draft choice from Bowling Green University, Hershiser did not strike fear into the hearts of batters when he joined the Dodgers organization. Nor did he appear to be the kind of pitcher who would dominate Major League hitters. Nonetheless, Dodgers manager Tommy Lasorda saw something special in Hershiser. Lasorda deftly used his unique motivational skills to instill in Hershiser the belief that he was special.

Lasorda would remind Hershiser to be aggressive and pound the strike zone. Lasorda initiated a practice of calling Hershiser "Bulldog." The moniker encouraged Hershiser's confidence and reminded him of who he could be rather than who he was at that point in his career.[333] Hershiser explains, "Every time Tommy bellowed 'come on, Bulldog' from the dugout, I believed more and more I was the Bulldog."[334] Lasorda's mentoring worked to perfection. In Hershiser's career year of 1988, he won 23 games and threw 59 consecutive scoreless innings, leading the Dodgers to the World Series championship.

Long-time scout Ben McLure views self-confidence as a gift, similar to having superior hand-eye coordination. "I think you are born with it," McLure says. He adds, "Once you get some success, you just build on that." Conversely, McLure concludes, "If you don't have the gift, the inability to handle failure can bring a promising career to an abrupt end." McLure recalled a story from his days with the St. Louis Cardinals. He had gone into the Cardinals' clubhouse after a game to visit with a top prospect who had not fared well in the game. The prospect was packing his bags to leave. McLure asked, "Where are you going?" The player replied, "I'm going home."

McLure tried to console the youngster by telling him that every player has bad days. "It happens to everyone," McLure told him. The player's reply is imbedded in McLure's memory. "That's never happened to me before," the player said, "and it will never happen to me again." "The ability to handle failure is a big thing in baseball," McLure notes.

Jim Riggleman has been involved with professional baseball as a player, coach and manager for almost half a century. Very little in the game surprises him. Yet Riggleman still becomes very animated when discussing confidence. He was particularly perplexed upon learning that one player who had experienced a long and successful Major League career had lost confidence. The player in question was the late Jim Fregosi, who starred for the expansion Los Angeles Angels in the 1960s.

Fregosi was considered the top-hitting shortstop in the American League. He represented the Angels in six All-Star games between 1964 and 1970. Despite having already proven himself as a top-flight Major League shortstop and an accomplished hitter, Fregosi struggled at the plate in 1971, hitting only .233. Fregosi confided that he was losing confidence in his ability to hit. "Maybe I was just lucky all those years," he said. Riggleman, a career minor leaguer who never made it to the majors as a player, was stunned. "A month's slump overrode all those years of success," Riggleman recalls, "It got into his head."

Fregosi was not alone. Many established major leaguers have experienced similar doubts, even after having proven themselves at the Major League level. Perhaps the most storied case is that of Steve Blass, the ace of the Pittsburgh Pirates pitching staff from 1968 to 1972. Blass helped lead the Pirates to the 1971 World Series championship and was runner-up in the 1972 Cy Young balloting. Inexplicably, Blass found he was unable to throw strikes consistently in 1973.

Blass describes the frustration in his autobiography. "I was lost as a pitcher. Just dangling," he wrote. "Now the doubt was there. What is causing this? Am I going to get out of this? I was starting to feel anxious about going out on the mound." As Blass's problems continued, his anxiety soared. He explained, "I knew I shouldn't be pitching in Major League games. I was embarrassed and humiliated. Those are the worst two things a professional athlete can ever experience. … I went out to pitch to an avalanche of doubt."[335]

The Pirates released Blass during the 1975 spring training. His ten-year Major League career was over. He was 32 years old. So dramatic was his decline that similar cases of the "yips" are commonly referred to as "Steve Blass disease."[336]

In another infamous case, the yips affected the 1982 Rookie of the Year, Steve Sax. As the starting second baseman for the Dodgers, Yankees and White Sox from 1982 to 1992, Sax was a five-time All-Star with a potent bat. Never a stellar fielding second baseman, Sax developed a very distressing throwing problem early in the 1983 season. His difficulties started on April 8, during the Dodgers' home opener. "I took a relay throw from the outfield," he said, "and I chucked it home past the catcher. Next day, I made another error. Pretty soon, the monkey was on my back."[337] He accrued 30 errors in 1983, 24 of them in the first half of the season. Unlike Blass, Sax was able to overcome the yips and went on to have a fine fourteen-year Major League career.

The most celebrated case of the yips from the draft era involves St. Louis Cardinals bonus baby Rick Ankiel, who was the 1997 High School Player of the Year. Ankiel was on a steady trajectory to become a dominating pitcher for the Cardinals. The script appeared to be unfolding perfectly for the Redbirds. In 2000, Ankiel made the St. Louis roster out of spring training at the age of 20. He won eleven games for the Cardinals that season and was voted the *Sporting News* Rookie Pitcher of the Year. Despite his regular season success, Ankiel "lost the plate" in the postseason, walking four batters and throwing a record five wild pitches in two innings. Inexplicably, Ankiel looked as though he could not throw the ball within ten feet of the strike zone. He never regained his control and his once promising pitching career was over in a blink of an eye.[338]

Former Major League pitcher Bob Tewksbury is the mental skills coach for the San Francisco Giants. Previously, he occupied the same position for the Boston Red Sox, where he helped Red Sox ace Jon Lester navigate the mental challenges of the game.[339] Tewksbury credits the seminal work of the late Harvey Dorfman, *The Mental Game of Baseball: The Guide to Peak Performance*,[340] as the genesis of the mental coaching movement. It is widely recognized that the understanding of the mental side of the game remains at a very fundamental and undeveloped level.

Dorfman encouraged players to develop specific goals and to write the goals on paper. He stressed keeping the goals simple. The goals, he said, were "one-pitch-at-a-time-goals." For a hitter, the ideal goal would be, "See the ball." The theory behind Dorfman's approach was to allow a hitter to focus on picking up the spin on a pitch and avoid thinking about anything else. In a sense, Dorfman had arrived at the same conclusion that Yogi had reached years earlier when he said, "You can't hit *and* think at the same time."[341]

A Veteran's Approach to Dealing with Adversity:
Stay on Your Toes, Stay Humble

Former player agent Bill Moore maintains that the two biggest reasons that players do not succeed in professional baseball is, first, because of injuries and, second, because they give up. From stars such as Ron Guidry to solid major leaguers such as Frank Menechino, many professional players have been tempted to quit the game in their younger years after enduring difficult times.

When veteran pitcher Craig Stammen was asked whether he ever considered quitting during his early years in the minor leagues, he replied, "Many times." For Stammen, a 12th round pick of the Washington Nationals in 2005, the challenge of playing in the minor leagues extended far beyond learning to master his array of pitches. Equally challenging was adjusting to playing in small towns in front of sparse crowds and sleeping in hotels that most people would avoid.

Stammen pitched with success in Class A and Double-A in 2008, recording a 2.01 earned run average in 107 innings and earning a spot on the Carolina League All-Star team. When promoted to Triple-A that same year, however, Stammen had an ERA of 7.33 in nine appearances. It was the dualistic yin and yang familiar to baseball players at every level.

As a first-grade student in North Star, Ohio, Stammen had printed his life goals in large block letters on a piece of tablet paper. Now yellowed with age but still intact, the paper is one of many treasured mementoes that Stammen's mother, Connie, keeps at the family home. On the paper Stammen listed three goals: play pro baseball, play pro football, and play pro basketball. Eventually, he settled on baseball as his chosen profession.

After signing with the Nationals, Stammen thought he was "destined" to play in the Major Leagues. However, he quickly found out that he had a long road ahead of him. Baseball, he learned, "is filled with adversity." On a pitch-by-pitch basis, he says, "somebody has failed."

After 12 years in the big leagues, Stammen has developed a philosophical acceptance of the ups and downs. "Baseball is funny," he told reporter Lisa Lane in 2018, "when things go your way, when the umpire is calling the pitch on the corner that you really need or they are hitting a line drive right at somebody, it may not necessarily be good pitching but good fortune." Stammen learned long ago that "There's good times and bad times within baseball. They shape each other. You learn when things are going good that the bad stuff may be not too far away."

"At some points," Stammen concludes, "it gets so low, you just have to decide that I'm going to put up a brick wall and everything on the other end of that wall is going to be a little different than it was on the other side." For Stammen, faith plays a role in his acceptance of adversity. The key, he says, "is to stay on your toes and stay humble and get ready to play every day." *

* Lisa Lane, Fox Sports San Diego, interview with Craig Stammen, April 23, 2018.

Postscript

[Teams] will embrace anything that helps you win. A guy in the field isn't going to say, 'Stay away from me with your analytics. No, bring the analytics on.' But the analytics guy better be able to really sell it. You've got to question everything and if it helps the team win, use it.

— Buck Showalter, former Major League manager

Scouting in the Age of Analytics

The 2019 off-season was dominated by revelations about the 2017 World Champion Houston Astros' electronic cheating scandal. The investigation by Major League Baseball into Houston's malfeasance was swift and led to significant punishments and the firing of Astros general manager, Jeff Luhnow, and field manager, A.J. Hinch. Luhnow was the primary architect of "Astroball," which had propelled the Astros to prominence in 2017. However, the success that Houston had experienced since the 2017 season has become tainted. The rapidity with which the Astros have fallen in stature is difficult to comprehend and impossible to overstate.

Irony and surprise have long reigned as baseball's constant companions. In the days before the scandal broke, the possibility that the well-respected and analytically savvy Hinch would be replaced as Astros manager by a laid-back 70-year-old, Dusty Baker, was unfathomable. Yet on January 29, 2020, the Astros hired Baker as their new manager. Hinch was out of a job.

Baker is one of the most respected and successful managers in the game and leads all active managers with 1,863 career wins (as of January 2020). However, the irony of his hiring is off the charts. After leading the Washington Nationals to two successive post-season appearances in 2016 and 2017, the team let him go in part because he was not considered to be sufficiently versed in the analytical aspects of the game.

In hindsight, the rush to praise the success of the analytically driven Astros in 2017 seems unwarranted. The effect of the hoopla was to devalue the contributions of the scouting community. By 2017, the overly negative criticisms of scouts perpetuated by "Moneyball" had been in circulation for fifteen years. Even so, Houston's sabermetric "revolution" resulted in real and painful consequences. Numerous scouts lost their jobs. The 2019 World Championship of Mike Rizzo's "old school" Washington Nationals seems to have restored, to a degree, confidence in the value of traditional scouting. Moreover, with the revelation of the Astros' cheating debacle, the sabermetrics movement has been tarnished. Time will tell if these developments will lead to a resurgence in scouting.

Just as the rush to dismiss the contributions of scouting was unfair, it would be similarly unfair to dismiss the value and importance of analytics. The fact that the Astros violated both the spirit and the letter of the rules does not diminish the utility of analytics. As we will explain here, we believe that analytics and scouting will not only coexist but will work together to improve the game and amateur scouting.

In the view of Pittsburgh Pirates general manager Ben Cherington, scouting and analytics complement one another in an evolutionary manner. Cherington, a graduate of Amherst College, had started with the Red Sox as a summer intern in 1995. In 1998, fellow Amherst alumnus and former Red Sox general manager Dan Duquette hired Cherington as an area scout. Cherington rose steadily up the Red Sox's organizational chart. In 2011, when sabermetrics wunderkind Theo Epstein departed Beantown to run the Chicago Cubs, Cherington succeeded Epstein as Boston's general manager. Under Cherington's leadership, the Red Sox won a world championship in 2013. With a background in both scouting and sabermetrics, Cherington is well-positioned to offer insights on the complementary roles of scouting and analytics.

Cherington fondly remembers his first scouting assignment with the Red Sox. He had ventured down to North Carolina in 1999 to see uber prospect Josh Hamilton. Hamilton would be the first player chosen in the 1999 draft. Cherington recalls thinking, "Wow, scouting doesn't look that hard. He looked pretty good." To Cherington, Hamilton's size and skill made him seem like a different species.

Cherington quickly learned that Hamilton was indeed unique; from the perspective of both physique and tools, few prospects stood out in the manner of Josh Hamilton. Cherington also learned that a scout's job was filled with endless observations of countless players, most of whom would never become major leaguers. As an area scout, Cherington interacted with many old-time scouts, learning valuable lessons from and about the scouts. Perhaps foremost among the lessons that Cherington gleaned is that a scout can be, and perhaps has to be, very stubborn.

Cherington prefers to view scouting and player selection as an endeavor driven by data. For Cherington, the more information, the better. Taking it one step further, Cherington argues that the key is synthesis and refinement of the available data. Cherington views technological and video advances that provide data such as spin rates, launch angles and exit velocity as a continuing evolution from the days when radar guns were first introduced.

For Cherington, the information derived from analytics is merely a starting point. These days, he notes, teams commonly use regression analysis to create decision-making models. The regression analysis incorporates key data on players that a team has accumulated over time from a variety of sources. "The next step," Cherington says, "is for teams to run a backwards regression to identify how all those inputs should be weighed based on what has actually happened in the past with players." The thrust is to identify factors, including scouting grades, amateur performance, health data and much more, that have a high degree of correlation with success at the Major League level.

Cherington believes that the use of a decision-making model actually works to protect a scout's evaluation of an amateur player. "When a scout has been watching games for 30 years," Cherington says, "there's a whole lot of data inside their heads and they are using data to observe games and make judgments." There was a time in the draft room, Cherington notes, "where the area scout's opinion wasn't always weighted that heavily." This could result, he says, from a situation where the strongest advocate in the draft room possessed either a really loud voice or a really quiet voice. "Either way, that might change the player's position on the draft board," Cherington says.

In an attempt to bridge the divide between the "baseball people" and the analytics experts, the Rays have put their former director of analytics, Jonathan Erlichman, in uniform and on the bench. A fixture in Tampa Bay's dugout, Erlichman wears uniform number 97. The Rays list his position as the team's "process and analytics coach." The appointment of Erlichman as coach is noteworthy for several reasons. He had grown up on hockey in Canada. He had never before worn a base-ball uniform. His entire exposure to playing baseball consisted of one year of T-ball at the age of five. Erlichman's role is to create "organic conversations."[342] For the forward-thinking Rays, it is an innovative way to facilitate compatibility between the old school and the new school.

At least one "old-time" scout, John Tumminia of the Chicago White Sox, has become a true believer in the value of analytics. Tumminia sees analytics as the wave of the future. "Scouts will either incorporate the analytics or disappear," he says. Tumminia's conviction was heavily influenced by an experience in 2016. While evaluating Washington Nationals' pitching prospect Reynaldo López, Tumminia examined spin rate data from the TrackMan radar system. "If it wasn't for the help from analytics in evaluating Reynaldo López's breaking ball accurately," Tumminia revealed, "I might not have been able to see a breaking ball. I was thinking it was looking like a slider or a backup slider when, in fact, it was a power curveball."

Pittsburgh Pirates scout Matthew Burns is also an advocate for analytics. Before embarking on a career in scouting, Burns operated the TrackMan system at FNB Field in Harrisburg. "There are a lot of guys who throw a hybrid between a slider and a curveball," Burns says. He continues, "what the data helps you see is the release point of the pitch and then it shows the break angle of the pitch. So you can look at that break angle and see which way it is breaking and if it has more horizontal break or more vertical break. If it has more horizontal break, that would be the slider. If it has more of a vertical break, it's a power curveball."

Veteran Major League manager Jim Riggleman suggests that analytics complements, rather than competes with, traditional scouting. "Sabermetrics is really interesting. It's great information," he says. Riggleman finds that much of the available sabermetric data simply confirms what the scouts have already seen. "I don't think we should ever get to the point where we pit analytics against scouting," Riggleman says, because "the two systems can work together and they do work together. They basically confirm each other's thought." "If you are a believer in spin rate or a believer in launch angle or a believer in what TrackMan is telling you," he says, "you should draft the type of players with high spin rates and optimum launch angle."

Feeling A Draft

As baseball tracking technology proliferates at more parks throughout the country, it will allow scouts to incorporate analytics into their reports. At present, however, the cost of tracking technology restricts its availability at college and high school venues. The widespread availability of the technology may be still years away, except perhaps for the most prominent high school showcases and major college conferences such as the Pac-12 and the Southeastern Conference. At this stage, it is difficult to envision that advanced metrics technology will be available, in the near future, for the enormous number of high schools and smaller colleges throughout the nation.

Even if the technology were to be available at every stadium, there remain concerns about its applicability. Cincinnati Reds scouting director Chris Buckley questions the utility of data that is collected at the high school level. For Buckley, "When you are talking about a 17-year-old kid who is far and away the best player on the field and he's playing with a bunch of high school players, sabermetrics doesn't help much with the evaluation process. Many times you go to see a high school player and he will be the only player on the field who is going to have the opportunity to play past high school. To compare that kid's statistics with those of the other players does not help with projection."

J.P. Ricciardi, former general manager of the Toronto Blue Jays, appreciates the value of analytics but also is quick to notes its limitations. "I don't think there's an exact metric that can tell us who is going to be able to hit a baseball," he says. For Ricciardi, analytics is definitely playing a part in how the draft is run. Ricciardi takes issue, however, with the view that teams can rely exclusively on analytics when preparing for the amateur draft. "If that were the case," Ricciardi asks, "how come every team isn't hitting on all their draft picks? We have a hard enough time picking the number one pick in the first round and having those guys be successful. History will tell you that players come from different schools and different places and it is up to the scouts to evaluate those players with the backing of the analytics, but the analytics are not the end-all, be-all."

Will the proliferation of data in baseball lead to the extinction of scouts? Ben Cherington believes there will always be value in having scouts at high school and college games. For Cherington, "the opinions of scouts are also a form of data." In his view, the decision-making models used by Major League teams should and must include the scouts' opinions.

Baseball does not unfold in a linear manner. Rather, the game evolves with uneven twists and turns, rendering all predictions fraught with uncertainty. Scouting is, and always has been, an evolutionary process. That process has taken scouts from stopwatches and radar guns to TrackMan and other advanced analytical systems. Major League Baseball has passed the point where scouts can resist the sabermetrics movement. Scouts who refuse to stay current with the technological advances risk going the way of the dinosaur. Conversely, scouts who are able to harness the full potential of technology have much to offer.

The view from here is that scouts who are able to adapt to the age of analytics and employ metrics to their benefit will remain the lifeblood of the game.

The Intersection of Analytics and Scouting: The Reynaldo López Dilemma

Coming off the 2016 season, the Washington Nationals were looking for a way to return Trea Turner to his natural position at shortstop. Turner had spent much of 2016 in center field, providing much-needed offense after Ben Revere failed to hit.

The key to installing Turner at shortstop for 2017 was to acquire an everyday outfielder to play either right or center. As the 2016 winter meetings approached, the Nationals were targeting 27-year-old Adam Eaton, who in three previous seasons with the Chicago White Sox had split his time between center field and right field. The price for Eaton would be steep; the White Sox were seeking pitching prospects who would be ready to step in at the Major League level.

White Sox scout John Tumminia pushed for the Nationals' Reynaldo López to be included in the trade package. Months earlier, Tumminia had scouted López at Double A Harrisburg, where the 22-year-old right-hander spent the first two months of the 2016 season. Tumminia liked López from the start. However, he found it difficult to get a clear read on López's assortment of pitches. There was one pitch in particular that puzzled Tumminia – a ball that had the speed of a slider but with spin that made it look like a curve. The speed left some scouts convinced the pitch was a slider. Tumminia wasn't so sure.

To ensure accuracy in his report to the White Sox, Tumminia turned to a technology known as TrackMan. Over the past decade, as baseball has become increasingly reliant on analytics, TrackMan technology has emerged as a ubiquitous presence at FNB Field in Harrisburg and most other professional ballparks throughout the United States. TrackMan uses Doppler radar to capture spin rate, tilt and more than twenty other attributes for each ball that is pitched during a game.

It was the spin rate that provided clarity for Tumminia. "A scout," he says, "can know the look of a spin but not the rate of spin." The spin rate that TrackMan measured indicated that López's pitch was a power curveball, even though it had the speed of a slider.

Ultimately, when the White Sox pulled the trigger on the Eaton trade, Reynaldo López was one of three pitching prospects whom the Sox acquired. The transaction provided a unique example of the beneficial blend of traditional scouting and new-age analytics.

Appendix 1
*Hall of Fame Players Acquired Through
the Amateur Player Draft*

Draft Year	Name of Player	Round in Which Drafted	Year of Induction into Hall of Fame
1965	Johnny Bench	2	1989
1965	Nolan Ryan	12	1999
1966 (January)	Tom Seaver	1	1992
1966	Reggie Jackson	1	1993
1967 (January)	Carlton Fisk	1	2000
1967	Ted Simmons	1	2020
1969	Bert Blyleven	3	2011
1970	Rich Gossage	9	2008
1971	Mike Schmidt	2	1995
1971	George Brett	2	1999
1971	Jim Rice	1	2009
1972	Gary Carter	3	2003
1972	Dennis Eckersley	3	2004
1973	Robin Yount	1	1999
1973	Dave Winfield	1	2001
1973	Eddie Murray	3	2003
1975	Andre Dawson	11	2010
1975	Lee Smith	2	2019
1976	Wade Boggs	7	2005
1976	Rickey Henderson	4	2009
1976	Alan Trammell	2	2018
1976	Jack Morris	5	2018
1977	Ozzie Smith	4	2002

Appendix 1: *Hall of Fame Players Acquired Through the Amateur Player Draft*

Draft Year	Name of Player	Round in Which Drafted	Year of Induction into Hall of Fame
1977	Paul Molitor	1	2004
1977	Tim Raines Sr.	5	2017
1977	Harold Baines	1	2019
1978	Cal Ripken Jr.	2	2007
1978	Ryne Sandberg	20	2005
1981	Tony Gwynn Sr.	3	2007
1982 (January)	Kirby Puckett	1	2001
1984	Tom Glavine	2	2014
1984	Greg Maddux	2	2014
1985	Barry Larkin	1	2012
1985	Randy Johnson	2	2015
1985	John Smoltz	22	2015
1987	Craig Biggio	1	2015
1987	Ken Griffey Jr.	1	2016
1988	Mike Piazza	62	2016
1989	Frank Thomas	1	2014
1989	Jeff Bagwell	4	2017
1989	Trevor Hoffman	11	2018
1989	Jim Thome	13	2018
1990	Chipper Jones	1	2018
1990	Mike Mussina	1	2019
1992	Derek Jeter	1	2020
1995	Roy Halladay	1	2019

Appendix 2
Wins Above Replacement Values
(WAR values shown are as of 09/27/2020)

Top Three Players Ranked According to Wins Above Replacement (WAR) Values for the Duration of Player's Career			
Name of Player	**Draft Round**	**Years in Major Leagues**	**Career WAR**
1965			
Nolan Ryan	12	27	83.6
Johnny Bench	2	17	75.2
Graig Nettles	4	22	68.0
1966			
Reggie Jackson	1	21	74.0
Charlie Hough	8	25	39.0
Richie Hebner	1	18	33.0
1967			
Bobby Grich	1	17	71.1
Ted Simmons	1	21	50.3
Vida Blue	2	17	44.8
1968			
Thurman Munson	1	11	46.1
Cecil Cooper	6	17	36.0
Doyle Alexander	9	19	34.8
1969			
Bert Blyleven	3	22	96.1
Dwight Evans	5	20	67.1
Buddy Bell	16	18	66.3
1970			
Rick Reuschel	3	19	68.1
Rich Gossage	9	22	41.6
Darrell Porter	1	17	40.9
1971			
Mike Schmidt	2	18	106.8
George Brett	2	21	88.7
Keith Hernandez	42	17	60.4

Feeling A Draft

Name of Player	Draft Round	Years in Major Leagues	Career WAR
1972			
Gary Carter	3	19	70.1
Willie Randolph	7	18	65.9
Dennis Eckersley	3	24	62.2
1973			
Robin Yount	1	20	77.3
Eddie Murray	3	21	68.7
Dave Winfield	1	22	64.2
1974			
Dale Murphy	1	18	46.5
Willie Wilson	1	19	46.1
Lance Parrish	1	19	39.5
1975			
Lou Whitaker	5	19	75.1
Andre Dawson	11	21	64.8
Carney Lansford	3	15	40.4
1976			
Rickey Henderson	4	25	111.2
Wade Boggs	7	18	91.4
Alan Trammell	2	20	70.7
1977			
Ozzie Smith	4	19	76.9
Paul Molitor	1	21	75.7
Tim Raines	5	23	69.4
1978			
Cal Ripken Jr.	2	21	95.9
Ryne Sandberg	20	16	68.0
Dave Stieb	5	16	56.5
1979			
Orel Hershiser	17	18	51.4
Brett Butler	23	17	49.7
Don Mattingly	19	14	42.4
1980			
Darryl Strawberry	1	14	42.2
Eric Davis	8	17	36.1
Danny Tartabull	3	14	23.3

Appendix 2: *Wins Above Replacement Values*

Name of Player	Draft Round	Years in Major Leagues	Career WAR
1981			
Tony Gwynn	3	20	69.2
David Cone	3	17	61.6
Fred McGriff	9	19	52.6
1982			
Bret Saberhagen	19	16	58.9
David Wells	2	21	53.6
Dwight Gooden	1	16	48.1
1983			
Roger Clemens	1	24	138.7
Wally Joyner	3	16	35.8
Ron Gant	4	16	34.1
1984			
Greg Maddux	2	23	104.8
Tom Glavine	2	22	73.9
Mark McGwire	1	16	62.2
1985			
Barry Bonds	1	22	162.8
Randy Johnson	2	22	103.5
Rafael Palmeiro	1	20	71.9
1986			
Kevin Brown	1	19	68.2
Gary Sheffield	1	22	60.5
Matt Williams	1	17	46.6
1987			
Ken Griffey Jr.	1	22	83.8
Craig Biggio	1	20	65.5
Kevin Appier	1	16	54.9
1988			
Kenny Lofton	17	17	68.4
Jim Edmonds	7	17	60.4
Mike Piazza	62	16	59.5
1989			
Jeff Bagwell	4	15	79.9
Frank Thomas	1	19	73.8
Jim Thome	13	22	72.9

Name of Player	Draft Round	Years in Major Leagues	Career WAR
1990			
Chipper Jones	1	19	85.3
Mike Mussina	1	18	82.8
Andy Pettitte	22	18	60.7
1991			
Manny Ramírez	1	19	69.3
Mike Cameron	18	17	46.7
Brad Radke	8	12	45.6
1992			
Derek Jeter	1	20	71.3
Johnny Damon	1	18	56.3
Jason Giambi	2	20	50.5
1993			
Álex Rodríguez	1	22	117.5
Scott Rolen	2	17	70.1
Torii Hunter	1	19	50.7
1994			
Nomar Garciaparra	1	14	44.3
Javier Vázquez	5	14	43.4
Placido Polanco	19	16	41.9
1995			
Carlos Beltrán	2	20	70.1
Roy Halladay	1	16	65.4
Todd Helton	1	17	61.8
1996			
Roy Oswalt	23	13	49.9
Jimmy Rollins	2	17	47.6
Eric Chávez	1	17	38.3
1997			
Tim Hudson	6	17	56.5
Lance Berkman	1	15	52.0
Troy Glaus	1	13	38.1
1998			
CC Sabathia	1	19	62.0
Mark Buehrle	38	16	60.0
J.D. Drew	1	14	44.9

Appendix 2: *Wins Above Replacement Values*

Name of Player	Draft Round	Years in Major Leagues	Career WAR
1999			
Albert Pujols	13	20	100.6
Carl Crawford	2	15	39.1
Jake Peavy	15	15	37.2
2000			
Chase Utley	1	16	64.4
Adrián González	1	15	43.6
Cliff Lee	4	13	42.5
2001			
Joe Mauer	1	15	55.2
Mark Teixeira	1	14	50.6
David Wright	1	14	49.2
2002			
Zack Greinke	1	17	67.1
Joey Votto	2	14	61.8
Cole Hamels	1	15	58.4
2003			
Ian Kinsler	17	14	55.2
Nick Markakis	1	15	33.8
Adam Jones	1	14	32.5
2004			
Justin Verlander	1	16	72.3
Dustin Pedroia	2	14	51.6
Ben Zobrist	6	14	44.5
2005			
Ryan Braun	1	14	46.7
Troy Tulowitzki	1	13	44.5
Andrew McCutchen	1	12	44.4
2006			
Clayton Kershaw	1	13	67.0
Max Scherzer	1	13	60.6
Evan Longoria	1	13	56.5
2007			
Josh Donaldson	1	10	41.4
Giancarlo Stanton	2	11	40.9
David Price	1	12	39.7

Feeling A Draft

Name of Player	Draft Round	Years in Major Leagues	Career WAR
2008			
Buster Posey	1	11	41.8
Brandon Crawford	4	10	25.3
Lance Lynn	1	9	25.0
2009			
Mike Trout	1	10	74.4
Paul Goldschmidt	8	10	44.9
Nolan Arenado	2	8	38.9
2010			
Chris Sale	1	10	45.4
Manny Machado	1	9	39.5
Bryce Harper	1	9	33.4
2011			
Mookie Betts	5	7	45.2
Anthony Rendon	1	8	30.9
Gerrit Cole	1	8	25.5
2012			
Carlos Correa	1	6	26.0
Corey Seager	1	6	17.6
Marcus Stroman	1	6	14.6
2013			
Kris Bryant	1	6	24.1
Aaron Judge	1	5	20.1
Tim Anderson	1	5	10.9
2014			
Aaron Nola	1	6	22.3
Trea Turner	1	6	16.3
Kyle Schwarber	1	6	5.1

Appendix 3
Notes

Introduction

[1]Stan Zielinski worked as a professional baseball scout for 38 years. He began his scouting career with the Chicago White Sox in 1979 and worked for the Montreal Expos and Florida Marlins before joining the Cubs as an area scout in 2001. He was named the Cubs' scout of the year in 2015. He died in January 2017.

[2]Kevin Kerrane, *Dollar Sign on the Muscle: The World of Baseball Scouting* (New York: Beaufort Books, Inc., 1984).

[3]On-base Plus Slugging is the sum of a player's on-base percentage and his slugging percentage. Batting Average on Balls In Play depicts a player's batting average when taking into account only the balls that are hit in play, removing from the calculation home runs and strikeouts. Wins Above Replacement measures the number of additional wins that a team achieves by virtue of having a certain player on the team instead of a replacement-level player. Home Run to Fly Ball ratio, applied to both pitchers and batters, shows the percent of fly balls that result in home runs.

[4]"Sabermetrics" is the empirical analysis of baseball, especially focused on statistics that measure in-game activity. At its essence, sabermetrics is the use of statistics in baseball to determine why teams win or lose. The term is derived from the acronym SABR, which stands for the Society for American Baseball Research.

[5]Michael Lewis, *Moneyball: The Art of Winning An Unfair Game* (New York: W. W. Norton & Company, Inc., 2003).

[6]Keith Law, *Smart Baseball: The Story Behind the Old Stats That Are Ruining the Game, the New Ones That Are Running It, and the Right Way to Think About Baseball* (New York: HarperCollins Publishers, 2017), 231.

[7]Kevin Kerrane, *Dollar Sign on the Muscle: The World of Baseball Scouting* (Reston, VA: Prospectus Entertainment Ventures, LLC, 2013), 296.

[8]*Ibid.*, 297.

[9]Ben Reiter, "The Slugger and the Scout," *Sports Illustrated*, 8 May 2017, 58.

[10]Win Probability Added is a statistic that takes into account the importance of an individual play that occurs during the course of a game. As an example, a home run that occurs in a scoreless game has a higher WPA than a home run that is hit in the late innings of a rout.

[11]Kerrane, *Dollar Sign on the Muscle* (2013), 76-77.

[12]Jacques Barzun, *God's Country and Mine: A Declaration of Love Spiced with a Few Harsh Words* (Boston: Little, Brown and Company, 1954), 159

The Early Years of the Amateur Player Draft

[13]Anup Sinha and Bill Lajoie, *Character Is Not A Statistic: The Legacy and Wisdom of Baseball's Godfather Scout Bill Lajoie* (Xlibris Corporation, 2010).

1965

[14]Allan Simpson, *Baseball America's Ultimate Draft Book* (USA: TEN, The Enthusiast Network Magazines, Inc., 2016), 8.

[15]Bando was named the Most Valuable Player at the College World Series in 1965. The World Series ended a week after the draft. If the draft had been held one week later, it is probable that Bando would have been chosen much higher.

1966

[16]David Halberstam, *October 1964* (New York, NY: Villard Books, 1994), 5.

1967

[17]Atley Donald is remembered and celebrated in Yankee lore for recommending fellow Louisianan Ron Guidry, who was drafted by the Yankees in the third round of the 1971 draft. Guidry went on to have a stellar fourteen-year pitching career with the Yankees, including winning the Cy Young Award in 1978 and carrying the Yankees to a world championship that same year.

[18]Ron Blomberg and Dan Schlossberg, *Designated Hebrew: The Ron Blomberg Story* (New York, NY: Sports Publishing, 2006).

1969

[19]Simpson, *Baseball America's Ultimate Draft Book*, 82.

1970

[20]*Ibid.*

[21]Kerrane, *Dollar Sign on the Muscle* (2013), 103.

1971

[22]Mark Winegardner, *Prophet of the Sandlots: Journeys With a Major League Scout* (New York: The Atlantic Monthly Press, 1990).

[23]Art Stewart and Sam Mellinger, *The Art of Scouting: Seven Decades of Chasing Hopes and Dreams in Major League Baseball* (Olathe, KS: Ascend Books, 2014), 43.

1973

[24]Simpson, *Baseball America's Ultimate Draft Book*, 139.

[25]"Dave Winfield: The Favorite Pick," by the baseballegg.com.

[26]Hall of Fame shortstop Ozzie Smith was Murray's teammate at Locke High School in 1973.

[27]Steve Wulf, "Eddie Is A Handy Dandy," *Sports Illustrated*, 21 June 1982, www.si.com/more-sports/2011/03/21/Baltimore-oriolesrelated-march28.

[28]George Genovese, with Dan Taylor, *A Scout's Report: My 70 Years in Baseball* (Jefferson, NC: McFarland & Company, 2015).

1975

[29]Didier was named after New York Giants great Mel Ott. Didier's father was a banker by trade but was an avid semipro baseball player. The senior Didier had played both with and against the teenage Ott, who starred for a lumber company team in Patterson, Louisiana before signing with the Giants. Both of Didier's parents knew Ott well and greatly respected him for his talent and character on and off the field.

[30]Mel Didier and T.R. Sullivan, *Podnuh, Let Me Tell You a Story – A Baseball Life* (Baton Rouge, LA: Gulf South Books, 2007).

[31]Francis Damberger, *Scout's Honor: The Mel Didier Story* (Aquila Productions, 2014).

[32]*Lee Smith's Page* at the Baseball Hall of Fame.

1976

[33]Graham Couch, "Major League Baseball Super Scout Dick Wiencek 'Saw the Good in People'," *Kalamazoo Sports*, 22 May 2011, mlive.com/sports/kalamazoo/2011/05/major_league_baseball_super_sc.html.

[34]*Ibid.*

[35]Joseph Wancho, "Rickey Henderson," *Society for American Baseball Research Project*, 3 January 2018, sabr.org/bioproj/person/957d4da0.

[36]Steve West, "Wade Boggs," *Society for American Baseball Research Project*, 1 April 2016, sabr.org/bioproj/person/e083ea50.

1977

[37]Charles Faber, "Ozzie Smith," *Society for American Baseball Research Project*, 10 January 2016, sabr.org/bioproj/person/ozzie-smith/

1979

[38]Larry Stone, "Inside Pitch: No. 1 Pick in 1979, Chambers Looks Back At the Top," *The Seattle Times*, 13 June 2004, archiveseattletimes.com/archive/?date=20040631&slug=ston13.

The Golden Age of the Amateur Draft (1980-2001)

[39]Declaring Joe Mauer to be the best player of his 2001 draft class requires some explanation. We have used the commonly accepted WAR metric to rate each draft class. Mauer finished his career with a WAR of 55.2. Other players drafted in 2001 closed out their careers with comparable WAR values, most notably Ian Kinsler and Mark Teixeira. However, Mauer played 921 games, out of a total of 1,858, at catcher, the most demanding position in baseball. The experience of Mike Piazza suggests that the WAR metric understates the actual value of catchers. Piazza's career WAR of 59.5 is only the third highest in his 1988 draft class. Yet, he is the only member of the class to be elected to the Hall of Fame.

1980

[40]Larry Keith, "The Little Big Man for the Phillies," *Sports Illustrated*, July 24, 1978, vault.si.com/vault/1978/07/24/the-little-big-man-for-the-phillies-while-teammates-of-greater-stature-slumped-or-sat-shortstop-larry-bowa-used-his-bat-glove-and-guts-to-take-philadelphia-to-the-divisional-lead.

[41]Cy Slapnicka's most famous discovery was that of Hall of Famer Bob Feller for the Indians. In his 50 years in the game, he also signed Lou Boudreau, Roger Maris, Ken Keltner, Bobby Avila, and Herb Score.

[42]Kerrane, *Dollar Sign on the Muscle* (2013), 34.

[43]Lewis, *Moneyball: The Art of Winning An Unfair Game*, 16-17.

1982

[44]Simpson, *Baseball America's Ultimate Draft Book*, 263.

[45]*The Book of Blitzer* by Chuck Wasserstrom, https://medium.com/@chuck.wasserstrom/the-book-of-blitzer-2a9d074c5d25.

[46]Bill Simmons, "Remembering the Summer of Doc," *ESPN The Magazine*, 29 August 2005.

1983

[47]Simpson, *Baseball America's Ultimate Draft Book*, 273.

[48]*Ibid.*, 276.

[49]The Mitchell Report was an independent investigation into the illegal use of steroids initiated by the Commissioner of Major League Baseball, Bud Selig. The Report was prepared by former U.S. Senator George J. Mitchell. The Report consisted of 409 pages and was released in December 2007. A total of 89 Major League players, included Clemens, were implicated.

[50]Simpson, *Baseball America's Ultimate Draft Book*, 278.

Appendix 3: *Notes*

1984

[51]Lajoie drafted Whitaker in the fifth round of 1975. Whitaker, a native of Martinsville, Virginia, was shy and quiet. He was hesitant to sign a professional contract because his wardrobe was quite limited. Whitaker agreed to sign after Lajoie bought him two suits. "Bill Lajoie Obituary," legacy.com/ns/bill-lajoie-obituary/147478940.

[52]Sparky Anderson and Dan Ewald, *Bless You Boys: Diary of the Detroit Tigers' 1984 Season* (Chicago, IL: Contemporary Books, Inc., 1984).

[53]The *Los Angeles Times* offered one criticism, noting that Anderson had confused Daniel Webster with Noah Webster when he wrote, "I've heard or read all of the adjectives old Daniel Webster put in his dictionary, and none of them does my bullpen justice."

[54]The other five would enter the 1985 Major League Baseball Draft and dominate the early first round in that year.

[55]Simpson, *Baseball America's Ultimate Draft Book*, 290.

1985

[56]*Ibid.*, 305.

[57]*Ibid.*

[58]*Ibid.*, 306.

[59]E. M. Swift, "Will Power," *Sports Illustrated*, May 28, 1990, 76.

[60]Richard Cuicchi, "Will Clark," *Society for American Baseball Research Project*, 6 November 2018, sabr.org/bioproj/person/3bcff907.

[61]Nick Peters, "Bottom Line on Clark Contract: $25,000 a Hit!" *The Sporting News*, February 25, 1990, 32.

[62]Angela Henderson Bentley, "Bennett heading to Cooperstown for Larkin's Hall of Fame Induction," *The Lawrence Herald*, March 22, 2012.

[63]Jeff Pearlman, *Love Me, Hate Me: Barry Bonds and the Making of an Antihero* (New York: HarperCollins, 2006), 48.

[64]Hank Hersch, "30/30 Vision: Pittsburgh's Barry Bonds Sees Those Numbers Coming," *Sports Illustrated*, June 25, 1990.

[65]Tracy Ringolsby, "Incaviglia Paying Dues as Independent League Skipper: Former Slugger, Who Bypassed Minors as a Player, Now Earning Managerial Stripes," August 29, 2014, MLB.com.

[66]Simpson, *Baseball America's Ultimate Draft Book*, 308.

[67]Recollections of former Mets general manager Joe Mcilvaine, February 13, 2018.

[68]John Stubel, "Gregg Jefferies, Rotten Apple," July 18, 2017 (blog).

[69]Gene Wojciechowski, "Scouts Weren't Always On the Mark," ESPN.com, April 25, 2009.

[70]Joseph Wancho, "Randy Johnson," *Society for American Baseball Research Project*, 2017, sabr.org/bioproj/person/e905e1ef.

1986

[71]Stewart and Mellinger, *The Art of Scouting: Seven Decades Chasing Hopes and Dreams in Major League Baseball*, 26, 32.

[72]Simpson, *Baseball America's Ultimate Draft Book*, 320.

[73]Stewart and Mellinger, *The Art of Scouting*, 24-25.

[74]*Ibid.*, 23.

[75]Simpson, *Baseball America's Ultimate Draft Book*, 321.

[76]*Ibid.*, 318.

1987

[77]Emily Hawks, "Ken Griffey Jr.," *Society for American Baseball Research Project*, 9 November 2015, sabr.org/bioproj/person/3e8e7034.

[78]True Grich: "Talking Baseball with Marlins Scout Roger Jongewaard," February 13, 2010.

[79]Tracy Ringolsby, "Q and A, Balderson Discussed Drafting Griffey," July 23, 2016, MLB.com.

[80]Emily Hawks, "Ken Griffey Jr.," SABR project.

[81]Alan Shipnuck, "Junior Comes of Age: Ken Griffey Jr has Matured Into More than a Star— He's the New Straw that Stirs the Game," *Sports Ilustrated*, 8 August 1994, https://vault.si.com/vault/1994/08/08/junior-comes-of-age-ken-griffey-jr-has-matured-into-more-than-a-star-the-new-straw-that-stirs-the-game.

[82]*Ibid.*

[83]E.M. Swift, "Bringing Up Junior: Young Ken Griffey Jr., Son of a Baseball Star, Is Already the Kind of Player that Candy Bars Are Named After," *Sports Illustrated*, 7 May 1990, https://vault.si.com/vault/1990/05/07/bringing-up-junior-young-ken-griffey-jr-is-already-the-kind-of-player-that-candy-bars-are-named-after.

[84]Jim Rodenbush, *Sporting News*, June 5, 2017.

[85]Albert Belle Scouting Report from 1991, Eddie Bockman, Busted Coverage.com https://busted-coverage.com/2014/05/28/albert-belle-scouting-report-1991/

[86]https://www.si.com/vault/1996/05/06/212584/he-thrives-on-anger-albert-belle-is-all-the-rage-in-cleveland-because-he-can-turn-his-fury-into-prodigious-power-at-the-plate

[87]*Ibid.*

[88]Tom Wancho, "Albert Belle," *Society for American Baseball Research Project*, 12 November 2018, sabr.org/bioproj/person/1d993b9b.

[89]*Ibid.*

[90]Thomas Boswell, "On His Way Out, Belle Takes a Swing At Introspection," *The Wash. Post*, March 7, 2001, D1.

1988

[91]Simpson, *Baseball America's Ultimate Draft Book*, 349.

1989

[92]Richard Justice, "Orioles, Everyone Else Decide Ben McDonald Is the One in the Draft," THE WASH. POST, May 21, 1989.

[93]Simpson, *Baseball America's Ultimate Draft Book*, 362.

[94]"The Sad Failure of Donald Trump's Desperate Attempt at a Baseball League." https://deadspin.com/the-sad-failure-of-donald-trumps-desperate-attempt-at-a-1797451274.

[95]Simpson, *Baseball America's Ultimate Draft Book*, 364.

[96]Overthinking It: What scouts Said About 2014's Top Cooperstown Candidates, *Baseball Prospectus.* https://www.baseballprospectus.com/news/article/22528/overthinking-it-what-scouts-said-about-2014s-top-cooperstown-candidates/

[97]https://www.washingtonpost.com/news/nationals-journal/wp/2014/01/08/frank-thomas-becomes-the-first-hall-of-famer-mike-rizzo-signed/?utm_term=.d8d31a77a722

[98]*Ibid.*

[99]Simpson, *Baseball America's Ultimate Draft Book*, 366.

[100]*Ibid.*, 365.

[101]Jake Kaplan, "Tom Mooney Knew He Scouted Special Player in Jeff Bagwell," *Houston Chronicle,* July 27, 2017, 6-7. https://www.houstonchronicle.com/sports/astros/article/Tom-Mooney-knew-scout-special-player-Jeff-Bagwell-11525775.php

[102]*Ibid.*

[103]https://www.cleveland.com/pluto/index.ssf/2018/07/jim_thome_the_making_of_a_hall.htm; "Terry Pluto, "Jim Thome: The Making of a Cleveland Indians Hall-of-Famer," Cleveland.com, July 29, 2018.

[104]Joseph Wancho, "Jim Thome," SABR Project, 24 January 2018, https://sabr.org/bioproj/person/a2bb6366.

[105]https://www.pjstar.com/article/20131123/news/131129754 One Cleveland Scout Said Watch This Kid Hit. Dave Eminian, Journal Star, posted Nov 23, 2013.

[106]https://www.cincinnati.com/story/sports/mlb/reds/2015/11/13/longtime-reds-scout-jeff-barton-dead-50/75701346/

[107]*Ibid.*

[108]Max Mannis, "Trevor Hoffman," SABR Project, 30 April 2018, https://sabr.org/bioproj/person/740006e2.

1990

[109]Simpson, *Baseball America's Ultimate Draft Book,* 377.

[110]Fred Mitchell, "Pitching Prospect May Shake Off College," *Chicago Tribune,* June 4, 1990. https://www.chicagotribune.com/news/ct-xpm-1990-06-04-9002160686-story.html.

[111]*Ibid.*

[112]Simpson, *Baseball America's Ultimate Draft Book,* 377.

[113]https://www.foxsports.com/south/story/chipper-jones-todd-van-poppel-012418

[114]Chipper Jones and Carroll Rodgers Walton, *Chipper Jones, Ballplayer* (New York, NY: Dutton Publishing, 2017), 52-53.

[115]Simpson, *Baseball America's Ultimate Draft Book,* 377.

[116]*Ibid,* 379.

[117]https://www.si.com/vault/1994/07/18/106786720/the-mm-boys-plain-and-peanut.

[118]Ryan Brecker, "Mike Mussina," SABR Project, https://sabr.org/bioproj/person/d79f7a98.

[119]https://www.baseballamerica.com/stories/how-the-baltimore-orioles-scouted-mike-mussina-in-1990/

1991

[120]Andrew Marchand, "Brien Taylor Unmade: An Oral History," ESPN,go, June 4, 2014, 3; https://abcnews.go.com/Sports/brien-taylor-unmade-oral-history/story?id=23991124.

[121]*Ibid.*

[122]Simpson, *Baseball America's Ultimate Draft Book,* 393.

[123]*Ibid.*

[124]*Ibid,* 397.

[125]*Ibid.*

[126]Stewart and Mellinger, *The Art of Scouting: Seven Decades Chasing Hopes and Dreams in Major League Baseball,* 139.

1992

[127]Simpson, *Baseball America's Ultimate Draft Book,* 407.

[128]The Yankees' selection of Jeter is discussed in greater detail in the chapter on The New York Yankee Dynasty and the Unsung Role of Scouts.

[129]Simpson, *Baseball America's Ultimate Draft Book,* 409.

[130]*Ibid.*

[131]Stewart and Mellinger, *The Art of Scouting: Seven Decades Chasing Hopes and Dreams in Major League Baseball,* 105.

1993

[132]Simpson, *Baseball America's Ultimate Draft Book*, 419.

[133]Stewart and Mellinger, *The Art of Scouting: Seven Decades Chasing Hopes and Dreams in Major League Baseball*, 219.

[134]Alan Schwarz, "A-Rod, Griffey Not Obvious Overall No. 1's," Special to ESPN, http://www.espn.com/mlb/columns/schwarz_alan/1560103.html

[135]Alan Simpson, *Baseball America's Ultimate Draft Book*, 421.

[136]*Ibid.*

1994

[137]Claire Smith, "Baseball: Gooden, Seaver, Ryan and Now Wilson?" *The N.Y. Times*, June 3, 1994, https://www.nytimes.com/1994/06/03/sports/baseball-gooden-seaver-ryan-and-now-wilson.html

[138]Ben Grieve is the son of Tom Grieve, who was drafted by the Washington Senators in the first round of the 1966 draft. When the Athletics drafted Ben Grieve, he and his father became the first father-son duo to be selected in the first round of the draft.

[139]Josh Dubrow, "A-Rod, Nomar and Jeter: Stars at Shortstop," Associated Press, March 26, 2000, Peoria, AZ. https://www.latimes.com/archives/la-xpm-2000-mar-26-sp-13004-story.html

1995

[140]Simpson, *Baseball America's Ultimate Draft Book*, 449.

[141]Sally Jenkins, "Darin Erstad," *Sports Illustrated* Vault, April 24, 1995. https://www.si.com/vault/1995/04/24/8093592/darin-erstad.

[142]*See*, for example, the 1995 Scouting Report by Paul Provas. https://collection.baseballhall.org/PASTIME/darin-erstad-scouting-report-1995.

[143]"A Foot in the Box: The Strange Career of Ben Davis," http://www.afootinthebox.com/peter/the-strange-career-of-ben-davis.

[144]Simpson, *Baseball America's Ultimate Draft Book*, 450.

[145]Ben Davis Scouting Report, April 06, 1995, Scout Mark Bernstein. https://collection.baseballhall.org/PASTIME/ben-davis-scouting-report-1995-april-06.

[146]Ben Walker, "A Phenom If Ever There Was One, Wood Zooms From High School to the Hall, " LAS VEGAS SUN, May 16, 1998. https://lasvegassun.com/news/1998/may/16/a-phenom-if-ever-there-was-one-wood-zooms-from-hig/.

[147]Simpson, *Baseball America's Ultimate Draft Book*, 452.

[148]*Ibid.*

[149]Carrie Muskrat, "Scout Who Drafted Halladay Shares '95 Report, November 8, 2017, https://www.mlb.com/news/scout-shares-roy-halladay-s-95-draft-report-c261023984.

1996

[150]Simpson, *Baseball America's Ultimate Draft Book*, 470.

1997

[151]https://www.mlb.com/news/phillies-drafted-but-did-not-sign-j-d-drew-c278287718.

[152]Simpson, *Baseball America's Ultimate Draft Book*, 480.

[153]Ed Pebley, Matt Anderson Scouting Report, June 6, 1997. https://collection.baseballhall.org/PASTIME/matt-anderson-scouting-report-1997-june-06.

[154]https://retrosimba.com/2017/06/08/how-cardinals-gambled-on-rick-ankiel-in-1997-draft/"How Cardinals Gambled on Rick Ankiel in 1997 Draft," RetroSimba.

[155]*Ibid.*

[156]Scouting report on Tim Hudson by Ross Bove, Milwaukee Brewers, March 7, 1997. https://collection.baseballhall.org/PASTIME/tim-hudson-scouting-report-1997-march-07.

[157]*See* e.g., https://collection.baseballhall.org/PASTIME/lance-berkman-scouting-report-1997-february-23 Lance Berkman Scouting Report, February 23, 1997.

1998

[158]https://www.mcall.com/news/mc-xpm-1998-06-01-3197049-story.html.

[159]https://retrosimba.com/2018/05/31/how-j-d-drew-found-a-home-with-cardinals/

[160]*Ibid.*

[161]https://www.foxnews.com/wires/2006Nov10/0,4670,BBNDodgersDrew,00.html.

[162]https://www.chicagotribune.com/news/ct-xpm-2007-11-19-0711180575-story.html.

[163]*Ibid.*

1999

[164]https://www.newsobserver.com/sports/high-school/article147086394.html.

[165]https://www.si.com/more-sports/2012/07/02/josh-hamilton-tim-crothers.

[166]https://www.si.com/ vault/ 2004 / 04 / 12/ 367411/180-degrees-of-separation-in-1999-josh-hamilton-and-josh-beckett-were-so-close-in-talent-and-potential-that-they-were-drafted-1-and-2-now-theyre-worlds-apart.

[167]*Ibid.*

[168]*Ibid.*

2000

169Simpson, *Baseball America's Ultimate Draft Book*, 524.

170*Ibid.*

171Boggs Interview, https://www.sun-sentinel.com/news/fl-xpm-2000-06-04-0006040095-story.html

172Simpson, *Baseball America's Ultimate Draft Book*, 527.

173https://www.chicagotribune.com/news/ct-xpm-2000-07-29-0007290097-story.html.

174Simpson, *Baseball America's Ultimate Draft Book*, 526.

175Timothy C. Davis, *The Knights' Joltin' Joe: Joe Borchard, Pro Baseball's All-Time Richest Bonus Baby, Battles Injuries and His Own Expectations, Creative Loafing,* June 30, 2004, 31.

176https://uclabruins.com/news/2013/4/17/208182149.aspx.

177https://www.mcall.com/news/mc-xpm-2000-06-06-3304641-story.html.

178Simpson, *Baseball America's Ultimate Draft Book*, 530.

179https://www.inquirer.com/philly/sports/phillies/20120221_Phillies_Notes__Exploring_the_Joe_Jordan-Cliff_Lee_connection.html.

2001

180Simpson, *Baseball America's Ultimate Draft Book*, 538.

181*Ibid.*, 540.

182https://www.twincities.com/2013/05/31/twins-scout-who-signed-joe-mauer-you-knew-hed-be-special/

183Simpson, *Baseball America's Ultimate Draft Book*, 538.

184http://www.startribune.com/sixteen-years-after-no-1-pick-no-regrets-for-twins-or-joe-mauer/426194721/

185*Ibid.*

186*Ibid.*

187https://www.foxsports.com/mlb/story/former-cubs-ace-mark-prior-i-dont-blame-dusty-baker-for-what-happened-to-me-080516.

188https://www.minorleagueball.com / 2008/5/7/482090/review-of-the-2001-baseball-season.

189https://www.usatoday.com/story/sports/mlb/2015/10/27/the-wright-stuff-mets-captain-treasures-world-series-debut/74667692/

190In author Michael Lewis' telling of the incident, "When Grady [Fuson] leaned into the phone to take Bonderman, Billy, in a single motion, erupted from his chair, grabbed it, and hurled it through the wall. When the chair hit the wall it didn't bang and clang, it exploded." Lewis, *Moneyball: The Art of Winning An Unfair Game*, 16-17.

The "Moneyball" Era of the Amateur Draft (2002-2014)

191https://americanrhetoric.com/MovieSpeeches/moviespeechfieldofdreams.html.

192https://sports.yahoo.com/10-degrees-moneyball-caused-largest-changes-baseball-since-integration-050601410.html.

193*Ibid.*

194Brian Kenney, *Ahead of the Curve: Inside the Baseball Revolution* (New York, NY: Simon and Schuster, 2016), 280.

195*Ibid.*, 283.

196Lewis, *Moneyball: The Art of Winning An Unfair Game*, 18.

2002

197Simpson, *Baseball America's Ultimate Draft Book*, 552 (quoting Dan Jennings, "This is a good draft depth-wise.")

198*Ibid.*

199Upton is now known as Melvin Upton Jr., a name he began using in 2015.

200*Baseball America* Scouting Report, https://www.baseballamerica.com/draft-history/mlb-draft-database/

201https://www.espn.com/mlb/story/_/id/23903194/bunt-zack-greinke-one-small-skill-world-best.

202*Ibid.*

203Simpson, *Baseball America's Ultimate Draft Book*, 556.

204https://www.espn.com/mlb/columns/story?id=1578263.

205Mark Reynolds, "Matt Cain's Perfect Game Is a Testament to the San Francisco Giants Front Office," https://bleacherreport.com/articles/1222243-matt-cains-perfect-game-is-a-testament-to-the-san-francisco-giants-front-office.

206Lewis, *Moneyball: The Art of Winning An Unfair Game*, 115.

207*Ibid.*, 110 (emphasis added).

208*Ibid.*, 116.

209Simpson, *Baseball America's Ultimate Draft Book*, 554.

2003

210*Ibid.*, 569.

211https://www.jockbio.com/Bios/N_Markakis/N_Markakis_bio.html.

212*Ibid.*

2004

[213]Simpson, *Baseball America's Ultimate Draft Book*, 581.

[214]*Baseball America* Scouting Report, https://www.baseballAmerica.com/draft-history/mlb-draft-database.

2005

[215]Dan Martin, *How Yanks Accidentally Found the Forever Ignored Brett Gardner*, THE N.Y. POST, July 13, 2015, https://nypost/2015/07/13/how-yanks-accidentally-found-the-forever-ignored-brett-gardner/

[216]https://www.wsfa.com/story/3442893/former-biscuit-bj-uptons-brother-goes-1-in-mlb-draft/

[217]Simpson, *Baseball America's Ultimate Draft Book*, 598.

2006

[218]Simpson, *Baseball America's Ultimate Draft Book*, 611.

[219]*Ibid*, 600.

[220]https://bleacherreport.com/articles/2642794-how-prep-phenom-clayton-kershaw-became-an-la-dodger-10-years-ago.

[221]https://www.si.com/vault/2008/07/07/105709341/how-tiny-tim-became-a-pitching-giant.

[222]Simpson, *Baseball America's Ultimate Draft Book*, 614.

[223]https://www.eastbaytimes.com/2008/07/15/with-lincecum-giants-gambled-on-a-freak-of-baseball-nat.

[224]*Ibid.*

[225]https://bleacherreport.com/articles/654139-can-i-get-a-mulligan-re-drafting-the-2006-mlb-draft#slide1

[226]https://www.youtube.com/watch?v=1rDXwvY-INVQ.

2007

[227]Simpson, *Baseball America's Ultimate Draft Book*, 626.

[228]*Ibid.*

2008

[229]Simpson, *Baseball America's Ultimate Draft Book*, 648.

[230]*Ibid.*, 644.

[231]https://www.latimes.com/sports/la-sp-world-series-20141021-story.html.

[232]https://www.si.com/mlb/2014/10/30/madison-bumgarner-giants-world-series-mathewson-burdette-gibson.

[233]https://www.latimes.com/sports/la-sp-world-series-20141021-story.html.

2009

[234]https://www.espn.com/mlb/columns/story?columnist=crasnick_jerry&page=starting9/10601.

[235]https://www.si.com/vault/2009/03/30/105792766/stephen-strasburg-is-ready-to-bring-it.

[236]Simpson, *Baseball America's Ultimate Draft Book*, 656.

[237]https://www.washingtonpost.com/news/dc-sports-bog/wp/2015/06/08/stephen-strasburg-will-never-be-as-good-as-he-was-on-the-first-strasmas-and-thats-okay/

[238]https://www.ocregister.com/2012/11/10/scout-saw-trouts-potential/

[239]http://www.knbr.com/2019/05/31/farhan-zaidi-discusses-scouting-and-passing-on-mike-trout-with-billy-beane-and-the-as/

[240]https://www.nbcsports.com/bayarea/athletics/how-angels-stopped-picking-mike-trout-back-2009-mlb-draft. The Peter Principle holds that individuals in a hierarchy tend to rise to their "level of incompetence." A scouting director who excels at his or her job will often be in line for promotion to general manager for the team. The fact that the individual is competent as a scouting director, though a factor in the promotion to general manager, does not ensure success as a general manager, particularly if the promotion places the individual beyond his level of competence. Laurence J. Peter and Raymond Hull, *The Peter Principle: Why Things Always Go Wrong* (New York, NY: HarperCollins Publishers, 2009).

[241]https://www.si.com/vault/2012/08/27/106225913/kid-dynamite.

[242]Jeff Trout, a five-foot-nine infielder, spent four years, 1983-1986, as a Twins' farmhand. He topped out in Double-A. Jeff's best season came with the Orlando Twins in 1986, when he hit .321 with seven home runs. He finished with a cumulative batting average of .303, with 22 home runs, for his four minor league seasons.

[243]https://www.si.com/vault/2012/08/27/106225913/kid-dynamite.

[244]*Ibid.*

[245]https://www.espn.com/mlb/story/_/id/26864123/draft-heist-century-how-mike-trout-fell-angels.

[246]https://www.si.com/vault/2012/08/27/106225913/kid-dynamite.

[247]*Ibid.*

[248]https://www.5280.com/2018/03/nolan-arenados-big-season-starts-now/

[249]*Ibid.*

2010

[250]https://www.si.com/vault/2009/06/08/105822135/baseballs-lebron.

[251] *Ibid.*

[252] https://theathletic.com / 1306780 / 2019 / 10 / 23/at-some-point-stephen-just-said-enough-how-freshman-year-at-san-diego-state-reshaped-the-career-of-stephen-strasburg/

[253] https://www.si.com/vault / 2009 / 06 / 08 / 105822135/baseballs-lebron.

[254] *Ibid.*

[255] *Ibid.*

[256] https://www.baseballamerica.com/stories/christian-yelichs-epic-80-grade-power-surge-was-years-in-the-making/

[257] https://twitter.com/mlbnetworkradio/status/1063265326983520256

[258] https://nypost.com/2018/10/15/christian-yelichs-monster-season-hasnt-changed-him-at-all/

[259] https://en.wikipedia.org/wiki/Matt_Harvey#cite_note-32.

[260] https://www.si.com/vault/2013/05/20/106324253/the-dark-knight-of-gotham.

2011

[261] Joe Frisaro, "Beloved Star Fernandez Dies in Tragic Accident," www.mlb.com, 2016/09/25.

[262] https://www.si.com/mlb/2019/10/11/houston-astros-gerrit-cole-new-york-yankees.

[263] https://www.si.com/mlb/2019/02/19/trevor-bauer-cleveland-indians-training-tools-twitter-controversy-cy-young.

[264] https://www.baseballamerica.com/stories/dylan-bundys-stats-stuff-turns-heads/

[265] https://www.washingtonpost.com/sports/nationals/2011-mlb-draft-nationals-pick-anthony-rendon-with-no-6-pick-in-surprise/2011/06/06/AGPt5dKH_story.html.

[266] https://www.nytimes.com/2019/10/31/sports/world-series-anthony-rendon-nationals.html.

[267] The Brewers selected left-handed pitcher Jed Bradley at number 15, and the Red Sox drafted outfielder Jackie Bradley Jr. with the 40th pick.

[268] https://www.cleveland.com/tribe/2012/05/cleveland_indians_prospect_fra.html.

[269] https://www.foxsports.com/mlb/story/former-scouting-directors-faith-in-javier-baez-pays-off-for-chicago-cubs-101416.

[270] https://theathletic.com / 841538 / 2019 / 02 /28/he-was-miraculous-the-jose-fernandez-free-agency-that-never-was/

[271] https://www.mlb.com/video/journey-of-a-season-for-nationals.

[272] https://theathletic.com / 841538 / 2019 / 02 /28/he-was-miraculous-the-jose-fernandez-free-agency-that-never-was/

[273] https://www.masslive.com/redsox/2015/07/boston_red_sox_mookie_betts.html.

[274] *Ibid.*

[275] https://www.si.com/vault / 2015 / 06 / 01 / 106755724/moveable-beast.

[276] *Ibid.*

[277] *Ibid.*

2012

[278] https://www.espn.com/blog/sweetspot/post/_/id/62869/how-the-pirates-stole-roberto-clemente-from-the-dodgers.

[279] Simpson, *Baseball America's Ultimate Draft Book*, 701.

[280] https://climbingtalshill.com/2015/08/01/houston-astros-scouting-carlos-correa-with-joey-sola-interview/2/

[281] https://footer.mlblogs.com/twas-a-long-eventful-day-for-carlos-correa-next-up-his-high-school-graduation-and-then-baseball-6092a8fd6a7b.

[282] https://www.si.com/mlb/2018/11/30/edwin-diaz-mets-mariners-robinson-cano-trade.

[283] Seager's brother, Kyle, was drafted by the Seattle Mariners out of the University of North Carolina in 2009. In July 2011, the Mariners promoted Kyle to the Major Leagues and installed him as the team's regular third baseman.

2013

[284] https://www.kwbaseball.com/mlb-scouts-look/

[285] www.espn.com/blog/chicago/cubs/post/_/id/30805/bryants-college-coach-i-had-a-front-row-seat.

[286] https://www.si.com/mlb/2017/05/09/aaron-judge-new-york-yankees, 78.

[287] https://www.mlb.com/news/oral-history-of-yankees-drafting-aaron-judge-c278026828.

[288] *Ibid.*

[289] https://www.si.com/mlb/2017/05/09/aaron-judge-new-york-yankees, 78.

[290] *Ibid.*, 76.

2014

[291] Simpson, *Baseball America's Ultimate Draft Book*, 727.

[292] https://abc13.com/sports/astros-will-win-19-world-series-says-writer-who-predicted-17-win/5639511/

[293] Simpson, *Baseball America's Ultimate Draft Book*, 729.

[294] *Ibid.*

[295] https://bleacherreport.com/articles/2838859-can-brady-aiken-save-career-from-being-worst-mlb-draft-bust-of-all-time.

[296] https://www.si.com/vault/2017/05/02/slugger-scout.

[297] https://www.chicagotribune.com/sports/cubs/ct-cubs-stan-zielinski-death-20170105-story.html.

[298]Simpson, *Baseball America's Ultimate Draft Book*, 728.

The New York Yankee Dynasty and the Unsung Role of Scouts

[299]Jonathan Eig, *Luckiest Man: The Life and Death of Lou Gehrig* (New York: Simon and Schuster, 2005), 30.

[300]McGraw became manager of the Giants midway through the 1902 campaign and held that position until midway through 1932. In those 31 seasons, the Giants won ten national league pennants, the last coming in 1924. In seven of their ten pennant-winning years, the Giants led the National League in stolen bases. By the 1920s, the Giants had added a few power hitters of their own, most notably first baseman George "Highpockets" Kelly, who clubbed 97 home runs in the five years from 1921 to 1925. Nonetheless, under McGraw, the Giants relied primarily on solid defense and wearing opponents down with stolen bases.

[301]Harold Rosenthal, "Instant Stardom," in *Joe DiMaggio: The Yankee Clipper*, ed. Mike Pagel (Dallas, TX: Beckett Publications, 1998), 23-24.

[302]Kevin Kerrane, *Dollar Sign on the Muscle: The World of Baseball Scouting* (1984), 16.

[303]Halberstam, *October 1964*, 5.

[304]From roughly 1880 to the mid-1970s, player contracts allowed baseball's owners to "reserve" the services of a player in perpetuity. Free agency was non-existent; players were effectively bound to a team until the team decided to release them. The reserve system ended in 1975 when arbitrator Peter Seitz ruled that the reserve clause was contrary to established principles of law. Ultimately, players and owners agreed on a system that allowed players to become free agents, and thereby offer their talents to other teams, after a period of six or more years of Major League service.

[305]Bill Madden and Moss Klein, *Damned Yankees: A No-Holds-Barred Account of Life with "Boss" Steinbrenner* (New York: Warner Books, 1990), 205.

[306]*Ibid.*, 125. (Emphasis in original). Madden and Klein point out that even future All-Star Don Mattingly "was the victim of the usual treatment at first: after first making the team to open the 1983 season, he was returned to [Triple-A] Columbus after seven at-bats in 23 games."

[307]The ban was the second time that baseball had removed Steinbrenner from active involvement in running the team. Baseball commissioner Bowie Kuhn had suspended the owner for fifteen months in November 1974 after he pleaded guilty to making illegal campaign contributions to the re-election campaign of President Richard Nixon and to obstruction of justice charges.

[308]"Draft and follow" was a concept that allowed teams to maintain exclusive rights to sign a high school player until a week before the next draft, if the player chose to attend junior college. Under other circumstances, if a player went to a four-year college or was returning to a four-year school, teams lost their rights to the player as soon as he attended his first college class of the subsequent semester. "Draft and follow" allowed clubs to follow a junior college player for the next 51 weeks before making a commitment to signing him. Changes made to the draft procedures in 2007 essentially eliminated the use of "draft and follow."

[309]Ian O'Connor, "Andy Pettitte Turned His Fire into Ice," ESPN.com, 4 February 2011, http://www.espn.com/new-york/mlb/columns/story?-columnist=oconnor_ian&id=6088090.

[310]Unlike Jeter, Pettitte, and Rivera, Posada was not a key component of the 1996 championship team. He spent the bulk of the 1996 season with the Columbus Clippers. He appeared in only eight games with the parent club during the regular season and was not on the World Series roster. Posada's first significant action with the Yankees would come the following season, when he spent the entire year on the Major League roster and played in 60 Major League games.

[311]Rob Neyer, "When a Hall-of-Famer Quit Because of Derek Jeter," *SBNation*, 6 June 2013, https:// www.sbnation.com/hot-corner/2013/6/6/4403582/derek-jeter-draft-hal–newhouser-scout-astros. Dan O'Brien, scouting director for the Astros at the time, denies that the selection of Nevin caused Newhouser to retire. O'Brien contends that Newhouser had planned his retirement date long before the day of the draft.

[312]Steven Marcus, "Five Teams Passed on Derek Jeter; Here's What They Think About That Now," *Newsday*, 5 July 2014.

[313]Bennett was both an experienced and insightful evaluator of baseball talent. He was responsible for drafting, among others, Barry Larkin, Paul O'Neill, and Chris Sabo.

[314]Marcus, "Five Teams Passed on Derek Jeter; Here's What They Think About That Now."

[315]*Ibid.*

[316]Larkin declined to sign with the Reds and, instead, accepted a scholarship to play at the University of Michigan. The Reds would draft him again in 1985, this time as the fourth overall pick. He signed with the Reds shortly thereafter.

Diamonds in the Rough: Hidden Gems Uncovered in the Draft

[317]Kelly Whiteside, *A Piazza with Everything*, *Sports Illustrated*, July 5, 1993, 13.

[318]Mike Piazza, with Lonnie Wheeler, *Long Shot* (New York: Simon & Schuster, 2014), 34.

[319]*Ibid*, 40.

[320]Gib Bodet and P.J. Dragseth, *Gib Bodet, Major League Scout: Twelve Thousand Baseball Games and Six Million Miles* (Jefferson, NC: McFarland & Company, Inc., 2013), 67.

[321]Jonah Keri, *The Extra 2%: How Wall Street Strategies Took a Major League Baseball Team from Worst to First* (New York: ESPN Books, 2011).

[322]Only four of the 13 players drafted by Tampa Bay in rounds 1 through 13 actually made it to the Major Leagues: Josh Hamilton (1st round), Carl Crawford (2nd round), Doug Waechter (3rd round), and Seth McClung (5th round).

[323]Keri, *The Extra 2%: How Wall Street Strategies Took a Major League Baseball Team from Worst to First.*

[324]Rany Jazayerli, "The Curious Case of Mark Buehrle," 17 July 2014, http://www.grantland.com/features/mark-buehrle-surprising-success/

[325]Sam Miller, "Hudson & Buehrle: Two 'Non-Prospects' Who Hit It Big," http://www.foxsports.com/mlb/just-a-bit-outside/story/tim-hudson-mark-buehrle-top-100-lists-baseball-america-hall-of-fame-retire-prospects-111215.

The Sixth Tool: Confidence

[326]https://www.washingtonpost.com/sports/2018/12/26/baseball-mental-coaches-were-once-seen-weak-minded-now-theyre-essential/

[327]Jesse Dougherty, *Kieboom Is Eager For A Second Chance*, THE WASH. POST, February 26, 2020, D1.

[328]http://davidkrell.com/uncategorized/even-willie-mays-had-slumps/

[329]In 1979, Mario Mendoza, a shortstop, played in 148 games for the Seattle Mariners and hit .198 for the season. Mendoza's struggles as a hitter were highlighted when a teammate referred to a .200 average as "the Mendoza Line." The quip stuck. Ever since, "the Mendoza Line" has been synonymous with a batter's struggles at the plate.

[330]*Moneyball: The Art of Winning An Unfair Game*, 46.

[331]https://www.barrypopik.com/index.php/new_york_city/entry/cornerbacks_need_short_memories.

[332]https://www.latimes.com/archives/la-xpm-1992-08-20-sp-6123-story.html.

[333]https://www.latimes.com/archives/la-xpm-1985-03-31-sp-19010-story.html.

[334]https://www.youtube.com/watch?v=ChlX-0GKLsYoT.

[335]Steve Blass and Erik Sherman, *Steve Blass: A Pirate for Life* (Chicago, IL: Triumph Books LLC, 2012), 2-3.

[336]Blass recalls the day he told Pirates manager Danny Murtaugh that he was going to have to quit. "I don't want to go through it anymore," he said to Murtaugh. Blass wrote, "I had decided to shut it down. I was succumbing to what would later become a part of the American lexicon – *Steve Blass Disease*, the inexplicable loss of control when throwing a baseball." *Steve Blass: A Pirate for Life*, 28-29.

[337]Alan Cohen, "Steve Sax," *Society for American Baseball Research Project*, 2016, sabr.org/bioproj/person/1ebe8065.

[338]A versatile athlete, Ankiel recast himself as an outfielder after his pitching woes and spent seven seasons in the Major Leagues as a position player. He finished his career with a lifetime batting average of .240.

[339]https://www.si.com/edge/2018/05/02/bob-tewksbury-mental-coaching-baseball-jon-lester.

[340]H.A. Dorfman and Karl Kuehl, *The Mental Game of Baseball: The Guide to Peak Performance* (Lanham, MD: Diamond Communications, 1989).

[341]https://quoteinvestigator.com/2011/07/13/think-and-hit/

Postscript

[342]https://www.si.com/vault/2019/04/30/amazing-rays.

Printed in the United States
by Baker & Taylor Publisher Services

Printed in the United States
by Baker & Taylor Publisher Services